Critical Reading and Writing

'Goatly's book provides lucid, clearly illustrated, concise explanations and well thought out exercises that will give students the competence, confidence and motivation to engage critically with texts. An invaluable coursebook.'

Chris Christie, *Department of English and Drama, Loughborough University*

'For the first time we have a teaching tool for truly international, cross-cultural English Studies, that will work across a wide range of university faculties and class work ... a much needed synthesis of the "what and why" of critical language study and the "how-to" of critical writing instruction. We have waited long enough for a book like this. I'm very glad it's finally here.'

David Stacey, *Associate Professor, Humboldt State University*

'This is a comprehensive and eminently comprehensible introduction to the basic terms, tools and techniques of discourse analysis. At the same time, unusually, it offers systematic yet sensitive guidance in practices of critical writing as well as reading.'

Professor Rob Pope, *English Studies Department, Oxford Brookes University*

Critical Reading and Writing is a fully introductory, interactive textbook that explores the power relations at work in and behind the texts we encounter in our everyday lives.

Using examples from numerous genres – such as popular fiction, advertisements and newspapers – this textbook examines the language choices a writer must make in structuring texts, representing the world and positioning the reader. Assuming no prior knowledge of linguistics, **Critical Reading and Writing** offers guidance on how to read texts critically and how to develop effective writing skills.

Features include:

- activities in analysis, writing and rewriting
- an appendix of comments on the activities
- further-reading sections at the end of each chapter
- a glossary of linguistic terms

Written by an experienced teacher, **Critical Reading and Writing** has multi-disciplinary appeal but will be particularly relevant for use on introductory English and Communication courses.

Andrew Goatly has taught English Language and Linguistics in colleges and universities in the UK, Rwanda, Thailand, Singapore and Hong Kong and is currently Associate Professor at Lingnan University, Hong Kong. He is the author of *The Language of Metaphors* (Routledge, 1997).

Critical
Reading
and Writing

An introductory coursebook

Andrew Goatly

LONDON AND NEW YORK

First published 2000
by Routledge
11 New Fetter Lane, London EC4P 4EE

Simultaneously published in the USA
and Canada
by Routledge
29 West 35th Street, New York,
NY 10001

*Routledge is an imprint of the
Taylor & Francis Group*

© 2000 Andrew Goatly

Typeset in Times and Futura by
J&L Composition Ltd, Filey, North Yorkshire
Printed and bound in Great Britain by
TJ International Ltd, Padstow, Cornwall

*British Library Cataloguing in
Publication Data*
A catalogue record for this book is
available from the British Library

*Library of Congress Cataloging in
Publication Data*
Goatly, Andrew
    Critical reading and writing: an introductory
coursebook / Andrew Goatly.
        p.   cm.
    Includes bibliographical references (p.   )
and index.
    1. English language–Rhetoric.
2. Literature–History and criticism–theory,
etc.   3. Criticism–Authorship.   4. Authors
and readers.   5. Critical thinking.
6. Academic writing.   7. Literary form.
I. Title.
PE1479.C7G55   2000
808'.0427–dc21   99–16628

ISBN 0–415–19559–4 (hbk)
ISBN 0–415–19560–8 (pbk)

Contents

Illustrations

Plates

Figures

Tables

Style and usage in this book

Throughout this book

- The pronoun *she* is used to refer to a writer or speaker and the pronoun *he* to refer to the reader or hearer, except in cases where the gender of actual readers and writers is known.

In the main text

- Double quotation marks are used either as scare quotes for contested terms or to indicate a meaning rather than a form e.g. 'Grant deplores the "bimbos" in the White House'; '*choice* can mean "the act of choosing" or "what is chosen"'.
- Italics are used to refer to types of words, e.g. 'the modal *can* has several different meanings'
- Bold is used for technical terms where the term is first introduced, defined and explained, e.g. 'By **ideology** I mean "knowledge in the service of power"'. These items appear in the Index and Glossary of linguistic terms (see p. 329), where there is also a cross-reference to where they are defined and explained.
- Initial capital letters are used for technical terms which might be confused with the same form having a non-technical meaning, e.g. 'Theme', 'Object'. Terms which are obviously technical, e.g. 'rheme', 'declarative', 'naturalisation', are not capitalised. All these technical terms, which are in bold at first occurrence, can be found in the Index and Glossary of linguistic terms on p. 329.
- Shaded areas of text include direct and useful practical hints on writing, and can be useful for revision/review purposes.

n examples and activities

- In transitivity analysis, the verb referring to the process is in bold, and the participants are underlined, e.g. <u>John</u> (Actor) **smoked** (Material process) <u>a cigarette</u> (Affected).

An asterisk * is used to indicate that it would be useful for students to bring to class an overhead transparency (OHT) or multiple copies of the text to be discussed. OHTs with water-soluble ink are more environmentally friendly, especially for large groups.

Acknowledgements

This book would never have been written without the stimulus of Anneliese Krämer-Dahl, with whom I was lucky enough to share the teaching of the courses Professional Writing at the National University of Singapore and Language and Education at Nanyang Technological University (NTU). Besides the general education she gave me in Critical Discourse Analysis and Critical Literacy, I owe her a particular debt for Activity 33 in this volume, for which she provided the text. Other colleagues at NTU were also good enough to read early drafts of the book and give me their comments: Peter Teo, Antonia Chandrasekaran and Brendan Buxton, and I would like to express my gratitude to them. The students on the module Critical Reading and Writing 1 at the National Institute of Education in Singapore were very diligent in filling in the survey feedback form which helped me to make necessary revisions to the content. I regret not having an opportunity to use this book to teach them that course, but wiser heads decided this was not to be.

The readers recruited by Routledge were exceptionally committed and helpful. I would like to single out Thomas Huckin, David Stacey and, above all, Rob Pope for their sympathetic responses, and eminently reasonable and constructive suggestions, many of which I have been able to incorporate. The book is much better as a result. Louisa Semlyen, my commissioning editor at Routledge, has, as usual, been as efficient as one could hope for.

My family, Mathanee, Julia and Thomas have, in the times of professional crisis when this book was written, provided a vital alternative focus of attention and helped, I hope the reader will agree, to keep me sane, as well as putting my work in perspective.

Thanks are due to the following copyright owners for allowing me permission to use their texts as examples for analysis.

America Online for the advertisement 'Try America Online' which appeared in *Popular Science* magazine June 1995 (pp. 16/17). 'America Online,' 'AOL' and the Logo design are all Registered Trademarks of America Online Incorporated.

I.B. Tauris & Co. Ltd for their kind permission to reproduce part of the poem 'Sorties' from The *Newly Born Woman* by Helen Cixous: London, England 1986.

Emirates airlines for the advertisement 'Mary Cheung, award-winning photographer, on Emirates (award-winning airline)' that appeared in *Asiaweek* magazine February 1997 (p.19).

The *Financial Times* newspaper for the article 'Greater wealth of nations' that appeared 16 December 1993. Copyright © The *Financial Times* 1993: London, England.

The *Guardian* newspaper for the article 'I'm sorry teenagers, you are not the centre of the universe' by Linda Grant that appeared 3 February 1998. Copyright © The *Guardian* newspaper 1998: Manchester, England.

'The Dish – What's all the buzz about?' article that appeared in *Jump* magazine August 1998 (pp.46-8). Reprinted with kind permission from Weider Publications, Inc.: California, USA.

The *Sun* newspaper for permission to use a 93 word extract by David Kemp entitled 'Britain faces a war to stop pedlars, warn MP's call up forces in drug battle!' that appeared in the *Sun* 24 May 1985. Copyright © The *Sun* newspaper 1985.

'16 lines from Toads' by Philip Larkin is reprinted from *The Less Deceived* by permission of The Marvell Press: England and Australia.

Laurence Pollinger Limited and the Estate of Frieda Lawrence Ravagli for permission to use excerpts from 'Nottingham and the Mining Country' from the *Selected Essays of D. H. Lawrence*, published by Penguin: London, England.

The *Times* newspaper for the articles 'Tube drivers ran over injured dog to avoid delays' by Carol Midgley and 'Birdbrains fight ruff justice in court' by Robin Young that both appeared 2 May 1996. Copyright © *Times Newspapers Limited* 1996: London, England.

Punch magazine for the reproduction of Caption competition cartoon No. 887, that appeared on 7 January 1987 (p.54). Copyright © *Punch Publications* 1987.

Starwood Hotels & Resorts Worldwide, Inc. for allowing use of their advertisement for Sheraton Hotels that appeared in *Asiaweek* magazine June 1997 (p.7)

Toyota *Tacoma* advertisement 'The Arrival of the Fittest' that appeared in *Popular Science* magazine June 1995 (p.125). Reproduced with kind permission from Toyota Motor Sales USA, Inc.: Torrance, USA.

Every effort has been made to contact copyright holders for their permission to reprint material in this book. The publisher would be grateful to hear from any copyright holder who is not here acknowledged and will undertake to rectify any errors or ommissions in future editions of this book.

Introduction

0.1 Who is this book for?

This is a practical textbook on reading, writing and *critical* thinking designed for undergraduate, college and pre-university students in the UK, North America and the Asia-Pacific region. It will be very useful for those who are going on to major in English studies, communication studies, media studies/journalism, cultural studies and education. However, it has been designed for and tested on students who may not specialise in those areas, but who are taking a university/college foundation course in critical reading and writing.

0.2 What is critical reading and writing?

Critical reading and writing is an ambiguous title. *Critical* is, for a start, used to mean many things in an educational context. To some *critical thinking* simply means the ability to see logical flaws in arguments or to weigh up the evidence for explicit claims. In this coursebook we take a wider view. *Critical* partly means resisting the assumptions on which "rational arguments" are based, by explaining and questioning how common-sense "logic" establishes its categories in the first place. And this leads us to an even wider meaning for *critical*: "explaining how the world and our relationships within it and to it are constructed through reading and writing". By what *criteria* do we judge discourse and its claims, assumptions and values?

Another meaning for *critical* sees it as derived, not from the noun *criteria*, but from *crisis*. The world and its inhabitants face a number of crises. For many, life is still critical from day to day, with either unemployment or persistent food shortages threatening one billion. Others, especially perhaps women, find the relationships within the family and the

1

demands of conflicting social roles increasingly intolerable. Meanwhile, whole populations in modern urban society have been subjected to scientifically-based technological experiments. Some of these – like using plastic with its mimic oestrogens, putting CFCs in aerosols, feeding old sheep meat to cows, or allowing the car to be used as the primary means of transport – have turned out to have disastrous consequences, and have led to a crisis in confidence for science and technology. Linked to this is an ecological crisis, which calls into question the systems of economic and technological development of the last 200 years, and the culture of consumer capitalism which has established itself in the last 50. How the ideology, the way of thinking that causes these crises can be detected in text and discourse is one of the themes running through this book.

0.3 How can I use this book?

Used intelligently, this textbook can provide a comprehensive introduction to the language choices which writers consciously or unconsciously make in composing and revising texts. And it should also raise critical awareness of how these choices structure our thought processes and affect our social and environmental behaviour. With this in mind, it is not supposed to be read in one go or even, necessarily, from cover to cover, but is designed as a practical and interactive textbook incorporating the following features.

- Many activities in analysis, writing and rewriting, which help to clarify the concepts introduced, and give practice in applying them to the production of texts. These might form the basis for class or seminar discussion on taught courses, or as exercises for self-study.
- Comments on these activities in an appendix, which may be referred to by teachers and students, but which can often be the basis for debate. They will be especially useful for students studying on their own.
- Further-reading sections at the end of each unit, which give guidance on how to explore the topics in greater depth.
- A glossary of linguistic terms, which defines the technical linguistic terms introduced and used in the text.
- Suggestions for five extended writing projects, which will be written for a real readership – schoolchildren, editors/readers of newspapers, fellow students and so on.

This book explores ideology. It aims to develop an understanding of how we are socially positioned by the discourse in which we participate, of how discourse enacts the power relations and conflicts within society. Since we only discover ourselves and our ideologies in relation to others, the writing projects suggested in this book should have a real readership. So they are designed to give experience of analysing and producing the kinds of texts which will be important in everyday life and professional life, or which, for future teachers, are likely to be relevant to pupils.

0.4 Describing Text, interpreting Discourse and explaining Ideology

There are three levels at which we understand and analyse what we read and write (Fairclough 1989: 25-7). First of all, we decode the surface forms and meanings of a text, and these meanings can be described. By **text** we mean "the physical form which the writing (speaking) takes on the page (in the air) and the meanings which this physical form encodes". This decoding depends upon Semantics and answers the question 'What does the Text mean?'

At a second level, we have to interpret what we have decoded, as part of discourse, working out, for example, to whom it refers and guessing what inferences we are expected to make. By **discourse** we mean "the act of communication in which the writer intends to affect a reader, and the reader attempts to work out the writer's intentions". This interpretation of intention depends upon Pragmatics, and answers the question 'What does the writer mean by this Text?'

The third level, which we often ignore, is explanation, the end of critical discourse analysis, showing why the discourse and Text are the way they are. It asks the question 'What social and ideological forces underlie or determine Text and discourse meanings?' By **ideology** we mean "the ways of thinking which (re)produce and reflect the power structures of society", or, more briefly, "meaning in the service of power" (Thomson 1984).

Table 0.1 Three levels of Text analysis

Level	Text analysis	In this book
1	coding and describing	Part one
2	interpreting and inferencing	Part two
3	explaining the ideology behind 1 and 2	Part three (Parts one and two)

An example will make this clearer. Let's look at the news report '"Superman" may never walk again', (see pp. 4–5) from the *International Express*, 1–7 June 1995. At the first level, description, we could, for example, note that the first two lines of the report and the headline are in a larger point size, and that almost every sentence takes up a whole paragraph. These are features that help us to place the text in the genre of news report. Or we might note a shift in formality between sentence 4 and sentence 5, with 92 per cent single-syllable words in sentence 4, and only 60 per cent in sentence 5. We could also analyse the phrases used to refer to and to describe the named characters in this text, noting incidentally that these characters are generally given first position in the sentence/paragraph:

Christopher Reeve	Superman star, partially paralysed, horse-mad, 43 and 6ft. 4in.
Lisa Kastelere	the actor's publicist, upset
Gael Exton	British lover
Dana Morosini	singer

Moving to the second level, discourse interpretation, it's quite clear that we have to make several inferences in order to understand this passage. We would infer, for example, that the events described in the last two paragraphs took place before those in the first six. Or that Reeve's hitting the ground hard (sentence 4) was the cause of his suspected broken back (sentence 1), since this is not actually stated. These two inferences are quite uncontroversial, but inferencing is a risky business and a more controversial inference may be suggested by the information in sentences 8 and 9. These may imply that Reeve somehow deserved this 'punishment' for abandoning his British lover and their two children and striking up a relationship with Dana Morosini.

The description and interpretation levels of understanding and analysis lead to ideological explanation. For example the description phase shows that Lisa Kastelere is depicted as 'upset'. This fits neatly into the stereotype of women as prone to emotions or unable to hide them (Fowler 1991: 101). In addition, the only nationality adjective used in the passage is 'British', used to describe Gael Exton. We can explain this if we know the ideological position of the newspaper. Express Newspapers are British with a capital 'B', unashamedly nationalistic, featuring the Union Jack flag and a medieval crusader as masthead adjacent to their title. Reeve's former partner – who was a 'lover', by the way, not just someone like Dana Morosini with whom he had a 'relationship' – was British. This might make Britain somehow more important, or at least enable the British reader to relate more closely to the story. Such a nationalistic background also provides an ideological explanation for the doubtful interpretation – that the accident was deserved as a punishment for infidelity.

'Superman' may never walk again

(1) SUPERMAN star Christopher Reeve is in hospital with a suspected broken back.

(2) His family ordered hospital officials not to give out any information –

but sources say he is partially paralysed.

(3) The actor's publicist, Lisa Kastelere, was plainly upset as she revealed that horse-mad Reeve was hurt show-jumping in Virginia.

(4) Witnesses saw him hit the ground hard as his horse shied.

(5) As doctors evaluated his condition in the acute-care ward at the university of Virginia's Medical Centre in Charlottesville, it was not known whether he will walk again.

(6) Reeve, 43 and 6ft. 4in. was flown to the hospital by air-ambulance after doctors at the competition decided he needed special care.

(7) Reeve, who starred in 4 *Superman* movies, lived with his British lover Gael Exton for 11 years.

(8) They had two children.

(9) Reeve then began a relationship with singer Dana Morosini.

0.5 The organisation of this coursebook

The way this book is organised roughly reflects these three levels of analysis (see Table 0.1, p. 3). In Part one, at level 1, we analyse the forms and meanings that the text explicitly gives us. At this level we will be looking at Text from three perspectives of meaning:

- **Textual meaning**, to do with the ways in which texts can be organised, both in sentences, paragraphs and according to structures of a genre (Chapter 1). Examples are the headline and paragraphing of the 'Superman' report.

- Conceptual or **ideational meaning**, in which the language of the Text represents, sorts and classifies the outside world and the mental world (Chapter 2). This is exemplified by the descriptions which are used of Reeve, Exton and Morosini.

- **Interpersonal meaning**, in which the Text sets up relationships between readers and writers (Chapter 3). For instance, we noted the shifts in formality between sentences 4 and 5.

These three perspectives on the meanings encoded in texts derive from the functional grammar associated with Michael Halliday (Halliday 1994). He sees grammar as designed to perform three functions within a social context – textual, ideational and interpersonal – and so his grammar is particularly suitable for describing naturally-occurring, socially-situated texts. It is also distinctive in the attention it gives to interpersonal meanings; most traditional treatments of semantics concentrate almost entirely on logical or conceptual meaning.

In Part one, Chapters 4, 5 and 6, we move to the discourse perspective, the production and interpretation of Text as a social act. If Part one was about what the Text means, then Part two is about what the writer means by and does with the discourse, or what meanings and effects are felt and created by the reader. Texts are by-products of this social interaction. As cues and traces of discoursal acts, texts have to be produced and interpreted by reader and writer (Chapter 4). Irony and metaphors are prime examples where inferencing and interpretation are essential in getting at the writer's intended meaning. In discourse we do things to each other with texts, we position each other socially (Chapter 5). For instance, the 'Superman' report positions the reader as someone interested in the private life of a show-business personality. But texts do not work in isolation from each other. We make texts out of other texts, we use information from previously encountered texts to interpret the current one, in a web of intertextuality (Chapter 6): we notice that the news report is made up of texts first produced by, among others, the 'sources' (sentence 2) and the 'witnesses' (sentence 4).

Parts one and two show how the structures and the stated and implied meanings of texts can be analysed and then related to ideologies. But Part three starts at the other end by considering ideologies and how they are expressed in texts. We look at four case studies from different ideological perspectives: advertising texts as an expression of consumerism (Chapter 7); romantic fiction as an expression of sexism (Chapter 8); news reports as an expression of institutional power and neo-imperialism (Chapter 9); and poetry/news in their relation to environmentalism (Chapter 10).

0.6 Pathways through this book

Though the careful organisation of the book suggests that the most straightforward way of reading is in the order given, for students whose interests are less in the English Language, and more in these various ideological perspectives, there is the possibility of beginning with Part three, with its ideological background and analysis of media texts. If this option is taken, then there would have to be selective reference back to Parts one and two or to the Index and Glossary of linguistic terms in order to understand the relevant technical terms in the analysis. See also, Introduction to Part three, p. 181, for suggestions on how to read that section.

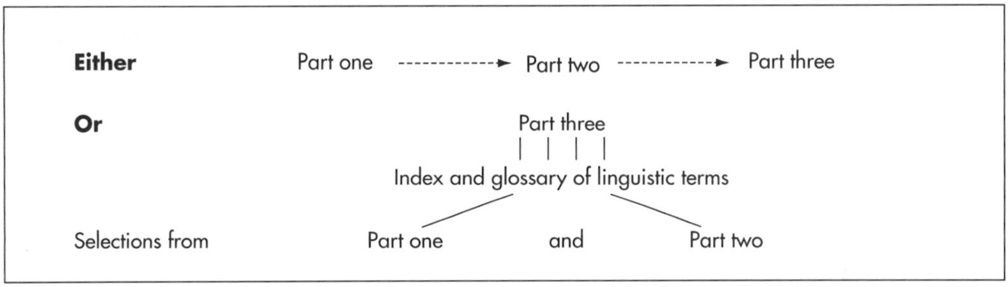

```
Either          Part one  ----------▶  Part two  ----------▶  Part three

Or                                  Part three
                                    |  |  |  |
                            Index and glossary of linguistic terms


Selections from         Part one          and          Part two
```

Figure 0.1 Pathways through this book

Suggestions for further reading

- Ulrich Beck's *Risk Society: Towards a New Modernity* is a socio-political account of the critical state of modern German and European society and culture. Besides locating the crises of the environment, the family and the status of science and technology within political and economic theory, he takes a remarkably positive attitude to the political awareness and participation which these crises have brought about.

- In many ways this present book takes the same perspective on discourse as Norman Fairclough's *Language and Power* and derives from it its underlying theoretical linguistic framework. However, that is a more advanced textbook without any emphasis on the writing of texts. For the reader whose appetite has been whetted by the present book it would be excellent follow-up reading at a more challenging level.

- Fairclough is himself very dependent on Michael Halliday's *Introduction to Functional Grammar* which is the inspiration and source of most of the grammatical theory of Part one.

- There are various derivatives of Functional Grammar designed for students at different levels. Suzanne Eggins's *An Introduction to Systemic Functional Linguistics* is clear and comprehensive, and explains and uses the notion of system: a framework for modelling linguistic choices, a concept which underlies Halliday's *Grammar* but to which he makes no explicit reference.

- An equally accessible, but no less comprehensive textbook, is Angela Downing and Philip Locke's *A University Course in English Grammar*. One advantage of this text is that although Hallidayan in spirit it preserves much of the traditional terminology of grammatical analysis. It also includes many interesting texts.

- The easiest introduction is David Butt *et al*'s *Using Functional Grammar*:

An Explorer's Guide designed specifically for teachers using Hallidayan grammar in the classroom.

I shall refer to specific parts of these grammar books in the further reading sections of Chapters 1 to 3.

An outline of the book

Part one: Critical linguistics: reading meanings from the text

Chapter 1: Genre and the organisation of text

Shows how texts are organised at the level of the sentence, paragraph and genre, and explores the use of visual information and graphics.

Chapter 2: Text and conceptual meaning

Explains how the language in texts, sorts, classifies and represents the phenomena in the outer world and the inner world of the mind, and explores the use of stereotyping.

Chapter 3: Text and interpersonal meaning

Surveys the main ways in which the text's language sets up relationships between readers and writers, reflecting and creating social distance, and expressing emotion.

Part two: Critical discourse: reading meanings into the text

Chapter 4: Interpreting discourse

Shows how the meanings of texts are never complete without inferences on the part of the reader, and that in some cases like irony and metaphor, we cannot take the meaning of the text at face value.

Chapter 5: Reading and writing positions

Views the production of texts as an action performed by the writer on the reader and as a means of setting up roles and positions for the reader and writer.

Chapter 6: Intertextuality

Exemplifies how texts interpenetrate and influence each other, how a prior text provides information which influences the interpretation or production of later texts; and how through experience of varieties of texts we develop a sense of genres.

Part three: The ideology behind the text

Chapter 7: Advertising and consumerism

Explores the ideology behind advertising and consumer capitalism, and analyses three magazine advertisements to see how this ideology is reflected in their language and visuals.

Chapter 8: Fiction and feminism

Gives a brief background to the ideology of romantic and "courtly" love, and, by linguistic analysis of a women's-magazine romantic short story, shows how persistent are the themes of courtly love, and the stereotypes of women as dependent on men.

Chapter 9: News and institutional power

Argues that the notion of "unbiased news" is a myth, given the ownership of the press, the institutionalised racism in the selection of news and the access to the media of the rich and powerful; these arguments are supported by surveying the content and analysing the language of newspapers and magazines.

Chapter 10: Nature, vocabulary and grammar

Makes the case for an ecological critical discourse analysis, suggests how linguistic resources can be most helpfully exploited to reflect, more faithfully, modern ecological theory, and shows how, in this respect, Wordsworth's *The Prelude* is superior to *The Times* of London.

Part one

Critical linguistics: reading meanings from the text

Chapter 1

Genre and the organisation of text

The aim of this chapter

To show how we can organise information in texts, through language, visuals and the structure of different genres.

- **1.0 Introduction: the need for organisation**
  Underlines the fact that texts will be judged not only on their content but also on their organisation and textual impact.

- **1.1 Information in the clause and sentence**
  Analyses the language resources for distributing old and new information in sentences, and patterns of organisation over sequences of sentences.

- **1.2 The structure of the paragraph**
  Introduces four basic kinds of paragraph structure, and explores the differences between point-first and point-last structures.

- **1.3 Visual information in texts**
  Surveys the devices at our disposal for making texts more visually interesting, and discusses their effects on reading.

- **1.4 Generic structure**
  Introduces the notion of generic structure, concentrating on narratives and news reports and showing how the latter's structure gives scope for bias.

As well as many small-scale activities, there are two major activities on

- making a text more visually attractive

- rewriting a narrative as a news report

1.0 Introduction: the need for organisation

Supposing you were a student living in university accommodation near Tottenham Court Road in London, and someone gave you the following directions to get to their house:

> It's 4 Hills Road, Buckhurst Hill. It's in Essex. There's a pond opposite it, and beyond a pond a church called St. John's with a spire. It's in a cul-de-sac. You go up Palmerston Road from Buckhurst Hill tube station, turning right and then left as you come out of the station. It's a Central Line station, the Epping branch, not the Hainault branch. You'll need to go to Tottenham Court Road station and take the eastbound train. When you get to the top of Palmerston Road you turn right at the T-junction, cross over the High Road and take a path with the pond on your right. It's the second house, on the left.

Though there is probably enough information here to get you to your destination, it's so hopelessly organised that it will be difficult to remember or to use. In fact it violates two principles of the organisation of information. The first is that a speaker/writer should start with what the hearer/reader already knows. The second is that when a sequence is described, its elements should be given in the order in which they take place. So it would be better to start with going to Tottenham Court Road Station, which you, the student, already know and which is the first part of the journey, and then to tell which train to take in which direction, where to get off, how to proceed from the station, how to recognise the location of the house, and finally to give the house number.

Spoken text is entirely linear, and written text is predominantly so. We have to listen in the order in which the words are spoken, and we often read the text in the order in which it is presented to us, though, as we shall see, this varies with the kind of text, and how visual it is. Because language text is largely linear, the order in which we present information is crucial in organising our material effectively.

In fact, reading a text is very much like making a journey from one point to another. If a longish text is well organised it will be possible for the writer to give a map and visual cues to the reader; indicate in advance and by graphic devices how the text is sectionalised; what point in the text we have reached; and where we are going next. These are a courtesy to the reader and make the organisation clear. But without an underlying organisation, a map is impossible.

1.1 Information in the clause and sentence

First of all, let's look at how information can be ordered and organised in the sentence or clause. To analyse clauses for their information structure we can divide them into two parts called **Theme** and **rheme**. Assuming the basic elements of the clause can be labelled Subject, Object, Verb, Adverbial, the Theme will be the first of these elements to occur in the clause. Let's look at some examples.

(1)

Subject	Verb	Object	Adverbial
John	ate	the tomatoes	on Wednesday

Theme.......... | Rheme..

(2)

Object	Subject	Verb	Adverbial
The tomatoes	John	ate	on Wednesday, (the spinach on Friday)

Theme.......... | Rheme..

(3)

Adverbial	Subject	Verb	Object
On Wednesday	John	ate	the tomatoes

Theme.......... | Rheme..

There are various additional grammatical tricks we can use to redistribute information. First, we can use the Passive:

(4)

Subject	Verb	Adverbial	Adverbial
The tomatoes	were eaten	on Wednesday	by John

Theme.......... | Rheme..

Or we can introduce a second clause:

(5) What John did to the tomatoes on Wednesday was to eat them.

(6) It was the tomatoes that John ate on Wednesday

(7) It was on Wednesday that John ate the tomatoes

(8) It was John who ate the tomatoes on Wednesday

Theme–Rheme and Given–New

The most straightforward way of organising information in a text is to put old or given information, information we already have, in the Theme position, and new information towards the end of the rheme. We can see this if we imagine the sentences above are replies to questions.

ACTIVITY 1

Which of the above sentences 1–5, uttered with normal intonation, are the most appropriate answers to the following questions?

(a) Those tomatoes, did you say that on Wednesday John *picked* them?
(b) When did John eat the tomatoes?
(c) Who ate the tomatoes?
(d) But the tomatoes, when did John eat *them*?
(e) What did John eat on Wednesday?

NB: Comments on most of these activities are given at the end of the book. But they are only suggestions and you are free to consult them as you wish.

The guiding principle is, then, that the most important new information goes at the end of the rheme, and given or old information goes in the Theme. If, in your writing, you bend this rule then you should have very good reasons for doing so.

ACTIVITY 2

Look at the following extracts (slightly modified) from an abstract/summary of a mini-dissertation, and say what you think is wrong with them. How could you rewrite them to distribute given and new information better? (You can make a few adjustments by adding a word or two if necessary as in examples 5–8.)

ABSTRACT

(a) That persuasion depends on the interrelationships between discourse and society is generally recognised.

(b) The idea that ideological persuasion can be repeated, so that later it becomes taken for granted, is argued in this study.

(c)   Essentially, the framework for studying discourse proposed by Fairclough (1995) will be used.

1.2 The structure of the paragraph

Thematic strings or thematic development

Besides looking at the Themes of individual clauses, we can consider the pattern of Themes over a whole paragraph or passage. A clear pattern of **thematic development** will often be a sign of good organisation. Look back at the text concerning the horse-riding accident to Christopher Reeve (see p. 4). Notice that the Themes are as follows:

> *Superman* star Christopher Reeve
> His family
> Sources
> The actor's publicist Lisa Kastelere
> She
> Horse-mad Reeve
> Witnesses
> Doctors
> Reeve, 43 and 6ft. 4in.
> Doctors
> Reeve
> They
> Reeve

There is an obvious pattern here. The Themes always refer to people, in step with the dictum that news is about people and has human interest. Almost half of the Themes refer to Reeve. The other people referred to are those who have reacted verbally to the accident or its aftermath.

ACTIVITY 3

Look at the following two paragraphs, which convey the same information but distribute it differently by having different Themes. Identify the first Themes of each sentence in both passages. Which passage is most successful, and how is this related to the patterning and progression of Themes?

1   Spring and fall are the most beautiful time of the year here in the Blue Mountains. Millions of wild flowers and trees are in bud, and the many planned gardens in the region start to flourish in springtime. The North American species of trees introduced long ago into the region – oak, elm, chestnut, beech and birch – do the same in the Blue Mountains as they would in the Catskills: turn brilliant reds, oranges and yellows in fall. Campers and hikers are found descending on the mountains in throngs in summer, and the mountains are at their quietest and most peaceful in winter, offering perfect solitude for city escapees.

2   Spring and fall are the most beautiful time of the year here in the Blue Mountains. In springtime millions of wild flowers and trees are in bud, and the many planned gardens in the region start to flourish. In fall the North American species of trees introduced long ago into the region – oak, elm, chestnut, beech and birch – do the same in the Blue Mountains as they would in the Catskills: turn brilliant reds, oranges and yellows. Summer finds campers and hikers descending on the mountains in throngs, and winter is the time the mountains are at their quietest and most peaceful, offering perfect solitude for city escapees.

(Quoted in Matthiessen 1992, p. 58–9)

We have seen that the words in the Theme of sentences and clauses have a very important role in making a text hang together, technically, giving it **cohesion**. Or to put it another way, repeated references to the same people or semantic areas throughout a text may well help the text cohere; but if the expressions which refer to them are in Theme position this cohesion will be more obvious and more organised.

We have seen such patterns of referring to persons in the 'Superman' text, and to seasons in passage 2 of Activity 3.

Paragraph structure

Thematic development is one area to pay attention to in organising our text, but equally important is paragraph structure. Walter Nash (1980) has suggested that there are four quite typical ways of organising paragraphs in continuous prose, which he calls the Step, the Stack, the Chain and the Balance. These are not rigid patterns, and may be combined or modified, but they often give a basic shape to paragraphs and sections of writing.

The Step

Heat fat in frying pan. When hot add peas. Turn and stir-fry slowly over a medium heat. Add chicken broth and continue to stir-fry for one more minute. Sprinkle with salt, sugar and sherry and stir-fry gently for one further minute and serve.

This is part of a recipe, one example of a **procedure** – a text type that tells you how to carry out a process step by step in the right order. The **step** is probably the basic design which underlines procedures, as well as **narratives**, both of which depend upon an ordering of events in time. Notice that, in this recipe, there is very little attempt to make the text hang together internally, not much cohesion: only the means of cooking is repeated – 'stir-fry' – but none of the ingredients is mentioned more than once; and there is no pattern of thematic development. Rather it is the external activity which gives it coherence, along with the repetition of commands or imperatives: 'heat', 'add', 'stir-fry', 'sprinkle,' etc.

The Stack

As the metaphor suggests, stacks amount to lists of arguments or facts which are piled up, as it were, to support a position. (The following example probably only makes sense if the reader knows the Singapore context, where the government controls the number of cars on the road by issuing limited numbers of Certificates of Entitlement, and has several current campaigns, among them to save water, and to adopt a healthy lifestyle.)

Topic Sentence

There are many things illogical and self-contradictory about the Singapore government's giving way to public pressure and allowing more cars on to the road just before an election. [First], this ill-thought-out move will inevitably result in more fatalities on Singapore's highways – there were already ninety deaths in the first quarter of 1997. [Second], if the government believes in a healthy lifestyle for its citizens, then discouraging walking, even if only to the bus stop, is a step backwards. Who knows how much car use might contribute to heart disease through obesity in years to come? The [another] government campaign – to save water – would achieve some success if there were fewer cars about that had to be regularly washed. [Furthermore], with world-wide oil reserves likely to halve in the next fifteen years we must be sensible enough to prepare ourselves for transport like the underground system, buses and bicycles which use non-renewable energy more efficiently or avoid using it altogether. Frankly, increasing the population of cars, while politically pragmatic, seems quite irrational.

This is quite a common paragraph structure in exposition or argument. It begins with a **topic sentence**, announcing the main idea or point at issue. Then it proceeds to give a stack of amplifying comments, all of which can be related back to the topic sentence. Such stack patterns also have the option, taken up here, of ending with a restatement of the writer's main point, nicely rounding things off.

The fact that these are stacked is clear from the option of enumerating the arguments, as indicated by the enumerators in brackets. These would be an example of signposts given to the reader to make the organisation of the text clear. However, quite apart from these, the paragraph displays cohesion through using vocabulary with related and contrasting meanings. 'Illogical' in sentence one is echoed by 'ill-considered' in sentence two and 'irrational' in the last sentence and contrasts with 'sensible' in the penultimate sentence. The word *government* recurs three times, and the related words *election* and *political* occur in the first and final sentences. The word *self-contradictory* is expanded in sentences three and four, which claim that the increase in the number of cars works against two government campaigns.

The Chain

The two paragraph patterns we have looked at so far show very tight organisation. But the **chain** has a more exploratory or rambling feel about it. It is a design where the sentences appearing in succession are linked most obviously only to the previous sentence.

Mosquitoes are the greediest creatures I have ever met, my children not excluded. They combine the vice of greed with the virtue of persistence, and buzz around for hours in the darkness seeking out those few patches of bare white flesh I negligently leave uncovered. Under that flesh, as they well know, flow pints of that red juicy food known as blood. Blood is to mosquitoes, what Fosters lager is to Australians. However, it is only the females which suck blood, the males feeding on nectar. If they both fed on blood there would be no hope. But, as it is, providing we can live far enough away from flowers there is some hope that, to find a mate, the blood-sucking sex will have to keep away from us.

The chain-like structure links one sentence to the next. This cohesion is achieved by repeating vocabulary, or using pronouns to refer "back" to something which has come in the previous sentence; for example

Sentences 1–2	*mosquitoes*	*they*
	greediest	*greed*
Sentences 2–3	*bare flesh*	*that flesh*
Sentences 3–4	*blood*	*blood*
Sentences 4–5	*mosquitoes*	*males, females*
	blood	*blood*
Sentences 5–6	*males, females*	*they both*
	blood	*blood*
	feeding	*fed*
Sentences 6–7	*blood*	*blood-sucking*
	no hope	*some hope*

The Balance

The last basic design for paragraphs or texts is the **balance**. The metaphor suggests a weighing up of descriptive facts, or arguments for and against a proposition, giving equal proportion to each side, without coming down firmly in favour of one or the other.

> The Institute of Education certainly has a more human scale than the National University, both in the size of student population and in its architecture. On the other hand, the University, being more modern in its buildings and larger in size, can afford better resources than the Institute. Its library is one of the best in the region, and the computing facilities are second to none. However it is sprawled over Kent Ridge, with narrow bending walkways which never allow you to see anyone else from a distance, and this, coupled with its long, bare, windowless corridors gives it a rather impersonal and sinister atmosphere. The Institute, by contrast, may have decaying, termite-infested buildings, cave-like offices, and uneven floors, but it has a more homely, if messy, human feel to it. And while a larger proportion of students at the University are just after a certificate to improve their chances of material success, the undergraduate at the Institute of Education is more likely committed to a worthwhile career, and may be a kinder kind of soul.

There are several Balances in this paragraph. Very often one sentence is weighed against another by using words or phrases specifically to point contrasts, 'on the other hand', 'by contrast', 'however'. At other times the fulcrum of the Balance occurs in mid-sentence through use of a **conjunction** like *while*. More generally, the frequent use of comparatives – 'better', 'kinder', 'more' – gives an overall sense of weighing up two things in opposition.

Sometimes the Balance is unequal. We may have made up our mind already which side we come down on, and simply concede one or two contrary arguments to make us appear reasonable. For example

> Although pet cats and dogs are invaluable companions for old people, and are creatures 'for children to learn benevolence upon', these advantages cannot outweigh the negative impacts they have on the environment. They consume huge amounts of protein in a world where a quarter of the popula-

tion is hungry. They spread diseases and parasites to human populations, particularly when negligent owners do nothing to control their defecation in public parks and on pavements. There are numerous instances of young children being attacked, maimed and disfigured by 'guard' dogs. And the industry of dog and cat breeding simply reinforces and displaces snobbishness about human ancestry with snobbishness about canine and feline pedigree.

Here the first clause, 'Although ... upon', makes a couple of concessions to those in favour of pets. This makes the writer appear reasonable, before the crushing weight of arguments against is 'stacked' up against them.

This example, in fact, makes it clear how the paragraph design of Balance and stack can be combined in practice. There is a very small stack of two items on one side of the Balance, but a much bigger and weightier one on the other side. There's no doubt which way the scales are supposed to tip:

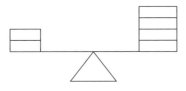

ACTIVITY 4*

Find a short paragraph from a book or magazine text that is written in continuous prose. Try to analyse it by seeing what kinds of paragraph structure it incorporates. Remember that most real paragraphs will mix at least two of the basic designs – Step, Stack, Chain and Balance. How useful are Nash's categories of paragraph type?

*Activities which are asterisked are particularly useful for discussion in class, in which case multiple copies or OHTs of the text could be produced.

The point of paragraph or text

Another crucial aspect of paragraph and text structure is the position of the point, or topic sentence. The main idea, the most essential new information, can appear in at least two positions. It may come in the first sentence as it does in the example of a stack. In other paragraph or discourse types it may come last, towards the end of the paragraph or text.

Point-first structures are called **deductive**, and point-last structures **inductive**. Deductive structures are generally easier to absorb than Inductive ones. They allow skimming, or allow the reader to abandon reading half-way through the text, while still understanding the gist of it, and so are less time-consuming. Inductive structures, on the other hand, are more enigmatic, suspenseful, demand more time, and place an emphasis on the process of reading rather than simply the information as a product. Good writers will always be careful to adopt the most appropriate structue, Inductive or Deductive, to match their purposes and the likely reading syle.

ACTIVITY 5

Which of the following genres is generally Deductive, point first, and which Inductive, point last? murder mystery; research article; classified advert; sophisticated advert in a glossy magazine; joke; news report

1.3 Visual information in texts

So far we have been assuming the organisation of a text lies primarily in the words and clauses, its language. But, in fact, when we considered paragraphing, we were already paying some attention to the use of white space to indent the text. This is just one of the means available for making a text, what Bernhardt (1985) calls, **visually informative**. Visual aspects of the text can be ways of imposing organisation on it, or highlighting an existing organisation. These graphical devices, such as choice of font, use of bullets, importing of graphs, are, with the widespread use of word processors, within reach of most of us. So in this section we will be considering some of the resources for visual information, and the consequences which they may have for text organisation, including the Inductive–Deductive distinction.

Resources for visual informativeness

In the past, linguists have often insisted that the spoken language, with features like stress and intonation, speed variation, rhythm, loudness and voice quality, is much richer than the written language. This is only partially true. There are a range of graphic resources which, for instance, a desktop publisher will have to decide on when she comes to creating printed text, and which give an extra layer of textual meaning.

(1) At the global level she will decide if she is going to import graphics – pictures, graphs, pie charts.
(2) She will consider how these can be integrated with global layout features – page size, number of columns, use of white space or colour.
(3) At a slightly more detailed level, she has the opportunity to use graphics for making textual organisation clear, for example by bullets, asterisks, dashes, enumeration (such as numbering or lettering).
(4) More locally, she has the choice of text features or highlighting: font type, font size, capitalisation, bolding, italicisation, underlining, outlining, shadowing.

ACTIVITY 6

- Compare the Geographical Society circular (GS) with 'What's all the buzz about' (WB), both below. In what ways do these two texts differ in their global layout features (2), use graphics to make textual organisation clear (3), or use local text features or highlighting (4)? Which of the two texts is more visually informative?

- Word-process the Geographical Society circular to make it more visually informative, like the WB feature on coffee.

4th November 1990   Geographical Society
                                         c/o Dept. of Geography

Dear Sir/Mdm

SALE OF APA INSIGHT GUIDEBOOKS

It is my pleasure to inform you that the Geographical Society will be selling APA Insight Guidebooks at a very special rate of only $22-00 each. These books provide up-to-date information on more than a hundred destinations world-wide. Such books are excellent pre-trip reading material and focus on customs, culture, history, art and architecture, religion, wildlife and food, thus setting them apart from all other guidebooks on the market today.

Enclosed is the latest title list for your perusal.

This special offer is valid until the end of the academic year 90/91. Should you want to purchase any of the listed guidebooks, please complete the reply slip below and mail it back to us together with a cheque made payable to the NUS GEOGRAPHICAL SOCIETY.

Do call me on 7723862 should you require further information.

Yours sincerely

Adeline Tan
Treasurer

the **Dish**

What's all the buzz about?

Whether you're a quivering caffeine junkie or just a casual sipper, there's more to that hair-raising jolt than meets the eye

By Cindy Waxer

What would you say if someone offered you a steaming hot cup of 1,3,7-trimethylxanthine? "Thanks, but no thanks." Well, guess what. You just refused a cup of coffee. 1,3,7-trimethylxanthine is the fancy-schmancy name for caffeine, that go-go ingredient in everything from sodas to Snickers. Yet, despite its overwhelming presence, there are many myths brewing about caffeine. So, before you declare yourself a mocha maven, test your caffeine chutzpah to see if you're really full of (coffee) beans.

True or False

A cup of coffee a day will keep the love handles away. **True or False?**
False. Sure, we've all felt that first blast of energy after drinking a fat mug of coffee, but that doesn't mean you're blasting the pounds away. While a moderate dose of caffeine might temporarily jump-start your metabolism, it's not an appetite suppressant. In fact, in 1991 the FDA banned the use of caffeine in over-the-counter diet pills because, unlike proper nutrition and exercise, it has no proven long-term affect on weight.

Chemically, caffeine is in the same family as poisonous compounds such as strychnine, nicotine and morphine. **True or False?**
True. Caffeine is found in the leaves, seeds and fruits of more than 60 plants, including coffee, cacao beans, kola nuts and tea leaves. But, despite caffeine's *au naturel* origins, its chemical makeup belongs to the same family of potentially lethal compounds as emetine. But fear not the hot black brew. A recent study suggests that women who drink two or more cups of coffee per day are less likely to commit suicide than those who don't drink coffee at all.

46 JUMP

PHOTOGRAPHED BY THOMAS CARD.

Plate 1 'What's all the buzz about?' (Article from *Jump*, August 1998, pp. 46–8)

Genre and visual informativeness: localised and progressive texts

Bernhardt (1985) suggests a scale of visual informativeness ranging from, for example, the homogeneous text of the average novel, whose only visual features are paragraph indentation and chapter headings, to instructions for self-assembly furniture, which, unfortunately, are often almost entirely visual in their information.

ACTIVITY 7*

Which of the following discourse types or genres would you regard as most visually informative? List them in order of informativeness.

1 poem   2 form   3 recipe   4 textbook   5 magazine advert
6 newspaper report

*You might bring an example into class and be prepared to identify the kinds of visual informativeness it displays.

Degrees of visual informativeness are likely to match reading styles. In particular, if graphic devices of types (2) and (3) are employed to sectionalise the text, then the text can be described as **localised**. These sections can be read selectively, and in any order one chooses. For example in 'What's all the buzz about' the reader can home in on the True or False section and choose to look at just one of the questions and answers without reading the other.

By contrast, texts that are not visually informative tend to be **progressive**. They only reveal their structure through reading in their entirety, which enables the text to form one large unit, with, perhaps, a point-last, Inductive structure. Novels and poems are normally Progressive; you are not supposed to turn to the last page of a murder mystery to find out who was the murderer. The homogeneous print of literary texts doesn't encourage this kind of scanning either.

Assured and non-assured readers

When deciding on how much visuality is appropriate for a text we have to take into account another factor – how motivated or assured our readers are. A reader looking through a telephone directory for a number, or reading the latest novel by their favourite author, does not need to be encouraged to continue reading, and can be described as an **assured** reader. But someone flicking through a magazine, nonchalantly looking at the adverts as he turns the pages, or glancing at brochures in a travel agent's, needs to have his attention grabbed and sustained, and can be called a **non-assured reader**. The non-assured reader will need to be attracted by the visuals, so one would expect texts designed for him to be more visually informative. By contrast, the texts for an already motivated reader can afford to dispense with the range of graphic devices we have been considering.

ACTIVITY 8

Look back at the previous activity. Does your ranking of the different text types tell anything about the degree to which the readership for these is assured?

1.4 Generic structure

If we glance at a newspaper in a foreign language, the graphic design and page size will tell us straight away what kind of text it is. A discourse type or genre, as we have seen in the previous section, will have various conventions for graphics and layout, which will help to structure the text. So it would be wrong to assume that, when we are organising the texts we write, we somehow start from scratch. In fact, each discourse type or genre has a more or less conventionalised **generic structure**, a kind of template into which we can fit our words and sentences. For example, look at these adjacent entries from the telephone directory.

Johnson Anne	10A Brighton Ave.	280 8093
Johnson Bill	4A Ardmore Park #02 – 00	733 5146

The generic structure for each entry is quite clear. (The carat, $^\wedge$, means 'followed by' and the parentheses indicate that these elements are optional):

SURNAME $^\wedge$ GIVEN NAME $^\wedge$ ADDRESS ($^\wedge$ FLOOR – FLATNUMBER) $^\wedge$ TELEPHONE NUMBER

And the larger generic structure simply involves listing each person alphabetically by SURNAME.

Genres in education

There has been much research interest, especially in Australian applied linguistics, in the kinds of genres that are or are not required or taught in schools. If we assume that writing in schools should be a preparation for writing in the real world, it does appear that in the past there has been a misguided emphasis on narrative. How often do adults write narratives in their everyday life?

Nevertheless, Martin, Rothery and others (Martin and Rothery 1981, 1982) have identified a range of other genres which *do* seem to surface in the classroom. Based on their work, the education authorities in New South Wales came up with a list of text types or genres for curriculum development purposes (Table 1.1).

Table 1.1 Narrative genres in the classroom

Genre	Purposes of language use
Narrative	To tell a story as a means of making sense of events and happenings in the world. It can be both entertaining and informing
Recount	To construct past experience by retelling events and incidents in the order in which they occurred
Information report	To represent factual information about a class of things usually by first classifying them and then describing their characteristics
Discussion	To present information and opinions about more than one side of an issue: it may end with a recommendation based on the evidence presented
Explanation	To explain why things are as they are or how things work
Exposition	To advance or justify an argument or put forward a particular point of view
Procedure	To show how something can be accomplished through a series or steps of actions to be taken

Source: *English K-6 in the classroom* New South Wales Department of School Education

We do not have the space here to go into the various structures inherent in all these different genres, but we can link them back to Nash's paragraph designs. Narrative, **recount**, and procedure (e.g. recipes) all involve sequences of events, so that the ordering of clauses which represent these events is going to be a crucial part of their structure. They are likely to make extensive use of step (and chain) structures. Information **report**, **exposition**, **discussion**, and **explanation**, on the other hand, involve things or ideas rather than events. An information report will obviously structure itself around categories and subcategories, and their definitions/descriptions, probably with many stacks embedded in other stacks. Exposition, arguing only one side of an issue, is likely to use stacks too. By contrast, Discussion, having different sections to do with the opinions for and against, will need to develop some Balance structures. Explanation, if involving a series of causes and effects, might well make use of chaining devices. Though these are general patterns, remember that most genres will mix their basic design and freely combine it with others, as we saw in the case of the Balance combining with the stack.

In the following sections we will concentrate on the structure of two genres, narrative and news reports. I choose these because they are widely read, and because, although they often deal with sequences of events, their structures are markedly different.

The generic structure of narrative

Investigating oral narratives, William Labov discovered the following elements of their generic structure (Labov 1972).

Abstract

The **abstract** is a short summary of the story that narrators generally provide before the narrative begins. It encapsulates the 'point' of the story, or what the story exemplifies. It is not compulsory, but it provides a signal that a narrative is about to commence, and that the speaker wishes to hold the floor uninterrupted until it is over. And it is also a bridge to make the narrative relevant to the preceding conversation. For example, the conversation might be about how frightening childhood experiences can give you phobias. To make the transition to narrative you could say 'There's this kid I knew when I was young who had a dreadful experience with bears, and it has still affected her behaviour for years afterwards'.

Orientation

The **orientation** gives information about the time, place, persons and situation/activity type they are engaged in. Typically, this section will include Adverbials of time and place and **relational** verbs like *to be* which describe states/ relations rather than actions, for instance, describing the place, time, weather or characters. When the reference is to an action that is going on at the time the narrative commences, then the **progressive** *-ing* forms of the verb will be used. An example would be:

> relational   relational
> verb   verb
> *Her name <u>was</u> Goldilocks and she <u>was</u> very adventurous.*

> time adverbial   progressive   place adverbials
> *<u>One June day</u> she was <u>walking</u> <u>to school along the edge of the wood</u>*
> *<u>behind her house.</u>*

31

Strictly speaking this Orientation element is not compulsory either, but is normal in written narratives.

Complicating Action

The **complicating action** and the Resolution are the essential elements in a narrative. In fact, all a narrative needs is two or more clauses describing a pair of linked events or actions, ordered chronologically, such as 'Goldilocks went into the bears' house. The bears frightened her away'. These clauses will be in simple present or simple past tenses, in contrast with the Progressive forms in the Orientation, e.g. 'went' not 'was going'. If the order of clauses is reversed, the interpretation of the sequence of the events changes, and we have a different narrative. For instance, 'The bears frightened her away. Goldilocks went into the bears' house'. Even nowadays, 'She had a baby and got married' is a different story from 'She got married and had a baby'.

Resolution

The **resolution** is provided by the last of the narrative clauses which began with the Complicating Action, bringing the sequence of actions and events to an end, for example 'Goldilocks ran away from the house of the three bears and back home'.

Coda

The **coda** is the means by which the narrative is completed and the listener is brought out of the past back into the present time. Just as the Abstract was a bridge from the surrounding conversation to the narrative, this is a bridge out of the narrative and signals that the speaker no longer has the right to the floor. Often it is changes of tenses and time adverbs that bring us back to the present, as in 'So, she <u>still</u> *doesn't* eat porridge, play with teddy bears or rock on chairs, and she *prefers* to sleep on the floor'.

Evaluation

Although these previous elements should occur in a particular order, Evaluation may occur at any point in the narrative, scattered throughout the text between the Abstract and Coda. Labov defined **evaluation** as those clauses which don't belong to the narrative action, but which, on the contrary, delay its forward movement. These comprise:

• comments by narrator	'At that moment Goldilocks looked like a little Russian doll'
• evaluative comment of character	'Eating my porridge was a horrible thing to do'
• evaluative comments attributed to a third party	'Mama bear told you it was naughty not to lock the door'
• emotive devices:	
– exclamations	'What a soft bed it was!'
– interjections/swear words	'<u>Oh my God</u>, look at my chair!'
– emotionally laden vocabulary	'The <u>horrible greedy slut</u>!'
• comparators:	
– if clauses	'<u>If</u> Goldilocks had cried,
– comparisons	<u>more like</u> a stereotypical girl
– modals (*can*, *shall*, *must*, *might*, etc.)	Baby Bear <u>might </u>have pitied her.
– negatives	But she did<u>n't</u>.
– futures	<u>Will </u>she ever go walking in the
– questions	woods again<u>?</u>'

We can sum up Labov's model in the following formula, with optional elements in parentheses.

(ABSTRACT^)(ORIENTATION^) COMPLICATING ACTION ^ RESOLUTION (^ CODA) + (EVALUATION).

This diagram means that a minimum narrative consists of two linked clauses, the first belonging to the Complicating Action and the second constituting the Resolution.

Why does the narrative genre have this particular structure? We might answer this question by comparing and contrasting it with a Recount. In Table 1.1 we see that one of the main differences is that a narrative is a story (possibly fictional) which is an attempt to 'make sense of events and happenings in the world'. By contrast, a Recount simply tells events from experience (non-fictional) in the order in which they occurred. The Genesis creation myth, as an example of narrative, not only tries to make sense of the origins of life on earth, but more particularly explains why there are seven days in the week, why snakes have no legs, why women have one rib more than men and suffer in childbirth, why we wear clothes and why work is necessary. This requirement that narratives make sense of the world provides some explanation for the elements of their structure. The Abstract suggests that the story has a point, some topic or proposition which it illustrates; or to put it the other way around, the Abstract makes sense of the story. The same role may be fulfilled by the Coda, for instance the moral at the end of a fable. The Resolution also contributes to

33

'making sense' – it gives a feeling of 'closure', a conclusion to the episodes, a neat tying up of the narrative strands, or a solution to a problem. Real life, of course, seldom has such neat or final solutions – the marriage that ends a Shakespearean comedy would, in real life, be as much a beginning as an ending. In a similar way, whereas the clauses of a Recount could describe unrelated events or actions, the clauses of the Complicating Action of narrative are defined as linked in some way, for example by cause or effect, or condition and response (Montgomery *et al.* 1992: 177-8).

ACTIVITY 9

Look at the following short narrative. Try to identify the narrative moves Abstract, Orientation, Complicating Action, Resolution, Coda and Evaluation.

I think Peter's always been a bit foolhardy. I remember once we were on holiday in Cornwall, and it was one of those lovely sunny breezy days which are just right for a picnic. So we'd decided to go down to Clodgy point, the rocky cliffs of the Atlantic coast. After a picnic lunch, Peter and his brother asked if they could go for a walk while me and my husband had a nap. So off they went. They hadn't come back in two hours, so we went to look for them. We walked quickly along the cliff for half an hour, and, as we came round a promontory we caught sight of them at the foot of the cliff on the rocks at the opposite side of the cove. I was terrified. How had they got down there? We called frantically for them to come back. They climbed up the steep grassy slope, which must have been about 60 degrees. I don't know how they did it. When they met us at the top I said,

'Why did you go down there. Don't you know it's dangerous?'

Peter held out a black and white striped snail shell, and all he said was

'If we hadn't gone down there I would never have seen this.'

So nowadays I'm never surprised to hear he's involved in some dangerous adventure or other.

We notice that in narrative we have a basically Inductive structure. In one sense, of course, an Abstract, if there is one, might give a hint of the point of the story, which would make it a point-first, Deductive story. But the Inductive movement towards the resolution is essential to the specific instance that proves the point. Unlike really Deductive structures, the narrative cannot be abandoned part-way through and still convey the gist of the story. As we shall see, this is one of the main differences between the generic structure of Narrative, and that of News Reports.

The generic structure of news reports

The structure of news reports in 'serious' newspapers is quite different from narrative, though popular newspapers tend to be more narrative like. In this section, we will be following the pattern of generic structure worked out by van Dijk (1986), somewhat simplified and diagrammed in Figure 1.1, see p. 36.

The **summary**, to be distinguished from **the news story**, comprises the **headline**, and the **lead**, generally the first paragraph (or two). The headline, and sometimes the Lead too, will be graphologically prominent, in bigger or bolder type. The Summary announces the main topic, and also includes a concise version of the main point, the main event. This makes the news report skimmable. A basic guideline for reporters is that the Lead should contain information about who did what, when, where and how. However, it stops short of answering the question *why?*. For example:

Chips down again for Mir [HEADLINE]

The main computer on the Russian space station Mir malfunctioned on Monday, plunging the ageing vessel into a new crisis. [LEAD]

(This and the following extracts illustrating news report structure are adapted from an article in the Singapore newspaper the *Straits Times*, 20 August 1997, p. 9)

The news story comprises the **episode** and **comments**. The Episode is made up of **events** and **consequences**.

Dealing with the events first, these divide into the **main event** and the **background**. The Main Event(s) by van Dijk's definition, based on a daily newspaper, must have taken place within the last two days. For example:

An unexplained error in the computer made Mir lose its proper position as it spun around earth, meaning the station was no longer orientated toward the sun and its solar energy panels did not generate electricity. [MAIN EVENT]

If the event is one of a series in a previously reported ongoing story, then the last important event constitutes the Main Event. In short reports, the Main Event and the Lead may be one and the same paragraph or sentence.

35

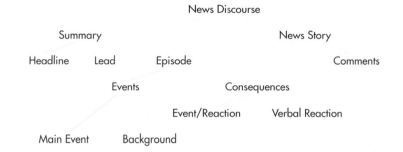

Figure 1.1 The discourse structure of news reports

The **background**, most fully developed in broadsheet papers, helps us to activate or update the knowledge held in memory, thereby making the news intelligible. Here, we find references to previous events sometimes stretching back even into history, and details of the physical circumstances in which the event took place. This section has much the same function as Labov's Orientation. For example:

> There was a collision between Mir and an unmanned cargo vessel in June. [BACKGROUND]
> The computer failure came just after the crew successfully docked a new progress cargo vessel, using manual controls. [BACKGROUND]

Turning from Events to Consequences, these latter may be almost as important as the Main Event, but they tend to come later in the report. The Consequences are anything which was caused by the Main Event, namely another event, or a human physical **reaction** or **verbal reaction**. For example:

> The three-man crew shut down all electrical instruments, including the faulty onboard computer. [REACTION]
> Mission control chief, Vladimir Solovyov told reporters that with the guidance system down, the 11-year-old vessel was spinning erratically in its Earth orbit. [VERBAL REACTION]

As we shall see in Chapter 9, the verbal reactions are usually those of powerful authority figures, stars, politicians, government spokespersons, police, lawyers or scientists and other professionals.

The Comment part of the Episode comprises evaluations of the other elements and speculations about what might happen next. When doing analysis it is important to remember that these Comments are those of the reporter or the editorial team producing the newspaper, and are different from the verbal reactions of eyewitnesses, politicians, etc. Generally news reports try to maintain the illusion of impartiality. It is only in the Comments section that the hidden ideology comes more or less to the surface. For example:

> Mir, which has been plagued with problems [COMMENT: evaluation] over the last six months, is probably coming to the end of its useful life. [COMMENT: speculation]

Van Dijk's model is strictly applicable only to News Reports, not to other articles in the newspaper such as editorials and features. In fact, newspaper feature articles can be viewed as an expansion of the Background and Consequences of newspaper reports, and editorials as an expansion of Comments.

The elements or moves of news report generic structure have a certain amount of ordering built into them. Providing the Lead and the Main Event are kept distinct, which is not always the case with shorter reports, the Summary must precede the Main Event, which may be followed by the Background, Consequences and Comments. These last three categories do not, however, have to appear in any particular order. This could be diagrammed as follows:

SUMMARY ^ MAIN EVENT ^ (BACKGROUND) (CONSEQUENCES) (COMMENTS)
[Less strictly ordered]

We need to add a couple of optional elements to van Dijk's model: the **dateline** which intervenes between headline and Lead, and the **attribution** which comes at the very end, and identifies the news agency from which some reports are compiled.

Sample analysis

To make the application of this analytical model clearer, here is a sample analysis of a news story about the Pope. The labels follow the preceding discourse element. Double brackets indicate one discourse element inside another.

Pope in hospital for tests after intestinal pains

[HEADLINE]

ROME – [DATELINE] A team of 15 doctors and nurses carried out a series of tests on Pope John Paul II yesterday to find out what is causing the abdominal pains that made him enter hospital for treatment. [LEAD/MAIN EVENT]

He may need surgery [COMMENT] but there was no immediate news of what ails him. [lack of VERBAL REACTION] The Gemelli clinic where the Pope is warded [BACKGROUND] did not plan to issue any formal bulletin before today or even tomorrow. [lack of VERBAL REACTION]

On Sunday, Vatican spokesman Joaquin Navarro-Valls said the 72-year-old pontiff's ailment had an 'intestinal dysfunction'. [VERBAL REACTION] It may be linked to the stomach wound he received during an assassination attempt in 1981. [COMMENT[BACKGROUND]]

Prayers were said for him throughout the Roman Catholic world yesterday. [VERBAL REACTION]

On Sunday a small crowd of well-wishers saw his entourage enter the hospital. Well-wishers jammed its balconies. [REACTION]

Inside the lobby he shook hands with nurses, patients and visiting families. [REACTION] He was smiling [BACKGROUND] and looked relaxed. [COMMENT]

It was in this clinic that he recovered from the 1981 assassination attempt under the care of Francesco Crucitti who will attend to him again. [BACKGROUND]

Always a robust figure, the Pope maintains a gruelling schedule and sleeps only a few hours. [COMMENT/BACKGROUND]

Although he has looked tired in recent years, his health has not been a cause of concern. [COMMENT]

(AP/UPI/Reuter [ATTRIBUTION])

The parts of this analysis which are a little tricky or debatable deserve explanation. Notice, first of all, that the Main Event and the Lead are combined into one sentence/paragraph; this is quite common in short news reports. In any analysis, it is crucial to try to define the Main Event: is it the Pope going into hospital, or the carrying out of tests? Presumably, strictly speaking, the latter, so that some of the later Reactions, such as the crowd jamming the balcony, and so on, are really responses to a Previous Event, his admission to the hospital.

Second, notice that life was made difficult for the reporters, because there was no Verbal Reaction by the hospital authorities. They solve this problem by reporting the lack of Verbal Reaction instead, which doesn't exactly make the report more interesting!

Third, there are cases of one element of the discourse embedded in another. For example, Background, the assassination attempt, is embedded in a larger sentence, which is Comment. Towards the end, Comment, in the form of the adjectives 'robust', 'gruelling' is combined with what might be Background, the

Pope's habit of sleeping little and having a busy schedule. This Background also implies a positive evaluative Comment on the Pope as someone who works hard and relentlessly to achieve his mission.

ACTIVITY 10

Look back at the news report about Christopher Reeve (p. 4). Can you identify the different elements of van Dijk's model in that text?

Values and ideology in the ordering and selection of news

News is a manufactured and processed product. This is quite clear if you listen to the radio news late at night and then early the following morning. Very often it will be the same, since the people who manufacture news have been sleeping. In the BBC's early years, the announcer would sometimes declare 'there is no news tonight' (Bell 1991: 2), meaning there was not sufficient manpower available, or no raw material had been found worthy of selection and processing into a story.

Let's look at the processing first. Because the generic structure of news reports is Deductive and relatively visual compared with narrative, it allows for reordering, prioritising and highlighting of the events reported. This processing gives scope for bias. With its point-first structure the reader can abandon the reading and still get the gist of the report. At the most extreme, he might just glance at the headline or look at the Lead, before moving on to something else. The copy-editor's selection of what goes into the headline and or the Lead, then, can set up distortions by giving prominence to one aspect of the story rather than another (Davis and Walton 1983; Bell 1991: 80)

For example, in the *International Express* 1–7 June 1995, p. 18, there was a report about a speech made by President Clinton at a conference on investment in Northern Ireland. The conference delegates included the leader of Sinn Fein, the political wing of the Irish Republican Army (IRA). The report begins with the following Summary, all in a larger point size than the remainder of the report.

Disarm, Adams is urged by Clinton

President Clinton has called on the IRA to give up its weapons.
In a speech which delighted British diplomats and Ulster Secretary Sir Patrick Mayhew, he repeated his call for talks on IRA disarmament.

However, later in the news report we have Clinton's words actually quoted:

> Paramilitary [sic] on both sides must get rid of their bombs and guns for good.

This quote appears some paragraphs down. And a reader who simply read the headline and Lead would be misled into thinking that Clinton had singled out the IRA, and Adams in particular, and had said nothing to the Protestant paramilitary groups in Ulster. Besides which, Adams is a politician, not part of the paramilitary IRA, so that the headline's presupposition that he controls arms is extremely manipulative. A more accurate headline would be:

Clinton urges Ulster paramilitaries to disarm

This example shows that the organisation of a news story has great potential for distorting and misrepresenting the news. The headline foregrounds one sort of information rather than another, and gives a false interpretation of what comes later (see Bell 1991: 224). The reader who only skims the headline and Lead in this Deductive text will come away with a very inaccurate idea of what Clinton actually said.

The selection of the raw material out of which news is processed has nothing particularly objective about it either. Galtung and Ruge identified a number of factors or biases that determine what events get into the news and which get left out or 'spiked'. These include:

(a) reference to élite persons;
(b) reference to élite nations;
(c) cultural proximity;
(d) intensity;
(e) unexpectedness;
(f) negativity.

If a news story refers to powerful or famous people it is more likely to get in the news (a). If you or I broke our back in a horse-riding accident, we wouldn't get six column inches on the front page of the international edition of a British newspaper. But Christopher Reeve did. If President Yeltsin has a heart by-pass operation, it is in the national and international newspapers for weeks. If your grandmother were to have one, I doubt it would even make the local paper. The newspaper texts quoted so far figure the famous show-business personality Christopher Reeve, alias 'Superman', and the powerful pontiff Pope John Paul II.

The appearance of these two in the news also illustrates the factor of cultural proximity (c). Hollywood culture has spread worldwide, as has the Catholic Church. So the wide dissemination of these cultures makes the stories more understandable, relevant to existing knowledge in readers' heads. By contrast, a Malaysian takraw star wouldn't mean much to readers of the *International Express* or to many readers of this book.

It is quite obvious that citizens of Europe, Japan and North American nations are more prominent in the news than citizens of poorer countries such as those in Africa, China or the Indian subcontinent (b). Seventy-four Western and Japanese tourists killed in a "terrorist attack" in Luxor, Egypt, got 12 column inches on the front page of the Singapore *Straits Times* 17 November 1997, while the same edition gave only 2 column inches, tucked away on page twenty-three, to the 87 coal miners killed in Anhui China, despite the latter's cultural, ethnic and geographical proximity. The *Straits Times* for 9 July 1997, reported a bomb blast in Punjab which killed 25 people in 20 column inches, as against 32 column inches devoted to an Australian political rally in which there were a few injuries to whites, with a single 60-year-old member of the One Nation party having to stay in hospital overnight. Such bias in the degree of coverage, which is endemic in newspapers worldwide, might be considered as an institutionalisation of racism (see van Dijk 1988a, 1988b).

In other words, for citizens of non-élite nations, the Event has to have more intensity (d), as measured by numbers, to be considered newsworthy. And perhaps accidents in Chinese coal mines and bombs in the Punjab are so common that one more is hardly unexpected, which is another news value (e).

In most newspapers in Western countries, negativity is an important value (f); disasters, accidents and any threats to the public are more common than good news. However, in countries where the media is under state control, the home news, especially, is likely to be more positive.

ACTIVITY 11*

Take the following text, which has a discourse structure typical of narrative, and transform it into a news report (200–250 words).

- Concentrate on reproducing the typical discourse structure of a news report in a quality newspaper, including as many of van Dijk's categories as possible, in an appropriate order. Indicate how the different parts of your text realise these categories. You may have to invent some material, especially for the Consequences (Verbal Reaction) and Comment category, and, of course, you do not have to include all the details of the original.
- You should also modify other aspects of style besides discourse structure.

Typical news report features include juxtaposition (or apposition) of two phrases referring to the same person, e.g. 'Janet Lee 32, a receptionist with Peat Marwick', inclusion of detailed precise facts like ages or exact numbers, complicated noun phrases, e.g. 'the judge in the mail-train robbery trial in Aylesbury', and short paragraphs of one or two sentences. Look at a few newspaper reports as models.

- Make your text more visually informative than the original, in ways that are appropriate to News Reports.
- Be prepared to discuss the changes that have been made to the discourse structure and visual informativeness of the original narrative. Why does the new discourse structure seem ludicrously inappropriate for this material? Does this story contain the news values necessary for newsworthiness?
- How could you have given a different emphasis and a different value to the news reported by selecting a different headline and Lead for your story?

Little Red Ridinghood's mother was packing a basket with eggs and butter and homemade bread.

'Who is that for?' asked Little Red Ridinghood.

'For Grandma,' said Mother. 'She has not been feeling well.'
Grandma lived alone in a cottage in the middle of a wood.

'I will take it to her,' said Little Red Ridinghood.

'Make sure you go straight to the cottage,' said Mother as she waved good-bye, 'and do not talk to any strangers'.

Little Red Ridinghood meant to go straight to the cottage but there were so many wild flowers growing in the wood, she decided to stop and pick some for Grandma. Grandma liked flowers. They would cheer her up.

'Good morning!' said a voice near her elbow. It was a wolf. 'Where are you taking these goodies?'

'I'm taking them to my Grandma,' said Little Red Ridinghood, quite forgetting what her mother had said about talking to strangers.

'Lucky Grandma,' said the wolf. 'Where does she live?'

'In the cottage in the middle of the wood,' said Little Red Ridinghood.

'Be sure to pick her a nice BIG bunch of flowers,' said the wolf and hurried away.

The wolf went straight to Grandma's cottage and knocked at the door.

'Who is there?' called Grandma.

'It is I, Little Red Ridinghood,' replied the wolf in a 'little girl' voice.

'Then lift up the latch and come in,' called Grandma.

Grandma screamed loudly when she saw the wolf's face peering around the door. He was licking his lips. She jumped out of bed and tried to hide in the cupboard, but the wolf, who was very hungry, caught her and in three gulps ate her all up. Then he picked up her frilly bedcap that had fallen to the floor and put it on his own head. He pushed his ears inside her cap, climbed into Grandma's bed, pulled up the bedclothes and waited for Red Ridinghood to come. Presently there was a knock on the door.

'Who is there?' he called, in a voice that sounded like Grandma's.

'It is I, Little Red Ridinghood.'

'Then lift up the latch and come in.'

She opened the door and went in.

'Are you feeling better, Grandma?' she asked.

'Yes dear, I am. Let me see what you have in the basket.'

As the wolf leaned forward the bedcap slipped and one of his ears popped out.

'What big ears you have,' said Little Red Ridinghood.

'All the better to hear you with,' said the wolf, turning towards her.

'What big eyes you have, Grandma!'

'All the better to see you with,' said the wolf with a big grin.

'What big teeth you have!'

'All the better to eat you with!' said the wolf and threw back the covers and jumped out of bed.

'You are not my Grandma!' she screamed.

'No I'm not. I'm the big bad wolf,' growled the wolf in his own voice, 'and I'm going to eat you up.'

'Help! Help!' shouted Little Red Ridinghood as the wolf chased her out of the cottage and into the wood.

The woodcutter heard her screams and came to the rescue. As soon as the wolf saw the woodcutter's big wood-cutting axe, he put his tail between his legs and ran away as fast as he could.

'What a lucky escape I had,' said Red Ridinghood to the woodcutter. What a lucky escape indeed.

1.5 Summary and postscript on genre, culture and ideology

In this unit we have been exploring the ways in which text is organised or knitted together, its cohesion. We looked at how:

- to organise information within the clause or sentence, to preserve a given–new order in Theme and rheme, and how to relate Themes throughout paragraphs;
- to organise information and ideas in four basic kinds of paragraphs – Step, Stack, Chain and Balance – patterns which in practice we can blend;
- to position the point first or last in the discourse to give a Deductive or an Inductive structure;
- to use visual information to help with the organisation of text, in order to produce Localised rather than Progressive structures, and to make texts more attractive, so that they appeal to non-assured readers;
- specific genres have their own organisational conventions, which may or may not be required or taught in schools;
- the generic structure of narrative contrasts with news reports, which provides opportunities for distortion of news.

Genres are discourse types which have achieved importance within a particular culture, society and institution. Another way of looking at it is to say that the culture values these particular forms of discourse, so that to be part of that culture and to participate fully within it one needs to master their linguistic and generic conventions. An imaginary person who was restricted in competence to the genres of sales encounters, jokes, conversation and chatting up members of the opposite sex, would have less power, and be less valued and lower paid than a person who could, in addition, give public talks or lectures, write letters to the editor of a quality newspaper, conduct employment interviews, chair committee meetings, and so on.

In an educational context it becomes important for students to be taught to operate successfully within the highly valued genres of a society, by being acquainted with their generic structures. This is part of what is meant by 'empowering' students and it necessitates abandoning the overemphasis on narrative writing: 'stories are for those who, because of their social status and education, are denied the power of exposition' (van Leeuwen 1987: 199). It is hoped that, if you missed out on explicit teaching of genre in school, this book will help at least to raise your awareness of the features of different genres.

Genres are, however, seldom absolutely distinct – one text will often include elements of different genres (Fairclough 1995: 88–90), and genres and generic combinations are evolving and emerging all the time. For example 'What's all the buzz about' exemplifies a relatively new genre combining elements of the more traditional popular science feature article and interview/conversation. So school, college and university students should not simply learn to reproduce generically "pure" texts but also to experiment with combining and modifying genres. This will give an opportunity to question their structural and linguistic conventions, in order to explore their communicative justifications, if any, or their ideological underpinnings.

Suggestions for further reading

- Halliday (1994) chapter 5, Downing and Locke (1992) chapter 6, and Eggins (1994) chapter 9 all provide a comprehensive account of the grammar of Theme and rheme. Butt *et al.* (1995) chapter 6, give a simpler version. Eggins (1994) chapters 2 and 3 has a clear and detailed account of the theory of genre and register, and Butt *et al.* (1995) deal with the same concept in a very simplified way in chapter 8.

- Halliday and Hasan's *Language Context and Text* chapter 4, explains the idea of generic structure and gives clear examples of how it is related to social context. Tony Bex's *Variety in Written English* provides a useful overview of written genres.

- Walter Nash's *Designs in Prose* chapter 1, pp. 9–19 is the source for the accounts of paragraph structure given in this chapter. Although, or because most of his examples are made up, they are often humorous and entertaining. This book has been perhaps superseded by Nash and Stacey's *Creating Texts: An Introduction to the Study of Composition*. Both are very useful rhetorical manuals, though they have little to say about the ideological dimensions of texts.

- Colomb and Williams' 'Perceiving structure in professional prose' is a very useful article. It is the source for the point-first and point-last distinction, but elaborates many other aspects of prose structure, such as the way texts hang together through lexical patterning to form discourse units of various extents.

- Stephen Bernhardt's 'Text structure and graphic design: the visible design', is the source for the features of visual informativeness mentioned in this chapter. It makes an interesting comparison between grammatical–lexical features of texts and their visual equivalents, within a functional framework. Goodman and Graddol's *Redesigning English*, chapter 2, has interesting work on the visual aspects of texts.

- Ronald Carter and Walter Nash's *Seeing through Language*, chapter 3 is a useful exploration of narrative structure, as is chapter 18 of Montgomery *et al.*'s *Ways of Reading*. William Labov's original account of the structure of oral narratives can be found in *Language in the Inner City*. The major introduction to narrative is Michael Toolan's *Narrative: A Critical Linguistic Introduction*.

- Van Dijk's 'News schemata', from which the model of generic structure of news reports is taken, has an extremely interesting later section which explores convincingly the ideological potential of news structures.

- There is a considerable literature on genre and its teaching, mainly within an Australian context. Most useful and accessible is probably Frances Christie and Jim Martin's *Genre and Institutions: Social Processes in the Workplace and School*. Also valuable is Clare Painter and Jim Martin's edited collection *Writing to Mean: Teaching Genres Across the Curriculum*.

Chapter 2

Text and conceptual meaning

Aims of this chapter

To show how vocabulary and grammar represent the state of the world, and, through stereotyping and obscuring responsibility, reflect underlying ideologies.

To demonstrate how to analyse the vocabulary and grammar of a longer text and relate the findings to ideological concerns.

- **2.0 Introduction: language as a tool for thinking**
  Argues that the way we think about and perceive the world around and inside us is more or less determined by the language we speak, and the choices we make within that language.

- **2.1 Ideology and vocabulary**
  Shows how vocabulary is used to classify the objects and phenomena of our world, with such classification leading to stereotyping, and explores in particular the representation of women.

- **2.2 Ideology, grammar and transitivity**
  Gives a detailed explanation of how clauses represent states, actions, speech and mental processes; the section includes a substantial analysis of a feature column from the *Guardian* newspaper linking the analysis of vocabulary and grammar to the ideological concerns of the writer.

- **2.3 Complications to transitivity**
  Explains how grammatical structures like the Passive, and the changing of verbs into nouns, can be used to hide agency and responsibility.

2.0 Introduction: language as a tool for thinking

If chapter 1 was about packaging, the thrust of this second chapter is content – the ideas we convey to our readers through language. One of the main assumptions of critical linguistics is that the language in the text affects the way we think. In a trivial sense this is obviously true – most people would agree that the main reason for communication is to influence the thoughts of others by what we say. Practitioners of critical discourse analysis, however, consider the effect of language on thought in more important senses:

(1)   The vocabulary and grammar of a particular language predispose the speakers/writers of that language to think in certain ways about themselves, other members of society and the world around them.

(2)   The grammatical and vocabulary choices which a speaker/writer makes within the resources of that particular language *construct* a representation of the world, rather than simply *reflect* a pre-existing reality.

(1) is known as the theory of **linguistic relativity** (Whorf 1956: 57–65). The strong version of the theory claims that our language completely determines the way we think about the world and ourselves. But the weak version, which I accept, simply says that speaking one language makes it difficult to think as the speakers of another language do.

ACTIVITY 12

If you or anyone in the class speaks a non-European language, compare the different vocabulary for family members available in English and the other language. Is there one word which exactly conveys the meanings of the word *brother* 'male sibling' or *uncle* 'brother of mother or father'? If you speak French as well as English, consider whether there is any precise equivalent for the meaning of the words *chair* or *brown* in French.

The assumption (2) suggests that the 'same' event may be represented in many different ways. Look at this extract from a news report about riots in the English city of Bristol (*Straits Times*, 20 July 1992):

> The trouble erupted on Thursday night after two men were killed when the stolen police motorcycle they were riding was involved in a crash with an unmarked police car.

(a) Two men were killed when the stolen police motorcycle they were riding was involved in a crash with an unmarked police car.

(b) Police murdered two 17-year-olds on a motorcycle by ramming them with their unmarked police car.

(c) Two youths killed themselves by driving their motorcycle into an unmarked police car.

The choice of (a), (b) and (c) represents or constructs the event in quite different ways.

ACTIVITY 13

In which of the above reports, (a), (b) or (c), are we most inclined to blame the police and sympathise with those who die? And in which do we shift responsibility for the event onto the victims? What aspects of the language (grammar and vocabulary) create these differences in assigning responsibility and creating sympathy?

Further evidence that language has a strong effect on the way we perceive reality, comes from captions to photographs or pictures. The satirical magazine *Punch* used to run a competition for the caption to a picture/cartoon which interpreted it in the most humorous way (see Plate 2).

Another insight of critical discourse analysis is that the influence of language upon our thought and perception of reality is most powerful when we are unaware of it, when it expresses hidden or, technically speaking, **latent ideology**. We may be aware of alternative ways of conceptualising reality because we speak a second language (1) or are sufficiently alert to notice the choices made within the language we speak (2). But, if not, the texts we encounter may seem the only natural way of representing experience. This mind-set is known as **naturalisation**. It is quite common for people to talk about "objective", "unbiased" description, as though our language and texts can simply and faithfully reflect a pre-existing reality. In fact we have no direct access to the world or reality out there. Even in the act of perception we interpret rather than simply register sensations of the world. For example, our brains invert the upside-down image on our retina, and we often interpret the size of that image as a cue to distance rather than an indication of the dimensions of the object. But language is even more important than perception as a distorting medium, coming between the reality "out there" and our perceptions/thoughts of it.

Plate 2 'I've never been to a nuclear power-station open day either' (Cartoon, *Punch*, January 1987, p. 54)

A particular problem might arise for the less dominant groups of society when they have an experience which they cannot articulate, because the vocabulary of the language includes only the terms of the dominant group. The feminist, Betty Friedan, for example, put forward the concept of *the problem without a name*, the alienated and oppressed experience which women felt as members of a patriarchal society. Her claim was that the lack of a term to describe this condition made it impossible for women to talk about it, and so to recognise that the problem was shared by the oppressed group (Mills 1995: 122). Sociologists use the term *anomie*, borrowed from the French.

The conceptual or representational dimension of language shows itself in two ways: first, in the vocabulary we use to categorise and refer to phenomena; and, second, in the structures of clause grammar which set up relationships between the objects we refer to. We'll start with vocabulary and then move on to discuss the grammar of the clause.

2.1 Ideology and vocabulary

First of all I want to demonstrate that the reality we experience has no inherent categories or classes and can therefore be categorised in any number of different ways. Let's sketch out what goes on in an act of classification with the following simple exercise. Look at the six boxes below, and separate them into two classes containing three boxes each.

Figure 2.1 Alternative classifications – ideology and vocabulary

There are several valid ways of grouping these boxes in categories. You could divide them into 1, 3, 6 and 2, 4, 5 on the criterion of containing one letter or two. Or into 1, 2, 6 and 3, 4, 5, because 1, 2, 6 contain only Os and no Xs. Or into 1, 3, 4, which have an upper-case letter in the centre, and 2, 5, 6 with their lower-case letters. Or any number of other alternatives. Adopting any one criterion for classification means excluding other possible criteria.

The question is: why might we categorise in one way rather than another? The answer is that the features we select as criteria for classification reflect our value system. You may have discovered earlier that the vocabulary for siblings in non-European languages pays attention to seniority in classifying relatives of the same generation. This shows that seniority is an important value in these societies. Elder brothers and sisters often take responsibility for younger siblings, make demands on them and expect a certain degree of obedience in ways unlikely to occur in mainstream Western cultures.

Another way in which vocabulary reflects ideological values is by the invention of categories through new words. The new word or phrase, especially if a noun, assumes that this is a useful, valid, or "real" category for referring to things, so this is a very clear example of language constructing rather than simply reflecting reality. The categories invented will sometimes reassure us or sometimes alarm us. Once upon a time, doctors invented the term *colitis*. It may be that if your doctor can diagnose your bowel problem as *colitis* this will give you some reassurance. Certainly you might begin to doubt her competence or feel that there is something very serious if she said 'I don't know what disease this is'. However, when we probe a little deeper we realise that the label *colitis* really only means "inflammation of the colon" and is a description of the symptoms, rather than a diagnosis of the cause. If, as I once did, you push further and ask what causes the inflammation you may well be told it is *ideopathic* which more or less means "the cause is unknown". So perhaps our faith in the doctor should not necessarily be restored simply because she could find these labels. By contrast, the press are quite adept at inventing categories of people who are perceived as some kind of threat to themselves, their family or society: 'couch potatoes', 'chain-smokers', 'shopaholics', 'wife-beaters', 'road-bullies', etc. And advertisers are very fond of inventing *ad hoc* categories of the market they are targeting – to parody: 'toast-lovers', 'mosquito-haters', etc.

ACTIVITY 14

Try to find examples of the invention of labels for such classes of people in adverts or popular newspapers. Can you invent any parodic terms?

Categorising the categories

Ideology also comes powerfully into play when the categories established by vocabulary are themselves categorised into more general groups. In contrast with the first level of classification, these more general categorisations are less obvious and more debatable. So, on some occasions we might want to group dogs in a more general class with mammals like cows and whales, but on another occasion to classify them as pets, along with goldfish and budgerigars. Very often these super categories will be established or negotiated in particular texts or discourses.

The following extracts are taken from the report of a seminar on the physical abuse of women. Participants in this seminar obviously disagreed over the members of the more general category:

(1) 'Road-bullies and wife-beaters are the same type of criminals and should be treated with equal severity,' pronounced Dr Alfred Choi.

(2) 'If counselling doesn't work, then drastic measures are called for. But let's not go overboard and equate the wife-beater to the road-bully, child-abuser and rapist,'– Mrs Ruby Lim-Yang.

(3) 'There is a big difference between the road-bully and the wife-beater,' Professor Anne Wee said. 'When you are punishing the road-bully you don't have to think in terms of the long-term relationship between the bully and victim ... tougher measures could worsen the situation ... in most cases wife-battering is not premeditated.'
(From 'Beating the wife-beater', *Straits Times*, 14 August 1992)

What is clear from the wife-beater debate is that the decisions we make about these general categories are not simply academic; they have practical consequences. We tend to treat the people we group together in the same way, a point made very clear by comments (1) and (3). This is most obvious in legal cases where classification will have crucial consequences for sentencing or the allocation of damages and entitlements, e.g.

A retired policeman won a unique court ruling to have his stress-related depression classed as an "injury" in the line of duty. The case means Bob Pickering, 52, of Brighton will be entitled to increased pension payments and may open the way to more claims against police authorities.

(*International Express*, 1–7 June 1995, p. 6)

ACTIVITY 15

Discuss how the following extract from a letter to *Newsweek* uses categorisation as an argumentative strategy.

Pol Pot and his henchmen were responsible for the evil of his tyrannical regime, but the Jane Fondas, Ramsey Clarks and other '60s hippies share the responsibility for Cambodia. In Southeast Asia as in South Korea, America tried to save a nation from tyranny.

Word-class, value and action

When classification leads to action the choice of a noun rather than a verb or adjective is important. Nouns represent categories of things, adjectives represent relatively permanent qualities, and verbs quite temporary qualities. Consider for example the following possible ways of criticising your lecturer:

(1) The lecturer **bored** me	verb (past tense)
(2) The lecturer **bores** me	verb (present tense: habitual)
(3) The lecturer is **boring**	adjective
(4) The lecturer is a **bore**	noun

In (1) this may simply be a one-off failure to be interesting; perhaps the lecturer was tired, or hadn't enough time for preparation of audio-visuals. (2) is more damning, suggesting that he is in the habit of being less than interesting. (3) damns him still more, since the capacity to bore is one of his relatively permanent qualities. Worse still is to label him a 'bore' (4), since this equates his very existence with boredom. The solutions to this problem will be less or more drastic according to the word-class used. In the case of (1) there is perhaps no need to do anything, since he will probably return to form on subsequent performances. (2) and (3) are more problematic, but student feedback may induce him to make changes to his style. (4) indicates that being a bore is part of his nature, and he is irredeemable. The only solution may be to remove him.

Stereotyping

One by-product of the categorising systems underlying vocabulary is **stereotyping**. Stereotyping occurs when, on the basis of some members of a class having a characteristic or belonging to another class, other members are assumed to have that characteristic or belong to that other class.

For example, because many Chinese students are short-sighted, we might assume that all Chinese students are short-sighted. Or, because most nurses belong to the female class, we might assume that all nurses are female. Stereotyping is a particular problem when we have no first-hand knowledge of the class members or their assumed characteristics. If we have never met a Nigerian in the flesh, then we will pick up our stereotypes second hand.

Similarly, when judging someone's character or inner state of mind we simply have to make assumptions on the basis of their observable behaviour. For example, in some cultures people queue for buses and in others they do not. Does this indicate that the latter are competitive or lack a sense of justice?

--- **ACTIVITY 16**

Make a list of adjectives which you associate with any three of the following nationalities:

Italian, Jamaican, Mexican, Swedish, Hong Kong, USA

To what extent are these qualities the result of first-hand experience, and to what extent are they second hand? If second hand, where do you think they come from?

Vocabulary, stereotyping and women

We can now take a look at more concrete examples of how vocabulary serves ideology, either by labelling and the categorisations it involves and/or the stereotyping it makes possible. Let's consider the ways in which vocabulary is used for women.

ACTIVITY 17*

Look at a recent copy of a tabloid newspaper. List the vocabulary used to describe women and compare it with the vocabulary used to describe or categorise men. You might look both at <u>adjectives,</u> and the *classes* to which women are assigned e.g. Benazir Bhutto is an <u>exceptional </u>(adjective) *politician* (class). What differences do you perceive in the portrayal of the sexes?

There are perhaps three main areas where the stereotyping of women is most obvious in newspapers and magazines.

- First, you may have found certain subcategories or subclasses to which women are typically assigned by nouns. Very often these subclasses define them in terms of their family relationships rather than in terms of their jobs. 'Jane Martin, 28, mother of two', is much more likely to occur in a newspaper report than 'John Martin, 30, father of two'. On the few occasions when women are defined by occupation rather than as wives and mothers, we might find that certain occupations are stereotyped as female, and others as male. This means that a longer form has to be used for what is regarded as exceptional, giving rise to phrases like *lady doctor*, *male nurse*, *women MPs*. One other linguistic symptom of the stereotyping of women's roles is the use of suffixes to distinguish women from men, and convey different connotations, for instance *act<u>ress</u>, auth<u>oress</u>, host<u>ess</u>, steward<u>ess</u>, poet<u>ess</u>, comed<u>ienne</u>, ush<u>erette</u>* (Mills 1995: 94–5).
- Stereotyping can also be observed in the way that verbs and adjectives are used of women, so that possible qualities come to be seen as expected or even inevitable, e.g. physically weak, emotional, irrational. Linked to the previous point, you may have noticed that the selection of vocabulary will emphasise the non-occupational qualities of women in society. The result is that many words, and visuals, concentrate on describing women's looks, youth, sexuality and desirability for men. A particular semantic area which is **overworded** is in the vocabulary for hair colour, some of the terms hav-

ing no equivalent for male hair: *brunette, blonde, auburn, redhead, peroxide blonde, ash blonde, natural blonde* (Mills 1995: 162). This suggests that women are still constructed in the media as objects for satisfying men's desires and, as a by-product, for producing children to keep the nation or human race going. For instance, female secretaries are unlikely to refer to managers as 'the boys along the corridor', but managers might well refer to secretarial staff as 'the girls in the office'. This emphasis on youth in relation to women is also reflected in the popular press's use of first names and diminutives. Though male politicians and others in power are sometimes referred to by a diminutive form, e.g. 'Little Johnny Howard' (Australia), the tendency does seem stronger in the case of women, e.g. '*Winnie*' not '*Winifred Mandela*', and '*Maggie*' for Margaret Thatcher, but not '*Johnny*' for John Major (Fowler 1991: 96, 100–101); 'The name is Bond. Jimmy Bond' sounds ridiculous. Of course politicians pre-empt this if they already use the shortened form for themselves, like Tony Blair.

ACTIVITY 18

Look at the following vocabulary, which depicts humans as food. Are these words used equally of men and women? You may need to use a dictionary, such as the *Cobuild English Dictionary*.

Nouns: cookie, tart, the cream in my coffee, crumpet, sugar, honey, sweetie, cheesecake, mutton dressed as lamb
Adjectives: tasty, dishy, insipid, refined, sour, bitter, vinegary

- Finally, there is a widespread use of metaphors for women, especially in Japanese (Hiraga 1991: 55), which depicts them as commodities, consumer goods or food. The ideological implications behind these metaphors are quite clear: commodities are inanimate objects; their sole purpose is to be used by consumers; they can be bought and then become the property of their rightful owners. All these assumptions suggest a social system in which women are expected to be passive, powerless, valuable and desirable objects, whose role in society is to be purchased, owned, used, consumed, and enjoyed by men.

A rather interesting development of stereotyping theory can be seen in a poem by Hélène Cixous, who shows that a binary opposition such as male/female can become a way of organising other oppositions.

> *Where is she?*
> Activity/passivity
> Sun/Moon
> Culture/Nature
> Day/Night
> Father/Mother
> Head/heart
> Intelligible/sensitive
> Logos/Pathos
>
> Man/Woman
>
> (Cixous 1981: 90)

These analogical oppositions seem to mutually reinforce each other, for example nature (not culture) will come to be seen as both a woman (not a man) and passive (not active). Obviously enough, these oppositions cluster to produce strong stereotypical associations for women and men, as well as for nature.

The strength of the male–female opposition and obsessive insistence on its application leads to quite cruel and pernicious medical practices. An article in the *New Internationalist* reports:

> According to the Intersex Society of North America one in every 2,000 infants is born with ambiguous genitalia from about two-dozen causes. There are more than 2,000 surgeries performed in the US each year aimed at surgically assigning a sex to these intersex patients. The Intersex Society campaigns against what it sees as an unethical medical practice of performing cosmetic surgery on infants who cannot give consent.
>
> (Nataf 1998: 23)

What is happening here is that the increasingly widespread phenomenon of uncertain sex, which makes the categorisation into male and female difficult to apply, prompts surgeons to change the phenomenon so that it more neatly fits the desired classification. There could hardly be a more telling example of the relationship between linguistic classification and (abuse of) power, unless it were Clinton's attempt to pin down the meaning of 'sexual relations' as a synonym of 'sexual intercourse'.

2.2 Ideology, grammar and transitivity

The conceptual aspects of ideology are not simply reflected in the vocabulary of a language, however. They are at work in the grammar and probably more dangerous there precisely because they are more latent. The part of the grammar of the clause which is relevant to conceptualisation, the representation of the world, is called **transitivity**. Let's see how it works.

Table 2.1 Process types in Hallidayan grammar

Process	Meanings	Participants	Example
Relational	existence, states, relationships	Token, Value	John (T) is sick (V) Peter (T) remained *a teacher* (V)
Material	actions, events	Actor, Affected, Beneficiary	Snow (Act) blocked *the road* (Aff) *Jane* (Act) handed *me* (Ben) *a waffle* (Aff)
Mental	perception, emotion, thought	Experiencer, Experience	*The cat* (Exr) saw *the bird* (Exp) *Mat* (Exr) hated *dogs* (Exp) *He* (Exr) decided *to go home* (Exp)
Verbal	speaking, writing, comunicating	Sayer, Receiver, Verbiage	*Paul* (S) told Mindy (R) *he would go home* (V) *Deidre* (S) whistled

Key
(Act)	= Actor		(Aff)	= Affected
(Ben)	= Beneficiary		(Exp)	= Experience
(Exr)	= Experiencer		(R)	= Receiver
(S)	= Sayer		(T)	= Token
(V)	= Value			

We can divide verbs and the processes they represent into four basic categories, Relational, Material, Mental and Verbal. **Relational processes** are those which describe states of affairs, static situations. They relate two things, or a thing and a property, the **token** and the **value**, e.g. 'John (Token) is a teacher' (Value), 'John (Token) is poor' (Value). They include verbs like *to be* and *to have* e.g. 'I have two houses', 'that penknife belongs to Jim', 'the hairbrush is in the drawer', 'there are ants in this cupboard'. Other Relational verbs are *remain, stay, equal, comprise, constitute, include, contain*, etc. And, as used in the following sentences, though not always, they include the verbs *stand, surround, occupy*: 'Big Ben stands next to the Houses of Parliament', 'a moat surrounds the castle', 'an oak tree occupies most of my back garden'.

Material process verbs are those which describe an action or event, and answer the question *what happened*? These are perhaps prototypical verbs, the "doing words" which we were taught in primary school e.g. 'John **hit** the teacher', 'John **smoked** dope', 'Mary **kissed** the referee', 'Jemima **died**', 'Harry **ran** fast', 'the cat **vomited**'. But Material processes also include verbs without an animate agent, e.g. 'snow **fell** heavily and **blocked** the driveway', 'the car **slid** over the black ice', 'the avalanche **buried** three skiers'. Whether animate or not, the thing responsible for causing the action or event is called the **actor**: John, John, Mary, Jemima, Harry, the cat, snow, the car, and the avalanche, respectively. Some of these verbs will have an Object, the thing that the action or event affects, and we can call this the **affected.** In the previous examples the teacher, dope, the referee, the driveway and three skiers are the Affected parties. There may sometimes be two Affecteds, one of which can be called the **beneficiary**. For example John in 'Mary gave John a potato'.

Mental process verbs are of three types, perception, cognition and emotion, e.g. 'Madeline Albright **saw** the Israeli Prime Minister', 'Samantha **heard** the birds singing'; 'Bach **considered** resigning', 'computers **think** fast'; 'Saddam Hussein **loves** waffles', 'the boss **annoyed** me'. The "person" who experiences these perceptions, thoughts, or emotions we can call the **experiencer**, in the previous examples Madeline Albright, Samantha, Bach, computers, Sadam Hussein and me. Sometimes the **experience** (perception, thought or emotion) will be referred to by a noun phrase, 'waffles', 'the boss'. But often it is represented by a whole clause (underlined): 'Blair **wondered** whether he should accept 1 million pounds for the Labour party. He **decided** not to accept the money, because he **thought** it might compromise his integrity.'

Verbal process verbs are verbs of saying or writing, e.g. 'He **demanded** an apology', 'he **nominated** a gorilla as chairman of the committee', 'the Indonesians **prayed** for rain', '"Help me," he **cried**. "How, exactly?" she **asked**'. The person doing the saying or writing will be called the **sayer**. The person addressed is the **receiver**. Sometimes what is actually said, the **verbiage**, can be represented by a whole clause or sentence, as with Mental processes: 'He said he would come on Monday.' '"I ate the chocolate cakes," she confessed'.

ACTIVITY 19

Look at the sentences below and decide what processes the verbs in bold represent. In Material processes what things or people are the Actors and Affected? In Mental processes who are the thinkers and the Experiencers of emotion, and what thoughts or feelings are they experiencing? In Verbal processes who are the sayers?

(1) Rebel Myanmar group **sets up** radio station in Norway

(2) Thatcher **to be** consultant with tobacco company

(3) She **disgusts** me

(4) Iraq **denounces** world population conference

(5) Japanese parents **reconsider** cram school system

(6) I was **given** a present by John

(7) I **love** the present

(8) He **said** she should be more careful

A sample of transitivity and vocabulary analysis

I will now demonstrate how to apply these lexical classifications and grammatical analyses to a longer text, to show the ways in which linguistic patterns can be used, deliberately or not, to construct a version of reality, and reflect ideological conflicts. The text I have chosen is a comment column taken from the Internet version of the British newspaper the *Guardian*, 3 February 1998. The text runs as follows:

I'm sorry teenagers, you are not the centre of the universe

Whether it's lovers on the Titanic or the White House bimbos, youth isn't so cool

By Linda Grant

Tuesday, 3 February 1998

Just as the lights were going down in the Odeon Leicester Square on Friday night, I said, 'Who's the hunk factor in this apart from Leonardo DiCaprio?' No one knew. Not Billy Zane, obviously. It turned out there wasn't one. We had to sit through three-and-a-half hours staring at the 10-foot features of a baby-faced 23-year-old whose puppy fat still filled his cheeks. The kid is barely out of zit cream. Where, we wanted to know, was Alan Rickman, smouldering erotically in a pea jacket? Or Sean Connery in captain's cap, head-butting the iceberg for its presumption? Or Liam Neeson in steerage, heavy in his boots in the Irish dancing? Or Sam Shepard as transatlantic gentleman card sharp from Missouri, making his own luck? In Schindler's List you got Liam Neeson and Ralph Fiennes. That's what I call a picture. The next day, the Turkish dry cleaner told me she wasn't going to bother to see Titanic. 'What's in it for us?' she demanded. 'My daughter here, she's going next week. But she likes Leonardo DiCaprio, don't you?' The girl sighed meaningfully and rolled her eyes. 'Ye-es' she breathed. 'You see? He's for teenagers. This is a teenage film.' I agreed.

In Titanic you see how completely the world has been taken over by adolescents and adolescent values. Here's a blockbuster movie for all the family – enjoyable tosh with great special effects – with absolutely no sex appeal for any woman over the age of 35 and in which no one over the age of 20 has any morality or goodness or courage apart from the unsinkable Molly Brown, here transformed into Young Love's accomplice.

For a good two bum-numbing hours the plot hinges around the escapades of a couple of naughty adolescents trying to evade the authority of the grown-ups in order to have sex, which eventually takes place, as most of it does at that age, in the back seat of a car. Meanwhile the ship plunges on towards its terrible destiny and the teeny-weeny, self-important world of the adolescents is overtaken by events, and indeed, reality.

Does this remind you of anything? Ring any bells? Any resonance here? All last week political commentators with lines and the odd grey hair, giving every appearance of being adults, were asking each other whether the approaching war with Iraq was being got up as a smokescreen to shift attention away from what really mattered: the US President's sex life. It seemed to occur to no one that it might be the other way round: that the 'me, me, look at me,' cries of the young women who may or may not have gone down on Bill Clinton were distracting us from potential military action against a mad dictator with an arsenal of chemical weapons. Whether you are for or against war with Saddam Hussein, you have to concede that if there is a burning issue of the moment it isn't the shape of the President's penis. That metaphor about rearranging the deckchairs on the Titanic has never seemed so freshly-minted.

Madeleine Albright is touring the Middle East to drum up support for air strikes and here we all are, fixated and focused on Clinton's extramarital affairs with women just about young enough to be his daughters. Like Clinton himself, we are mesmerised by the teenagers. With a grown-up wife beside him in the White House – and smart enough to get him off the hook – he still prefers the fleeting company of bimbos. I know I shouldn't call them that – Monica Lewinsky was a White House intern, after all – but if you spend your time giving blowjobs to older men instead of memorising the US Constitution and its many amendments, that's the label you are going to get stuck with.

The sexual power of young women is a force which seems capable of pulling the whole world off kilter. Adolescence has many, many attractions

– one need spend almost nothing on moisturiser (just as well, as the pocket money doesn't stretch to it); you can stay up all night energised by a tab of E and a bag of chips and still look ravishing in the morning; and you can endure the discomfort of a treetop camp for days on end while you stop a bypass. But in the virtues of adolescence lie its faults. Its condition is to see things in black and white, never to be plagued by uncertainty, or submit to expediency and compromise, and never, ever have to worry about mortgages, pension plans, household contents and building insurance or whether or not remembering where you put your keys is an early warning sign of senile dementia.

The downside to this ruthless confidence in the self-evident correctness of whatever moral high ground you have chosen is that it can fall easily into fundamentalist error, such as the date-rape frenzy which took over American campuses a few years ago in which teenage students singlehandedly attempted to abolish the uncertainty of the sexual encounter by the institution of a written code of behaviour.

Teenage radicalism is a product of the mistaken belief that yours is the first generation that ever lived to discern that the world teems with injustice. When Swampy's mum looks at him, does she also see Kevin the Teenager and his ancestral cry – handed down through the genetic pathways and emerging with the first pubic hair – of 'It's not fair' and 'I didn't ask to be born'? I'm sorry, teenagers, you are not the centre of the universe. I do not care about your doomed love affairs, whether they take place fictionally on board the Titanic, in a cupboard in the White House, or under the concealing darkness of the local bus shelter. I know you think your life will be ruined if you are made to come home no later than midnight by your cruel and oppressive parents but you don't know what ruined means until you've seen a chemical weapon in action.

Last week Peter Mandelson asked an eight-year-old to hold forth on his views about the contents of the Dome. Hey, why not ask him to run America's foreign policy, too? Put him in charge of the whole shooting match; let those Sony Play Station reflexes zap the baddies. Put Baby Spice in charge of United Nations weapons inspection. Give Kate Moss the presidency of the European Union. If youth is so cool, let them try running a few countries and see if the rubbish gets taken out, the beds made and there's something to eat in the cupboard.

The Iranian Revolution was carried out by the teenage zealots of the Revolutionary Guards, zipping around on motorbikes spray-painting the arms of anyone wearing a T-shirt. Who winds up in cults? Teenagers.

Vocabulary and the population of the text

We noted earlier that vocabulary classifies and categorises, and that texts often invent their own supercategories in order to construct a representation of experience. One important facet of this column is its categorising of the people mentioned in the text, technically called the **text population** (Talbot 1992).

The primary axis of classification is into the young and the middle-aged, or children and parents, with an emphasis on the younger. At one point this amounts to an age divide at the age of 35, though in relation to the characters in *Titanic* the division is set at 20, i.e. teenagers or older than teenagers. A lexical analysis of the text gives us 'teenage'/'teenager(s)' (12 times), 'adolescent(s)'/'adolescence' (6 times), 'young'/'youth' (6 times), 'daughter(s)' (twice), 'baby' (twice), 'bimbos' (twice) and 'kid', 'an eight-year-old', 'girl', and 'puppy' (each once). The word *teenager*, by the way, demonstrates quite clearly the arbitrariness of the linguistic categorisation process. There are many possible ways of dividing up the continuum of time, but to take those numbers of years which happen to end in *–teen* as a criterion appears quite *ad hoc*.

The frequency and variety of terms to refer to the young is an example of **overwording**, showing 'preoccupation with some aspect of reality–which may indicate that it is a focus of ideological struggle' (Fairclough 1989: 115). Less frequently represented is the older generation with 'adults', 'grown-up' 'older men', 'senile', 'mum', 'ancestral' and 'parents' all occurring once.

Other categories of people are perhaps not so clearly lexicalised, and have to be to some extent inferred. First, there are (film) stars: 'Leonardo di Caprio', 'Kevin the Teenager', 'Kate Moss', 'Baby Spice'; 'Alan Rickman', 'Sean Connery', 'Liam Neeson', 'Ralph Fiennes', 'Sam Shepard'. In line with the primary axis of classification by age these can be supercategorised into the young (the first four) and the older (the last five).

Second, we have politicians: the US President 'Bill Clinton', (5 times), 'Saddam Hussein' (3 times), 'Madeleine Albright' and 'Peter Mandelson'. These politicians in power are contrasted with teenagers who, in their 'radicalism' and vulnerability to 'cults' have rebelled against authority. These were either the 'teenage zealots of the Revolutionary Guards' who brought about the Iranian Revolution, or those 'teenage students' who campaigned 'to abolish the uncertainty of the sexual encounter'. Note that the use of plural forms often has connotations of threats, as when in right-wing circles during the Cold War the Soviet Union would be referred to as *The Soviets* and the communist block as *Reds*. Remember how the letter writer quoted in Activity 15 uses the phrase 'the Jane Fondas, Ramsey Clarks and other '60s hippies'? Does referring to youngsters fighting for power in the plural illustrate a hostility to the young?

A major character in the text population is, of course, the writer herself,

Linda Grant. She projects herself as in the older population, and belongs to the group she refers to as 'commentators with lines and the odd grey hair'. However, the point of the column is actually to question whether these people are behaving more like teenagers or like adults. 'All last week political commentators with lines and the odd grey hair, giving every appearance of being adults, were asking each other whether the approaching war with Iraq was being got up as a smokescreen to shift attention away from what really mattered: the US President's sex life'. Given the choice of identifying with adults or commentators she opts for the former and distances herself from the latter.

Besides the populations of the text we can look at the different social worlds they inhabit and how vocabulary represents these worlds. Three important areas seem to be the public world of geo-politics ('war', 'military action', 'chemical weapons', 'airstrikes', 'US constitution', 'the White House', 'the Middle East', 'foreign policy', 'radicalism', 'Revolution'); the family world of domesticity ('mortgages', 'pension plans', 'insurance', 'household contents', 'beds', 'cupboard', 'rubbish', 'keys'); the private world of sex ('sex'/'sexual' (5 times), 'affairs' (twice), 'erotically', 'penis', 'date-rape' (once)) . The world of film ('Odeon', 'picture', 'film', 'blockbuster movie', 'special effects', 'Titanic', 'plot') makes the fictionally private world of sex public, and the media ('we' ('commentators')) make it political.

Grammar and ideology: transitivity analysis

Now we have identified the major population groups in the text and their social worlds, we are in a position to explore how they function as participants in clauses as parts of those worlds. We will examine, in turn, interesting patterns in the Relational, Mental, Material and Verbal process clauses in this text. The large number of examples quoted and analysed here give you a model for any analysis you may wish to do yourselves, but you might wish to skim over some of them.

Relational clauses

Relational clauses will be used to describe and explicitly categorise the participants in the text. The relevant kinds of question when we perform a critical reading will be 'what participants attract these relational descriptions?', and 'what kinds of qualities or categories are assigned to them?'.

Along with the overwording, the number of Relational clauses devoted to describing teenagers and the state of adolescence betrays a fascination with the young, and perhaps an attempt to exorcise their power.

> Adolescence (Token) **has** <u>many, many attractions</u> (Value)

The fascination, and perhaps envy, focuses, to start with, on their sexuality.

> <u>The sexual power of young women</u> (Token) **is** <u>a force which seems capable of pulling the whole world off kilter</u> (Value)

And having acknowledged young people's power in that department, it proceeds to debunk the adolescents' claims to moral superiority, describing it as simplistic overconfidence, which leads easily into excess or error.

> But <u>in the virtues of adolescence</u> (Value) **lie** <u>its faults</u> (Token). <u>Its condition</u> (Token) **is** <u>to see things in black and white</u> (Value)

> <u>The downside to this ruthless confidence in the self-evident correctness of whatever moral high ground you have chosen</u> (Token) **is** <u>that it can fall easily into fundamentalist error</u> (Value)

These errors can take the form either of idealistic radicalism:

> <u>Teenage radicalism</u> (Token) **is** <u>a product of the mistaken belief that yours is the first generation that ever lived to discern that the world teems with injustice</u> (Value)

Or, more sinister, religious deviance:

> <u>Who</u> (Token) **winds up** <u>in cults</u>? (Value) <u>Teenagers</u>. (Token)

Obsessively, the columnist casts doubt on the superiority of the young and on their importance,

> <u>If youth</u> (Token) is <u>so cool</u> (Value)
> <u>youth</u> (Token) isn't <u>so cool</u> (Value)
> <u>you</u> (Token) **are** not <u>the centre of the universe</u> (Value)

This last protest, dramatised by its positioning as headline, is paradoxically negated by the column's obsession with adolescents. If not the centre of the universe they are, in this column, the centre of attention.

Mental processes

Mental processes indicate internal or perceptual processes, which are, strictly speaking, only accessible to the Experiencer. One question to ask is who the

Experiencers are – whether the writer claims to know the Experiences of other Experiencers, other characters, as is common with all-knowing narrators in some kinds of fiction. Another important question might be whether the Mental processes are to do with thinking, feeling or perception.

Mental process clauses with teenagers as Experiencers display three clear patterns. First, there are Mental processes which teenagers have never experienced.

> but you (Experiencer) don't **know** <u>what ruined means</u> (Experience) until you've (Experiencer) **seen** <u>a chemical weapon in action</u> (Experience)

Then there are processes which they have experienced but which are misguided or dangerous in some way.

> The downside to this ruthless confidence in the self-evident correctness of <u>whatever moral high ground</u> (Experience) <u>you</u> (Experiencer) have **chosen** is that it can fall easily into fundamentalist error

And third, there are Mental processes which they believe are unique to them but which actually adults have experienced too.

> Teenage radicalism is a product of the mistaken belief that yours is <u>the first generation that ever lived</u> (Experiencer) to **discern** <u>that the world teems with injustice.</u> (Experience)

We notice that in all these examples the writer is claiming knowledge of the thought processes of the young, which perhaps is rather presumptuous.

When we look at Linda Grant's less presumptuous representation of her own and other adults' Experiences, we notice that she confesses to a fascination with the young:

> Like Clinton himself, <u>we</u> (Experiencer) are **mesmerised** by <u>the teenagers</u> (Experience)

However, youngsters are often seen as a dangerous irrelevance:

> <u>the 'me, me, look at me,' cries of the young women</u> (Experience/Actor) . . . were **distracting** <u>us</u> (Experiencer/Affected) from potential military action against a mad dictator with an arsenal of chemical weapons.

(There is a slight problem in analysing this last example. Some verbs seem to have a foot in more than one process, and so we can label them with pairs of labels. *Distract* is one which seems to be partly Material and partly Mental (perception), as is *endure*, (emotion) analysed below.)

Material processes

The main reason for analysing Material processes is to uncover who is represented as the most powerful participants in the text. Crudely speaking, if the clause has an Actor and an Affected, this Actor is being represented as relatively powerful and responsible for the action. If there is only an Actor, and no Affected, the Actor comes over as less powerful. Affected participants come over as passive and powerless.

As we noted when discussing Relational processes, the writer acknowledges the sexual prowess of the young and particularly of young women. The alleged affairs between Clinton/Lewinsky/Jones, etc., provide a link between the two generations, the primary groups established through lexical classification, and between the private world of sex and the public world of politics.

> if <u>you</u> (Actor) spend your time **giving** <u>blowjobs</u> (Affected) to <u>older men</u> (Affected: beneficiary) instead of memorising the US Constitution

Notice that these alleged sexual acts are portrayed with women rather than Clinton as Actor; for example, this event could have been represented as 'Clinton taking blowjobs from younger women'. As it stands the President seems more passive and less responsible for the sex, and the young women more active and blameworthy. The writer's most extreme claim about the power of women's sex appeal is:

> <u>The sexual power of young women</u> is a <u>force which</u> (Actor) seems capable of **pulling** <u>the whole world</u> (Affected) off kilter

Women as sexual protagonists affect not only "the most powerful man in the world" but the world itself.

Youngsters' sexual activity seems to be one aspect of their physical energy and resilience, qualities which the author also recognises and perhaps admires:

> And <u>you</u> (Actor/Experiencer) can **endure** <u>the discomfort of a treetop camp</u> (Affected/Experience) for days on end

> <u>You</u> (Actor) can **stay up** all night

However, in the political sphere, teenagers are portrayed as not amounting to much. Their actions seem largely to be ineffectual, gratuitous and negative:

> The teenage zealots of the Revolutionary Guards (Actors) **zipping around** on motorbikes, **spray-painting** the arms of anyone wearing a T-shirt (Affected). While you (Actor) **stop** a bypass (Affected)

Prefacing the main verb with *try* and *attempt* (*) is a clear signal of potential failure:

> Teenage students (Actor) singlehandedly attempted* to **abolish** the uncertainty of the sexual encounter (Affected)

Other clauses suggest they are quite helpless and incapable, whether in the political or domestic sphere:

> If youth is so cool, let them (Actors) try* **running** a few countries (Affected) and see if the rubbish (Affected) gets **taken out**, the beds (Affected) **made**

In this last example, and the following ones, the opportunity for teenagers to take political responsibilities is subject to the permission of mature adults, to whom the imperatives 'let', 'give', 'put', and, indeed, the whole article are addressed.

> **Let** those Sony Play Station reflexes zap the baddies
>
> **Give** Kate Moss (Affected: beneficiary) the presidency of the European Union (Affected)
>
> **Put** Baby Spice (Affected) in charge of United Nations weapons inspection

In fact what we notice is how frequently teenagers are Affecteds in Material process clauses. Often the Actors will be adults, as in the examples above, and sometimes more specifically their parents:

> I know you think your life (Affected) will be **ruined** if you (Affected) are **made** to come home no later than midnight by your cruel and oppressive parents (Actor)

Summing up the portrayal of the young in the Material process clauses, we can say that their main prowess, especially of women, is in the sexual field, though they also devote their resilient energies to ineffectual and negative revolutionary or rebellious acts. They are portrayed as ultimately unable to take responsible domestic action, let alone political action, even if adults were to give them the chance. In fact their lives are represented as under adult control. We can add to this what we discovered from Mental and Relational processes, that teenagers are depicted as dangerously misguided, ill-informed and conceitedly, overconfidently, idealistic.

These then are the adolescent values which are symbolised by the film *Titanic*:

> In Titanic you see how completely <u>the world</u> (Affected) has been **taken over** by <u>adolescents and adolescent values</u> (Actor).

However, the sinking of the Titanic reverses this, suggesting that in the end the serious, realistic, world of mature adult values destroys the unreal, frivolous, sexual adolescent world:

> <u>the teeny-weeny, self-important world of the adolescents</u> (Affected) is **overtaken** by <u>events, and</u> indeed, <u>reality</u> (Actors)

Verbal processes

What is the point of analysing Verbal processes? One reason is to see who gets to hold the floor, to have their words (Verbiage) reported. Another is to see what kinds of effect the Sayers might have on those listening, whether they come over as dominant, for example, or what speech acts they perform (see also unit 5). Analysis of the Verbiage will also tell us the main concerns of the Sayers, and be an expression of their Mental processes.

In a way the pattern of representation of teenage roles and values we observed in Material and Mental processes applies equally to Verbal. The Verbiage of the young is either an expression of sexual desire, sense of injustice, or, it is implied, ill-informed, a 'mistaken belief':

> '<u>Ye-es</u>' (Verbiage) <u>she</u> [the Turkish cleaner's daughter] (Sayer) **breathed**
>
> '<u>It's not fair</u>' (Verbiage) and '<u>I didn't **ask** to be born</u>' (Verbiage)?
>
> Last week Peter Mandelson asked <u>an eight-year-old</u> (Sayer) ... **to hold forth** on <u>his views about the contents of the Dome</u> (Verbiage)

In the last example, as with Material processes, it is the adult politician, through speaking, who controls the young speaker.

> Hey, why not **ask** him to run America's foreign policy, too?

Ideological factors in and behind the Text

The purpose of performing such a detailed analysis of the lexis and clauses of a Text is to reveal patterns which might be cues to the underlying ideology, or ideological conflict. This amounts to explanation, at level 3 in Table 0.1. It is, of course, rather more problematic than pure description of the text's meanings, so my explanation may be highly disputable.

I think the main ideological areas are the struggle between the rebellious young and the conservative old, and the protest against the ageism and trivialising tendencies of the media.

We have seen that the older generation's obsession with youth and young women is reflected in their overwording. The writer as Experiencer admits that the older generation is, in fact, 'mesmerised' by the Experience the young represent. And this obsession is also clear in the frequent relational clauses devoted to the description of the state and values of adolescence. The reason for this obsessive description and overwording might be the threat that the younger generation represents. This perceived threat has a long history going back to the New Comedy of Ancient Greece, where we find the same antagonism between the generations, the younger's (sexual) rebellion against the authority of the elder generation and parents (Frye 1957: 163). As this text puts it 'naughty adolescents trying to evade the authority of the grown-ups'.

The threat or rebellion is constructed as mainly sexual and physical by the Material process clauses with the young (women) as Actors, a distracting interference with the world of adult politics. But it is also seen in terms of resisting parental regulations, in terms of morality, and in terms of deviance. While there could be subconscious envy of the young for their physical resilience and sexual powers, a member of the 1960s' generation may also feel some guilt at the way its idealism has fizzled out amongst the mundane concerns like household management and the practical financial matters of insurance and pensions. She may resent the young having idealistically taken the moral high-ground. And an inherent conservatism seems manifest here too.

The detailed analysis has shown how the writer copes with the threat that the younger generation represents. While admitting their sexual prowess, the writer insists on how ignorant and ineffectual they are in the political sphere, by the way they are positioned as participants in Mental and Material processes. By so often making them Affecteds, the writer reassures herself and the middle-aged reader that the young are, after all, under control. The Mental process analysis also allows the writer to construct them as misguided, mistaken in their beliefs, and prey to the latest cults, rebellious to the extent of zealotry and deviance. The writer's last defence mechanism seems to be the emphatic insistence, in headline form, that, as much as the film industry constructs them as the centre of the universe, in the important affairs of war and geopolitics they are really only marginal.

To represent social groups as marginal, deviant or eccentric is a powerful weapon for conservatives in resisting change. The key words in the passage are probably *zealot* and *cult*. These seem to be an echo of the conservative popular press in England, who demonise non-conformity: unorthodox religious movements and lifestyles such as Scientology, The Children of God, New Age Travellers; or unorthodox sexual practices and family groupings like lesbian parents; or non-mainstream political parties such as the Socialist Workers' Party or more generally "the loony left".

The text can also be seen as a site of struggle over the ideologically contentious issue of the role of the media in modern society. Besides the long history of struggle between the generations, there is also a considerable European tradition of conflict over highbrow and popular culture. Often this took the form of the educated despising popular entertainment, for example the Roman poet Juvenal despising the (bread and) circuses which, like sex stories involving Clinton, distracted the population from more important matters (Juvenal Satires viii, 80). More recently, books like Postman's *Amusing Ourselves to Death* have deplored the pernicious effect of television on education and its lowering the level of political thought and debate. Critical discourse analysts, including myself (unit 8), often belong in this tradition and bemoan the ways in which serious political issues are turned into or eclipsed by entertainment in the modern media (Fairclough 1995: 148–9).

Teenagers and the media, the dual butts of the writer's protest, are, of course, linked by the financial realities of the film industry. Media economics recognises the size of the teenage movie-going market, and this explains why *Titanic* is a much greater box-office success than more serious films like *The Twilight Zone* about an older generation. Teenagers are a group without the responsibilities of work and family, and considerable leisure time, and, at least for the middle classes, spending power. This economic reality is one symptom of the ageism against which the text most explicitly protests. Grant struggles to insist on the importance of adult political values and concerns. This is why she portrays the young as arrogant in their Mental processes, and as basically ineffectual and irrelevant in Material process terms, whether in the domestic or political sphere. The headline might be glossed 'Teenagers, you've tried to project yourselves, your world, your values, and your sexual activity as most important, but I'm sorry to say you have been unsuccessful, because you and what you stand for are relatively trivial'.

ACTIVITY 20

Try to apply the kind of grammatical analysis just demonstrated to the following text of an advertisement for a perm (see Plate 3). This appeared in the magazine *Good Housekeeping* and the visual accompanying the text depicts a woman running her fingers through long black curly hair. The verbs representing processes have been underlined to help you. I have also unpacked the more complicated clauses and put them in brackets. Analyse these too, which will give you fourteen analyses in all.

If you need guidance in the analysis, ask yourself the following questions:

• Which six verbs represent actions, Material processes? Who are the Actors in these processes? Which things or people are Affected, if any? Who or what is represented as most powerful in this text? Who or what as least powerful?

• Which five verbs represent Mental processes? Are these of perception, emotion or thought? If the Experiencers (perceivers, thinkers and emoters) are identified, who are they? In cases where they are not identified, can we supply them easily?

• Which two verbs represent Relational processes or states? Who/what are being described or categorised?

• Which verb represents a Verbal process? Who does the speaking and who do they speak to?

• What explanation can you give for these patterns in the text, i.e. how are women, hairdressers and the product represented? What might be the underlying ideological explanations?

(1) <u>Feel</u> the difference vitality makes
(2) [vitality <u>makes</u> a difference]
(3) Dulcia Vitality <u>is</u> a perm for you to enjoy
(4) [you <u>enjoy</u> a perm]
(5) It <u>gives</u> your hair a superb feel and a new vitality
(6) As your L'Oréal hairdresser <u>perms in</u> Dulcia Vitality,
(7) every single hair <u>receives</u> a thorough beauty treatment through its conditioning agent Ionene G
(8) Just <u>imagine</u> the difference
(9) Your hair not only <u>has</u> vitality – lasting body, bounce and curl,
(10) but [your hair] also <u>shines</u> with a soft natural silkiness that feels as good as it looks.

73

Feel the difference vitality makes.

Dulcia Vitality is a perm for you to enjoy. It gives your hair a superb feel and a new vitality.

As your L'Oréal hairdresser perms in Dulcia Vitality, every single hair receives a thorough beauty treatment through its conditioning agent Ionene G.

Just imagine the difference. Your hair not only has vitality – lasting body, bounce and curl, but also shines with a soft, natural silkiness that feels as good as it looks.

So ask your hairdresser for Dulcia Vitality. Because only he can add that finishing touch of brilliance to your hair style with Dulcia Vitality.

The perm at your L'Oréal hairdresser today.

HAIR TECHNOLOGY
EXCLUSIVE TO YOUR L'ORÉAL SALON.   133

Plate 3   'Dulcia Vitality' (Advert for a perm, *Good Housekeeping*, May 1987, p. 33)

(11) [a soft natural silkiness <u>feels</u> good]

(12) [a soft natural silkiness <u>looks</u> good]

(13) So <u>ask</u> your hairdresser for Dulcia Vitality.

(14) Because only he can <u>add</u> that finishing touch of brilliance to your hair style
with Dulcia Vitality.

(Good Housekeeping, May 1987, p. 133)

Summary

We have now explored how the choice of vocabulary to categorise and the choice of
processes and participants in the clause display underlying ideological positions
and conflicts. Some of these analyses might simply reinforce the obvious meanings
which a reader gets from the text anyway. But in other cases the linguistic analysis
will reveal latent patterns which escape an ordinary reading. Critical reading can
benefit greatly from such analyses, precisely because it brings to light what is ordinarily latent or hidden. We would do well therefore, to apply such critical reading
to the drafts of our own writing, to reveal the categories we think in and the way we
have represented participants.

2.3 Complications to transitivity

At this unconscious or latent level, we often fall for two major transformations
or complications to the grammatical system: nominalisation and passivisation.
We'll devote this next section to them since, unconsciously or not, they are powerful ideological and manipulative tools.

Passivisation

Passivisation allows you to leave out the Actor in Material processes, Experiencer in Mental processes, and Sayer (speaker) in Verbal process clauses:

Material: Poachers killed the elephant → the elephant was killed

Mental: Rangers noticed the vultures → the vultures were noticed

Verbal: The marksmen told the poacher to freeze → the poacher was told
to freeze

Sometimes this enables newspapers, for instance, to protect sources by omitting the sayer, or to retail their own opinions as though they were someone else's : e.g. 'It is widely believed the BJP will not survive the confidence vote in the Indian Parliament'. The omission of an Actor will avoid apportioning blame or responsibility.

ACTIVITY 21

Take the following passage and turn the underlined verbs into the Passive leaving out the actors, sayers, etc. This will mean making the Object of the sentences (italicised) the Subject of the Passive clause. The first two clauses would work out as follows:

> Her horse was given to me and she was set on it ...

> They <u>gave</u> me *her horse* and I set *her* on it and so I <u>brought</u> *her* down the mountain.

> As I walked I <u>heard</u> behind me *the sound of wailing*. I <u>observed</u> *her face*, but she stared straight ahead.

> We rested at the hamlet till daybreak. I told *the men* to take enough for their meal, no more. I <u>sat</u> *her* down in the headman's house, and <u>lit</u> *the lamp*. Then I <u>brought</u> *some supper*.

Nominalisation

Nominalisation is the turning of a verb or an adjective into a noun. It is brought about most obviously by adding a suffix (e.g. *rough→roughness, imply→implication*), but less obviously by using a noun which has the same form as a verb, e.g. *a catch*. Nominalisation allows you to go further than passivisation and omit both things in a clause, e.g. Actor and Affected participant in Material process clauses:

> Hutus killed one million Tutsis in the Rwandan civil war → There were one million killings in the Rwandan civil war

Here, not only is the Actor lost sight of but also the Affected, the victims of the killings.

In addition, nominalisation gives a sense of timelessness, since tense is no longer needed. Supposing we nominalise the clause 'People are dissatisfied with the government policy on new golf courses' to make it part of the following sentence:

(x)   *Dissatisfaction with the government policy on new golf courses* will cause a loss of popularity

The hearer doesn't simply remain ignorant about who is dissatisfied, but lacks the crucial information about when they became dissatisfied, and whether they are still dissatisfied. The dissatisfaction sounds permanent.

Furthermore, noun phrases carry with them an **existential presupposition**. That is to say, since a noun phrase refers to things, when we come across one we will assume something exists which is being referred to. So nominalisation can be a means of smuggling in presuppositions. The transformed sentence above presupposes:

>>'There is dissatisfaction with the government's policy on new golf courses'

Nominalisation here is a sleight of hand which assumes propositions without stating them. If presupposed they cannot be easily argued against. For instance, if you say 'No' in reply to the statement in (x) then you are arguing against the claim about loss of popularity not about whether anyone is dissatisfied with the government policy. To argue against or disagree with a presupposition is much more difficult; you'd have to say something like: 'What do you mean by dissatisfaction with government policy on golf courses? Who's dissatisfied with it?'

ACTIVITY 22

(a) Nominalise the following verbs and adjectives, that is, turn them into nouns:

fail	demand
attract	export
deny	sensitive
inflate	complain
silly	end
	safe

(b) Combine the following pairs of sentences by nominalising the underlined verb or adjective. You might have to add the verb (if you like try the one provided in brackets), e.g.

If you <u>word-process</u> at the keyboard for long periods this <u>stresses</u> your eyes and wrists. It is very <u>exhausting</u> (leads to) → Word-processing at the keyboard for long periods leads to stress of the eyes and wrists and to exhaustion.

(i)   People <u>applauded</u>. The play <u>ended</u>. (follow)
(ii) John <u>ate</u> the banana skin. This shows he is <u>stupid</u>.
(iii) We <u>stayed</u> in Switzerland. It was wonderful.
(iv) The jury agreed with the judge. He <u>suggested</u> that I was guilty.
(v)   The mountains are <u>cool</u>. When moist air goes over them it <u>condenses</u>. (cause)

A sample analysis

Nominalisation and passivisation are put to strategic use in the following news report. If we look carefully at paragraphs 1–5, 10 and 13 we can see a large number of examples.

Armed Muslim fundamentalists clash with Algerian forces

ALGIERS – (1) Security forces fought with armed Muslim fundamentalists on Saturday, killing one person as dozens of arrests were reported a day after violent anti-government protests. (2) Three people were killed and 15 injured in fighting on Friday with police during protests against prison sentences imposed on seven leaders of the Islamic Salvation Front (FIS).
(3) On Wednesday, FIS president, Abassi Madani and vice-president Ali Belhadj each received 12-year prison terms. (4) Five others were jailed for between four and six years.
(5) State-run radio reported fighting with armed 'Islamic fundamentalists' in Djmila forest near Setif, 300km east of here since Friday.
(6) No other details were given.
(7) In a separate gunbattle, police killed a leader of an armed fundamentalist group, the official APS news agency reported. (8) He was identified as Shei Azzeddine.

(9) The prosecutor in the case against the FIS leaders said on Saturday that he would appeal against the sentences which he considered too light, said sources.
(10) The FIS leaders were convicted of fomenting riots last year that killed 55 people.
(11) Unofficial estimates said 36 people were arrested between Friday morning and Saturday night. (12) Witnesses said they were caught trying to set fire to cars or public buildings, blocking streets or distributing fundamentalist tracts criticising the government.
(13) Gunfire echoed through the fundamentalist neighbourhood of Belcourt late on Friday as security forces tried to disperse crowds setting fire to rubbish in the streets, they said.
(14) The riots in the middle of last year led President Chadli Bendjedid to postpone legislative elections and declare a six-month state of emergency. (15)

When the elections were held in December, the FIS came out ahead and was expected to take control of Parliament in the second round of voting. (16) The military blocked that by forcing Mr Benjedid out of office in January, and installing a five-member ruling council led by Mohammed Boudiaf, who was shot dead last month. – AP.

The passivisations are:

- five others were jailed (4)
- the FIS leaders were convicted (10)
- dozens of arrests were reported (1)
- three people were killed and 15 injured (2)

The first two of these are not particularly significant, since we can infer who the actors are likely to be – the police and the courts. The third, omitting a sayer, may be an attempt to protect sources inside a country against a repressive government. The most important omission is the Actor for the killing and injuring. Readers would be very interested to know who was responsible for these deaths. The reason for the omission is not clear – perhaps the news agency didn't know; or perhaps the editor didn't wish to offend some politically powerful interests.

The nominalisations are:

- arrests (1) (cf. X arrested Y)
- protests (2) (cf. X protested against Y)
- fighting (2) (cf. X fought Y)
- riots (10) (cf. X rioted)
- gunfire (13) (cf. X fired a gun)

Again we can infer who is doing the arresting, the police, but exactly who was arrested we cannot tell. More important is our ignorance about who is protesting and most important who was rioting, since the riots, rather than the rioters, are held responsible for the fifty-five deaths in the previous year: 'riots last year that killed 55 people'. Are these protesters and rioters a small section of the Algerian population, a minority of armed Muslim fundamentalists, as the headline suggests? Or is this a mass uprising of the Algerian people against a non-democratic military government? The subsequent history of Algeria, with 30,000 killed since the cancellation of the elections, might suggest the latter. 'Gunfire', 'fighting' and 'riots' similarly give us no clues about the actors: who is firing guns, who was it that was responsible for the fighting in which three people were killed?

Although nominalisation provides opportunities for manipulation, vagueness and failure to allot responsibility, there is no doubt of its importance in academic writing. One study shows that educated native speakers of English use nominalisation much more successfully than foreign students. Compare for example this paragraph written by a foreign student studying educational psychology, with its rewrite by an educated native speaker:

Original

They (teachers) should know some of these students are misbehaving because they have problems coping with the life they lead at school. Because they can't solve it themselves they behave in ways that are totally foreign to them.

Rewrite

Student <u>misbehaviour</u> may be caused by problems with life at school. The student's <u>inability</u> to solve these problems may lead to kinds of <u>behaviour</u> that are totally foreign to them.

The nominalisations have been underlined in the rewrite. Importantly, nominalisation gives opportunities to vary the Theme of the sentence. Whereas the original generally sticks to 'they' as the Theme, the rewrite has 'student misbehaviour' and 'the student's inability to solve these problems' (Jones 1991: 181). Reinforcing this view, research has found a correlation between highly rated literature essays in schools and the use of nominalisations in the Theme (Tan 1993: 86).

ACTIVITY 23*

Try rewriting the second paragraph of the news report, *Armed Muslim fundamentalists clash with Algerian forces* in order to apportion agency and responsibility more clearly. This might mean denominalising *protests*, *fighting* and depassivising *killed* and *injured*. You can discuss the changes you have made, using the appropriate terminology, and say what differences in meaning the changes make.

As readers and writers we should be careful not to be enslaved by grammatical structures like nominalisation, but to use them consciously, remaining aware of how they leave out participants or mystify the processes to which they refer. They are an important and powerful resource, but, in so far as they muddle our thinking about causes and responsibilities can be dangerously abused. Warning: nominalisation and passivisation can seriously damage your mental health.

2.4 Summary

In this unit we looked at the conceptual or representational dimension to ideology. We saw that:

- the language we use predisposes us to think and act according to certain value systems and ideologies, and to represent the world in certain selective ways;
- we encode value and ideology by vocabulary, which assigns to categories, categorises these categories, stereotypes, and 'invents' new categories, exploring how lexis represents women in newspapers;
- we can convey value and ideology less obviously by the choice of processes and participants in the clauses of texts, a choice which inevitably biases representation of the "facts"; an example was how ideological protests against ageism and the power of the media were reflected in the different representation of the young and the old in the clause structure of the 'Sorry teenagers . . .' article;
- we can use nominalisation and passivisation for strategic purposes such as avoiding assignment of responsibility for statements or acts, or for preventing argument, and, textually, for allowing more choice of themes

Suggestions for further reading

- Perhaps the best introduction to the Whorfian hypothesis is to go back to the original and read Whorf's 'An American Indian model of the universe' and 'The relation of habitual thought and behaviour to language' both in *Language, Thought and Reality*. Though his hypothesis has gone out of fashion in mainstream North American Linguistics, with its emphasis on universals of language (see Pinker's superficial rejection on pp. 59–66 of *The Language Instinct*) there have been more or less successful attempts to defend, explain or reclaim the hypothesis by John Lucy and Penny Lee.
- Fowler gives a useful account of how vocabulary is used to describe women in newspapers in *Language in the News* chapter 6, 'Discrimination in discourse'. Sara Mills's *Feminist Stylistics* (chapter 4) also provides interesting strategies on how to analyse at the level of the word.
- The grammatical details of process types, participants and transitivity can be found in Halliday (1994) chapter 3, Eggins (1994) chapter 8, Downing and Locke (1992) chapter 4, or the more elementary treatment in Butt *et al.* (1995) chapter 3.

- My own 'What does it feel like to be a single female 20 something Singapore graduate' applies transitivity analysis to a newspaper column and relates the analysis to the ideological position of women in Singapore. This is useful reading for South-East Asian students, who could well substitute this for the analysis of the Linda Grant column.
- Chapter 4 of Simpson's *Language Ideology and Point of View* and Mills's *Feminist Stylistics*, chapter 5, show how transitivity analysis can be applied to literature, and Fowler (1991), pp. 70–80, to news headlines. The final, new chapter, of Hodge and Kress's *Language as Ideology* includes an incisive analysis of the media coverage of the Gulf War.
- Halliday discusses the grammar of nominalisation on pages 343–53 of his *Introduction*. Martin gives a rather negative view of nominalisation on pages 29–32 of *Factual Writing* and in 'Life as a noun: arresting the universe in science and humanities'. I dispute some of his value judgements in my 'Green grammar and grammatical metaphor'.

Chapter 3

Text and interpersonal meaning

Aims of this chapter

To show how the vocabulary and grammar of texts reflect and create social relationships between reader and writer.

To give practice in the rewriting of texts with similar content but for different readerships.

- **3.0 Introduction: understanding social relationships**
  Provides a framework for understanding how our social relationships vary in terms of Power, Contact and expression of emotion.

- **3.1 Regulating behaviour**
  Shows how the grammar uses commands and expresses obligations as a way of influencing others' behaviour.

- **3.2 Assertiveness**
  Shows how degrees of dogmatism in a text depend on the linguistic resources for expressing probability, frequency, universality and subjectivity.

- **3.3 Pronoun use**
  Gives an overview of the choices of pronoun and how their use reflects different kinds and extents of personality.

- **3.4 Contact and the imitation of speech**
  Demonstrates how certain features of spoken language, like minor sentences and rhythm, can be incorporated into written texts to make them less formal and more expressive.

- **3.5 Formality of vocabulary**
  Explores the varying strands of vocabulary in English from the informal Anglo-Saxon, to the more formal French, to the most formal Greek and Latin, and relates them to style markers in dictionaries.

- **3.6 Emotional meaning in lexis, and contested terms**
  Illustrates how vocabulary can be used to express emotion, or euphemism to hide it, and the need for sensitivity to politically contested/incorrect terms.

- **Activities**
  Besides small-scale exercises, there is one major activity – a rewrite of a formal information letter as though addressed to a friend.

- **Project 1: Simplifying an academic text**
  The first suggested project involves taking a short extract from an academic text, then adapting/simplifying it for schoolchildren, and testing the resulting text on a real readership.

3.0 Introduction: understanding social relationships

In Chapter 1 we discussed how writers organise information within a text, and, in Chapter 2, how the texts we read and write create a value-laden representation of reality. We now shift to the third aspect of description, how texts convey and create interpersonal relationships. If Chapter 1 was about packaging, and chapter 2 about "content", then Chapter three is about exchange.

We have all had the experience of reading articles or books whose content would be interesting enough, but whose author's personal style is off-putting. We might respond with adjectives like *stuffy*, *distant*, *unenthusiastic*, *unengaged* or if the author errs in the other direction, *over-familiar*, *juvenile*, *condescending*, *patronising*. The appropriate interpersonal stance is quite difficult to judge, but this chapter will make you more aware of the language choices you have available to construct relationships between yourselves as writers and your readership.

Before we begin we should take a look at the different dimensions of relationships. Cate Poynton (1991), in her book *Language and Gender: Making the Difference*, suggests that interpersonal relationships can be analysed along three dimensions: **power**, **contact** and **emotion** (Figure 3.1). Let's take Power first. The Power someone has over you might be a matter of physical strength or force, for example Mike Tyson; or the authority given to a person by an institution, such as the vice chancellor of a university; or status which depends on wealth, education, place of residence, for instance the person in the Jaguar who lives in a smart suburb and has an MBA; or expertise, the possession of knowledge or skill, such as the expert cook rather than the novice, the authority on bee-keeping compared with the person just starting up a couple of hives.

As far as Contact is concerned, we will communicate with some people more often than others, and so they will be more familiar to us. Members of our family we might see every day and provide a lifelong relationship. Fellow students whom we have just met we might also see every day at the moment, but perhaps our relationship won't last a lifetime. We might consult our dentist regularly but with long time intervals in between. We recognise the bus driver whom we see several times a month, but hardly talk to. And at the extreme there will be total strangers who we have never met, and if we do meet them do not expect to meet again.

On the face of it we might think that there is only need for one dimension here, that those who have higher status and power are not the sort of people we will have much Contact with. A moment's thought, however, indicates that this is not the case. Parents and their children are very close, seeing each other frequently on the Contact axis, but there is clear inequality in terms of Power. The same may be true of the relations between teachers and pupils.

The third dimension is Emotion or affect. In some relationships we are

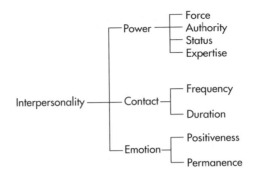

Figure 3.1 Dimensions of interpersonality

unlikely to express emotion at all. If we do express it, emotion can be positive or negative, and fleeting or permanent; for example feeling annoyed with someone and then quickly forgiving them, or, by contrast, holding a grudge against them for years.

To sum up we can think of interpersonal relationships as depending on Contact, or horizontal social distance, Power, or vertical social distance, and the kind and amount of emotion expressed. Emotion is partially dependent upon the Contact and Power dimensions; we tend not to express strong emotion to people of higher status or Power, or those who are distant on the horizontal axis. The expression of emotion will often in itself be an attempt to change the horizontal distance between discourse participants.

ACTIVITY 24

It might be interesting for you to make a note of the individuals you interact with on any one day, and figure out:

- whether they are superior to/more powerful than you, and if so why;
- what degrees or kind of Contact you have with them, and
- whether they are the sort of people to whom you would expect to express strong emotions.

One way of helping you judge the right interpersonal tone is to find the person in Activity 24 that best matches your ideal reader, and to visualise them as a reader while you are composing. This unit surveys the linguistic means by which we express the appropriate interpersonal meanings in the text.

Any writer should, then, be asking herself the following questions:

- Do I wish to come over as an authoritative expert or not?
- Do I wish to set myself up as of higher status than my reader?
- Do I wish to appear friendly/close to my reader or more distant and formal?
- Am I going to express feelings in my writing, and will they be positive or negative?

3.1 Regulating behaviour

The most obvious way in which we show our Power is by regulating the behaviour of other people in accordance with our wishes or the wishes of the institution we represent. If we wish to regulate their physical behaviour then the most straightforward way of doing this is to issue commands or insist on the reader's obligations. If we wish to regulate their verbal behaviour we will, of course, tend to use questions, demanding a reply. In either case there are more and less forceful ways of achieving compliance with our wishes.

Commands and obligations

The strongest demand is conveyed by a command, what is known technically as **imperative** mood. For example: 'wash the dishes'; 'have a drink'; 'take a bath'; 'come on Tuesday morning'. However there are other systematic resources in the grammar for telling or reminding people of what they are obliged to do. These are verbs and adjectives that are inserted before the verb referring to the action the speaker/writer wants done. They are known as **modal constructions**. Here are some examples, 1–8, in ascending order of strength of obligation. I have put some equivalent phrases to the right.

(1) You **can** use a condom for casual sex	You are allowed/permitted to ...
(2) You **may** use a condom for casual sex	
(3) You **might** use a condom for casual sex	It is suggested that you ...
(4) You **need** to use a condom for casual sex	It is necessary for you to ...
(5) You **will** use a condom for casual sex	You are required to ...
(6) You **should** use a condom for casual sex	
(7) You **are to** use a condom for casual sex	You are obliged to ...
(8) You **must** use a condom for casual sex	

Even (8), the strongest of these modal constructions, is less forceful or demanding than the imperative 'use a condom for casual sex'.

ACTIVITY 25*

Rewrite the following text from a teachers' handbook, replacing the imperatives with modals of obligation. To help you the imperatives are underlined. What effect does the rewriting have on the interpersonal relationship between the writer and teacher? And what does the frequency of imperatives in the original suggest about the role or autonomy of the teacher in this particular education system and classroom?

Getting started

Discuss the concept of the four dimensions with your pupils. This will prepare them for the reading as well. According to *Collier's Encyclopaedia* the four dimensions are length, width, height and time. The fourth dimension, which is time, also refers to any additional quality beyond what is ordinarily expected. *Ask* pupils to think about the fourth dimension in this less specific sense, and discuss the possibility of life on other planets.

The poem is provided as a stimulus. Check pupils' comprehension of it.
Assign pupils to read on the topic ahead of the lesson, so that they can contribute to the discussion of aliens. You may choose to focus the topic as an oral book-review session.

Alternatively, use the kit to introduce pupils to science fiction, in particular the work of H. G. Wells. (Clue 2 Teachers' Guide, p. 12)

Imperatives and modals of high obligation generally indicate that the writer/speaker is in a position of greater power than the reader/listener. This Power may be a question of authority or status, especially when the action to be performed is for the benefit of the writer or the institution that the writer represents and that gives her authority. In cases where the action is for the benefit of the reader, as, for example, procedural texts like manuals and recipes, the authority of the writer comes more from expertise. Either way, the Power asymmetry is clear. As far as the horizontal axis is concerned, bare imperatives tend to be used either when we have a high degree of Contact, or to people with whom we have very little Contact, perhaps having met them once, and never expecting to meet them again. We reserve the politer forms where there is a medium degree of Contact, but where we anticipate that Contact may increase, for example people you quite like in your class, but who are not yet close friends (Wolfson 1989).

Questions

The most direct way of demanding verbal behaviour of a listener or reader is to use questions, technically, the **interrogative** mood: 'Have you ever been to Sweden?' 'What time is it?' 'Can you swim?'

The effect of interrogatives on interpersonal relationships is not as clear as in the case of commands. On the one hand, on the Power dimension, questioning assumes authority, the right of the writer to demand information from the reader, as, for example, in the composition and filling in of forms. On the other hand, a typical question assumes that the reader possesses knowledge which the writer does not have but wishes to have, so that the reader is something of an expert. (Albeit in the case of forms this is an expertise which only extends as far as personal details.) Horizontally, on the Contact dimension, written questions can often be ice-breaking or a social lubricant. This is because they ask for a reply, which keeps the channels of communication open, and show some interest in the state of the reader or what the reader is engaged in, as in a personal letter or e-mail. However, in mass-produced texts, interrogatives are something of an anomaly, because there is no opportunity for the reader to reply to them. What kinds of question, then, might be used in such texts?

First, there are **expository questions**, like the one at the end of the previous paragraph. This is a question which the writer herself goes on to answer. It is a way of introducing or stimulating interest in an issue or discourse topic, of providing textual scaffolding for the discourse which follows.

Then there are **rhetorical questions**, which, unlike expository ones, do not demand an answer. This could be because the answer is supposed to be common knowledge in the first place. For example if I say 'Is Tony Blair a real socialist?' I may expect that everyone believes he isn't. Or sometimes the point of the question is really to make an indirect statement. For example 'Doesn't the government realise that we no longer need the Official Secrets Act?' is really a way of saying 'We no longer need the Official Secrets Act'.

In this section on regulating behaviour it was suggested that commands and questions are the main grammatical ways of getting other people to act or speak in accordance with our wishes. Consequently, written texts which use commands and questions assume, or pretend, the presence of the reader. This makes them more personal than texts which simply make statements. Often this personality is a fake, what Fairclough called **synthetic personalisation**, that is treating a mass audience as though they are individuals being directly addressed (Fairclough 1989: 62, 1995: 11). For example 'Have a nice day', the kind of notice used at the exit points of public buildings or by the roadside at the boundaries of towns, tries to give the impression that whoever reads it is being personally and individually addressed. In fact it is quite general and indiscriminate, especially when you read it at 11 p.m.

3.2 Assertiveness

Most commonly writers make statements (rather than issue commands or ask questions), using what is technically known as the **declarative** mood. When these are published, writers are claiming higher status or expertise than the reader, setting themselves up as an 'authority'. James Thurber said 'reason is six sevenths of treason' but he might also have said, '*author* is two-thirds of *authority*'. For example, if the writer makes informational statements or advances arguments, we expect from her a high degree of expert knowledge or rationality. If the writer is an entertainer then we assume that she has the special ability to amuse the readership. But this expertise and authority/status will be reflected in the degrees of dogmatism or assertiveness with which statements and arguments are made, the topic of this next section.

The grammar of English provides plenty of resources for us to make our statements less assertive or less dogmatic. First, there are other modal structures, besides those used to regulate behaviour, which encode different degrees of certainty or probability. Then there are words which are used to claim different degrees of frequency or universality, how generally true the statement is. Finally there are markers of subjectivity.

Modals of probability

(1)	This 10-year-old car doesn't have a smoky exhaust.	
(2)	This 10-year-old car is unlikely to have a smoky exhaust.	probably doesn't have
(3)	This 10-year-old car may have a smoky exhaust.	possibly has
(4)	This 10-year-old car will have a smoky exhaust.	is likely to have
(5)	This 10-year-old car must have a smoky exhaust.	certainly has
(6)	This 10-year-old car has a smoky exhaust.	

(1) to (6) are statements about a particular car rather than cars in general. At the two extremes, (1) and (6), we have the bare negative and positive statements. Sentences (2) to (5) express increasing degrees of probability/certainty. Sentence (6), the bare statement, can be seen as a kind of extreme pole for the scale of probability, as it allows no doubt about how possible it is for the car to have a smoky exhaust. You might think that sentence (5) with its *must* is more assertive or dogmatic than (6). However, think about a sentence like 'The millennium dome must be finished by now'. This actually expresses some uncertainty; it is as though the speaker is trying to reassure herself that it is finished.

Frequency

(7)   This 10-year-old car occasionally has a smoky exhaust.
(8)   This 10-year-old car sometimes has a smoky exhaust.
(9)   This 10-year-old car often has a smoky exhaust.
(10) This 10-year-old car frequently has a smoky exhaust.
(11) This 10-year-old car always has a smoky exhaust.

Sentences (7) – (11), like (1) – (6), are also about one particular car. They become progressively dogmatic because they make increasing claims about the frequency with which the car exhaust is smoky.

Universality

(12) No 10-year-old cars have smoky exhausts.
(13) A few 10-year-old cars have smoky exhausts.
(14) Some 10-year-old cars have smoky exhausts.
(15) Many 10-year-old cars have smoky exhausts.
(16) Most 10-year-old cars have smoky exhausts.
(17) All 10-year-old cars have smoky exhausts
(18) 10-year-old cars have smoky exhausts.

By contrast with (1) – (11), which were statements about an individual car, sentences (12) – (18) make statements about members of the class of 10-year-old cars. So they use quantifiers like *few*, *some* and *many* to indicate the rough proportion of the class. As with (1) and (6) in our first group, (12) and (18) are dogmatic statements, and even more dogmatic than (1) and (6) since they are universal generalisations.

ACTIVITY 26*

The following is a rather dogmatic and assertive text, as is often the case with D. H. Lawrence. What kind of interpersonal relationship does it convey between writer and reader? Rewrite it, making it less dogmatic by adding or changing modal features, frequency expressions and quantifiers.

As a matter of fact, till 1800 the English people were strictly a rural people – very rural. England has had towns for centuries, but they have never been real towns, only clusters of village streets. The English character has failed to develop the real urban side of man, the civic side. Siena is a bit of a place, but it is a real city, with citizens intimately concerned with the city. Nottingham is a vast place sprawling towards a million, and it is nothing more than an amorphous agglomeration. There is no Nottingham in the sense that there is a Siena.

('Nottingham and the Mining Country' p. 21, *Selected Essays*, Harmondsworth: Penguin 1950)

Table 3.1 Markers of subjectivity

Certainty	Expression (personal)	Expression (impersonal)
High	I believe/I think/in my opinion/ to my mind	it's obvious that/obviously the plant is dead it's clear that/clearly she is tired it's evident that/evidently the food was bad
Medium	I presume I suspect I expect	it's apparent that/apparently she is tired it seems that the plant is dead it looks dead she sounds tired the plant feels dead the plant smelled bad

Markers of subjectivity

It has been suggested by Simpson (1993: 50–1) that verbs of thinking and perception reduce the assertiveness of statements, just like modals. In other words, instead of saying 'it may rain' we can say 'I think it's going to rain', or 'in my opinion it will rain', and 'it seems about to rain'.

Summary

This section has shown how we can tone down or reduce the strength of the claims which we make when we write statements. The devices for this are modals of probability, frequency adverbs, quantifiers–which indicate degrees of universality–and subjective markers. All these devices have consequences for the Power dimension of interpersonal relations, because, generally speaking, the more universal or dogmatic the statement the higher the degree of authoritativeness or expertise the writer is assuming. Contrast, for example, 'I think this 10-year-old car may have a smoky exhaust', which is a very tentative statement about one particular car, with the rather bold and assertive generalisation 'All 10-year-old cars have smoky exhausts'.

It is important for you, as writers near the beginning of your academic career, to judge the degree of dogmatism or assertiveness to use in academic writing. Obviously, if you are making use of a well-known and widely accepted formula or theorem in science or mathematics you can afford to be dogmatic. You would be unlikely to say 'The square on the hypotenuse may sometimes be equal to the sum of the square of the other two sides'. Similarly, you will be quite sure about the figures for results of an experiment. However, in the conclusion section of an experimental write-up you may want to make tentative explanations, or in a history or literary criticism essay you might consider being far less dogmatic: 'It seems to me that when Lady Macbeth says "I have given suck" etc. this could be a confession to Macbeth of a previous marriage he knew nothing about.' In a sense, being tentative about scientific conclusions does not diminish authority because scientists are self-assured enough to be cautious in their conclusions, and this is a feature of scientific writing

ACTIVITY 27

Compare and contrast these two letters and replies which are rewrites of letters which appeared in *Woman's World* (14 January 1997), with the essential inter-personal linguistic features preserved. (Permission was refused to quote the original letters and replies.)

- What different relationships do the replies set up between the questioner and the expert who replies? How do these replies differ, if at all, in levels of assertiveness, i.e. in which are generalisations made or modal devices used? Which comes across as more dominant, for example in use of imperative commands or modals of obligation, the doctor in Doc's Corner or the psychotherapist in Helping the Kids?
- Can you suggest an explanation for any differences here, perhaps to do with the relative social status of doctors and psychotherapists?
- What modal devices and moods do the questioners use? What does this convey about their predicament?

Doc's Corner
'Work gives me the runs'

Q *I get diarrhoea, but only on Sundays, the day before I go back to work. My job is more stressful recently, since I now have to work without an assistant. Could my work and my stomach be connected?*

A Certainly! One of the most common types of diarrhoea is stress-related, and known as Irritable Bowel Syndrome. Those who suffer feel pain most intensely in the lower abdomen, and have a looseness of the bowels. Some people get relief by massage, taking long deep breaths and meditating. Strenuous exercise on weekends may help as well.

Neurologist **Algernon Rathbone M.D.**

Helping the Kids
'He's too devoted to his girlfriend'

Q *My son Paul, 16, calls his girlfriend Maggie a lot and dotes on her when she visits. But Maggie rarely calls Paul and doesn't say much to him when she's here. I think Paul puts too much in and gets too little out. She's his first girlfriend and I'd hate this to become a pattern. What can I do?*

A Being sensitive to Paul's feelings get him to consider what he likes in a relationship. What is his idea of a good girlfriend? How does his relationship to Maggie compare with that? Let him realise that he has a right to have his needs met. Encourage him to talk about this with Maggie.
Then stand back. Your first relationship with a girl is a learning experience. Experience is often a better teacher than a worrying parent.

Adolescent psychotherapist **Obadiah Merton C.S.W.**

3.3 Pronoun use

You can see that in our list of modal devices, some do not use the personal pronouns *you* and *I* – examples (1) – (18), and column 3 in Table 3.1 – and some do – column 2. This section explores further how the degree and kind of personality relates to choice of pronoun.

In English we have a number of choices in the pronoun system which will affect the degree of Contact expressed by the Text. The pronouns available are listed in Table 3.2 and will differ between singular and plural, and between first, second and third person. But, if we want to be very formal and distant, we can reduce the need for these choices by using impersonal constructions. In Table 3.1, column 3, we have already seen how constructions using *it* can avoid mentioning the Experiencer in Mental processes. And in Chapter 2 we also

Table 3.2 The personal pronouns of English

Person	Singular			Plural
1st	I			we
2nd	you			you
3rd	she	he	it	they
	one			

introduced passives and nominalisation which may also reduce personality. By using the Passive, we avoid mentioning one of the participants in the clause, and by using nominalisation we can avoid mentioning either.

Active	Our submarine sank your aircraft carrier
Passive	Your aircraft carrier was sunk
Nominalisation	The sinking [took place on Wednesday]

So the first choice we have is between avoiding the expression of personality through nominalisation and passivisation, or making our texts relatively personal. This choice between mentioning or avoiding mentioning participants is represented farthest left in Figure 3.2, as we read from left to right.

In certain genres, like scientific and academic writing, teachers often recommend an impersonal style through the use of the Passive, and in this genre nominalisation, too, is widespread. The resulting impersonality presents science and academic work as the supremely objective endeavour: as though a body of knowledge somehow exists independent of the scientist who makes the observations, and of the people who read the scientific report. However, I'm not sure I entirely agree with this recommendation. There are strong arguments for rejecting the claim of scientific objectivity. For one, scientific discovery takes place in institutions and academic communities where struggles for funding, power, prestige and promotion make science political and personal. In addition, the physical theory of quantum mechanics implies that the observed object and observer/observing instrument can no longer be separated, a point demonstrated by Heisenberg (Bohm 1980: 134).

If we opt to mention participants we can either use the explicit noun phrase or use pronouns (see Figure 3.2). With pronouns the first major choice we have as writers is to decide whether we wish to represent ourselves and the reader in the Text (absence or presence of writer in Figure 3.2). If not, we should stick to third-person singular or plural pronouns, or general *you*. In fiction the distinction between first and third person depends on whether the narrator participates in the events of the fiction. If she does so she will be bound to use the first-person singular pronoun *I*. A writer who confines herself to the third person automatically represents herself as less involved in the world she is representing. We are all

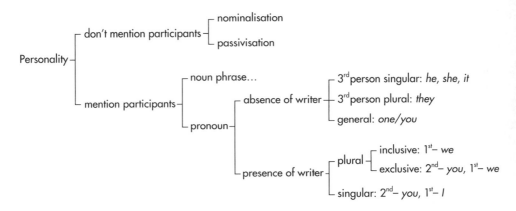

Figure 3.2 Personality and personal pronoun choice

familiar with complaints against the United Nations, the Government, Parliament which take the form of 'Why don't they do something about it'. More surprising, but quite common, is for people to complain in the same terms about institutions of which they are members as though they don't belong – this amounts to a shift of responsibility onto and criticism of the leadership of the institution.

Incidentally, the choice of singular third-person pronoun is problematic and ideological in gender terms. The use of *he* as a default pronoun, for example in university regulations, to refer to any student whether male or female should have been discontinued long ago. In such contexts it is quite acceptable nowadays to use *they* rather than the slightly clumsy *s/he* e.g. 'If a student is ill on the day of the examination they should provide a medical certificate and lodge it with the registrar's office within one week'. The association of certain high-status jobs with males by using the masculine pronoun, is, however, still quite widespread. For example in this extract from a secondary-school textbook:

> A supervisor assigns a lighter workload to **his** friend than he does to another worker with whom **he** doesn't get along, although both workers share the same job description.
>
> (*New Clue 4 Normal Academic*, p. 163)

In the present book I have avoided the problem by consistently using *she* when referring to a writer (speaker) and *he* to refer to the reader (hearer).

A further ideological controversy may arise from attempts to humanise and feminise nature by referring to the earth as *her* rather than *it*. You may be familiar with James Lovelock's Gaia theory, the idea that the earth's crust, the rocks and soil, the living things on them, and the atmosphere are one large organism, *Gaia* the earth goddess. And that this goddess positively regulates the environment so that life can continue (Lovelock 1988). Abolishing the distinction between 'living' and 'non-living' matter makes *he* or *she* sensible for referring to the earth, and the reconceiving of the earth as a goddess makes *she* the 'natural' choice (providing this does not reinforce the stereotype of passivity).

Once the writer decides to signal her presence she has the choice of using *we*, *you* and *I*. But there are complications in the use of these pronouns. *You* immediately gives the impression of being in Contact and of addressing her reader(s) and opens the way for more Contact devices such as rhetorical questions and commands. But it is ambiguous between singular, plural and general, appearing at the end of three pathways in Figure 3.2. *You* can refer to

- one individual addressee   e.g. *When did you first feel this pain?*
- a group of addressees   e.g. *When did you as a family move to Washington, DC?*

- people in general   e.g. *When you run fast your heart-rate increases*

In the last of these, *you* is the informal equivalent of *one*.

These ambiguities in the use of *you* become another resource for synthetic personalisation. We defined this, remember, as addressing a mass audience (the general or plural *you*) as though they were individuals, and it is particularly common in advertising. Consumer capitalism uses advertising to appeal to consumers as individuals; a consumer normally buys goods as an individual for themselves or other individuals, or sometimes for their immediate family. It would be disastrous for consumer capitalist economies if whole streets or blocks of flats got together to buy and then share computers, lawnmowers and washing machines. Not only advertisers, but any published writer must, in fact, be addressing more than one reader, and would often like to extend the readership widely, and yet, since silent reading is an individual activity, the reader will be positioned as though they are the only reader and will cooperate with this illusion. The ambiguity of *you* facilitates this, in ways which *one* never could because of its insistence on singularity.

An extremely important choice in terms of Contact and solidarity is between *you* and *we*. *We* may include the writer and the reader together in the same group, whereas *you* unambiguously separates them. The teacher who begins a lesson: 'Today *you*'re going to find out more about the discovery of North America by the peoples of East Asia' constructs the finding out as an activity of the pupils. The teacher who begins 'Today *we*'re going to find out more about the discovery of North America by the peoples of East Asia' represents the learning as a joint enterprise. This is somewhat disingenuous, of course, since she is likely to know roughly what she is going to find out before she starts! Contrast this with 'In the next unit we're going to discuss inferences' which equally disingenuously presumes the reader is as much involved in the discussion as the writer.

The main ambiguity in the use of *we* can be spelled out as follows, reflected in the options in Figure 3.2.

- Inclusive *we* to varying degrees includes the reader/hearer in the group referred to, as in the teaching/discussion examples above.
- Exclusive *we* refers to a group to which the reader does not belong. This is especially common when the writer represents an institution of which the reader is not a member, e.g. 'We at Toyota do our best for you'.

Finally, there is the option of using *I*. This is the most personal way for the writer to refer to herself, the only other option being the rather formal or distant noun phrase like *the present writer*, *this writer* or *the writer of this article*. *I* is informal, individual, and 'personal' too, though note that writers, especially entertainers, can use *I* as a persona or mask.

I've always found myself challenged, not visually, mentally, physically or, as far as I know, sexually, but by the little mundane tasks of life. In the morning I have to remember to turn on the hot-water switch outside the bathroom before entering to take my shower and to bring a towel into the bathroom with me. Next I must ensure that the socks I put on are a pair, neither of them inside out, and that I've done up my flies. I need to adjust the toaster accurately so that the bread comes out nicely browned, and if it's under-toasted adjust the control to a low level before re-toasting it. I try to avoid, not always successfully, having the porridge in the microwave boil over and ooze down the sides of the bowl so that it messes up the place mat on the table. It's a miracle if I ever leave the house without some trivial disaster or other. And did I shave? And have I got my umbrella?

The *I*, the persona of this passage, is a self-caricature of the real person of the writer, as synthetic as the synthetic personalisation of *you*.

The text you are reading is an academic textbook. I have, however, let myself as an 'I' intrude in places, with anecdotes about student pranks, travelling to Cyprus, my Christian evangelical upbringing, colitis and other examples of personal self-disclosure. Some of the reviewers of this manuscript welcomed these personal interludes while others thought them inappropriate to an academic style of writing. I kept them because I do not wish to disguise my own identity and subject position as writer, nor the fact that my own ideological position is only one of many and is determined partly by personal history. I hope this recognition of personality makes it easier for you to resist my position when it differs from yours.

Look back at the column 'Sorry teenagers, you are not the centre of the universe' (on p. 61) and analyse the use of first- and second-person pronouns.

- How do the pronouns change in the course of the passage?
- Do they always refer to the same groups? For example, the *we* and *you* of paragraph one and the *we* and *you* of paragraphs four and five, and the *you* of paragraphs six to eight?
- When *you* is used, who does it refer to? Is it used oddly, i.e., does it, as we would expect, always refer to the intended readers of the column? If not, what is the purpose of its unusual use?
- Is *we* used inclusively or exclusively? If it includes the reader what kind of reader would that be? We would expect it to include the writer, but is there some doubt about this?

3.4 Contact and the imitation of speech

The Contact dimension depends on the frequency and duration of meeting and talking face to face. So we might wonder how Contact could apply to the print medium, which is, of course, rather impersonal compared with, say, radio or television. But anything in a written text which gives the flavour of speech will be more personal and simulate some degree of Contact. We have already seen how questions and commands are used for such purposes, and how pronouns like *you* and *we* are used for synthetic personalisation. Another linguistic device which is related to the imitation of dialogic speech is the use of incomplete sentences, technically, **minor sentences**.

Minor sentences are stretches of text punctuated as sentences but with the main verb or Subject missed out. In dialogue, obviously, such utterances or "sentences" occur quite naturally, for example in response to questions. Look at this extract from a policeman interviewing a witness. The minor sentences have been underlined.

P: Did you get a look at the one in the car?
W: I saw his face, yeah.
P: What sort of age was he?
W: About 45. He was wearing a…
P: And how tall?

w: <u>Six foot one.</u>

p: <u>Six foot one.</u> <u>Hair</u>?

w: <u>Dark and curly.</u> Is this going to take long? I've got to collect the kids from school.

p: <u>Not much longer, no.</u> <u>What about his clothes</u>?

w: He was a bit scruffy looking. <u>Blue trousers, black</u> ...

p: <u>Jeans</u>?

w: <u>Yeah</u>

(Fairclough 1989: 18)

So one way of imitating speech will be to write in minor sentences. This is a particularly common convention for advertisement copywriters as illustrated by Plate 4.

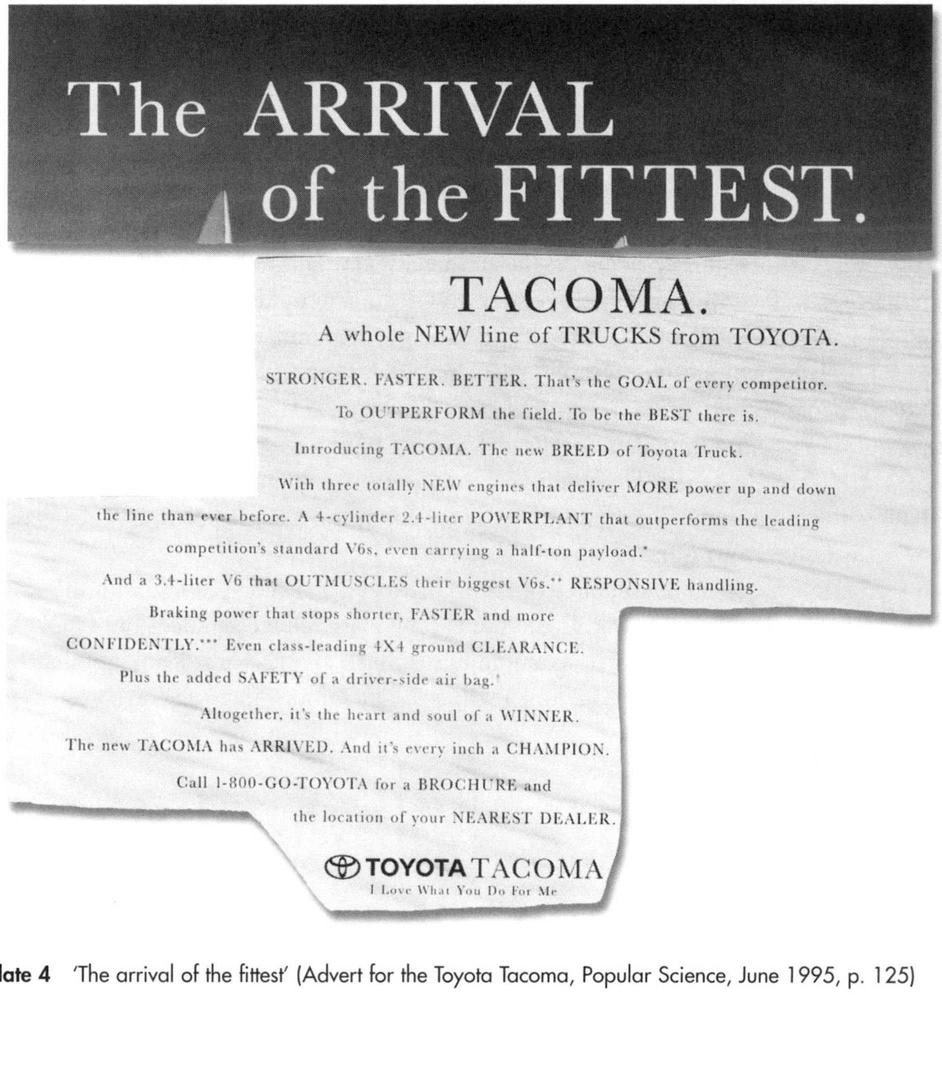

Plate 4 'The arrival of the fittest' (Advert for the Toyota Tacoma, *Popular Science*, June 1995, p. 125)

Which of the sentences in Plate 4 are complete sentences?

The minor sentences are very concentrated at the beginning of this advert, and suggest the writer (W) is voicing one half of a dialogue. Imagining a rather unsympathetic reader (R) we might fill in as follows:

W: The ARRIVAL of the FITTEST
R: What's arrived that's so fit?
W: TACOMA
R: It doesn't sound very fit to me. More like a nasty disease, a sarcoma, or something that gives you a coma. What on earth is it?
W: A whole NEW line of TRUCKS from TOYOTA.
R: How are they different from other trucks?
W: STRONGER. FASTER. BETTER. That's the GOAL of every competitor.
R: What is?
W: To OUTPERFORM the field.
R: What the hell does that mean?
W: To be the BEST there is. Introducing TACOMA.
R: Sorry I wasn't concentrating. What's that again?
W: The new BREED of Toyota Truck.
R: What does it come with?
W: With three totally NEW engines that deliver MORE power up and down the line than ever before.
R: So? What does it use to do that?
W: A 4-cylinder 2.4. liter POWERPLANT that outperforms the leading competition's standard V6's, even carrying a half-ton payload.
R: How extraordinarily interesting. So that's it, is it? Any other exciting features that make it more attractive than its wimpish opposition?
W: And a 3.4 liter V6 that OUTMUSCLES their biggest V6's.

When an utterance is incomplete, as in answers to questions or minor sentences, then the reader/hearer has to supply the missing information. This will either come from the previous question or from knowledge brought to the Text by the reader. Incomplete sentences assume that writer and reader share a good deal of information which does not need to be explicitly spelled out. This is typical of postcards: 'On Monday went to the Eiffel Tower. Drizzled all day' where the Subjects of the clause can be understood. Or of commentary on sporting events where the actions, such as kicking the ball are so obvious they need not be mentioned 'Beckham to Owen'. This presumption of shared information is why minor sentences suggest a high level of Contact between writer and reader. Of course, another feature of connected speech is that words are often contracted, *can't* for *cannot*, *I've,* for *I have*, *it's* for *it is,* (contrast *its* meaning 'of it' by the way). Contraction might be considered another kind of incompleteness.

ACTIVITY 30[*]

Find an advertisement in a magazine or newspaper. Bring it to class and discuss its use of commands (imperatives), pronouns and minor sentences. What interpersonal effects do their uses have? What other purposes might these features serve?

How much shared knowledge to assume

In fact one of the persistent problems of writing is judging how much knowledge your average reader possesses, how much can be left out. If we compare the following two texts A and B, we notice that A is written for a more specialist readership than B.

A

An appreciation of the effects of calcium blockers can best be attained by an understanding of the activation of muscle groups. The proteins actin, myosin, troponin and tropomyosin make up the sarcomere, the fundamental unit of muscle contraction. The thick filament is composed of myosin, which is an ATPase, or energy producing protein.

B

The contraction of muscle depends on calcium. If we can understand how calcium activates muscle groups, we can appreciate how those groups are affected by calcium blockers.

The fundamental unit of muscle contraction is the sarcomere. In the sarcomere are two filaments, one thick and one thin. They contain proteins that prevent contraction and proteins that cause contraction. The thick filament contains the protein myosin, which is an ATPase, or energy producing protein.

(quoted in Colomb and Williams 1985)

There are various pieces of knowledge which (A) assumes, but which (B) makes more explicit.

> The contraction of muscle depends on calcium.
> Calcium activates muscle groups
> In the sarcomere are two filaments, one thick and one thin.
> They contain proteins that prevent contraction and proteins that cause contraction.
> Myosin is a protein.

We might remark, incidentally, the differences between the first sentence of (A) and the second sentence of (B). (B) is more personal and less formal because 'appreciation' and 'understanding' have been denominalised into 'we [can] understand', 'we can appreciate', which also gives the opportunity to use the first-person plural pronoun 'we'. And (A)'s 'the activation of muscle groups' becomes (B)'s 'how calcium activates muscle groups', removing the nominalisation to make clear the Actor (calcium) and the Affected (muscle groups).

Rhythm

In Chapter 1 we surveyed the graphic devices available for making texts visually informative, to give the kind of richness to the written medium which the spoken medium has by virtue of its loudness, tempo, voice quality, stress, intonation and rhythm. But writing can also borrow rhythm from the written medium, assuming that the text is read aloud or sub-vocalised. Prose writers, popular newspapers, and above all advertising copywriters, often write rhythmically as though the written medium is to be translated into the spoken, with implications of higher Contact. But what exactly do we mean by 'rhythm'?

Rhythm is a regular pattern of stressed (louder) and unstressed (softer) syllables. In words of two syllables (or more) one syllable will be stressed and the other unstressed e.g. NEver, reMAIN, alLOW, ALLergy. In addition, one-syllable nouns, verbs (not auxiliaries), adjectives and adverbs will tend to be stressed. So the following sentence, with the stressed syllables marked /, and the unstressed x, has an observable rhythm, a recurring pattern of two unstressed syllables followed by a stressed syllable:

> x x / x x / x x / x x / x x / x x / x x /
> I can never remember the months of the year when the eating of oysters is safe.

You can find plenty of examples of the rhythms of speech by flicking through the adverts of magazines. These below come from *Popular Science*

```
/   /  x
Just surfaced
  /  /  x
Skyy vodka
  x  x /
the intell-
x x     /
igent drink
```

```
 / x   x  /  x  / x  /
buying a more expensive paint
 /  /   x  x / x  /
won't buy you a better paint
```

In the last example the rhythm is not quite so clear, but notice that the rhythmical pattern of the first six syllables is repeated exactly in the last six syllables. And the two clauses each have four stressed syllables like the lines in nursery rhymes.

```
 /   /   x / x  /
Tom, Tom the piper's son
 / x / x  x  / x /
Stole a pig and away did run
 x  /  x  / x   /  x  /
The pig was eat and Tom was beat
  x   /   x  / x   /   x  /
And Tom went roaring down the street
```

Perhaps this rhythmical tendency in written adverts is a pale imitation of the rhythmical slogans and jingles of TV adverts, which pretend a heightened emotion: the euphoria produced by the product becomes so powerful that one can only express it in song.

A general rule with rhythmical writing is that the higher the proportion of stressed syllables the slower we read and the more emphatic the effect. Conversely the higher the proportion of stressed syllables the faster the words flit by, and the more exciting or light-hearted it feels. You might like to compare the rhythmic effects of the second and third stanzas of the extract of the Larkin poem quoted on page 106 below.

Table 3.3 Stylistic variations in vocabulary

Core	Positive emotion	Negative emotion	Formal (technical)	Informal	Dialectal
house	home	hovel	residence	pad	pad
dog		cur	canine	pooch, doggy, bow-wow	pooch
	[motion, – negative]	shit	excrement, faeces	poo	
therefore			thus	and so	
thin	slim, slender	skinny	emaciated		
determination	perseverance	obstinacy stubbornness	motivation	will-power	
ear, nose and throat			otorhinolaryng-ology	ENT	
bear			tolerate	stand, put up with	
help		interfere	aid, assist	give a hand to	
prostitute	[comfort woman, – negative]	whore, slag		slag	slag

3.5 Formality of vocabulary

The vocabulary of English is largely made up of three strata. There is a bedrock of basic **Old English** words, which are the most frequent, occurring as they do across the whole range of genres. These are generally quite short and either core or informal. Then there is a thick sediment of the many French words of medium formality, which flooded into English in the fourteenth century. And finally, as topsoil, we have the more cultivated, learned and technical Greek and Latin words which were borrowed into the language from the sixteenth to eighteenth centuries.

Let's look at Table 3.3. The items in each row of the table convey the same logical concept, but differ stylistically, either in terms of positive/negative emotion, formality or geographical dialect. We can see how formal/technical vocabulary and informal vocabulary is distinguished from core vocabulary by looking at columns 1, 4 and 5. Good examples of the connection between borrowed words and formality are the quartet of informal *give a hand to* (all Old English words), core *help* (Old English), slightly formal *aid* (French) and the more formal French *assist*, originally from the Latin *adsistere*. Or consider the words *town* (Old English), *city* (French), and *metropolis* (Greek), though these are not listed as they do not have exactly equivalent logical meanings. Notice, too, that formality applies to all parts of speech – nouns, adjectives, verbs and even conjunctions like *therefore,* v. *thus,* v. *and so*.

Old English words are on the whole shorter than those from French or the classical languages. No doubt *supercalifragilisticexpialidocious* is not Old English. Consider in 3.3 the perfectly understandable Old English *ear nose and throat*, which any patient looking for the hospital department can understand. And contrast this with the formal, technical Greek *otorhino-laryngology*, incomprehensible for most outpatients, though this has not deterred some hospitals from snobbishly substituting it for the Old English terms. Notice *ENT* as well, which, as an acronym, is much shorter, and assumes a degree of familiarity or professional Contact with medical specialisation.

We can see that many informal equivalents use compounds and phrases rather than single words, *will-power* for *determination*, *put up with* for *toler-ate*, *give a hand to* for *aid*. This is another way of reducing the length of words, and preserving the informal Old English flavour. Word length has, in fact, been used as one factor for computing the technicality and difficulty of a text. Readability measures are generally based on a combination of word length and sentence length. If you use Microsoft Word 7 as a word-processing program you can select the spelling and grammar facilities on the tools menu, and when the grammar and spelling has been checked you will obtain readabil-ity statistics. This will give you two indices to tell you the grade level or read-ing level for which the text is appropriate (Grade 1 is that of a 6-year old).

We notice from the rightmost column that many informal words are also dialectal. The reason for this is that dialect is an expression of Contact: dialects can only be preserved if the speakers meet and use them. On the one hand dialec-tal usages affirm solidarity between speakers; on the other hand they deliberately exclude potential interlocutors who are not familiar with that dialect, or, for that matter, the latest slang.

It would be misleading to think that texts always keep up a consistent level of formality and informality throughout. Some writers even deliberately mix lev-els of style for poetic effect. Philip Larkin, for example, at the end of his poem 'Toads' recognises that the toad of work which oppresses him is matched by a psy-chological toad of conformity and timidity which ties him to his work. He expresses this in a mixture of styles – slang, archaic in a quote from Shakespeare's *Tempest* ('we are such stuff as dreams are made on'), the formal and the colloquial.

Ah, were I courageous enough	
To shout 'Stuff your pension!'	SLANG
But I know, all too well, that's the stuff	ARCHAIC
That dreams are made on:	|
For something sufficiently toad-like	FORMAL
Squats in me too;	NEUTRAL
Its hunkers are heavy as hard luck	
And cold as snow,	|

And will never allow me to blarney	COLLOQUIAL
My way to getting	|
The fame and the girl and the money	
All at one sitting.	
I don't say, one bodies	FORMAL
The other one's spiritual truth;	|
But I do say it's hard to lose either	COLLOQUIAL
When you have both.	|

On the other hand we would generally want to avoid the ludicrously inappropriate mixing of styles in sentences like 'They cast a stone at the fuzz and absconded with the loot' or 'They chucked a missile at the police officers and did a bunk with the money' (Leech 1974: 15). You might want to stop and think what kinds of style are being mixed in these sentences.

However, one of the features of modern media discourse is the hybridisation of texts, especially the conversationalisation of public discourse in order to make it sound or read like private discourse. Fairclough (1995: 9–14) cites the following example from the British tabloid the *Sun*, which packages and retails a parliamentary report for the British working-class reader.

Notice how the headlines and Lead have informal items like *pedlars/pushers*, *call up*, *forces* whereas the later paragraphs have more formal equivalents like *drug-running*, *ordering*, *security forces*. Or contrast the pair of sentences

Britain faces a war to stop pedlars, warn MPs

CALL UP FORCES IN DRUG BATTLE!

BY DAVID KEMP

The armed forces should be called up to fight off massive invasion by drug pushers, MPs demanded yesterday.

Cocaine pedlars are the greatest threat ever faced by Britain in peacetime – and could destroy the country's way of life, they said.

The MPs want Ministers to consider ordering the Navy and RAF to track suspected drug-running ships approaching our coast.

On-shore there should intensified law enforcement by customers, police and security forces

Figure 3.3 'Call up forces in drug battle!' (Extract from the *Sun*, 24 May 1985)

'Britain faces a war to stop drug pedlars' and 'Call up forces in drug battle' with the later sentence 'On shore there should be intensified law enforcement by Customs police and security forces'. You might like to consider, as revision, what it is about the first two sentences that makes them less formal than the third.

3.6 Emotional meaning in lexis, and contested terms

There are perhaps three main ways of encoding emotion in our choice of lexis. First, there is what one might call emotive "**spin**". If we look at the first three columns of Table 3.3 we notice that words may share the same conceptual meaning but differ in emotive meaning. A famous example is:

POSITIVE	NEUTRAL	NEGATIVE
slim	*thin*	*skinny*

It is as though these words are three identical balls, three identical concepts, but *slim* spins positively, *skinny* negatively and *thin* doesn't spin at all.

These words with emotive "spin" are different from a second class of words which are empty of conceptual meaning, what one might call **affective** words. Here we would include swear words. The fact that these are drained of any conceptual meaning is obvious when we consider that, as a swear word, *fuck* has no reference to copulation, *bloody hell* no connection with blood, and *piss off* nothing to do with urination. They are simply strong expressions of negative emotion. Less strong expressions of negative emotion include *terrible, horrible, awful, disgusting, pathetic*. At the positive end we have *nice, fine, cool, good, great, wonderful, smashing, fabulous* and so on. Because these are evaluative terms expressing individual taste, likes and dislikes, they are subjective and cannot be verified or challenged. Perhaps this is one reason they are so often used in advertising copy, where they are difficult to contradict or disprove. Look back at the use of *winner, champion* and *best* in the Tacoma advert.

Many of these conceptually empty Affective words can be used as adjectives/adverbs which add emotional intensity to the adjectives/adverbs they modify: *a **terrible** miss/**terribly** misguided, a **dreadful** experience/**dreadfully** hot, an **awful** mistake/**awfully** exciting*. These are called **intensifiers** and they also include *very, especially, complete/completely, absolute/absolutely, amazingly, madly, confoundedly*, and so on.

A further aspect of emotive meaning is illustrated in the second column of Table 3.3. Here in brackets are terms which are **euphemisms**, i.e. words used to avoid a direct reference to something considered impolite. Because the more common core word is taboo or has negative emotive spin, these terms are substituted, for example *comfort woman* is substituted for *prostitute* or *sex slave*, and *motion* is substituted for *faeces/shit*. They are in brackets because, rather than being positively emotive, they avoid the negative emotion of the core, formal or informal equivalents. Sex, urination and excretion, and death are the commonest topics for euphemism. It's quite usual to use the phrase *sleep together* as a euphemism for sex, though sleep is precisely what the sexual partners don't do! My favourite euphemism for a funeral wake is *cold meat party*, partly because the attempt at euphemistic disguise (deliberately) fails.

A third way of conveying emotion is to conceptualise it. This is when you use words like *despair*, *depression*, *nervous*, *amazement* to describe, rather than express, one's own or other people's feelings as it were objectively and from the outside. These contrast with Affective interjections (swear words) and adjectives (*nice*, etc.) because there is a degree of objectivity in their use, for example there are ways of measuring degrees of clinical depression. Emotional attitude can also be conceptualised through the use of **modals of (dis) inclination**: e.g. *need*, *want to*, *am inclined to*, *am keen to*, *would like*, *would rather*, *unfortunately*, *hopefully*, etc.

ACTIVITY 31

The following letter was printed in *Newsweek* on 1 June 1998. Comment on the use of emotional vocabulary. Are there any words which would appear emotionally neutral out of context but in this letter take on a negative spin? Are there any terms here which are used euphemistically?

> Pol Pot was a genocidal monster but your article 'Pol Pot's Last Days' (ASIA April 27) failed to say that the United States helped to create and support him. From 1969 to 1975 the United States repeatedly bombed Cambodia, continuing even in the face of a congressional ban. CIA figures show that 1.5 million people were displaced and 600,000 were killed. Pol Pot's holocaust followed, lasting until Vietnam's 1978 invasion, when China and the United States directly helped his Khmer Rouge reconstruct and continue terrorist killing.

Contested terms

In the climate of political awareness where we live today there is a heightened sense that certain words may unintentionally cause negative emotion, offence. The word *bimbo* used in the Linda Grant passage (see Chapter 2, p. 61) is a good example. We can call these **contested terms**. Their avoidance gives rise to groups such as the following:

nigger v. black v. Afro-American v. person of colour

crippled v. spastic v. handicapped v. disabled v. challenged

poor v. underprivileged v. economically disadvantaged

poor countries v. the Third World v. developing nations v. the South v. The
majority world

Many of these groups display euphemism as we proceed to the right, as though calling something by a less transparent name disguises the negative emotion associated with the original term. But sometimes pressure groups, who wish to contest taken-for-granted practices and naturalised ways of speaking, do the opposite: deliberately replace quite neutral or positive terms with negatively emotive ones

economic growth v. economic cancer

settlement (of Australia/ North America) v. invasion

Property is theft

Summary on style of vocabulary

Any good dictionary will give you an indication of styles: whether a word is formal, informal, has positive or negative emotion, is offensive or is dialectal. The Collins *Cobuild* dictionary, for example, has the following style markers which tend to overlap. I have attempted to arrange them in some order in Figure 3.4.

What this diagram tries to indicate is that formal language tends to be written, technical language tends to be written, legal and medical language is technical; informal language tends to be spoken, as does emotive and offensive language, and dialect is most obvious in informal speech rather than in writing; literary and journalistic language tends to be less formal than the technical languages of medicine and the law. More generally, of course, informality corresponds to closeness on both the Power and Contact dimensions, but especially Contact. And informality, emotion, and geographical dialect tend to converge.

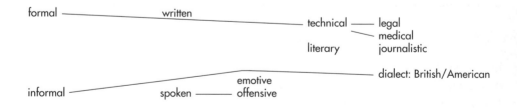

Figure 3.4 Style markers in the *Cobuild* dictionary

ACTIVITY 32

Use the beginning of the feature article on coffee from the teenage magazine *Jump* to try to apply what you have learned from the last three sections (3.5–3.7) on the imitation of speech, formality and emotional lexis. (See Plate 1, p.27)

1   How is speech imitated in the article? Are there minor sentences? How is a sense of (mock) dialogue created? Can you detect any rhythmical patterns, for example in Section 2?

2   This passage seems to almost exaggerate and celebrate the wide stylistic range of vocabulary from the formal to the informal. Can you illustrate this, using the labels from the *Cobuild* dictionary about different stylistic classes of words (see Figure 3.4).

3   Do you find any words which have positive or negative emotional spin, for example in Sections 1–3, and Section 6? Can you provide words which convey the same idea but with neutral or opposite spin? Is there any use of euphemism, for instance in Section 4? Do you find any contested words, perhaps in Sections 5 or 6? Is the author conscious of their potential contestation? What evidence do you have?

You might also like to use this passage to revise work done on degrees of assertiveness: how are probability, universality and subjectivity expressed?

The Dish'

(1)   What's all the buzz about?

(2)   Whether you're a quivering caffeine junkie or just a casual sipper, there's more to that hair-raising jolt than meets the eye.

(Cindy Walker)

(3)   What would you say if someone offered you a steaming hot cup of 1,3,7-trimethylxanthine? 'Thanks, but no thanks.'
Well, guess what? You just refused a cup of coffee. 1,3,7-trimethylxanthine is the fancy-schmancy name for caffeine, that go-go ingredient in everything from sodas to snickers. Yet, despite its overwhelming presence, there are many myths brewing about caffeine. So, before you declare yourself a mocha maven, test your caffeine chutzpah to see if you're really full of (coffee) beans.

True or false?

(4)   A cup of coffee will keep the love handles away. True or false?
       False. Sure, we've all felt that first blast of energy after drinking a fat
       mug of coffee, but that doesn't mean you're blasting the pounds away.
       While a moderate dose of caffeine might temporarily jump start your
       metabolism, it's not an appetite suppressant. In fact, in 1991, the FDA
       banned the use of caffeine in over-the-counter diet pills because, unlike
       proper nutrition and exercise, it has no proven long-term affect [sic] on
       weight.

(5)   Chemically, caffeine is in the same family as poisonous compounds such
       as strychnine, nicotine and morphine. True or False?
       True. Caffeine is found in the leaves, seeds and fruits of more than 60
       plants, including coffee, cacao beans, kola nuts and tea leaves. But, despite
       caffeine's *au naturel* origins, its chemical make-up belongs to the same
       family of potentially lethal compounds as emetine. But fear not the hot
       black brew. A recent study suggests that women who drink two or more
       cups of coffee a day are less likely to commit suicide than those who don't
       drink coffee at all.

(6)   The road to an Olympic gold medal is paved with coffee beans. True or false?
       Both. By revving up the central nervous system caffeine can temporarily
       enhance athletic performance. But while your gym teacher might applaud
       you for your effortless sprint, the International Olympic Committee could
       hand you your walking papers. Classified as a 'doping agent', caffeine
       intake is restricted by the committee. Some cardiologists also warn that
       caffeine before a workout can raise blood pressure.

       (*Jump*, August 1998, pp. 46, 48)

ACTIVITY 33*

Imagine that you are working as an administrative assistant in the Road Safety
Department of the Ministry of Communications. The fitting of baby seats in the
rear of cars has become compulsory recently, and you receive two letters enquir-
ing about how good the brand XXX car baby seats are. One of these letters is
from an unknown member of the public. The other one happens to be from an
old schoolfriend, who didn't know you worked in this department. The letter you
write to the member of the public goes as follows:

The Ministry of Communications
Land Transport Division
Road Safety Department
460 Alexandra Road
PSA Building #39
12 December 1999

Dear Mrs Jones

This is to acknowledge your letter of 5 December and your request for advice on the efficacy and local availability of XXX baby seats.

The Road Safety Department of the Ministry of Communications is involved in research aimed at increasing safety on the roads through vehicle safety testing, effective road construction and traffic redirection. Details of some of the studies and tests conducted are to be found in the enclosed November/December issue of *Safer Roads*.

Officers of the Department are, however, not aware of XXX vehicle baby seats and are thus unable to comment on their efficacy and availability. The Road Safety Department does not usually test commercial products; this role is more often undertaken by the Automobile Association. You can contact the association at 336 River Valley Road to ascertain whether it has tested the product.

Yours sincerely

Jane Lee

Write a letter to your old schoolfriend, conveying the same information as the letter above. Your letter should be in a more personal and informal style. To achieve this:

- change Passive constructions to Active;
- change nominalisations back into verbs and adjectives;
- use the appropriate first and second person pronouns where necessary (sometimes you may have to change the modal structures to do this);
- substitute informal for formal lexis where you can: you may wish to consult a dictionary, as well as a thesaurus to achieve a more or less consistent level of informality;
- use contractions, and minor sentences in places;
- introduce emotive vocabulary and intensifiers where appropriate;
- think about whether or not to use fully-blocked layout (everything set against the right hand margin) as in the formal version, and experiment with the salutation and valediction.

3.7. Summary

In this chapter we have looked at the various ways in which Text can encode interpersonal meanings, meanings associated with the social dimensions of Power, Contact and emotion. We saw that:

- we can demonstrate our Power by regulating behaviour through the use of commands and questions, presuming, synthetically, the presence of the reader and making demands on him; and we can regulate less strongly by using modals of obligation;

- we can vary the level of authority, assertiveness and dogmatism of our texts by employing the scales of modal probability, frequency, universality or by using subjective markers;

- we can increase the personality of our Text by the use of second-person pronouns or first person (exclusive and exclusive) or decrease it by using the third person, the Passive or nominalisation;

- we can suggest closer Contact and heightened emotion by imitating the rhythms and minor sentences of speech; though, with the latter, we must bear in mind the importance for the writer of correctly estimating the knowledge of the typical reader;

- we can create a closer Contact by choosing from the different strands of English vocabulary – the more formal and longer Greek/Latin words, the French words of medium formality, and the informal shorter everyday Old English words;

- we can use vocabulary to convey positive and negative emotion, or cause offence with contested terms.

Project 1

Take a passage of about two paragraphs from an academic textbook, which explains an important concept. Rewrite it for schoolchildren.

Try to:

- make the text less formal: get rid of nominalisations, and passives; choose less formal vocabulary where possible; use contractions;
- make your text more personal: introduce first- and/or second-person pronouns;
- be more explicit, by stating clearly some of the assumptions which the original text makes, but which your pupil readers may not know;
- make your text more visually informative than the original; this will also give you the opportunity to introduce minor sentences, e.g. in bulleted lists or diagrams;
- use one or more of the Microsoft Word readability indices when you have finished the first draft to see whether it is suitable for the grade level you have in mind;
- refer to Chapter 4 to see how you might use explanatory metaphor to get your ideas across more effectively.

It's useful to add footnotes or marginal notes to the text you create, indicating exactly what changes you have made and why you have made them. Include the original, unsimplified text.

Try the rewritten text out on some real pupils, and get some feedback through interviews or questionnaires to test their level of comprehension. How successful was your rewrite? Which parts still need improving?

Suggestions for further reading

- Poynton in the last chapter of *Language and Gender: Making the Difference*, gives an excellent overview of the resources for constructing interpersonal relationships, as well as the model of social relationships from which I borrow the dimensions of Power, Contact and Emotion (Affect). Martin gives a more theoretical and dense account in *English Text: System and Structure*, pp. 523–36.

- The grammatical dimensions of Mood and Modality have authoritative treatments in Halliday's *Introduction* chapter 4, Downing and Locke chapter 5 and Eggins chapter 6.
- Simpson chapters 2 and 3 develops the Hallidayan analysis of mood and modality into a theory of narrative point of view in prose fiction.
- Halliday and Hasan's *Cohesion in English*, pp. 43–57, discusses the English pronoun system in some depth. Rob Pope in *Textual Intervention*, pp. 51–3, 60–8, shows how complicated and ambiguous the reference of pronouns can become in lyrics. Montgomery (1986) does the same for DJ talk.
- Nash's *Designs in Prose* has an interesting chapter 6 on the relationships of a writer to his [sic] reader; pp. 152–4 discuss levels of formality and emotion in vocabulary, as does Leech's *Semantics*, pp. 12–18.

Part two

Critical discourse: reading meanings into the text

Introduction to Part two

In Part one of this coursebook we approached critical reading and writing through analysis of the surface grammar and vocabulary of texts. This is a semantic approach in which we examine what is encoded in the Text and explain it ideologically, in terms of the ideas and power structures of a society. However, for critical analysis to be complete and valid, we have to take a complementary discoursal approach in which Text is seen as a bridge between a writer and a reader. This is a more contextualised analysis which recognises the multiplicity of meanings that a Text can generate and the reader's work in constructing a meaning out of it. So in Part two the approach to Text will not be decoding or semantic description but making inferences and hypothesising. As a result, this part corresponds to level 2 in Table 0.1, p. 3.

There are three aspects of interpretation which are highlighted. Chapter 4 explains how the physical Text which links writer and reader fails to fully convey the intended meaning, but is simply a trace of the writer's meaning and a cue for the reader's meaning. The second idea we explore, in Chapter 5, is that writing is a form of action involving a writer and an implied or ideal reader. Another way of putting it is to say that the reader is being constantly positioned by the writer, and may to varying degrees accept or resist this reading position. Chapter 6 develops both the insights of Chapters 4 and 5 in the context of a discussion of various types of intertextuality. The end of the unit brings us full circle to the subject-matter of Chapter 1, by considering genre as one kind of intertextual phenomenon.

Chapter 4

Interpreting discourse

Aims of this chapter

To show how implicit knowledge supplied from outside the Text can interact with knowledge in the Text to create inferences.

To illustrate the ideological role of such implicit presupposition and inferencing.

To give practice in analysing presupposition and inferencing.

- **4.0 Introduction: the need for interpreting texts**
  Illustrates that meanings cannot simply be read off the Text but that inferences and attitudes have to be recognised to make sense of it.

- **4.1 Presuppositions**
  Surveys the main linguistic means for presupposing ideas rather than explicitly stating them, and gives examples of how presuppositions help to create the sense of an ideal reader, or are used to smuggle in ideology.

- **4.2 Propositional attitude**
  Points out how commands, orders and statements encode propositional attitude, and how inadequate visual codes are for conveying attitude.

- **4.3 Metaphor and irony**
  Identifies metaphor and irony as prime examples of language uses where we need to recognise propositional attitude, and explores the uses to which they are put in writing.

- **4.4 Inferences and existing knowledge**
  Shows how the background knowledge we supply for inferencing can be organised into stereotypical schemas; and illustrates how, in interpreting jokes, racist and value-laden schemas are evoked and given currency, even though we may not accept them.

- **4.5 Adverts, association and inference**
  Illustrates how sophisticated adverts can use visuals to create inferences about their products, so avoiding explicit and indefensible claims.

- **Activity**
  A major activity is to analyse magazine adverts for the inferences they make.

4.0 Introduction: the need for interpreting texts

The analysis of lexis, grammar, and their meanings only takes us so far in understanding how texts are composed or interpreted and what effects they might have on the reader. Some early code models of communication proposed that communication proceeds as follows: a writer has meaning in her head, she encodes this completely in her Text and the reader decodes it, resulting in a successful transfer of meaning from writer to reader. While, as we acknowledged in Part one, code is often important and necessary for communication, it is only one factor and is seldom sufficient. Reading is better modelled as 'a psycholinguistic guessing game', in which the Text provides clues for the reader, and in which not only the meaning of the Text but also the intentions of the writer have to be guessed (Sperber and Wilson 1995: 3–15, Mills 1995: 26–43).

Let's take a simple sentence like 'Shall I make a cup of tea?' uttered to your friend when she is visiting your flat or apartment. This won't be interpreted just by decoding. For a start you are not asking whether you should make a cup. Nor are you asking whether you are going to make tea (it grows on bushes), but rather whether to brew tea. Still, this doesn't take us far enough in our interpretation. You are not exactly asking about making enough tea to fill just one cup. You would have to leave some space for milk and sugar. Even more radically you would probably want a cup of tea yourself, so you are asking about brewing tea in enough quantities to fill at least two cups. In addition, since brewing two or more cupfuls of tea takes some time, this question could be an indirect way of asking whether your visitor has enough time to stay and chat, or will soon be leaving (Boutonnet, personal communication).

This example illustrates that codes are not sufficient for communication. But in fact, codes are not always necessary for communication. You might ask me whether I had a good holiday skiing in Canada, and instead of encoding an answer I could simply wave my broken foot in its plaster cast (Wilson and Sperber 1986: 25). There is no coded convention that suggests waving a foot means "I did not enjoy my holiday"; but probably I would have conveyed that meaning quite effectively.

What do we have to do to the decoded message in order to fully understand and interpret it? At least three things. We have to recognise propositions that are assumed rather than expressed. Then we must decide what attitude the writer has towards the propositions expressed or assumed. And, finally, we have to guess what inferences the writer intended us to make on the basis of the proposition. Let me give a small-scale example, borrowed from Wilson and Sperber (1986), before we go on to explore these questions in more detail.

Imagine the following scenario. Mary is sitting in the living-room reading the newspaper. John, who has been cooking dinner, comes in and puts two plates of food on the table and says: 'Your food will get cold'. First of all the sentence makes a certain **presupposition**, an assumption which is not explicitly stated, namely that the food is warm or hot. Second, we have to decide on the speaker's attitude to this proposition and the presupposed proposition, technically **propositional attitude**. If the food happens to be a hot dinner, then John will probably have the attitude of belief towards the presupposition >> 'the food is warm or hot' and towards the proposition that it will get cold. (The sign >> means 'presupposes'.) If it's ice-cream, he would obviously not believe the presupposition or the proposition, and not expect Mary to think he believed them, and this would be a case of **irony**.

Third, in order to fully interpret this sentence as discourse, we would have to guess what John intended by uttering it, what he is **implying**, what **inferences** he wanted Mary to draw (Thomas 1995: 58ff.). By saying 'Your food will get cold', John might be communicating

John wants Mary to eat the food at once

Inferences such as this are created by using contextual information, or **schemas**. John has access to a set of stored assumptions about 'eating dinner at home' which contains the information

John wants Mary to come and eat food at the time it is still hot

This assumption interacts with the full proposition/presupposition

The food on the table is warm/hot and will get cold

to create the inference

John wants Mary to eat the food at once

4.1 Presuppositions

In Chapter 2, we illustrated existential presupposition in discussing the means by which vocabulary constructs or confers a reality: if a new word or phrase is invented, such as *shopaholic*, then we assume that some people exist in the world who belong to this class. Also, when discussing complications to transitivity analysis, we mentioned nominalisation (turning verbs and adjectives into nouns) and the way this creates presuppositions. For example 'the ship sank' openly claims that the ship sank, whereas 'the sinking of the ship' simply presupposes it. We noted that arguing against a presupposition in noun-phrase form is far more difficult than arguing against the equivalent explicit statement, because presuppositions cannot be negated.

In fact, a defining feature of presuppositions is that they remain unaffected when we negate a sentence. For example, 'John's dog was killed' presupposes 'John has a dog'. If we negate this utterance to 'John's dog was not killed' it still presupposes 'John has a dog'.

Possessive presupposition

Presupposition is a large and complex area in the study of meaning, and we cannot deal with the theories in detail. So in this part we will only discuss those linguistic devices which are commonly used for ideological or manipulative purposes, to smuggle in, as common sense, assumptions which are debatable, controversial or simply inapplicable.

Close to existential presuppositions are **possessive presuppositions**. These occur when we use *'s* to indicate possession, or the pronominal "adjectives" *hers/his, their, my, our, your*. For instance, 'I looked under John's piano for your cat' presupposes >> 'John has a piano' and 'you have a cat'. To see how this works in practice look at the following extracts from a horoscope. This is based on a horoscope taken from *Woman's World*, a magazine primarily targeted at American women aged between 30 and 50 years old. (I have had to rewrite it to avoid copyright infringement, though I have preserved the essentials of the presuppositions.)

Aries   March 21 to April 19
With Mars in Libra's laid-back domain, you should consider letting your mate take the initiative in romance. Any diet you begin now will be successful, making you look and feel beautiful.

Taurus   April 20 to May 20
. . . be sure to take care of your pet's health in this period. On the 18th and 19th, your mate will find you overwhelmingly attractive.

Gemini   May 21 to June 21
. . . As your creativity blossoms, you'll become more self-assured and confident of your unique skills and talents.

Cancer   June 22 to July 22
. . . You could be eager for career challenges as Mars' stimulating aspect increases your ambition.

Virgo   August 23 to September 22
Your planetary rulers' positive aspects are giving you a sense of intense excitement. This energy spreads into your love life ...

Libra   September 23 to October 22
... Saturn's combative aspect perfects your diplomatic skills, preparing the way for career opportunities.

Scorpio   October 23 to November 21
... let the tiger inside you emerge from her cage.

Sagittarius   November 22 to December 21
Pluto's transforming power in your sign is stimulating you to rebuild your lifestyle to make it really comfortable for you.

Aquarius   January 20 to February 18
You could feel a strong desire for novelty as Uranus in Aquarius reawakens your adventurous nature.

Pisces   February 19 to March 20
... Fun becomes your top priority, as your inner child seeks your full attention.

(Adapted from *Woman's World,* 14 January 1997, p. 34)

The possessive presuppositions here make three sets of assumptions.

- First, that the readers have planetary rulers: 'your planetary rulers' >> 'you have planetary rulers', and that the effect of these rulers can be specified: 'Mars' stimulating aspect', 'Saturn's combative aspect', 'Pluto's transforming power' >> 'Mars has a stimulating aspect' etc.

- Second, that the readers have certain characteristics, presumably because they were born under a specific zodiac sign (e.g. 'Libra's laid-back domain'): 'your unique skills and talents', 'your diplomatic skills', 'your ambition', 'your adventurous nature', 'your inner child' >> 'you have unique skills and talents', etc. Notice too, in this respect, the existential and possessive presuppositions in 'let the tiger inside you emerge from her cage' >> 'there is a tiger inside you' and 'the tiger inside you has a cage'.

- Third, quite independent of specific zodiacal influence, one supposes, there are presuppositions about the general reader of these horoscopes: 'your partner', 'your love-life', 'your pet', 'your mate' >> 'you have a partner, love-life, pet and mate'. *Pet* comes as a bit of a surprise. I particularly like the juxtaposition of 'Be sure to take care of your pet's health in this period' and 'On the 18th and 19th your partner will find you overwhelmingly attractive'. Is this merely gauche or does the horoscope writer after all have a sense of humour? Are there two separate possessive presuppositions here?

In presupposing planetary influence, zodiacally determined characteristics, and the possession of partners/pets, this horoscope positions the reader as someone who takes astrology seriously and has a certain lifestyle. But in addition, there are frequent instances of another kind of presupposition – **change-of-state presupposition** – which construct the readers as unfulfilled in some way. We already illustrated change-of-state presupposition in the example 'Your food will get cold'. This presupposes that the food is not cold, i.e. it is hot or warm. Here are the examples from the horoscope which convey change-of-state presuppositions:

It'll make you look and feel beautiful
>> 'either you are not beautiful and/or you do not feel beautiful'

You'll become more self-assured and confident of your unique skills and talents
>> 'you are not completely self-assured and confident of your unique skills and talents'

Saturn's combative aspect perfects your diplomatic skills
>> 'your diplomatic skills are not perfect'

Pluto's transforming power in your sign is stimulating you to rebuild your lifestyle to make it really comfortable for you
>> 'your lifestyle has not been rebuilt and is not really comfortable for you'

Uranus in Aquarius reawakens your adventurous nature
>> 'your adventurous nature was once awake but has fallen asleep lately'

The horoscope seems to be reassuring women who are unfulfilled and dissatisfied with their lives that things are going to improve automatically under planetary influence. (Perhaps, at the end of the day, we won't need pets!)

To find examples of further presupposition devices, let's go from the sublime to the ridiculous, and look at the beginning of an editorial in London's *Financial Times*, praising the GATT agreement and the setting up of a World Trade Organisation.

Greater Wealth of Nations

Conclusion of the Uruguay Round is truly a triumph in adversity. Securing agreement among so many countries on such a complex raft of trade agreements frequently seemed an insuperable challenge in the past seven years. To have done it at a time of sluggish growth, political uncertainty and protectionist pressures is an extraordinary achievement.

Whatever the shortcomings of the result, the original vision of a broad expansion of international trade law is now much closer to fulfilment. More remarkably still, so is the dream that drove the founding fathers of the General Agreement on Tariffs and Trade: that of a liberal rules-based trading system overseen by an authoritative world trade organisation. Just as the Gatt helped foster economic integration and growth in the post-war decades, the new agreement should provide powerful underpinning for the world economy, fresh impetus to competition, and fresh hope for those developing and former communist countries that have been opening up to international commerce.

Several individuals deserve credit. Mr Peter Sutherland, and before him Mr Arthur Dunkel, Gatt directors general, worked tirelessly to cajole recalcitrants – especially the US and the EU – into settling differences. Mr Mickey Kantor, US trade representative, has dispelled the most serious doubts about his and the administration's commitment to multilateral free trade. Sir Leon Brittan, the European trade commissioner, played a difficult hand with consummate skill, and by luring France into the fold, arguably saved the Union from a political crisis of alarming proportions.

(*Financial Times,* 16 December 1993)

When we apply the negation test to diagnose presupposition, then it is only applied to the main clause of a sentence. This means to say that subordinate clauses regularly convey presuppositions. Look at this example:

Subordinate clause   *Main clause*
When John came in | the dog was alive

Applying negation we get:

Subordinate clause   *Main clause*
When John came in | the dog wasn't alive

The negation test preserves the presupposition >> 'John came in'.
Let's apply this to the following sentence of the editorial:

Subordinate clause
Just as the Gatt helped foster economic integration and growth in the post-war decades . . .

Main clause
. . . the new agreement should provide powerful underpinning for the world economy.

The first subordinate clause conveys a presupposition rather than being a clear statement. Only by changing it to a main clause would the claim become clear: 'The Gatt helped foster economic integration and growth in the post-war decades'. But as it stands, with the conjunction *just as* introducing the subordinate clause, the editorial has smuggled in a disputable claim.

Comparisons often automatically carry presuppositions. In paragraph two of the editorial '**More** remarkably still' assumes that the move towards a broader international trade law, mentioned in the previous sentence, is already remarkable. And if 'Mr Mickey Kantor, US trade representative has dispelled the **most** serious doubts about his and the administration's commitment to multilateral free trade' this suggests that there are other less serious doubts which remain.

Lastly there are some verbs and phrases which presuppose the truth or falsity of the statements they introduce, for example the verb *realise*: 'John realised that he had come to the wrong house' >> 'John had come to the wrong house'. In the editorial we have: 'Peter Sutherland deserves credit for tirelessly cajoling recalcitrants into settling their differences'. Here 'deserves credit for' presupposes the truth of 'he tirelessly cajoled recalcitrants into settling their differences'. And, similarly, 'cajoled into' presupposes 'recalcitrants settled their differences'. On the other hand, there are verbs, like *dream*, which presuppose that what follows them is false. So if we say 'the founding fathers of Gatt dreamed of a liberal rules-based trading system overseen by an authoritative world trade organisation', the verb carries the presupposition: 'a liberal rules-based trading system overseen by an authoritative world trade organisation did <u>not</u> then exist'. You don't need to dream of things which already exist.

If clauses and the main clauses they are paired with are particularly interesting in presupposing truth and falsity. To put it in a formula, 'If A had done X, Y wouldn't have happened' >> 'A did not do X'. Conversely, when the *if* clause is negative it presupposes that the positive equivalent did take place, 'If A hadn't done X, Y would have happened' >> 'A did do X'. In addition, the main clause in such pairs seems to presuppose its opposite: 'If A had done X, Y wouldn't have happened' >> 'Y happened'. And 'If A hadn't done X, Y would have happened' >> 'Y did not happen'. For example, although this does not occur in the passage, a sentence such as 'If Gore hadn't become Vice President the environment wouldn't be an important policy area' presupposes that Gore became Vice President, and that the environment is an important policy area.

ACTIVITY 34

Spell out the presuppositions of the following sentence. As well as the *if* clause, consider existential presuppositions, and how comparisons, and clauses which are not the main clause of the sentence, generate other presuppositions.

Seeing the bagloads of rubbish made this writer wonder how much more litter would be left behind if there had been no stiff $1,000 fine.

Before leaving the subject of presupposition, it is worth remembering and illustrating just how manipulative and disingenuous are the existential presuppositions brought about by nominalisation. For example, in the first paragraph of the GATT editorial, we have the nominalisation 'triumph'. The presupposition that someone or something has triumphed is very contentious. We would like to know very much who this is. The environment, which is having more growth(s) inflicted upon it? Poor villagers of India who now discover that their traditional medicinal herbs are a pharmaceutical company's patented intellectual property rights? The rich, with capital to invest, like the multinational companies and their chief executives? Or all of us? The ideological manipulation behind the use of presupposition could hardly be better illustrated – presupposing ideas assumes they are unquestionable truths.

4.2 Propositional attitude

In Chapter 3 we discussed commands, questions and statements. These are ways of encoding propositional attitude. In fact, linguists claim that the three sentences like (1) 'John, wash the dishes!' (2) 'Does John wash the dishes?', and (3) 'John washes the dishes' have the same underlying proposition. What distinguishes them is propositional attitude. The command (1) indicates that the speaker believes it is desirable for the hearer to wash the dishes. The question (2) expresses uncertainty about the proposition. And the statement (3), on the face of it, conveys the attitude that this proposition is true.

"Writing" is more and more visually informative in our modern Internet surf, and the global seaside village which demands language-neutral communication.

So it's worth pointing out that one of the major differences between visual and verbal communication is that only the verbal has the resources to effectively convey propositional attitude. When I was a student at a college which was predominantly Welsh, a non-Welsh friend and myself, on St David's Day, attempted to fly a flag as a light-hearted protest against the celebration of Welshness. The flag depicted Britannia spearing a Welsh dragon. The attempt to fly it was unsuccessful, but it struck me later that, in any case, the statement was unclear, precisely because it did not signal propositional attitude. The proposition conveyed pictorially was simply 'Britannia spears a Welsh dragon'. But whether it meant 'it's a scandal that Britannia is spearing a Welsh dragon', or 'I wish Britannia would spear the Welsh dragon' could not be conveyed graphically. Was it a statement or was it a command?

Of course, organisations like road traffic departments, airlines and multinational electronics companies, who communicate in ideograms to speakers of diverse languages, have managed to invent some crude markers of propositional attitude. They are, however, very crude. Although a diagonal bar usually means prohibition as in (A) below, I once encountered a sign like (B) in Figure 4.1 on the fold-down table of an Austrian Airlines plane going from Vienna to Cyprus. In the context, this could hardly have conveyed the negative command, 'do not bring pigs on board', but was in fact a statement of fact, 'we do not serve pork'.

(A)   **(B)**

Figure 4.1 Graphic attempts at propositional attitude

This Chapter concentrates discussion on two figures of speech in which propositional attitude is something less than belief. These are metaphor and irony.

4.3 Metaphor and irony

In one kind of irony, the writer expresses a proposition which she does not believe to be true, and which she expects the reader to know is not true. For instance, a friend of mine once wrote an ironic letter to the Forum Page of the

Singapore *Straits Times* newspaper (24 May 1990) complaining indirectly about the nuisance of barking dogs.

Barking dogs of Chip Bee Gardens

I WRITE to express concern about the growing number of 'burglaries' in the vicinity of my house in Chip Bee Gardens.

These burglaries occur at any time of the day or night. The burglars must work in large co-ordinated gangs because usually several houses are burgled at the same time. I wish something could be done about it.

One night last week was pretty typical. There were burglaries at 9.30 p.m., 10.15 p.m., 11.40 p.m., 1.30 a.m., 4.20 a.m., 5.10 a.m. and 6.30 a.m. Most of the burglaries were over in 10 minutes, but some took as long as half an hour to be completed. It is puzzling, but the owners of the houses being burgled did not seem to be particularly bothered.

I never saw them checking if their possessions were being loaded into a waiting van during any of the burglaries.

They didn't call the police to the scene of the crime.

Ah, I know the answer ... the poor unfortunates are probably deaf, and they slept through the din of their guard dogs barking furiously as the burglars went happily about their work.

P. E. CLIFFORD

Paul Clifford obviously did not believe some of the propositions he expressed (or presuppositions he made), notably

> These burglaries occur at any time of the day or night. The burglars must work in large co-ordinated gangs because usually several houses are burgled at the same time.

> One night last week was pretty typical. There were burglaries at 9.30 p.m., 10.15 p.m., 11.40 p.m., 1.30 a.m., 4.20 a.m., 5.10 a.m. and 6.30 a.m. Most of the burglaries were over in 10 minutes, but some took as long as half an hour.

> The poor unfortunates are probably deaf.

However, despite his signalling irony with scare quotes around the first occurrence of 'burglaries', at least one of the readers seemed not to detect his propositional attitude. The reply from the police (*Straits Times*, 7 June 1990) went as follows:

Two burglaries in Chip Bee this year

I REFER to the letter 'Barking dogs of Chip Bee Gardens' by Dr P. E. Clifford (ST, 24 May).

Our records show that there were only two cases of burglary at Chip Bee Gardens this year. Nothing was stolen in the first case and the second case resulted in the arrest of the culprit.

We would like to encourage Dr Clifford to help the police in apprehending the culprits by calling us if he witnesses any more burglaries in his neighbourhood.

ANG SIN PIN
for Director
Public Affairs Department
Republic of Singapore Police

Metaphor, too, runs the risk of not being recognised. In the film *The Mask*, we have a dialogue between the psychologist, Dr Neuman, author of the book *The Masks We Wear* and the hero, Mr Ipkiss, who possesses the magic mask.

Ipkiss: Loki? Who's Loki?
Neuman: The Norse god of mischief. Supposedly he caused so much trouble that Odin banished him from Valhalla for ever.
Ipkiss: Then he could have banished me with that mask.
Neuman: I'm talking about mythology, Mr Ipkiss. This is a piece of wood.
Ipkiss: But your book!
Neuman: My book is about masks as a metaphor, Mr Ipkiss. A metaphor, not to be taken literally. You're suffering from a mild delusion.

Given the risks of misunderstanding, what is the point of using irony and metaphor? Why do we complicate communication by saying things we don't believe, for example, saying our neighbours are deaf when they are not? Or, distracting with irrelevancies, like burglaries, when we are really talking about barking dogs, and by being deliberately ambiguous and indirect?

Table 4.1 sketches some of the more obvious functions of metaphor, listed according to ideational and interpersonal functions. Metaphor fulfils perhaps four significant functions. Explanation, ideological restructuring, cultivation of intimacy and the expression/hiding of emotion. The last two of these seem to be the main functions of irony as well.

Table 4.1 The functions of metaphor and irony

	Function	Examples
Ideational	(1) explanation/ modelling	_Electricity_ is like piped water. The pressure is _the voltage_, the rate of flow _the amperage_, and the width of pipe _the resistance_.
	(2) ideological restructuring	For mature economies growth amounts to economic cancer. Property is theft.
Interpersonal	(3) cultivating intimacy	_Myanmar_ is the Algeria of South-East Asia. What goes on four legs in the morning, two legs at mid-day and three legs in the evening? A man.
	(4) expressing/hiding emotion	Piss off. Europe's butter mountain. My mother passed away last year.

(1)   Metaphors are used in science and education both to build models and theories and to explain concepts to students. For example, physicists have two metaphors or theories for light, conceiving it either as wave or particle. And it is common to explain electricity to secondary school students in terms of water flow through a plumbing system.

(2)   Ideology and its restructuring probably underlie most uses of metaphor, and we have already had examples of this function when we discussed contested and offensive vocabulary. Metaphors of food for women, _cookie_, _honey_, _tart_, are a particularly noteworthy area ideologically, reducing women to objects for satisfying men's appetites. But if we call economic growth in mature economies _cancer_, and if we recategorise property as _theft_ we are trying to get our readers to reconceptualise and take a different ideological position. In this way, metaphor can become a creative force, undoing our received categories and transforming our perception of the world.

(3)   Partly because some people will accept these restructuring metaphors as literal, while others will reject them, metaphor can make radical divisions in society. But metaphor is also divisive because it makes allusions which some of our audience will understand and others will not. Some readers can interpret the metaphor in Table 4.1 because they know the recent history of Algeria and Burma and their foreign relations with the dominant trading blocks in their respective regions: the military take-over and cancellation of the second round of elections in Algeria in 1992, to be compared with a similar take-over in Burma in 1989 and the failure to respect the results of the elections; the connivance of France and the European Union in the take-over compared with the admission of Myanmar to ASEAN, etc. Those readers who have this background information feel included in the community of comprehenders. Whereas those lacking

enough political knowledge to make sense of it feel excluded. Similarly, riddles and jokes often depend on metaphors and when our readers get the joke or riddle, or have it explained to them, this strengthens the social bond between them and the writer. The riddle of the sphinx in Table 4.1, 'What goes on four legs in the morning, two legs at mid-day and three legs in the evening?' depends upon the metaphorical analogy

morning: mid-day: evening :: infancy: adulthood: old-age

and the metaphorical equation between a walking-stick and a third leg. Puns in adverts are a good example of jokes and humour which cultivate intimacy, and are probably used as part of synthetic personalisation to lower the defences of potential customers.

(4)   Lastly, metaphor has important relations to the expression of emotion. Some metaphors rely exclusively on emotional connotations, for example the swear words 'piss off' and 'shit'.

ACTIVITY 35

In Shakespeare's *Antony and Cleopatra*, Cleopatra applies a snake to her breast in order to commit suicide. She refers to the snake metaphorically as a baby.

Dost thou not see **my baby** at my breast that sucks the nurse asleep?
(Act V Scene 2, ll. 308–9)

Explain the conflicting emotions in this metaphor, our normal reactions to the two things being compared.

We will often use sensational or exaggerated metaphors if we wish to incite wonder or amazement in our hearers or readers. This is typical of popular newspapers:

Then he [Ian Botham] moved to a private bar upstairs and trouble **erupted**

Britain's butter **mountain**

Trouble doesn't just start it *erupts*, Britain doesn't have a few warehouses full of butter but a *mountain*.

Conversely, when the event or object referred to has unfavourable emotive connotations we will often resort to euphemism, one kind of metaphorical disguise (see Chapter 3, page 108). In American English, Louise Pound (1936) found the following metaphorical euphemisms for dying and funerals: *climbed the golden stair, called to the eternal sleep, crossed over the Great Divide, answered the last muster, planting, cold meat party* (quoted in Saville-Troike 1982: 201).

The metaphors we use, just like the other classifications, often have consequences for the actions we take. A disturbing case in point comes from the actions of police on the street children in Rio, Brazil:

> 'Street children' ... are often described as 'dirty vermin' so that metaphors of 'street cleaning', 'trash removal', 'fly swatting', 'pest removal' and 'urban hygiene' have been invoked to garner broad-based support for police and death squad activities against them.
>
> (*New Internationalist*, October 1997: 21)

When we turn to the functions of irony we see that they tend to be restricted to the interpersonal. One reason for using irony is akin to the euphemistic function of metaphor (4). It is to avoid responsibility for saying something that may cause offence or even bring legal punishment. Obviously, Paul Clifford used irony partly to soften his criticism of his dog-owning neighbours, but because it misfired it ended up potentially causing offence to the police! This avoidance of taking responsibility for claims can also apply to one of the meanings of metaphorical puns. The London bookshop, Dillons, advertised in the London Underground with the signature line *Go to Dillons. And be transported.* Given the ambiguity, Dillons could hardly be blamed by the Advertising Standards Authority for giving misleading information about the exciting qualities of their stock.

Irony often expresses disappointment that the actual state of affairs does not match up to the state of affairs described by the Text. If you say 'It's a lovely day for a barbecue' and then we go to the barbecue pit at the beach and there's a howling rain storm, you might ironically echo my earlier remark 'Yes, it's a lovely day for a barbecue'. Part of the function of this could be to express disappointment about the weather or to scorn my earlier statement. The more or less veiled expression of emotion (4) is then often an important function. Certainly, the 'Barking Dogs' irony cited in the previous paragraph is an indirect expression of disapproval.

But irony too can sometimes exaggerate emotion rather than hide it, deliberately setting out to shock the reader. Jonathan Swift in 'A Modest Proposal for Preventing the Children of Ireland from being a Burden to their Parents' ironically suggests that the problems of poverty in Ireland could be solved by eating the babies of the poor:

> I have been assured by a very knowing American of my acquaintance in London, that a young healthy child well nursed is at a year old a most delicious, nourishing and wholesome food, whether stewed, roasted, baked or boiled, and I make no doubt that it will serve equally well in a fricassee, or a ragout.

Swift's proposal amounts to hyperbole since he is implying that such a policy is only an exaggeration of the kinds of cruelty and oppression that had been inflicted upon the poor in eighteenth-century Ireland.

Irony, like metaphor, also cultivates intimacy (3) between the writer and reader who detects it, and even victimises those who fail to, like poor Ang Sin Pin. And irony seems to have humour as one of its main aims. According to Sigmund Freud (1960), a psychological sequence of initial bewilderment followed by a sudden flash of understanding is essential to jokes. This is just what happens when we process an ironic statement, being bewildered or puzzled by taking it at its face value, and then suddenly understanding that the writer believes the opposite of what she says.

ACTIVITY 36

(a)   What ironies do you detect in 'I'm sorry teenagers, you are not the centre of the universe' (on pp. 61–3)? You might look especially at paragraph nine. What is the purpose of the irony here?
(b)   Look at the following two passages, (1) is from a popular science text, (2) is from an advertisement. What functions do the metaphors serve in each?

> (1) Lymphocytes all originate from stem cells in the bone marrow. Some then migrate to the thymus where they mature into T cells (the 'T' means thymus-derived). As the T cells mature, an important process occurs known as 'thymic education', which prevents the immune system from attacking the body's own cells. Exactly what happens during thymic education is still uncertain. Many immunologists believe that any Th cells with receptors that bind to the body's own molecules are destroyed. This process is called clonal deletion. Others disagree and believe that the educative process may lie with the Ts cells, or elsewhere.
> [...]

If lymphocytes are thought of as a police force, patrolling the body, then the primary lymphatic organs are the police-training colleges where they originate and learn their skills. The secondary lymphatic organs are the local police stations where they congregate and deal with suspect antigens.

(*New Scientist*, 24 April 1988, p. 4)

(2) Picked daily there's a fresh edition of Dutch cucumbers on sale each day. Carefully harvested by hand, only Class-1 cucumbers are selected and packed by the grower for export to the United Kingdom. Firm crisp Dutch cucumbers straight from Europe's kitchen garden. They're good news indeed.

Your

daily Dutch

Dutch cucumbers

Fresh from Europe's kitchen garden   Holland

4.4 Inferences and existing knowledge

When we use metaphor and irony, then, we do not believe the proposition we utter. But in addition we make the reader infer our intended meaning, and this will often necessitate supplying information from outside the Text, as in the case of the Myanmar–Algeria metaphor.

The background information or assumptions which we bring to texts in order to draw inferences are generally organised in our long-term memory in structures known as **schemas**. These are the facilities for storing stereotypical knowledge. We will have schemas to refer to stereotypical information stored about objects and sequences of behaviour (Schank and Abelson 1979).

The extent to which we use schemas in ordinary understanding of language is obvious when we think of how we process a simple sentence such as 'I like apples'. Because our schema for apples includes the information that they are food, we will, by default, interpret this sentence to mean 'I like eating apples', rather than 'I have an emotional attachment to apples'. Remember the joke

Child: Mummy, mummy, I don't like grandma.

Mother: Well, leave her on the side of your plate and finish your potatoes.

Obviously it depends upon the fact that plates and potatoes belong to the schema for eating, and this forces us to abandon the default schema of family relationships cued by 'grandma'. In one sense understanding a text means finding a schema which accounts for it.

A famous example of a schema for eating at a restaurant was provided by Schank and Abelson (1979):

RESTAURANT

props:	tables, chairs, cutlery, food, plates, menu etc.
roles:	customer, owner, cook, waiter, (cashier)
entry conditions:	customer is hungry; customer has money
results:	customer has less money; customer is not hungry; owner has more money
Scene 1. <u>Entering</u>:	going in, deciding where to sit, sitting
Scene 2. <u>Ordering</u>:	(asking for menu, waiter bringing menu) choosing, signalling to waiter, giving order, waiter telling cook the order
Scene 3. <u>Eating</u>:	cook giving waiter food, waiter bringing customer food; customer eating food
Scene 4. <u>Exiting</u>:	customer asking for bill, waiter writing bill, taking bill to customer, (customer tipping waiter), customer going to cashier, paying cashier, leaving restaurant.

This is a pretty well-organised behavioural schema, reasonably stereotypical within Western culture. So that if you said 'I went to a restaurant yesterday evening' the hearer will probably infer that the standard schema was followed: this would be a default interpretation. It is only when there are non-standard occurrences that the speaker would think it worth her while elaborating on the restaurant visit. For example I remember a letter in a local newspaper complaining about a visit to a Pizza Hut restaurant. The event schema developed against expectations. Scenes 1 and 2 proceeded as normal. However Scene 3 was left out, despite the customers waiting an hour. Nevertheless, some of Scene 4 materialised, with the waiter writing and bringing the bill, and the customers leaving the restaurant, but without paying.

Miscommunication will occur when the reader evokes a different schema from the one the writer intended. The following is a famous example of classroom discourse in which the student mistook what the teacher was trying to achieve, what schema she was following when she said 'what are you laughing at'?

ACTIVITY 37 ━━━━━━━━━━━━━━━━━━━━━━━━━━━━━━━

Context: Teacher has just played a tape of a man with a strange accent as a way of introducing a discussion on accents.

> *Teacher*:   <u>What are you laughing at?</u>
> *Pupil*:   Nothing.
> *Teacher*:   Pardon?
> *Pupil*:   Nothing.
> *Teacher*:   You're laughing at nothing, nothing at all?   [line 5]
> *Pupil*:   No … It's funny really because they don't think as though they were there they might not like it and it it sounds rather a pompous attitude.

How does the pupil initially interpret the underlined utterance (up to line 4)? What does he think the teacher is trying to achieve by asking him the underlined question? Teaching involves both a content schema – what the lesson is about – and a regulatory schema – keeping order and discipline in class. Discuss this misinterpretation in terms of these two schemas.

━━━

What is the relevance of schema theory to writing? Well, as we have seen, understanding texts is largely a matter of invoking the right schema. So it is vital, especially in Deductive genres, for the writer to state clearly the topic or issue of the text adequately at an early opportunity so that the readers can supply the relevant schematic background information to make sense of it.

Newspapers face a particular problem with long-running stories, such as the hostage crisis at the Japanese ambassador's residence in Lima, which lasted several months. They cannot presume that every reader will have followed the story from its beginning, but they can probably guess that most have. There are two solutions to this problem. Introduce the earlier necessary background information in a shorthand way at the beginning. And/or have a Background section later in the article. We can see this in the newspaper article about the Pope quoted in unit 1. The Lead is

A team of 15 doctors and nurses carried out a series of tests on Pope John Paul II yesterday to find out what is causing the abdominal pains that made him enter hospital for treatment.

The clause 'that made him enter hospital for treatment', telling us more about the abdominal pains, is a shorthand way of giving us the information that he had already entered hospital. And later in the article more details of his admission are given:

On Sunday a small crowd of well-wishers saw his entourage enter the hospital.
Inside the lobby he shook hands with nurses, patients and visiting families.

For any writer the trickiest judgement to make is the state of the average reader's background knowledge, whether any particular schema exists for the topic of the piece of writing. She does not wish to tell the reader things the reader already knows, otherwise the writing will be laboured. On the other hand she does not wish to take the risk that the required inferences cannot be made because of inadequate background knowledge.

On which side did you err in preparing a simplified text for schoolchildren in your project in Unit 3?

It's worth emphasising the stereotypical nature of many of the schemas which we employ. The fact that we are constantly using such stereotypical information in our processing of Text gives horribly wide opportunities for ideologies to operate latently and, as it were, naturally or commonsensically.

Let's illustrate this point by thinking about jokes which depend upon racial stereotyping.

Q. What did the Japanese hostess say to the amorous stamp collector?

A. Philately will get you nowhere.

Or:

There were an Irishman and a gorilla, and they were both preparing for a voyage to a space station. It was the end of their six-month course of physical and scientific training, and the evening before the mission was scheduled to commence. The head of the programme invited them into his office for a final briefing, at the end of which he wished them luck for the trip and handed them each a sealed envelope containing instructions for their duties during the three-week trip.

When the gorilla got to his apartment on the base he opened his envelope and found five sheets of detailed instructions. They told him that he should perform experiments on crystallography and heat conductivity, take various complicated astronomical readings, and monitor his and the Irishman's bodily functions including performing CAT scans at various intervals.

When the Irishman opened his letter, there was one small piece of paper which read: 'Feed the gorilla'.

To understand these jokes we have to supply various assumptions from our schemas for Japanese and Irish: that Japanese pronounce [r] as [l] and that Irishmen are stupid. (We also have to be aware of the proverb 'Flattery will get you nowhere'.) Of course, we need not *believe* these assumptions to get the joke, but simply by entertaining them we are, in a sense, giving them currency, acknowledging that other people believe or at least entertain them. In fact, there is plenty of evidence that Irishmen are highly intelligent. Anyone who knows about the literature of the British Isles will realise that a major contribution has been made by the Irish – Swift, Goldsmith, Yeats, Oscar Wilde and George Bernard Shaw – who are famous for their wit, intelligence and verbal dexterity. How this myth of Irish stupidity arose is itself instructive. Apparently, during the nineteenth century, if workers in the English mills went on strike, it was the management's policy to import Irish labour to keep the factories going. The workers who were locked out had a vested interest in spreading the idea that the Irish were stupid and incompetent in order to dissuade the employers from substituting their labour. This case illustrates clearly enough that the common assumptions of a culture, which we supply to make sense of discourse, very often have ideological dimensions, even though in the course of history their origins may have been lost.

The reason that inferencing has such a powerful ability to reinforce ideology is that somehow we feel no coercion is involved in supplying the premises which lead to the inference. If an ideological position is stated baldly we recognise it, and even if it is conveyed through presupposition we can detect the manipulation involved. But supplying information appears to be something we are doing rather than something being done to us. However, although we seem to be acting freely, we are actually being created as subjects, subjects who can or are willing to entertain the assumptions necessary to make sense of the joke or advert.

4.5 Adverts, association and inference

Advertisements are particularly dependent for their effects and strategies on the inferencing process. In one kind of advertisement, the sophisticated ones which you find in glossy magazines, the product is more or less upstaged by the visuals, the setting, the characters and so on. These are notorious for using associations in a kind of behaviourist conditioning process in order to imply, most crudely, that by buying the product you buy other things as well. These things might be the "girl" who opens the door of the car being advertised, the kitchen in which the washing machine is located, the family and happy kids who are consuming the breakfast cereal. Another way of looking at this, less crudely, is to say that buying the product confers membership of the class of people for whom such a lifestyle is normal. By buying a Rolex watch you join a club which includes Arnold Palmer, Kiri Te Kanawa. The product becomes one prop in a schema for a stereotypical lifestyle.

Look at the advertisement for Dorma fabrics (Plate 5). While most space in the picture does indeed display Dorma fabrics, our attention is immediately drawn to the heads and upper bodies of the couple, because these are placed centrally and brightly illuminated. The caption above, 'One look creates perfect harmony', most obviously refers to the harmonious colours of coordinated fabric patterns, but the couple are looking at each other, she at his strong arm, he at her breasts. The advert promises, implicitly, then, not only cloth, but a harmonious relationship. What is the nature of the promised relationship? The pun 'Don't just sleep on it' implies that there are other things to do on the Dorma-sheeted bed – presumably to make love. It implies more too, certainly: that Dorma fabric can be admired as well as slept on, or, exploiting the idiom *to sleep on a problem/decision*, that the consumer shouldn't simply think carefully but go ahead and buy these fabrics. But the visual foregrounding of the couple primes us especially to the first implication. So we are implicitly promised a harmonious sexual relationship.

Further aspects of the visuals imply more than this. The other light area of the picture shows a curtain billowing in the breeze, and a rather basic old-fashioned lion-claw-foot bath tub, still two-thirds full, with a towel carelessly left over its edge soaking up the bathwater. This, we might thus infer, is a relationship in which the man and woman are too ecstatic to worry about closing windows or hanging up towels. And perhaps a slightly bohemian one – given that the bathtub is somewhat spartan.

The Pragmatic trick being played here is that the advertiser expects us to find a relevance for those foregrounded visuals which do not actually represent the products – the couple, the bathtub and towel. They can only achieve relevance if we accept some kinds of inferences, like those I have suggested. This

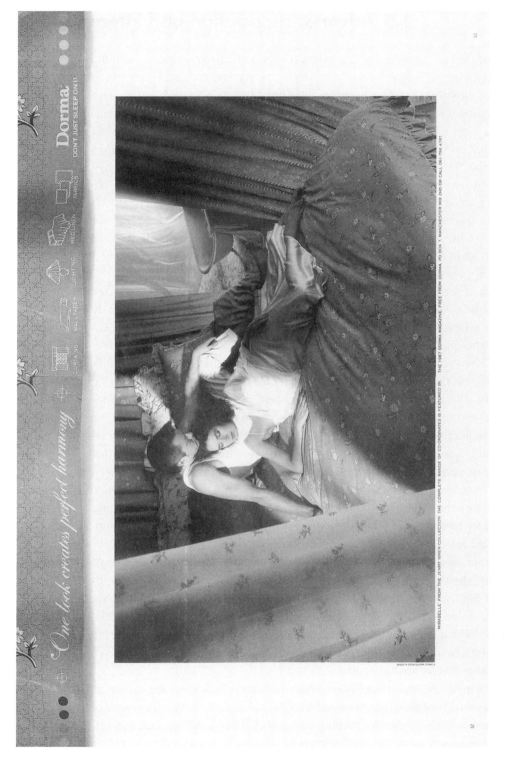

Plate 5 'One look creates perfect harmony' (Advert for Dorma Fabrics, *Good Housekeeping*, May 1987, pp. 52–3)

implicit message is a strategic device, too. The Advertising Standards Authority would, presumably, not allow the advertiser to claim explicitly that if you buy Dorma sheets you also get a passionate, bohemian, heterosexual partner (see Tanaka 1994: 40–3).

ACTIVITY 38*

Find an advertisement which depends heavily for its effect on inferencing, in the same way as the advert for Dorma sheets does. Bring along copies to class and be prepared to discuss the advertisement and how the inferencing works. Does the advert also exploit presuppositions to any extent?

4.6 Summary

In this chapter we elaborated on the fact that as readers we need to interpret texts as well as decode them. In particular we noted that:

- writers can use presuppositions to dangerously and unconsciously structure our thinking;
- writers may have attitudes towards the messages (propositions) of their texts which are not encoded in the Text;
- writers can use irony and metaphor to cultivate intimacy and express emotion, to explain the unfamiliar, or radically restructure thinking;
- writers expect readers to draw inferences by supplying background schematic knowledge;
- writers can exploit this schematic knowledge to reproduce ideologies and stereotypes and to make covert claims, for example in advertisements.

Earlier, we introduced the notion of latent ideology, and suggested that when ideology is explicitly stated it is far less dangerous. When it becomes natural or commonsense, a background assumption, it is extremely insidious. The degrees of presence of meanings in a Text might be represented on a scale (Fairclough 1995: 106):

Absent   Presupposed   Backgrounded   Foregrounded

Moving from right to left, foregrounded meanings are those which are explicitly stated. As for the backgrounding of information, in Chapter 1 we saw how this can be achieved through the generic structure of newspapers, or the sequencing of Theme and rheme in the clause. This Chapter has concentrated on the areas to the left of the scale; the presuppositions in the Text and the absent meanings and information we have to supply from outside the Text in order to make sense of it. It is in these areas that naturalised ideological assumptions are extremely powerful.

Suggestions for further reading

- Jenny Thomas's *Meaning in Interaction* is a very interesting and accessible introductory textbook on Pragmatics and it covers in more depth many of the topics dealt with briefly in Chapters 4, 5, and 6.
- Sperber and Wilson in *Relevance*, pp. 3–15, explain why the code model of communication is inadequate, and Mills, pp. 26–43, develops these ideas in relation to feminist critique.
- The best existing survey of presupposition theory is probably in Levinson's *Pragmatics*, chapter 4.
- Sperber and Wilson in *Relevance*, pp. 243–54, discuss propositional attitude in order to explain away speech-act theory.
- I have produced a detailed linguistic, Pragmatic and discoursal account of metaphor, *The Language of Metaphors*, chapter 5 of which discusses the functions of metaphor and the relationship between metaphor and irony. Wayne Booth's classic *The Rhetoric of Irony* takes a literary rather than linguistic approach.
- The philosopher Paul Grice was the first to stress the importance of inferencing in communication, in articles such as 'Logic and Conversation'. See Thomas (1995) chapters 3 and 4.
- Shank and Abelson elaborated the idea of scripts (which I include under schemas). A more accessible account of schemas can be found in Judith Greene. Fairclough in *Language and Power,* pp. 158–9, attempts to distinguish different kinds of schemas, which he calls *schemata*, *scripts* and *frames* relating them to discourse structure, interpersonal relations, and word meanings respectively.
- Keiko Tanaka's *Advertising Language* is an interesting account of advertising in Japanese and English, based on theories of Pragmatic inferencing, which analyses the strategies of latent or covert communication.

Chapter 5

Reading and writing positions

Aims of this chapter

To show the relationship between society's institutions and the sub-ject positioning of the reader.

To envisage written discourse as a writer acting upon a reader to con-struct a relationship.

To raise awareness of politeness factors in positioning the reader.

To encourage resistance against the reading positions foisted on us by texts.

reading position which the text invites us to adopt, and encourages this resistance when note-taking from written texts.

- **Activity**
  A major activity is to find a text which you wish to resist and explain/analyse your resistance to it.

5.0 Introduction: how texts position the reader

In Chapter 3, when we considered the interpersonal elements of the grammar of English, dealing with matters such as Power and Contact, we were already supplying one perspective on the relationships between the reader and the writer. In this Chapter, we are more specifically concerned with **subject positions**, the relative positions created for reader and writer through texts; here texts are seen as the means by which a writer performs an action on the reader. But before we embark on the details of how subjects are created by texts, we ought to glance at a theory of subjecthood which relates it to the underlying ideological concerns of this book.

Louis Althusser (1984) argues that we become subjects through subjection to societal institutions such as the educational system, religious organisations, the family and the media. The texts produced by these institutions map out a role for the subject. Recognising your role confers identity on you as an individual, thereby to some extent empowering you, but also subjects you to the state and authority. For example, in the first few weeks of school, children are taught and later internalise the rules of classroom interaction. Learning these enables them to act as subjects, for instance knowing how to raise their hand to attract the teacher's attention and ask for information, but also subjects them to the authority of the teacher and the institution. The fact that these rules become internalised and come to be regarded by pupils as obvious, unquestioned commonsense, shows the link between subject positioning and latent naturalised ideology (Mills 1995: 67–8). Let's now turn to discussion of how language is involved in creating subject positions for readers .

In written media texts, one aspect of subject positioning is the general question of who the ideal or average reader is imagined to be or invited to be. We saw an instance of this with the horoscope which we analysed for presuppositions in Chapter 4 (p. 123), where the ideal or typical reader will be a rather unfulfilled 30 to 50-year-old conservative American woman with a partner or a pet, who believes in the power of the zodiac signs to determine certain aspects of character and in the influence of the planets.

However there are more local aspects of subject positioning. Texts are seldom entirely homogeneous and writers will often adopt varying positions as the text progresses, and expect the reader to adopt reciprocal shifts in position. For example, in the article, 'I'm sorry teenagers, you are not the centre of the universe' (Chapter 2, p. 61) we might detect the adoption of the voices of a friend in conversation (paragraph 1), a reviewer (paragraphs 1–3), a journalist/political commentator (paragraphs 4–5), a pop social psychologist (paragraphs 6–8) and a parent (paragraph 8). The reader's subject positions vary in step with the writer's. The subject positions of friend in conversation would be matched by the subject position of another friend in conversation. A reviewer implies a movie-goer. A journalist/political commentator and a social psychologist imply an educated newspaper reader. A parent talks to a child; but as we saw when analysing pronouns in this column, this parent–child conversation is a kind of dramatisation, the audience for which are middle-aged parents.

More locally still, we can identify the particular sentence or utterance of writer/speaker and give this a label as a speech act, for example *inform, command, question, reprimand, warn, protest, dare, confide*. Again, using sentences to act on other people in these differing ways positions both writer/speaker and reader/hearer: the informed and the informant, the questioner and the questioned, the commander and the commanded, the warner and the warned, the confesser and the confessor, the confider and the confidant.

As writers, we should be alert to the kinds of positions we are taking up and the reciprocal positioning of our readers. This unit will help to raise awareness of the factors affecting this subject positioning by discussing it from four angles: speech acts; indirect speech acts and politeness; the heterogeneity of positions in texts; and the contesting or resisting of positioning.

5.1 Speech acts

Speech-act theory, beginning with Austin (1962) and elaborated by John Searle (1969, 1979), explores the notion that the sentences we utter and the texts we write are discourse acts which affect our addressees. From this perspective, Text is simply a trace of what we are attempting to do to other people.

In some kinds of speech act, assertives, the speaker/writer will be giving information, describing a state of affairs in the world, as in, 'There's a departmental meeting scheduled for tomorrow afternoon'. Examples are *state, inform, swear, remind*. In another type the writer/speaker attempts to make the reader/hearer do something, giving them a **directive**, as in 'Please type out the agenda'. Examples would be *ask, command, request, suggest, plead, beg*. In other speech-act types, commissives, the writer/speaker is giving a commitment to the reader/hearer that she will do something in the future, as with, 'I promise to type the agenda by tomorrow evening', for example, *promise, threaten, vow, volunteer*. At other times, the writer/speaker expresses an inner feeling in expressives, for example, gratitude when saying, 'Thanks for typing this so quickly'. Here we find acts like *thank, congratulate, apologise* and *condole*.

Look at the following letter written by the English poet John Keats to his younger sister, Fanny. Consider the underlined clauses, and decide which speech-act labels you would give them. (If you need help, you might use the following labels: *command, compliment, sympathising, condolence/commiseration, promise, undertaking, advice, apology, excuse.*) What do the results of this analysis suggest about the relationship between John Keats and his sister? How could you sum up the subject positions which he is setting up for himself and for her?

To Fanny Keats   *Tuesday 19th August*
                                                        1818

Miss Keats, Miss Tuckey's, Walthamstow

                                        Hampstead August 18th
My dear Fanny,

(1) <u>I am afraid you will think me very negligent in not having answered your letter</u> – I see it is dated June 12 – <u>I did not arrive at Inverness till the 8th of this month</u> so (2) <u>I am very much concerned at your being disappointed so long a time</u>. I did not intend to have returned to London so soon but have a bad sore throat from a cold I caught in the island of Mull: therefore I thought it best to get home as soon as possible and went on board the smack from Cromarty. We had a nine days passage and landed at London Bridge yesterday. I shall have a good deal to tell you about Scotland – I would begin here but I have a confounded tooth-ache. Tom has not been getting any better since I left London and for the last fortnight has been worse than ever – he has been getting a little better for these two or three days. (3) <u>I shall ask Mr Abbey to let me bring you to Hampstead.</u> If Mr A. should see this letter (4) <u>tell him that he still must, if he pleases, forward the post bill to Perth</u> as I have empowered my fellow-traveller to receive it. I have a few scotch pebbles for you from the Island of Icomkill – (5) <u>I am afraid they are rather shabby</u> – I did not go near the mountain of Cairn Gorm. I do not know the name of George's ship – the name of the port he has gone to is Philadelphia whence he will travel to the settlement across country – (6) <u>I will tell you all about this when I see you</u> – the title of my last book is *Endymion;* (7) <u>you shall have one soon.</u> (8) <u>I would not advise you to play on the flagolet</u>, however I will get you one if you please. (9) <u>I will speak to Mr Abbey on what you say concerning school.</u> (10) <u>I am sorry for your poor canary.</u> (11) <u>You shall have another volume of my first book.</u> My tooth-ache keeps on so that I cannot write with any pleasure

– all I can say now is that (12) <u>your letter is a very nice one without any fault</u> and that (13*)* <u>you will hear from or see in a few days,</u> if his throat will let him,

Your affectionate brother,

John

(Letters of John Keats, pp. 115–16)

5.2 Indirect speech acts and politeness

It is quite normal to use one kind of grammatical mood structure to perform indirectly a different kind of speech act. This is called an **indirect speech act**. Indirectness is quite common. You can use the grammatical structure of a statement (declarative) as an indirect Directive or command, e.g. 'The dog needs to be fed' instead of the direct 'Feed the dog'. You can use the grammatical structure of a statement (declarative) to indirectly ask a question, e.g. 'You went to Starbucks' last night?' Or the opposite, use a question (interrogative) form – as in one kind of rhetorical question – to make a statement. For example, 'Who left the door unlocked?' can be an indirect way of saying 'Someone left the door unlocked'.

    This section concentrates on discussing Directives, especially commands, requests and offers. We will consider when bald imperative commands should be avoided for the sake of politeness, and the various strategies of indirectness by which this can be achieved.

ACTIVITY 40

Rank the following in increasing order of politeness. What criteria did you use for this ranking?

(1)   Keep the umbrella I left behind last weekend for your own use.
(2)   Tell Mr A that I'll see him on Thursday.
(3)   Look after yourself in this cold weather.
(4)   Send me a cheque for $1,250 by return of post.
(5)   By all means use my car for the week of 20–27 March.

The degree of politeness has nothing to do with the grammatical form of these sentences, as they are all commands in the imperative mood. Rather the politeness depends on the costs and benefits to the writer and reader. The action demanded in (4) is very costly to the reader and benefits the writer. (2), involving simply speaking, is of little cost to the reader, and is of some benefit to the writer. The act in (3) would be of some benefit to the reader, but no cost to the writer. (1) would be of some benefit to the reader and a little cost to the writer. While (5) is the politest, because giving up the use of a car for a week is probably of considerable cost to the writer, and of great benefit to the reader.

First, then, in determining politeness it is crucial to take account of the difference in relative costs and benefits to writer/speaker and reader/hearer. And this is recognised in the distinction we have between requests and offers. Requested acts benefit the writer and offers are costly to the writer. Second, the writer will need to take more pains to be polite if the reader has more Power than her; she ought to be more polite in writing a memo to her boss than her subordinate. And third, as mentioned earlier, there is evidence to suggest that, at least in North America, a medium degree of Contact necessitates politeness: in other words, the writer can afford to be less polite with intimates and complete strangers, but she is likely to be more polite with those acquaintances she anticipates might develop into friends.

To sum up, there is a need to use the politer forms of language when:

- the reader is of greater Power than the writer;
- the reader has a medium degree of Contact with the writer;
- the action demanded is of relative benefit to the writer and of cost to the reader.

What exactly are these polite forms? Leech (1983) identifies, as major factors in politeness, the features of **optionality** and indirectness. Optionality means giving the reader the option of refusing. Indirectness gives the reader the opportunity to deny recognising that a request is being made. This becomes clearer if we look at these examples:

direct/no option less polite

(1) *Look after the kids.*

(2) *I want you to look after the kids.*

(3) *Will you look after the kids?*

(4) *Can you look after the kids?*

(5) *Would you mind looking after the kids?*

(6) *Could you possibly look after the kids?*

(7) *You couldn't possibly look after the kids, could you?*

(8) *The kids have a half-term holiday coming up.*

indirect/optional more polite

(1) is obviously the most direct of these requests. (2), (3) and (4) are less direct, not requesting the act itself. Of this trio, (3) and (4) are more tactful than (2) because they are in a question form and therefore allow for the possibility of a negative reply, the option to refuse. (5) and (6) are more tactful still: they recognise the reasons the hearer might have for taking the refusal option (he would mind it), and they are indirect because the *would* and *could* make them hypothetical, suggesting that the request has not actually been made (['If I asked you] would you mind looking after the kids?'). (7) is politer still, the question expecting the answer 'no', thereby making it even easier for the reader to take the option of refusal. (8) is the most indirect, simply being a hint, and cannot really be counted as an on-record request at all.

Leech has actually proposed a number of maxims that we more or less adhere to if we are being polite in our discourse (1983: 131–9). The first is **tact**, in Directives, which means, as we have seen, using indirectness and optionality when the action is costly to the hearer/reader. The second maxim is **approbation** or its converse **modesty**, when you praise others and underrate yourself. One way of being modest is to pretend that as a writer you are deficient in your communicative skills. You can use all the modal devices of uncertainty (Chapter 3) to suggest that you could be misleading your readers: *possibly, I think, sometimes*, etc. You can pretend that what you say is redundant: *As you know, of course*, etc. Or that you have a tendency to ramble on: *This may be beside the point, but . . . .* Or that you have put things more obscurely than need be: *In other words, or to put it more simply*, and *if you see what I mean . . . .*

Approbation is a telling strategy for effective communicators. We ought to take opportunities to praise or raise the self-esteem of the reader, especially when we have a potentially hostile or antagonistic readership.

Effective letters to the editor, for example, which are inherently critical or express disagreement, might at least show some approval or agreement. This is probably more important in cultures where a high value is placed on maintaining others' "Face". Look at the opening of the following letter 'Tough line must be taken to stop teenagers smoking' (*Straits Times*, 19 March 1997, p. 40) .

> I REFER to the report 'Community roped in to help smokers quit' (*ST*, 5 March).
>
> I applaud Mr Alex Chan, chairman of the Committee on Smoking Control, for involving the community in a bid to discourage smoking among teenagers.
>
> However, I disagree with his idea of dismissing the authoritarian approach when dealing with them.

The underlined sentence shows approbation before going on to criticise or show disagreement. In fact this gives us a clue to another strategy for being polite – to agree wherever possible, Leech's **agreement maxim**. The next letter, 'Sex scandals have a sordid tradition' (*Independent*, 9 May 1995) shows a Balance of agreement and disagreement in its opening paragraph:

> *From Mr David Turner*
>
> Sir: Our attitudes towards sex and marriage may well have changed over time, as Professor Carol Smart suggests ('Has adultery become a spurious issue?' 22 May), but the current stance taken by the popular media in its reporting of adultery is no recent development.

The last of Leech's maxims is the **sympathy** maxim. This suggests that one should at least take an interest in readers' problems, and ideally claim the feelings they have about their misfortunes or fortunes are matched by yours.

Typically, condolences and congratulations would figure here.

It should be clear from the last two maxims, concerning agreement and sympathy, that speech acts do not occur in isolation – you have to agree with a previous statement, or sympathise with good or bad news. Indeed, speech acts often form pairs, such as question/answer, greeting/greeting, inform/acknowledgement, statement/agreement, offer/acceptance, thanks/acknowledgement, command/compliance. The second act of the pair may be a **preferred second** or a **dispreferred second**. The ones I have listed above are the preferred seconds. But offers and commands could, for example, meet with refusals, and statements could meet with disagreements. These dispreferred seconds would be considered less polite.

Reflecting or constructing relationships

In our discussion of politeness we have assumed that the forms of language we choose simply reflect the existing dimensions of Power and Contact in our relationships. However, as we saw with ideational meanings in Chapter 2, language confers rather than reflects reality, and this is just as true of our social positions. It is through being talked and written to and by talking and writing in return that our social positions are established. For example, by using the imperative, advertisers constitute themselves as offering goods which are beneficial to the consumer, rather than requesting the reader to do them a favour. For there is, remember, no need to use less direct forms if the reader benefits. Or if a boss writes a note: 'I expect all members of the Division without exception to forward their comments to me on this matter by the end of next week' then this doesn't simply reflect a social positioning: it constitutes the relationship between boss and subordinates as an authoritarian one. In short, words create a social world rather than simply describing one.

5.3 Learning and resisting reading positions

Up to this point we have been discussing subject positions as if they were simply a matter of individuals interacting with other individuals. The fact is, however, that we learn or are taught both how to be good subjects, and how to read texts in a certain way, what we might call a **reading position**. This process inducts us into a community with shared reading habits. In particular, in literature classes we spend a great deal of time learning to imitate the valid/fashionable ways of reading and to avoid the less valid/unfashionable. And very often in ordinary English instruction, for example, in reading a comprehension passage in an English textbook, we were expected to be quite naïve readers, to accept the text as given and to answer "factual" comprehension questions on it. The very point of this present book is to help students to move away from this naïve position and to think about why the text is the way it is, how it could have been otherwise, and whose interests or purposes it serves.

The fact that different kinds of readers are expected of different kinds of texts is obvious enough from the following example. If you were given this text and were told it is a poem, you would read it in a particular way according to certain reading strategies.

> Black
> Fish
> Culler
> Leech
> White

You would, of course, initially apply the normal procedures for making syntactic and semantic sense of a sentence, which are not specifically literary ways of reading. Lines 2 and 4 of the poem are either nouns, in which case they represent two kinds of animal, or they are verbs meaning "to catch fish" and "to drain of blood". This last possibility makes sense for 'leech', since *to leech white* means "to drain of blood until it is white". 'Fish', on the other hand, looks like a noun since it has an adjective 'black' before it and presumably both premodify 'culler', someone black who culls, not, in this case, seals, but fish. Since 'culler' is singular, 'leech' would then be an imperative command, and the first three lines would be a vocative address. The poem could then be rewritten: 'Black fish culler, leech white!'

Moreover, having been taught to read poems you would do much more than simply work out the grammar and meaning of the Text. You might point out the symmetry of the poem, beginning with 'black' and ending with 'white', noticing that these words begin with sounds made with both lips, take special note of the pun on *colour*/'culler', and remark that this is the only two-syllable word and lies at the centre of the poem. You could also give some symbolic value to 'black' and 'white', perhaps good and evil, depending on how sensitive you are to political correctness . You might then arrive at an interpretation of some literary significance: the poem is an ironic exhortation to an evil (black) exploiter of nature (fish culler) to drain nature of its lifeblood (leech white); with the consequence either of giving natural victims a sacrificial sanctity (white), or, more cynically, of the culler (exploiter), by economic gain, whitewashing his own evil.

However, when you are told that this is a reading list for a class in stylistics, comprising just the surnames of the authors, you will read the text in a quite different way, not even trying to parse it as a sentence, let alone give it a literary interpretation:

> Black, Max 'More about metaphor'
> Fish, Stanley 'Is there a text in this class?'
> Culler, Jonathan *The Pursuit of Signs*
> Leech, Geoffrey *A Linguistic Guide to English Poetry*
> White, Hayden *Metahistory*

Resisting reading positions

On the whole, texts ask us to acquiesce in the position they set up for us. But there are various ways in which we can resist the position which a text places us in, and these are more or less radical. Most obviously and superficially we can resist the overt content of a text, the openly expressed ideational meanings. A few years ago there was an incident in my street in which my neighbour's dog was run over and left unconscious by a taxi who failed to stop. My neighbour chased the taxi and confronted the driver. The police arrived and charged my neighbour with grievous bodily harm. The dog was taken to the vet's and recovered fully after a few days. The case came to court two years later and my neighbour was acquitted. However, the two local newspapers both had factual errors in their reports of the court case. In one the dog died, in the other the dog was still recovering in veterinary hospital two years after the accident. Obviously, when I read those texts I resisted the overt misinformation which the newspapers gave. This first kind of resistance is pretty obvious and widespread, deservedly so (Bell 1991: 218).

Second, as Chapter 2 suggested, you can resist the text's ideological categorisations and the construction of reality, for example, patterns of the depiction of boys in teenage magazines (Fraser 1987). Turning to Chapter 3, one might resist the authority, dogmatism or level of formality of a text. More subtly, as Chapter 4 showed, one might resist its presuppositions, inferences or implications, and propositional attitudes. Finally, one might wish to resist the way of reading texts which seems to be natural, but which is in fact acquired through education and by example from other members of one's culture, sub-culture or community.

An example of how I, from my ideological perspective, might resist an author's presuppositions and propositional attitudes occurred when I read a feature article about the house of a socialite. Here is an extract.

> When you step into the home of X you enter a world of charmed gracious living.

The black and white marble-tiled foyer of the Cluny Park bungalow leads to a drawing room. Here, floor to ceiling French windows overlook a pool outside.

Broad white sofas line one side of the airy room, showing off a costly Persian carpet on the maple parquet floor. At one corner is a gleaming baby grand piano, at another a French-Vietnamese cabinet displays figurines of geisha girls, samurai, and Chinese deities – all carved from ivory.

Everything about the home, from the teak-framed modern Chinese paintings to a huge Filipino jade-bordered mirror in the toilet, reputed to belong to Mrs Imelda Marcos, is opulent but not ostentatious.

The home, you realise, is the sum of a determined woman, who took four years to tear it down and build it up again, until she could get it just so.

I assume that the ideal reader of this piece is supposed to admire the contents of this bungalow. More than this, he is supposed to accept that the character or identity of the woman is constituted by her valuable and tasteful possessions. And to accept the presupposition that she, despite the consequences for her fingernails, personally tore down the old bungalow and rebuilt it. However, I refuse to accept this ideal reading position. I have no admiration for furniture or *objets d'art* made of teak and ivory, because for me they symbolise reckless exploitation of the trees and animals in our environment. I feel slightly disgusted that a mirror should achieve a certain snobbish renown from having once belonged to Imelda Marcos, whose financial honesty has been seriously questioned. Even more strongly I resist the explicit claim that a person's value, identity and character is measured by their material possessions, 'The home is the sum of a determined woman'. And I can more easily believe that the original bungalow was torn down and rebuilt by poorly paid construction workers, than by the lady whose opulent lifestyle we are expected to admire.

Annotation and subject positioning

When you read texts, especially academic ones, you are probably in the habit of annotating them. Too often this annotation simply involves marking up the most important parts of the text by highlighting or underlining crucial points, in order to clarify or summarise the author's meaning. But annotation should involve more than that. It should involve your evaluative response to the text, your awareness of subject positioning, and your rejection, acceptance or qualification of that positioning. Charles Bazerman (1992) has listed a number of questions you can ask yourself to stimulate evaluative annotation, which have been modified below:

QUESTIONS	COMMENTS
Do I approve or disapprove?	*????, NO!, not bad, not exactly, yuk, nonsense, right*
Do I agree or disagree?	*I don't agree because ... No, the actual facts are*
Are there exceptions/counterexamples?	*Not true in the case of X ... Case Y is just the opposite*
Are there examples which support the argument?	*Exactly what happens in the case of Z*
Can this argument be extended?	*This might also apply to ... This explains why ...*
Do I accept the way the world/society is represented and categorised in this text?	*It's good to see X coming over as powerful.* *I don't like the use of the term Y as it suggests ...*
What relationship is the writer striking up with me?	*This text is too dogmatic/apologetic/patronising* *The writer is on my wavelength / treats me with respect*
Can I accept the presuppositions/ implications of this text?	*The presupposition X is unfounded* *I don't like the implications of this* *The inference depends on racist/sexist/ ageist, etc., stereotyping*
Can I accept the way of reading the text that I'm supposed to employ?	*What's so great about this Shakespeare/Keats/Melville? Why must I read this Z (advert) like a W (poem) when it's just a Z (cheap publicity)*

A good example of resisting the ways of reading expected by one's social group and subculture might be found in alternative readings of religious texts. I was brought up as a fundamentalist Christian, and taught that the Bible was true from cover to cover, that it was the inspired word of God, and was not written in a normal human way, but by divine dictation. I was encouraged to believe that it could give me spiritual guidance for my life and daily behaviour, and to use it as a devotional text. However, as a teenager, I noticed that the Bible had overt contradictions. Did Judas hang himself or simply fall over and break his neck? Did St Paul's companions, during his experience of God on the road to Damascus, see the light and not hear the voice, or did they hear the voice and not see the light? These overt contradictions led me to see the Bible in a quite different way. I could now no longer believe its texts were the result of God's Holy Spirit possessing the writers to produce an infallible text. I realised it was a flawed human product, like all other texts, and that it was written and edited/rewritten in a historical context, and had to be read in those terms, so that its injunctions could not simply be followed blindly in today's society. I came to the conclusion that it was only unique because it described a period of history in which God was particularly active or interventionary. This meant, of course, that I would read it differently and more critically. And, socially, it meant, though remaining a Christian, I could no longer feel at home in the fundamentalist church community where I was brought up.

ACTIVITY 41*

Find a text whose reading position you resist. Annotate it. Bring copies or an overhead transparency to class and tell the rest of the group why you resist the position the writer assumes you will take.

Explain what you are resisting:

- the ideological categorisations and the representation of reality?
- the authority, dogmatism or level of formality?
- presuppositions, inferences or implications?
- propositional attitudes?
- anything else?

Another example closer to your experience might be in the reading of magazines for women. There has been a great deal of work on the construction of femininity by teenage magazines. When you read the beauty sections of teenage magazines do you, if you are female, resist the way femininity is constructed there? Many such magazines reinforce and exploit the use of make-up as a ritual differentiating female adolescents from girls on the one hand, and adolescent men on the other. They suggest that a woman's status and identity depends upon her physical appearance. They tend to make girls dissatisfied with the natural changes to their appearance which accompany puberty, and introduce a sense of insecurity which can only be dispelled by buying a commodity. They also suggest a certain pleasure to be had from beauty rituals, once the commodity has been bought (MacRobbie 1991: 175–7).

Resisting reading positions entails resisting subject positions and challenging the beliefs, assumptions and authority figures of one's community. If one refuses to wear make-up as resistance to the kind of femininity constructed by magazines, this might alienate peers. Or if you idealistically resist, for example, the fetishism of economic growth and consumer capitalism then this might spoil friendships with those whose major pastime is shopping, and put you out of step with the rest of the community. Only by subsequently joining a subculture which to some extent shares one's ideological position could one maintain enough sense of belonging to remain mentally healthy.

ACTIVITY 42

Analyse the America Online advert (Plate 6) and the attached form primarily in terms of speech acts, politeness, and the way the reader is positioned. You might also look at presuppositions, inference and how the form will be used to categorise those who fill it out.

Questions to ask yourself include:

(1) How do adverts as a genre, position the writer and reader of the advert? What words could you give to label their subject positions? (e.g. adviser/advisee, confider/confidant . . .?).
(2) From the linguistic evidence, what kind of target reader do you think the advertiser had in mind?
(3) What kinds of speech acts does the writer perform in this advert? Does the pattern change from the main copy, to the form, to the small print of the form?
(4) Is the imperative mood used for Directives? Is this polite? Why or why not? In using these is the writer making a request or an offer?
(5) Are there indirect Directives? Do these use modals of obligation?
(6) Are there any questions? Are they direct or indirect? (Don't forget the form)
(7) Is the writer suitably modest about her product? What presuppositions are there about the product?
(8) How visually informative is this advert? What is the significance of the variation of the print?

5.4 Summary

In this chapter we explored the notion that texts create subject positions for readers and writers. We discovered that

Plate 6 'Try America Online' (Advert for America Online, *Popular Science*, June 1995, pp. 16/17) (The small print reads '*To use America Online for Windows, you must have a 386 PC or higher, 4MB of RAM, a VGA (256 color support recommended) monitor, a mouse, a modem, and a working copy of Windows 3.1. Use of America Online requires a major credit card or checking account. Limit one free trial per household. America Online is a registered service mark of America Online, Inc. Other names are service marks or trademarks of their respective owners.')

- the position created for readers will depend upon the kinds of speech acts we, as writers, perform on them;
- how polite we are affects the subject positioning of our readers. For Directives which are costly to the unfamiliar reader, we will have to use indirect speech acts in order to be polite. In speech-act sequences we will avoid dispreferred seconds.
- reading positions can be learned or resisted. Learning them confers community membership, and resisting them excludes us.

Suggestions for further reading

- Rob Pope's *Textual Intervention*, chapter 2, is an excellent resource for exploring more deeply how subject positions are set up and reproduced in discourse, and relating these to linguistic features such as agency, the vocabulary of self-description and pronouns. The whole book, as its title implies, encourages resistance against naïve subjection to positioning by the text.
- Fairclough's *Language and Power*, pp. 28–74, is an extensive and insightful account of subject positioning through the power structures of institutions in society, and how to resist it.
- The classic early text on Speech Acts is Austin's exploratory lectures *How to Do Things with Words*. John Searle in *Speech Acts* and *Expression and Meaning* consolidated the theory, and pp. 54–71 of *Speech Acts* provide the kernel of his ideas. Jenny Thomas gives a clear and accurate summary in chapter 2 of *Meaning in Interaction*.
- There are two major overlapping approaches to Politeness theory: Brown and Levinson's *Politeness* and Leech's in *Principles of Pragmatics*. Jenny Thomas in chapter 6 of *Meaning in Interaction* gives a thoughtful overview.
- For the concept of dispreferred seconds, a solid account, with the odd dirty joke, appears in Levinson's *Pragmatics*, pp. 332–45.
- Stanley Fish's *Is There a Text in This Class?* is a fascinating exploration of different ways of reading texts, and how readers are taught and so are inducted into discourse communities. The idea that a reading list might be read as a poem derives from Fish.

Chapter 6

Intertextuality

Aims of this chapter

To survey the various ways of representing another's text in one's own.

To show how deriving one text from another gives scope for "bias" in news reporting.

To illustrate how the meanings and purposes of texts depend on the previous texts they are reacting to, for example, in parody.

- **6.0 Introduction: textual interaction**
  Points out the importance of intertextuality for genre and inferencing.

- **6.1 Heterogeneity of subject positioning**
  Indicates how texts are not homogeneous but are often compounded of different text types.

- **6.2 The discourse of the other and reporting speech**
  Details the different modes of representing another's speech, and linguistic criteria for recognising them, showing how bias can be introduced in this representation.

- **6.3 The news-making process as an example of intertextual chains**
  Shows how news production depends on transmitting texts through a long series of readers and writers, with scope for distortion and changes to the original text.

- **6.4 Replies and reactions**
  Illustrates how meanings depend upon which texts are being reacted to, or which previous texts supply the background knowledge against which the present text is interpreted.

- **6.5 Parody**
  Explores the relationship between intertextuality and parody, and uses parody to underline the importance of attitude and purpose for making sense of texts.

- **Project 2: Letter to the editor**
  The second suggested project is a letter to a newspaper editor in which you explore your resistance and reaction to a text from that paper.

6.0 Introduction: textual interaction

This final chapter of Part two is a discussion of **intertextuality**. Intertextuality simply means the way in which one text impinges on other later texts, or, to put it another way, how texts feed off and relate to one another. In many ways, this chapter sums up the previous two chapters and the concluding section of Chapter 1 on genre. First, intertextuality is an aspect of inferencing. The "background" or "factual" knowledge, the assumptions and schemas which we bring to texts in order to infer meanings, are largely derived from other texts. Second, intertextuality relates to genre because it is through encountering examples of different texts in different social situations that we perceive typical text patterns and build up a mental model of the discourse structure of different genres. Within these genres or discourse types there will also be typical subject positions for readers and writers.

6.1 Heterogeneity of subject positioning

However, it would be naïve to think that one particular text demands only one single subject position from the reader. Texts are not homogeneous entities. Mary Talbot, in 'The construction of gender in a teenage magazine' took an article on lipstick and identified a multiplicity of voices: friend, interviewer, historian, advertiser, market researcher and facilitator (Talbot 1992). In the America Online advertisement (see Plate 6, p. 161) you probably noted that the small print at the end of the form read more like a legal text, in contrast with the conversational features of the main copy.

The multiplicity of voices and positions in texts is often a symptom of how one text type, discourse type or genre has colonised others. Fairclough has shown that conversational styles have colonised advertisements as an aspect of synthetic personalisation, as we saw in the Tacoma advert (see plate 4, p. 100) with its imitation of the omissions and minor sentences of conversation. And, in turn, bureaucratic discourse like forms have taken over some of the features of advertisements in order to become more reader-friendly (Fairclough 1989: 208–22).

ACTIVITY 43* ━━━━━━━━━━━━━━━━━━━━━━━━

Find a text which seems to be a combination of different genres. Pamphlets advertising financial services (credit cards, insurance, etc.), car adverts, food labels or official forms are good sources. What different genres (or voices) do you find overlapping or represented in the text? Bring in the texts for class discussion.

━━━

6.2 The discourse of the other and reporting speech

The most obvious way in which more than one voice can be introduced into a text is through the reporting of speech. The reporting text and the reported text belong to different voices. Briefly speaking, the choices we have for representing speech are as in Table 6.1.

Table 6.1 Ways of reporting speech

Mode of representation	Example	Defining features
Free direct speech	'I will come tomorrow.'	Words actually spoken. No reporting clause.
Direct speech	John said, 'I will come tomorrow.'	Words actually spoken. Reporting clause.
Free indirect speech	*He would* come/*go* tomorrow/ *the next day*.	Most of the words actually spoken, but some or all time, place and person shifters change. No reporting clause.
Indirect speech	John said *he would go the next day*.	Most of the words actually spoken but all time, place and person shifters change. Reporting clause.
Narrative report of speech act	*Mr J. Phillips indicated his intention of arriving on 21 November*.	Does not include most of the words actually spoken.

(Note: Italics indicate changes to words spoken)

The technical term **_shifter_**, used in the third column, needs some explanation. Some words will change their meaning according to who uttered them, when and where. For example *I*, *here*, and *now* mean something different if Bill Clinton utters them in Detroit on 12 November 1996 at 4 p.m., from what they would mean if Saddam Hussein uttered them in Baghdad on June 15 1992 at midnight. When indirect forms of speech representation are used these shifters change, for example the *I* of direct speech becomes *he/she* in indirect, *you* becomes *he/she/they*, *we* becomes *they*; *here* becomes *there*; *now* becomes *then* and present tenses shift to past tenses.

As we move down column two in Table 6.1 we notice that the words are changed more and more from the original actual utterance. We can see this change in terms of the reporter's voice becoming more dominant than the original speaker's voice. **Narrative report of speech act (NRSA)** entirely obliterates the voice of the speaker.

We may relate these speech representation choices to questions of ideology and power in the press. Research into the language of news has shown that the more élite or powerful the speaker, the more likely that their speech will be represented verbatim (Glasgow University Media Group 1980: 163). Less powerful Sayers are likely to have their actual words interfered with to a greater extent by being reported indirectly or paraphrased in NRSA form.

In addition, there is also less interference by the reporting voice in the case of free modes, where there is no reporting clause. The reporting clause allows the reporting voice to interpret, to give a speech-act label to the speaker's utterance, e.g. *she complained*, *they confessed*, *he promised*.

ACTIVITY 44

(1) Find examples of free direct speech in the following passage from a novel by Henry James.

(2) In direct speech, some of the underlined reporting phrases indicate the manner of speaking. Others label the speech act which the speech represents. Some do both. Try to decide which is which. (The sentences have been numbered for your convenience.) For example in (1) below *cried* indicates manner, (2) *gaily answered*, the *gaily* indicates manner, and *answered* is a speech-act label.

(1) 'How you talk to her!' <u>cried</u> Mrs Beale.

(2) 'No worse than you!' he <u>gaily answered</u>.

(3) 'Handsome is that handsome does!' she <u>returned in the same spirit</u>. (4) 'You can take off your things,' she <u>went on</u>, releasing Maisie.

(5) The child, on her feet, was all emotion. (6) 'Then I'm just to stop – this way?'

(7) 'It will do as well as any other. (8) Sir Claude, tomorrow, will have your things brought.'

(9) 'I'll bring them myself. Upon my word I'll see them packed!' Sir Claude <u>promised</u>. (10) 'Come here and unbutton.'

(11) He had beckoned his young companion to where he sat, and he

helped to disengage her from her coverings while Mrs Beale, from a little distance, smiled at the hand he displayed. (12) 'There's a stepfather for you! (13) I'm bound to say, you know, that he makes up for the want of other people.'

(14) He makes up for the want of a nurse!' Sir Claude <u>laughed</u>. (15) 'Don't you remember I told you so the very first time?'

(16) 'Remember? It was exactly what made me think so well of you!'

(17) 'Nothing would induce me,' the young man <u>said</u> to Maisie, 'to tell you what made me think so well of *her*.' (18) Having divested the child he kissed her gently and gave her a little pat to make her stand off. (19) The pat was accompanied with a vague sigh in which his gravity for a moment came back. (20) 'All the same if you hadn't had the fatal gift of beauty –!'

(21) 'Well, what?' Maisie <u>asked</u>, wondering why he paused. (22) It was the first time she had heard of her beauty.

(23) 'Why we shouldn't all be thinking so well of each other!'

(24) He isn't talking of personal loveliness – you've not *that* vulgar beauty my dear, at all,' Mrs Beale <u>explained</u>. (25) 'He's just talking of plain dull charm of character.'

(26) 'Her character's the most extraordinary thing in the world,' Sir Claude <u>stated</u> to Mrs Beale.

(27) 'Oh I know all about that sort of thing!'– she fairly <u>bridled</u> with the knowledge.

(28) It gave Maisie somehow a sudden sense of responsibility from which she sought refuge. (29) 'Well, you've got it too, "that sort of thing" – you've got the fatal gift: you both really have!' she <u>broke out</u>.

(30) 'Beauty of character? (31) My dear boy, we haven't a pennyworth!' Sir Claude <u>protested</u>.

(32) 'Speak for yourself, sir!' <u>leaped lightly</u> from Mrs Beale. (33) 'I'm good and I'm clever. (34) What more do you want? (35) For you, I'll spare your blushes and not be personal – I'll simply say that you're as handsome as you can stick together.'

(36) 'You're both very lovely; you can't get out of it!' Maisie felt the need of <u>carrying her point</u>. (37) 'And it's beautiful to see you side by side.'

(Henry James, *What Maisie Knew*, pp. 97–9)

The author's "interference" may not matter much in fiction, since, after all, it is made up by the writer. But when such interfering reporting clauses are used in newspapers and magazines to label and describe speech, this is capable of slanting the reader's interpretation, and is an aspect of the conferring of reality that we explored in Chapter 2. Several researchers have found that in stories about strikes, or arguments between the US and the Soviet government, verbs like *claim* were used for reporting the sayings of unions or the Soviet government, in contrast with the neutral *say* for management and the US government. Unions and the USSR were thereby represented as less credible than their antagonists (Glasgow University Media Group 1980: 184; Geis 1987; Short 1988).

Just as bad as interference and distorting the views of the second voice is plagiarism. This arises when you pretend to speak in your own voice but are really borrowing the voice of another, without acknowledging it. In one sense, of course, we can never speak entirely in our own words (Kress 1985: 49) since words, in order to be intelligible, have to be shared by a language community, but stealing text from another is an extreme appropriation.

> The standard way of referring to texts you quote has been used in this book, and in the previous sentence: the Harvard Reference System. Here you insert, in parentheses, the surname of the author, the date of the publication and the page number(s) at the point in your text most appropriate for acknowledgement. The reader can use your references at the end of the essay to identify the publication from which you have borrowed. For example
>
> Kress, G. (1985) *Linguistic Processes in Sociocultural Practice*, Oxford: Oxford University Press.

6.3 The news-making process as an example of intertextual chains

The texts we end up with often reflect a multiplicity of voices simply because they are the products of **intertextual chains**. Let's take newspapers as an example.

The news article 'Pope in hospital for tests after intestinal pains' from Chapter 1, p. 38, illustrates this point clearly enough. If we look at the third paragraph and consider the words 'intestinal dysfunction' we can trace the intertextual path by which these words reach the reader. Presumably one of the doctors, possibly Francesco Crucitti, or another member of the fifteen-member team, used this phrase to a Vatican official, who indirectly or directly conveyed it to a Vatican spokesman Joaquin Navarro-Valls, who in turn used it to reporters from one or all of the news agencies AP/UPI/Reuter, and similarly the news agency made it available to the Singapore *Straits Times* whose editorial team were responsible for the shape of the report as it appeared in the newspaper.

> Doctor → Vatican official → Vatican spokesman → UPI/AP/Reuters agency [X → Y → Z...] → *Straits Times* editorial team [A → B → C ...] → reader

Even a direct quotation like this is transformed in the process of transfer, at least to the extent of being translated from Italian into English. So just imagine what might happen with description of events rather than quotation. There is enormous scope for distortion by selection, omission and rewriting within such an intertextual chain, especially since, with tight time deadlines, the last person in the chain has little chance of checking for reliability with the initiator of the chain. Intertextuality and tight deadlines are two of the factors contributing to the kinds of factual misrepresentation illustrated by the story of my neighbour's dog, which I recounted earlier.

In fact, the chain we traced out considerably underestimates the number of links in the transmission process. The news team will include at least the journalist, the chief reporter, the news editor, various subeditors and printers. All these can make changes to the original report. Where international news is concerned, news agencies are also likely to pass the reports through quite complex internal chains of communications – their regional bureau, their central bureau, the bureau in the receiving country – even before they are received by the paper (Bell 1991: 44–50).

Sometimes in news reports it is not quite clear whose voice is being reported. It seems relatively common for an editor to save space by deleting the reporting clause, as in this example from Bell (1991: 71), datelined Tel Aviv:

An Israeli military force has crossed the border, an Army spokesman announced here, Agence France Presse reported	→An Israeli military force has crossed the border

The minimal interference of the free form and the failure to identify the speaker are blurrings of the distinction between the newspaper's voice and the Army's voice. Another trick is for newspapers to use a sort of direct speech form without quotation marks and with the reporting clause at the end.

> ELECTRONIC road-pricing is starting a
> month early on the Central Expressway, not

to generate extra income for the government, but to ensure a smooth extension of the system in September, Parliamentary Secretary (Communications) Yaacob Ibrahim said yesterday.

(*Straits Times*, 20 July 1998, p. 1)

This, at least initially, as though it were a free form, blurs the distinction between the voice of the paper and the voice of the government.

Whose voices, then, get reported in the newspapers?

─────────────────────────────────────── **ACTIVITY 45***

Take the news reports which appear on the front page of a recent copy of a popular tabloid newspaper and a more serious broadsheet newspaper. Whose words are reported? Ordinary members of the public? Entertainment stars? Politicians? Are the Sayers ever ambiguous because free forms are used without or with a delayed reporting clause?

6.4 Replies and reactions

Of course we may be free to react or reply to the voices of the media and the voices of the powerful, rich and famous reported in the media, though we seldom have the same degree of access to media as they do. Even if we did, through a letter to the newspaper, it is the originating voice which sets the agenda and makes various presuppositions which may be difficult to challenge.

We have already had an example of this specific kind of intertextuality, a reply or reaction to a previous text, in the letter about burglaries in Chip Bee Gardens, and the police reply. That pair of texts showed that the meaning of a text often depends upon whether it is reacting to an intertextual context, and, if it is, what this context might be. More precisely, a preceding text will evoke schemas which we use to interpret or draw inferences from the second text. The following text, for instance, could have a number of different meanings:

Organisms in order to survive all have to develop feedback mechanisms of one kind or another. In the case of the human organism not only do we have the brain sending out messages to the muscles, giving orders to the limbs, but we have messages passing in the opposite direction from the nerve-cells at the body's extremities to the spinal cord and up to the brain. If the brain makes a wrong or harmful decision, like telling the arm muscles to put the fingers in a fire, then the nerve cells experiencing intense heat will immediately send messages to the spinal cord/brain communicating pain, and the central nervous system will admit its mistake and withdraw the hand. It is difficult to see how any organism could remain healthy if these feedback messages to the decision-making centre were systematically stifled for long periods.

ACTIVITY 46 ━━━━━━━━━━━━━━━━━━━━

Imagine two intertextual contexts for this passage.

(1) A feature article on the advances in the effectiveness of the pain-killing sprays used by football players/athletes.
(2) A report showing that many politicians are devoting less and less time to their constituency surgeries/feedback sessions with the electorate.

How would the meanings of the text differ according to whether it was a reaction to (1) or (2)?

(Hint: In the context of (2), the 'organism' would be a metaphor for society, the brain would be the MP or government, etc.)

━━━━━━━━━━━━━━━━━━━━

Creative literature can also react against previous specific texts. As a secondary-school student you may well have read Golding's *Lord of the Flies*. This book can be viewed as a reaction to the "normal" Christian imperialist ideology inherent in *Robinson Crusoe*, *Swiss Family Robinson* and, especially, *A Coral Island*, where white boys or men subdue evil black natives. In *Lord of the Flies*, by contrast, the Christian white boys rapidly degenerate into savages, the most religious of them, the choirboys, degenerating the quickest.

6.5 Parody

Parody is a particularly interesting kind of intertextuality. The simplest form of parody is achieved by imitating the expression or style of a well-known text, author or genre and substituting an inappropriate content. You might, for example, take the content of a hairdresser's questions to a customer, and rewrite this in the style of a judge talking to a defendant: 'I put it to you that when you should have been washing your hair in anti-dandruff shampoo last night, you were in fact watching TV all evening, is that not so? Do you plead guilty or not guilty to having dandruff?' What distinguishes parody from the text being parodied is obviously propositional attitude – the writer of a parody does not seriously believe what she is writing, and the propositional attitude might range from light-hearted fun to scorn or disgust.

Back in the 1960s and 1970s there was a TV advertisement jingle that went:

```
x   /  x x /    x     / x   /
A million housewives every day
```

```
/    x  x /  x   /   x   /
Pick up a can of beans and say:
```

```
/      /      /
Beanz Meanz Heinz
```

The following parody of this imitates the expression and style of the original very closely. The rhythm is identical. And the only substitutions are 'students' for 'housewives', 'put down' for 'pick up', 'spraypaint' for 'of beans', and 'D' for 'B', 'F' for 'H' in the last line.

```
x /  x x /  x   / x /
A million students every day
```

```
/    x   x  /  x    /   x  /
Put down a spraypaint can and say:
```

```
/     /       /
Deanz Meanz Finez
```

The exact nature of the substituted content in parody is quite interesting. In the jingle above a whole different schema is evoked: students being dissuaded from spraypainting graffiti by the threat of fines from the disciplinary figure of the Dean, rather than housewives deciding to buy tins of Heinz baked beans. But we should also note that the content is at one point reversed where *pick up* is replaced by its opposite, *put down.*

Sometimes it may be difficult to decide whether a piece of writing is serious or is intended as a parody. The following letter to the editor 'Reading between the railway lines' *(Independent, 29* May 1995, p. 14) writes about the Thomas the Tank Engine books (substituted content) as though they are a moral and religious text.

From Mr Barney Jeffries

(1) Sir: I feel I must reply to your attack on my hero Thomas the Tank Engine. As one who has read and re-read the stories many times, I hope I will be able to put you straight on a few points.

This opening sentence refers to the text to which the letter is replying. Often such reference is more explicit – see letter openings on p. 153. Note the presupposition carried by the nominalisation *attack*. The writer also announces what he is about to do, useful in a long letter.

(2) You suggest that the morality which Thomas and friends offer is nothing more than Old Testament retribution. In fact, the message is that if you say you are sorry, you will be given 'another chance' (and probably end up pulling the special train). This surely represents a New Testament ethic of a loving Fat Controller who forgives all them who truly repent. And there are plenty of rewards for being good: a new coat of paint, a chance to pull the express or, the accolade, a branch line all to yourself.

Paragraph 2 has a kind of unequal Balance structure, hinging around the *in fact* where the original text's position is stated first and then demolished. The low-certainty verb *suggest* is outweighed by the modal devices of high certainty *in fact* and *surely*. Notice the lexical constrasts 'Old' v. 'New Testament', and 'retribution' v. 'reward'.

(3) The Fat Controller is not some distant, unapproachable ruler. He listens to the petitions of the engines (see Thomas and Gordon's alliance in *Gordon the Big Engine* and Percy's deputation in *The Twin Engines*).

A new paragraph (3), for the second point, which concerns the Fat Controller. This paragraph gives specific evidence for the point stated in its first sentence.

Paragraphs 3–5 are Deductive in structure moving from the general to the specific.

(4) The books also make us re-examine our prejudices; the likes of Daisy and Boo show that diesels are not all bad, and 'sinners' can often prove to be heroes.

(5) I can't agree with Thomas Sutcliffe's assertion that 'there's no altruism here'. Throughout the books, Thomas and friends continually work for the greater good of mankind (or, alternatively, enginekind). Often, the Fat Controller knows nothing of these deeds as the engines, being blessed with free-will make their own

Paragraph 5: the writer restates his position on Sutcliffe's views ... A bit of humour lightens the interpersonal tone.

The Themes of pararagraph 5 are carefully chosen to underline the move from the general to the specific 'throughout the books', 'often' and 'a good example' decisions. A good example of this is Douglas's heroic rescue of Oliver in *Enterprising Engines*.

(6) The value system nurtured in my impressionable mind (as a child born the year before Mrs Thatcher came to power) was obviously different from Mr Sutcliffe's son's. My favourite engine was always Toby the Tram Engine, perfectly content with his one faithful coach, Henrietta, rather than proud possessors of many coaches like Gordon and Henry. Blessed are the meek for they shall inherit their own stretch of branch line.

In paragraph 6 there is a telling presupposition that (storybooks) nurture value systems in impressionable minds; without such a belief this letter and the article which provokes it would be pointless or lack seriousness. There is a humorous inference that anyone born before Thatcher came to power is less likely to have a proud and competitive value system.

(7) Personally, I would like to wish Thomas and his friends a very happy 50th birthday, and best wishes for the next half century.

Paragraphs 6 and 7 are the most personal – 2 to 5 hardly mention the writer, but 7 climaxes in a personal birthday greeting.

Yours faithfully,
BARNEY JEFFRIES
West Grinstead
Wiltshire

ACTIVITY 47

As a way of revising and summing up the ideas of this chapter you might think about the following questions in relation to the Jeffries letter.

(1) How heterogeneous is this text? What different voices do you detect in it?
(2) When other writing ('speech') is represented how is this done (FDS, DS, FIS, IS, NRSA)? Are the sources acknowledged?
(3) Do you think it's a humorous parody, or is it serious? If you think it's a parody can you link this to your analyses in 1 and 2?

Parodies are likely to misfire, of course, if the text or style being parodied is not recognised by the reader. Without explanation I don't suppose many readers understood the parody of the Heinz advertisement. This reinforces two points we made earlier: first, a writer needs to correctly estimate the knowledge that readers can bring to the text being written; second, the originating text in any kind of intertextuality – quotation, reaction or parody – must represent a powerful voice, one which is important enough to be worth quoting or famous enough to be recognised by the readership. Parody, although apparently a humorous putting down of the powerful and their texts, in fact pays them homage.

The existence of parody is very clear evidence, too, that meanings cannot simply be decoded from a Text, and that very often Texts have to be interpreted according to the purpose and attitude of the writer, before we can go on to any ideological explanation. To what extent, do you think, was I too serious in my analysis of Linda Grant's 'I'm sorry teenagers you are not the centre of the universe', (see p. 61) and did I ignore an element of self-parody? Parody is evidence for the importance of factoring in purpose and attitude because on the decodable surface it is almost identical to the source text or genre. However, having humour as its main aim, it is by definition quite different in purpose and propositional attitude from the genre it imitates. In other words, parody highlights the difference between Critical Linguistics and Critical Discourse Analysis, Parts one and two of this book.

6.6 Summary

In this chapter we considered how:

- writers can make texts heterogeneous in terms of genre and subject positions;
- writers can introduce another voice into texts by the representation of speech, and to varying degrees merge it with their own, though always preserving and acknowledging the distinct voices in academic writing;
- journalists might (un)intentionally distort the news due to the long intertextual chains in the process of news reporting;
- writers can exploit intertextuality for humorous purposes in parody.

Project 2

You might like to write a letter to a national or local newspaper on an issue which has been mentioned in a recent news report or feature article in that paper. After conferencing with your peers/tutor you should really send it off to the paper, and see if they publish it. When you present it as an assignment it will be useful if it is accompanied by a commentary in note form in which you justify the choice of language you have made.

Obviously, it's best to choose an issue which interests you, and which you either know something about or can research to justify your opinions when necessary.

Though this letter will probably not be a parody, look at 'Reading between the railway lines' and the comments in the margin of that letter. Several discourse structure features are important in such letters:

- to refer carefully to the text you are reacting to early in the letter;
- to state your position on the issue clearly;
- to allocate a paragraph to each separate point, and usually, Deductively, to put the point first in the paragraph;
- to cite evidence for your opinions, generally towards the end of the paragraph;
- to carefully choose the Themes and develop the thematic progression of the paragraph and letter.

Particular areas of this book which you could apply to this letter will be Chapter 3 on interpersonal features of the text, the section on presupposition in Chapter 4, and that on politeness in Chapter 5. If you wish, you can also analyse how different participants are represented as powerful or powerless in your letter, using the kind of analysis done in Chapter 2.

I suggest that the whole project could be around 1,000 words, with the letter taking two-thirds and the commentary notes a third.

6.7 Summary of Part two

This chapter brings us to the end of Part 2 of the text which has been concerned with the level of Interpretation in Table 0.1 (see p. 3). It is worth recapping and drawing together the main gists of this section and showing how they relate to earlier sections.

I'd like to stress once again the importance of taking into account the ideal reader when one is writing. We can sum this up in a number of questions:

- How much knowledge can we presuppose – what schematic resources does the reader have?
- How much acquaintance has the reader with figures like metaphor and irony, and will these misfire?
- What kinds of opinions do we suspect in the ideal reader? What might cause offence? What might be contested terms for him? What kinds of pre-suppositional smuggling can we get away with?
- What kind of subject position is going to be most effective in communicating with him, based on our degrees of Contact, Power and emotion?

And, of course, if we are planning to be teachers and expect our students to write in various genres, we might well ask ourselves the question:

- How much knowledge do students have of the discourse structure of the genres we require?

Suggestions for further reading

- The theory of intertextuality originates with Julia Kristeva (1974: 59–60).
- There are many accounts of the representation of speech and thought. Leech and Short in *Style in Fiction,* chapter 10, provide a thorough and accessible account. A modification of their scheme can be found in Hutchinson's 'Speech presentations in fiction with reference to *The Tiger Moth* by H. E. Bates'.
- Allan Bell *The Language of News Media*, pp. 44–50, gives an insider's account of the different stages of transmission of messages in the news production process, and the opportunities for change and distortion which this communicative chain presents.
- Mary Talbot in 'The construction of gender in a teenage magazine' analyses a feature article on lipstick, and draws attention to the different voices heard.

Part three

The ideology behind the text

Introduction to Part three

The first two parts of this textbook started with language, Text and interpretation and moved towards ideological explanation. Part three, by contrast, moves in a different direction, overtly outlining and critiquing various ideological positions and then seeing how they are manifest in texts and discourses. The ideological positions are to do with

- the function and value systems of advertising in consumer capitalism (Chapter 7);
- the persistence of the ideology of romantic love in magazines for women (Chapter 8);
- the dominance of powerful political, ethnic and economic élites in the language of newspapers (Chapter 9); and
- classic physics perspectives of nature and modern scientific perspectives with their contrasting linguistic representations in Wordsworth's *The Prelude* and *The Times* (Chapter 10).

Chapters 7, 8 and 9 end with suggestions for projects – publicity material for an organisation to which you belong (Chapter 7), a short story for a student magazine (Chapter 8), and a news report (Chapter 9), also for a student newspaper.

Using Part three

There are various ways in which teachers and students can use Part three. It is possible simply to read the chapters through and (I hope) enjoy the analysis and commentary. However, it would be better to read with the projects in mind and to use the analysis, which revises Parts one and two, to inform the writing decisions necessary when composing the text for the project. More useful still would be to look at some of the texts analysed and respond to them before reading my detailed analysis, as this would lead to more interaction and engagement. For example in Chapter 7, you might read sections 7.1 to 7.8, and then analyse some or all of the four texts for yourselves before reading (and, I hope, resisting) my sometimes polemical and ideologically positioned analysis.

Alternatively, Part three can be read more selectively, choosing chapters and projects according to the interests of students. Or one could select which parts of a chapter's analysis to concentrate on. For example, one might want to look at visual informativeness and implicature in some of the ads in Chapter

7, narrative structure and politeness in the short story of Chapter 8, and transitivity analysis of the Hanson news report and the representation of women in the news from Chapter 9. This would give a coverage of the important concepts and practice in the analytical procedures introduced in Parts one and two, without necessarily following through all my thorough and detailed analysis.

Chapter 7

Advertising and consumerism

Aims of this chapter

To outline the obvious and less obvious ideological strategies in and behind the texts of advertisements.

To show how these ideologies are manifest by detailed analysis of three advertisements.

To give practice in the composition of promotional texts for a real readership.

- **7.0 Introduction: a brief historical perspective on consumerism**

Shows the importance of advertising to consumer capitalism and places it in its historical context.

The next sections outline six important aspects of consumerist ideology, used as strategies by advertising copywriters:

- **7.1 Desire and power**

- **7.2 Buying as problem solving**

- **7.3 Acquiring qualities**

- **7.4 Choosing an identity**

- **7.5 Distinguishing yourself: exclusivity, uniqueness and tradition**

- **7.6 Buying a lifestyle**

This is followed by three case studies:

(1) The car, the individual, and the road to success
  an Opel Vectra ad

(2) A match for the jet set and the good Chinese wife
   an advert for Emirates airlines

(3) Unnecessary words and welcoming in style?
   an advert for Sheraton hotels

- **Project 3: Promotional or publicity material**

Writing promotional or publicity material commissioned by a club, society, institution or company with which you are associated.

7.0 Introduction: a brief historical perspective on consumerism

Roughly speaking, we can look at the last two hundred years in Europe as representing a radical break with all the historic and prehistoric ages that preceded them. This is because technological advances of the Industrial Revolution made possible the mass production of manufactured goods and their quick and widespread distribution through modern means of communication such as the railways. Later, from the 1920s onwards, capitalist manufacturing industry became organised around highly mechanised production lines like the car assembly plants set up by Henry Ford, a kind of industrial organisation known as 'Fordism'. Because this system involved a great deal of capital investment the products produced had to be consumed *en masse*. The last forty years represent another important and distinctive 'post-Fordist' period. The development of electronic mass media, of radio and TV, allowed widespread advertising, even to illiterate people, so that most of the population could be targeted as potential consumers. These were the technological circumstances which enabled the development of modern consumer capitalism.

Current consumer capitalist economic models of growth depend upon a system with the following mechanisms and characteristics. In order to increase wealth economies and their industries have to produce more. And in order to sell more goods and services more people have to be persuaded to buy them, which is why advertising plays such a crucial role. Since the advent of the transnational corporation, market researchers have been able to recognise or create new modes of consumption; the market has been fragmented into numerous specialised niches according to income level, age, household type and locality.

Hand in hand with this fragmentation of the market has come the break up of mass culture. Instead of the two or three TV channels of the 1960s in the UK, and papers like the *Saturday Evening Post* in the States, which provided some common media experience, we have the diversity of cable and satellite TV, videos, the Internet and an abundance of specialised magazines. Instead of the rather conservative staple foods of the 1950s, the ordinary British high street and supermarket now boasts a diversity of cuisines: Chinese, Italian, Indian, Greek, Thai, Mexican, West Indian and vegetarian. Leisure and religion too have diversified with many exotic and eccentric options like t'ai chi, kung fu, judo, karate, taekwondo, Buddhism, Zen, Islam, Sufism, Hinduism, Scientology, Rastafarianism, Satanism, witchcraft and more (Faigley 1992: 12). Under these changed cultural circumstances, the modern person has a bewildering choice of lifestyle and identity, a position, as we shall see, that advertisers exploit (see sections 7.5 and 7.6). Truth and being true to oneself turns

185

out to be, like a commodity, a consumer choice. How significant is the metaphor *I don't buy that* to mean "I don't believe that"!

Choice in fact lies at the heart of consumerism, especially when shopping becomes a leisure activity rather than a chore. For it is in leisure that the modern urban population, especially the young, see their main area of freedom of choice. Work, and to some extent family, represent authority and discipline and various kinds of coercion and responsibility. But as consumers in our leisure time we seem relatively free (MacRobbie 1991: 86, 88).

There are many adverse consequences of this obsession with economic growth in general and consumer capitalism in particular. In Chapter 10 we will take an ecological perspective on this system of increasing production and consumption, and critique the now reactionary Newtonian world-view which underlies the Industrial Revolution. But even on the superficial level, it is obvious that manufacturing industry depends upon the use of raw materials, usually nonrenewable ones, and that when these consumer goods are broken, or outmoded, they are discarded, creating problems of waste disposal in a finite environment. Furthermore, a great deal of waste is created by the actual manufacture of the product. Very often obsolescence is deliberately built into these products, so that they do not last as long as they could – it is possible to produce a car tyre which never wears out, but to do so would obviously bankrupt Goodyear, Dunlop, Michelin and company, so that technological advance in this case is ignored in favour of profits. The clothing industry and its advertisements unashamedly create the concept of fashion, which changes from year to year. This, psychologically, makes last year's clothes obsolete, even though they may not be worn out. The flares I wore in the 1970s and which I went on wearing into the 1980s, much to the amusement of my students, have now, some twenty-five years later, and five years after I disposed of mine, come surging back into fashion. Obviously I should have hung on to them, or they to me.

7.1 Desire and power

But in this Chapter we will be concentrating more specifically on consumerism and the kinds of ideological effects that advertising has on society and the psychology of identity. First of all, in order to increase consumption, advertisers have to encourage human greed, envy and desire for power, no matter that most of the world's traditional religions and ethical systems would see these as antisocial, if not evil. Consumers have to be made to feel dissatisfied unless they buy a product or more of a particular product, whether they need it or not. If they needed it the advertiser would not have to put so much emphasis on attention grabbing, since the readership, as in classified adverts, would already be assured.

The problem is, of course, that when luxury goods, like cars, become widespread it is tempting for society to arrange transport around their ownership, so that what once was a luxury becomes a virtual necessity. I had a spare day in Los Angeles one summer and wanted to take my family to the zoo. This was almost impossible by public transport, so we were forced to hire a car for the day.

While buying a product directly satisfies (for the moment) the appetite and desires of the consumer, the link between buying the product and attaining power or competitive advantage is a little less obvious. This is perhaps why, especially in a magazine like *Popular Science* (June 1995), with a majority of male readers, the appeal to the desire for power is stressed, usually the power to make money or to win the competitive race.

> Introducing the fraction of an inch that will put you miles ahead.
> It's CompuServeCD. And it'll put you in the forefront of online technology, because of what it does and what it will let you do (...) they'll start you down the road to where you've always wanted to be. Ahead.
> Compuserve
> The information service you won't outgrow.
>
> (p. 33)

> 7 surefire ways to be your own boss. If you want the final say (...) if you want your name on the door (...) if you want the profits that come from running your own business... turn to the at-home training program that works: NRI
>
> If another ambitious person has already sent in the card write to (...)
>
> (pp. 40–1)

> You Need the Edge. We deliver.
> Every Edge product is covered by our famous lifetime guarantee.
>
> (p. 45)

> Slick 50 fuel system – more power to you.
>
> (p. 35)

Notice how the last two of these examples transfer power from the product to the consumer, and how the Edge advert promises that the lifetime of the tools will match the lifetime of the consumer.

By buying powerful products we acquire power, albeit at second hand. We have already seen in Chapter 2, in our clause analysis of the Dulcia Vitality Perm advertisement (see Plate 3, p. 74), that products are often represented as powerful, as the Actors. Perhaps this is not surprising when the product is a machine, which, after all, can cause things to happen and might be thought of as an Actor. For instance, an Olympus camera which '**creates** impressive reproductions ... **holding** as much as 80 images in its flash memory'(*Straits Times*, 20 August 1997, p. 27). But it's rather more surprising when the product is a substance like engine oil which, when the engine runs, is surely more of an Affected than an Actor: 'So every new Porsche comes filled with Mobil 1. Porsche believes that no other oil **performs** better'. When there might be doubts about the substance's efficacy, as with skin-cream cosmetics (usually made from the unwanted by-products of oil refining and the petrochemical industry), then its power as an Actor over Affected (your skin) tends to be stressed even more:

> It [Bella] successfully **revives** your tired looking skin and **restores** it to its natural glow. At the same time it **minimizes** the look of lines and wrinkles on your complexion, **leaving** it totally refreshed and strikingly radiant.
> (*Straits Times*, 20 August 1997, p. 29)

Very often the power claimed for the product is the power to solve a particular "problem", like the so-called problem of ageing skin.

7.2 Buying as problem solving

Second, therefore, consumerism encourages the idea that the way to solve problems is by buying a product, and this can undermine the possibility of social organisation and political action. Imagine the following crude scenario. An unemployed single mother is bringing up two small children on her own in a council flat, and suffers from headaches caused by stress. She might see advertisements for Panadol on the TV and treat her symptoms by buying and consuming them. Alternatively, she could attempt to remove the causes of the problem – contact other care-givers in the same position and try to set up a day-care centre for children, to give her and others a few spare hours' relaxation away from the children each day. Consumerism favours the first alternative. I had the tendency, when I was at college, to compensate for not working hard enough on my current essay by going out and buying a book on the subject. I now have a considerable collection of texts and criticism on English literature. This betrays a consumerist mind set. Look at the average beauty section in a teenage magazine to see to what extent readers are similarly encouraged to consume their way out of "problems" and "difficulties" with their appearance.

One consequence of seeing products as the way to solve problems is to depersonalise or disempower the consumer. Products, by being presented as achieving things that we cannot achieve, replace us. As Williamson illustrates:

> There is an advert for frozen vegetables which says 'Birds Eye peas will do anything to attract your husband's attention'. Presumably *you* would do anything to attract your husband's attention. A woman and a Birds Eye pea are made interchangeable. The peas represent what the woman can't do, they have the same aim: to make her husband notice something at dinner.
>
> (Williamson 1978: 38)

Michael Hoey, the text linguist, suggested that the problem–solution structure could be a basic template for many generic structures (Hoey 1973). Certainly, it figures widely and obviously in many advertisements where the product or service solves the consumer's problem. This structure may be overtly cued by the word *problem*

> If you have a hair problem, visit Glower, a leading trichological centre.
>
> (*Straits Times*, 20 August 1997, p. 3)

or the word *solution*

> Tailor made solutions available. (Give us your measurements) (. . .) So we take the responsibility of providing the most up to date communications solutions for voice, data and image, while you get on with what you do best.
>
> (*Asiaweek*, 14 February 1997, p. 11)

In other adverts, a negative state or state of mind is likely to be interpreted as problematic, even if the words *problem* or *solution* are not used.

> If you've been trying for a family and you haven't yet succeeded, don't worry, you're not alone. Every year at least 25,000 women try to get pregnant and fail. It doesn't mean there's anything wrong with them. It's usually just a case of bad timing. And that's when Discretest can be such a help.
>
> (*Good Housekeeping*, 8 May 1987, p. 10)

7.3 Acquiring qualities

The third psychological effect of consumer advertising is to conflate the product with the consumer. Just as the power of the product gives power to the buyer, so, more generally, any positive attribute of the product is supposed to transfer itself to the possessor, or to the possessor's relationships.

Sometimes these qualities will be feelings or mental qualities, as in the brand name for the shampoo Rejoice, or the slogan 'Happiness is a cigar called Hamlet' (Williamson 1978: 37). Since the product cannot literally have such qualities the pretence that they do is quite outrageous. A particular favourite with advertisers is the word *intelligent*, as in 'Skyy vodka, the intelligent drink'. These slogans can only sensibly be interpreted as meaning 'a cigar which gives you happiness' and 'a drink which makes the drinker intelligent', despite the fact that spirits befuddle the senses. Note how, in this next example, the transfer of the epithet *intelligent* from product to buyer is facilitated by the ambiguity of nominalisation.

> the intelligent choice for those shopping for high performance detection and highway safety combined.
>
> (*Popular Science*, June 1995, p. 21)

Here 'choice' can either mean 'the thing chosen' or 'the act of choosing'; the semantics and grammar of the phrase 'for those shopping …' suggests the first meaning; but, since the attribute 'intelligent' and the act of choosing are both mental, the second meaning emerges too.

The quality of a product might also be transferred to a relationship. A classic example is the series of De Beers' adverts with its slogan 'Diamonds are forever'. If diamonds are indestructible and forever, then presumably the relationship with the woman/man for whom one buys them will come close to being eternal too. The rings which partners exchange in a wedding as a token of their 'troth' or fidelity prepare the ground for this slogan, as they are made of the most enduring metal, gold. However, real human relations can often suffer from the advertisement-inspired drive to earn and consume more. Husbands, as well as wives, go out into full-time work in order, ironically enough, to be able to buy labour-saving devices, in addition to houses, cars, electronic audio-visual equipment, holidays. This work and spend system may leave little time for interaction with children – except for that spurious newly made category of "quality time" – and creates the kinds of tensions between work, housework and care-giving roles which strain relationships and may contribute to family break-up.

Rolex adverts play an interesting variation on transfers of quality between product and consumer. Here the stars – opera singers, golf champions, explorers and so on – share qualities of reliability and excellence with the watch, if not imparting these qualities to the product they buy. The direction of transfer is perhaps beside the point – either way the quality of the star matches the quality of the watch:

Clearly Cecilia Bartoli derives much pleasure from perfection. She knows that when every detail is flawless the performance will be perfect. Which is precisely why her Rolex gives her so much pleasure.

(*Asiaweek*, 14 February 1997, p. 3)

As far as the ordinary person in the street is concerned, the promised transfer will be from product to consumer. If a Rolex is a reliable watch then it might well turn you into a reliable person. It is a small step from this to suggest that one's identity, character and worth depend less on what one is and more on what one has. Even in cities like London or Hong Kong, where having a car is not absolutely necessary for most people, many demand to have one, simply as what we call a status symbol. This probably betrays a psychological syndrome in which we only feel important if we are seen as the possessors of valuable property, and the more we own the more important we are.

7.4 Choosing an identity

Given the pace of change, the fragmentation of mass culture, and the exploding numbers of possible lifestyles, modern people face an identity crisis. If advertisers can promise not only a product but an accompanying identity, then they have a very powerful strategy. As Lester Faigley (1992) puts it:

The desire to consume is predicated on the lack of a stable identity. Purchasing and using a consumer object is a temporary and unstable attempt to occupy an imagined identity provoked by an image.

(Faigley 1992: 13)

Some classes of advertisements – again the Rolex adverts are good examples – exploit the fact that we achieve identity by identification, so the celebrity who appears in the advert becomes the kind of person we wish to identify with. We'd all like to be able to sing like Cecilia Bartoli, enjoy her lifestyle, join her social set. This creates a kind of spurious social solidarity, a modern equivalent of totemism, in the form of "consumer clubs" – the collection of individuals who use or own an identical product (Williamson 1978: 45–7). In the late 1980s, a rally was arranged in southern England to which all the owners of original Austin Minis were invited. And the possession of an Apple Macintosh or IBM PC can, in some contexts, be seen as dividing people along social lines. When Apple Macintosh announced to its loyalists it had set up a deal with Microsoft, the news was received as something like treachery. These clubs are a rather desperate antidote to the increasing anonymity of modern society.

Products therefore become a badge of membership. For example the question 'Is your mum a Superfine mum?' is asking whether the child's mother belongs to the group who use Superfine margarine. This advert simultaneously casts doubt on whether a mother can do her job really well, can be superfine, unless she has joined that club. A similar technique is used in the following more extended advert:

IF THERE'S STILL A JAMAICAN BOBSLED TEAM, YOU'LL HAVE 350 CHANNELS TO FIND THEM

If you're a true sports buff, then get ready for a big change in your life. Or at least your weekends. Because with full-view satellite TV you get up to 35 glorious channels (including 100 radio). Which means you can watch virtually any football, basketball, hockey or baseball game. And darn-near any other televised sporting event in the nation – even if it's the Mexican ping-pong team. With hundreds of program packages, intense laser disc quality picture and CD quality sound. Call 1–800–778–4900 now for the nearest authorised Full View TV dealer, a free brochure and free basic installation at participating dealers. Hey, if having 350 channels is a guy thing, it's the ultimate guy thing.

FULL VIEW TV

THE SATELLITE SYSTEM WITH THE BEST VIEW

(*Popular Science,* June 1995, p. 19)

Notice in particular the opening and closing lines 'if you're a true sports buff' and 'Hey, if having 350 channels is a guy thing, it's the ultimate guy thing', with their unashamed appeal to the product as a membership badge.

Both through the individual qualities they promise to impart to us, and through the social groups they associate us with, advertised products are crucial in creating illusory identities in our consumerist capitalist culture. The ascendant New Right in the US and the UK see society simply as a collection of individuals, or, at the most, family units, with responsibilities only to themselves rather than to society as a whole. These individuals compete against each other and the most motivated and able earn and spend more. In this antisocial society, identification and self-definition are achieved through levels and kinds of consumption (Faigley 1992: 49).

7.5 Distinguishing yourself: exclusivity, uniqueness and tradition

So we cannot allow ourselves to identify with all the other members of society as though we were uniform. To define ourselves as more successful than average we must distinguish ourselves through the goods we consume. We must be permitted the luxury to feel different and superior since, after all, the goods we buy, often in fact very similar, are branded as *unique*, *unparalleled*, *special*, etc. This mindset explains the exploitation of the consumer's snobbishness, as in the following, with its appeal to the exclusiveness of royalty:

> EXCLUSIVELY FROM HARTMAN   Royal Club
> The Ultimate
> OUTDOOR LIFESTYLE
>
> *(Good Housekeeping*, May 1987, p. 220)

A more euphemistic word for snobbery is *discrimination*: as in 'for discriminating chocolate lovers'. This concept suggests that, like the Rolex superstars, we can match ourselves with the product, rather than simply deriving qualities from it, for instance: 'If you take pride in your handiwork, we think you'll appreciate the effort we put into ours'.

There is, of course, a deep paradox in pretending that products are exclusive, since they are mass produced and adverts are designed to increase the number of buyers, thereby making them less exclusive! So sometimes the appeal to exclusivity, taste and discrimination is social rather than individualistic, as in this Wedgwood advert, where the buyer is encouraged to start a little consumer club of their own to reinforce existing friendships:

> For richer for pourer. Wedgwood. If you can appreciate the finer things in life, you'll want your friends to do the same. Make someone's wedding day with a Windrush fine bone china dinner service.

Another way out of the exclusivity/mass-production paradox is to appeal to the individual's exceptionally good taste while locating it within a tradition of previous consumers:

> Jack Daniel's head distiller, Jimmy Bedford has lots of folk looking over his shoulder. Since 1866, we've had only six head distillers. (Every one a Tennessee boy, starting with Mr Jack Daniel himself.) Like those before him, Jimmy's mindful of our traditions, such as the oldtime way we smooth our whiskey through 10 feet of hard maple charcoal. He **knows**

Jack Daniel's drinkers will judge him with every sip. So he's not about to change a thing. The five gentlemen on his wall surely must be pleased about that.

In this, as in other whisky adverts, the appeal to an exclusive tradition is probably a reaction against the fetishism of the new: 'The Famous Grouse. Finest Scotch Whisky. Quality in an age of change'. It is an interesting question which categories of products have their value enhanced by being old, and which have to be touted as new. But the appeal of tradition is a strong one in a fragmented insecure society where things are changing so fast.

The following Sainsbury's wine advert is noticeable for playing on snobbery and inverted snobbery simultaneously. While it overtly rejects the idea of 'pride' based on wealth and the cost of the product, it nevertheless slips in the word 'pedigree' to cater to the taste for aristocratic tradition and exclusiveness.

It's a sparkling wine with a long and distinguished pedigree. It costs too little. At under $4 a bottle Sainsbury's Cava is something of a bargain compared to other sparkling wines. Perhaps at your next celebration you should pocket your pride and the difference.

(*Good Housekeeping*, May 1987, p. 8)

Chevrolet seems to go further, implying that there is no exclusivity about their products:

At Chevrolet we believe that everyone, no matter how much they have to spend, deserves a safe car.

(*Popular Science*, June 1995, p. 38)

Even so, the non-exclusivity would be clearer if they had said 'however *little* they have to spend'. Incidentally, this notion that the consumer 'deserves' everything the manufacturer has prepared for them alludes to one argument advanced in favour of advertising, especially in poor countries: adverts make the poor aware of a quality of life to which they have a right, the simple essentials of life, like soap, decent sanitation, bedding, housing and clothing, etc. I doubt this apologia for advertising can be sustained in modern advanced economies, unless, as I suggested earlier, we have structured our way of life around luxuries like cars to the extent that they are now necessities.

7.6 Buying a lifestyle

Back in the 1950s and early 1960s advertisers often used conditioning strategies, like Pavlov on his dogs, in which they paired the product with a desirable object (often an attractive female human). The result of the technique is either to transfer the desirable connotations of the accompanying image of object or person to the product, or, more crudely, to suggest that buying the product will bring you the desirable object too. In this latter case you are not just buying the product but what goes with it. For example the right toothpaste or perfume will bring you the attractive woman or hunky man. While this naïve technique is probably less common than it was, there is a similar technique which suggests that by buying the product you are adopting a certain 'lifestyle' or 'way of life'. Recall, for example, the analysis of the Dorma fabrics advert (see Plate 5, p. 142), which seemed to promise a bohemian lifestyle and passionate heterosexual relationship, not just cloth.

Judith Williamson in her book *Decoding Advertisements* explains how such appeals to a way of life achieve their signification:

> A product may be connected with a way of life through being an accessory to it, but come to signify it, as in the car advert which starts 'Your way of life demands a lot of a car' and ends by making the car signify the lifestyle: 'Maxi: more a way of life'. So the product and the 'real' or human world become linked in the advert, apparently naturally, and the product may or does take over the reality on which it was, at first, dependent for its meaning.
>
> (Williamson 1978: 35)

An explicit promise of a lifestyle also appears in the advert for AGA cookers (*Good Housekeeping*, May 1987, pp. 212–13; see Plate 7). Not only do we have AGA. IT'S A WAY OF LIFE, but the contact details at the foot of the advert read: 'if you'd like to find out more about life with a (...) Aga (...) send off this coupon', almost suggesting that your cooker is equivalent to your partner/spouse. Explicit the advert may be about selling a lifestyle, but it is not explicit about the kind of lifestyle. The advertiser cannot, of course, make overt promises that by buying the product you will also be buying something else. This has to be inferred from the accompanying visuals. The AGA advert seems to imply a simple and natural lifestyle. The substances in the kitchen are natural – the wicker basket, the wooden chest, chest of drawers and spoons, the stoneware vases, the fruit, the flowers, the leather sandals, the cotton nightdress, and the flagstone floor suggesting a country cottage. The simplicity is symbolised by the bare, homogeneous surfaces such as the whitewashed wall, with only

Plate 7 'AGA. It's a way of life' (Advert for AGA cookers, *Good Housekeeping*, May 1987, pp. 212–13)

a plain wood-framed mirror, the plain white nightdress, the woman's lack of jewellery or make-up.

Since lifestyle is not just a matter of our surroundings but also our behaviour we can infer a little narrative from the visuals as well. The weak sun slanting into the kitchen is quite low in the sky, which means it must be early morning or late evening. However the woman is dressed for bed, which suggests she has just got up in the morning. The flowers on the chest of drawers are the daisies of an English summer. The flowers lying beside her suggest that after rising early she went out into the garden to pick them, despite the chill of early morning, and returned, took off her sandals, and is blissfully warming her feet and dozing by the stove.

7.7 Summary

We have seen, in the first section of Part three, how, besides encouraging consumption, which is in some cases quite unnecessary, adverts appeal to and reproduce value systems and mindsets. Besides generating envy, greed and wastefulness, adverts also suggest that by buying a product or service we are:

- solving our problems;
- acquiring quality or qualities;
- choosing our identities;
- distinguishing ourselves;
- buying a lifestyle.

We now turn to look in detail at three advertisements, to illustrate how these psychological appeals are manifested in the linguistic texture of the copy, and also to apply many of the linguistic aspects which have been touched upon in Parts one and two.

Case study 1: The car, the individual, and the road to success

This advert for Opel (Plate 8) is a prime example of the blending of the personality of the consumer and the "personality" of the product. This is most apparent from the striking visual image – part woman, part car. The advert copy is, however, not quite sure about whether the qualities of the car – individuality and the power to make independent decisions – transfer from product to consumer

OPEL

VECTRA

WHEN YOU'VE MASTERED THE ART OF CONTROL

PEOPLE WILL KNOW.

(1) Remember all those moments when you wanted to say something, do something, but didn't?

(2) Times when you held back, because you were happier to let others take the lead.

(3) And yet, you know deep down that you wouldn't be who you are today, if it weren't for the decisions you'd made.

(4) Decisions that let you discover the power of individuality and the reward of independence.

(5) So why should your mode of travel be so different from your mode of thought?

(6) Why, indeed, should you follow the pack, when you could be leading it?

(7) When we designed the Opel Vectra, we set out to create a car that would sit

(8) at the very head of its class. A car that gives you the power to go where you want, when you want. And be capable of taking

(9) you the distance in comfort, safety and yes, we dare say it, *style*.

(10) You know what it is to be an individual, to move while others are stationary, to take control of a situation and direct it the way you want.

(11) When you drive the new Vectra you'll be reminded of all those moments when you pushed on with what you truly believed in.

(12) And when you move others will follow, as they come to realise that you have mastered the art of control.

OPEL ⊖

JAPAN TEL 0120-353-387 • TAIWAN TEL 886-02-507-5511 FAX: 886-02-507-5989 • THAILAND TEL 662-3606296 FAX 662-3611363 • INDONESIA TEL 62-21-4600847 FAX 62-21-4610538 • SINGAPORE TEL 65-4708760 FAX 65-4722474 • MALAYSIA
TEL 03-2419930 FAX: 03-2411303 • HONG KONG TEL 852-28818900 FAX 852-28828366 • CHINA TEL 86-10-5123618 • VIETNAM TEL 86-10-3121618 • VIETNAM TEL 84-8-2918600 FAX 84-8-231025 • SRI LANKA TEL 94-1-432838 FAX 94-1-446129

Plate 8 'When you've mastered the art of control, people will know' (Advert for the Opel Vectra car, *Asiaweek*, December 1996, pp. 2–3)

through the act of purchasing, or whether the buyer already has them. The opening of the copy suggests the first: 'Remember all those moments when you wanted to say something, do something, but didn't? Times when you held back, because you were happier to let others take the lead'. But later it is suggested that the car simply matches these pre-existing qualities of the consumer: 'And yet, you know deep down that you wouldn't be who you are today, if it weren't for the decisions you'd made. Decisions that let you discover the power of individuality and the reward of independence'. In either case the appeal is the match between mental characteristics and mode of travel: 'So why should your mode of travel be so different from your mode of thought?'

We notice, too, the appeal to three other consumer values identified earlier: power, identity and distinction. For the copy promises the following characteristics:

- decision-making power: taking control of a situation and directing it;
- individual independence: the power to go where you want when you want;
- personal 'advancement': leading the pack, being head of the class, moving while others are stationary.

Possible tensions between individuality and social membership are resolved by the notion of leading the pack; you are a member, but distinguished at the same time. Nevertheless, the main thrust of the advert is an appeal to identity and individualism. In the US, the car is almost synonymous with your rights and social identity. As Baudrillard puts it : 'Disenfranchising. You lose you rights one by one, first your job, then your car. And when your driver's licence goes, so does your identity' (Baudrillard 1989: 112). The car is, of course, the epitome of the individualism of *laissez-faire* consumer capitalism. It is individualistic, because it is private and designed for the individual or the nuclear family to use, rather than being a shared resource like public transport. It is *laissez-faire*, since it allows you to go where you like without making any messy or inconvenient social compromises. The problem is, of course, that it is not the most rational means of transport, given the problems of traffic, pollution and global warming. It is no accident that the most thoroughly consumer capitalist society, the US, is the most partial to the motor car, and also, though only four per cent of the world's population, responsible for forty per cent of carbon emissions.

The wording of the copy in this advert exploits a particular metaphorical equation in the vocabulary of the English language, which we might label SUCCESSFUL ACTIVITY = MOVEMENT FORWARDS (Goatly 1997: chapter 2). This equation gives rise to the following metaphors in the vocabulary of English (in bold):

Success is moving forwards:

> John has made great **advances** with his mathematics

So to develop or become more successful than others is to move ahead in a race:

> One element in the rat **race** is the desire **to get ahead**.

So failures cannot keep up with the front-runners:

> Paul is a **backward** child so it's difficult for him not to **get left behind**

Difficulty in succeeding is difficulty in going forward:

> Persuading Londoners to switch from cars to buses is an **uphill** task.

What prevents success is conceived of as an obstacle:

> Environmentalists are **obstructing** the government's attempts to manage Canadian forests effectively.

Solving a problem or avoiding failure is therefore passing through, round or over an obstacle:

> He **scraped through** his exam.
>
> Can't you **find a way around** that problem?

This metaphorical equation is obviously suited to the advertising of cars. It enables the car to symbolise independence, leadership and success, as we can see when we use it to interpret extracts from the copy:

> Times when you held back, because you were happier to let others take the lead =
> times when you were inactive and were happier for the others to do something first

> Why, indeed should you follow the pack when you could be leading it? = why should you imitate other people's behaviour instead of initiating or modelling an activity (or obey other people instead of giving orders)?

> A car that gives you the power to go where you want, when you want. And be capable of taking you the distance =

a car that gives you the power to do what you want when you want, and
is capable of making you succeed

To move while others are stationary, to take control of a situation and direct
it in the way you want =
to achieve things while others are doing nothing, to take control of a situation and make what you want happen

When you pushed on with what you really believed in =
when you did the difficult things you really believed in

And when you move others will follow =
when you do things others will imitate and obey

Besides illustrating these three kinds of psychological appeal, this advert
is also an exemplar of the use of interpersonal linguistic features. High Contact
is simulated by pronouns, interrogative mood "questions", fake dialogue, and
minor sentences or other shortenings.

First, the use of pronouns. Paragraph 1, sentences 1–6, uses just *you*. Obviously this has to be interpreted as an individual reader, given the emphasis on
independence and individuality. The concentration is, in fact, all on the psychology of the individual. The next paragraph, sentences 7 to 9, shifts to *we*, an
exclusive *we* which includes only the members of the Opel company and introduces the car, briefly. Sentences 10 to the end shift back to the potential customer, emphasising now not just her individual psychology, but also how she can
make a social impact, can be noticed by the *others*.

Turning to mood, we note the prevalence of the interrogative in the first
section (sentences 1, 5, and 6) which button-holes and engages the reader. In
fact, there is only one other complete sentence (3) which is a statement in
declarative mood, (2) and (4) being minor sentences. All interrogatives in this
section fail the tests for *bona fide* questions. The first (1) is really an indirect
statement or reminder. The second (5) and third (6) are another kind of rhetorical question, 'Why ...?', which everybody knows should be answered in the
negative, and amounts to an exhortation not to do something, in this case not
to 'follow the pack' or 'allow your mode of travel to be so different from your
mode of thought'. Later in the copy the flavour of dialogue is given by: 'and
yes, we dare say it, style', with its mock reply and its choice of the word *say*
rather than *write*.

If interrogatives give the flavour of speech, so does the use of compound
sentences, where clauses are joined by coordinating conjunctions like *and* and
but. Beginning a sentence with these conjunctions makes the copy even more
chatty as in (3), (5), (9) and (12).

In addition there are a number of shortenings and minor sentences which give the impression of conversational Contact. Contractions are everywhere: 'didn't', 'wouldn't', 'weren't', 'you'd', etc. Shortening of sentences is common: (1), really an interrogative, looks like an imperative, because the words *do you* have been missed out. (2) and (4), have been shortened into minor sentences – the major equivalents would begin: 'do you remember the times when …'; 'you'd made decisions that let you …'.

This use of shortenings and omissions in the first section contributes to a Chain-like rhetorical structure, because it demands a compensating repetition in adjacent sentences: moments (1) → times (2); decisions (3) → decisions (4). As Nash pointed out, chains give the impression of unplanned afterthoughts, and thereby contribute to the informality of this copy. These two chains are suspended on different ends of a Balance, of course, the fulcrum of which is the 'and yet' (3). Elsewhere in the copy stack structures seem to emerge: (7) (8) and (9) stack up positive claims about the car, for example.

In its affect there seems to be a growing confidence and heightening emotion towards the end of the copy. This is achieved by the repetition of grammatical structures, as in sentence (10), which suggest a rhythmical pattern – 4 beats per line, all starting with the infinitive form of the verb, with the x / pattern figuring prominently:

> You know what it is
>   x / x / x / x /
> to be an individual,
>   x /   x / x x / x /x
> to move while others are stationary,
>   x / x / x x / x / x
> to take control of a situation
>   x   x/ x / x /   x /
> and direct it in the way you want.

After this detailed analysis we can see the overall shape of the advert and how the linguistic details fit into the copywriter's strategic plan. The structure is that of problem–solution. The writer takes on the subject position of psychological counsellor, perhaps in assertiveness training or confidence building, beginning by establishing the patient's past. This accounts for the very personal beginning of the advert and the interrogatives. Having diagnosed the problem, though with a Balance structure which prevents the advert from being too insulting, and having given some interrogative advice, she provides the solution in the form of the Opel Vectra. This will afford the female buyer decision-making power, independence and noticeable success, a success underlined by the triumphant affective rhythms. And the metaphors of success for movement forward, along with the visual which blends car and person, vouch for the fact that cars confer identity and guarantee success.

Case study 2: A match for the jet set and the good Chinese wife

The selling point of this advertisement (Plate 9) is the matching of a famous personality with the service being advertised. This match is implied by the first two lines of the copy with its parallel syntactic structure of two apposed noun phrases:

(NP1) Mary Cheung, (NP2) award-winning photographer,
On (NP1) Emirates (NP2) (award-winning airline)

The parallelism of the second NP2 with the first NP2 is slightly obscured by using parentheses rather than commas. Presumably this is a gesture of modesty in the direction of politeness, an unusual self-effacement on the part of a company advertising. Once this link between product and famous personality has been achieved, buying the goods or service secures us identification with the famous and successful. The various real selling points of Emirates business class – the seatback video, the classy wine, the fax facility – are all mediated and validated through the eyes (camera) of Mary Cheung; as if they are not real until the famous photographer perceives and shoots them.

But besides this there is the appeal to distinction and exclusivity in the service provided. Particularly important for this effect is the mention of the wine Château Malescasse (or is it Malecasse?) '88, connoting French sophistication and exclusivity (wine of a certain château and vintage comes in limited quantities after all). This detail alludes to a whole way of life. We pick up on this detail, of course, because of the very visually prominent – it is in red – thumbnail sketch of 9D.

The previous Opel Vectra advert unashamedly celebrated the individualism of car transport. What then, is the ideological significance of air travel? Mary Cheung, though rich enough to enjoy the exclusivity of business class, cannot achieve the privacy and independence of private air transport. What does she feel about this enforced contact with two other members of the public, those sitting in seats 9D (a man) and 7E (probably an industrial chemist and therefore stereotypically a man)? 9D she just watches, but 7E's conversation on industrial polymers she regards as unfortunate. Apparently, industrial chemistry is not the kind

Plate 9 'Mary Cheung, award-winning photographer, on Emirates (award-winning airline)' (Advert for Emirates airlines, *Asiaweek*, February 1997, p. 19)

of topic which is likely to interest women, even those technically minded enough to invade the traditionally male preserve of photography. In any case, she does not find the company sufficiently engaging to dispel her homesickness, and therefore sends a 'love-you' fax back home.

This advert simultaneously breaks with gender stereotypes and reinforces them. It breaks them by presenting a woman who is successful in a traditionally male career and travels business class. But it reinforces them by insisting on her close ties with her family, as though separation from them does not really suit her fundamental instincts. Perhaps there is more to it than this. Within traditional Chinese culture there would be something suspect about a woman travelling alone in the presence of men with the opportunity to drink alcohol. Though she may have endured 7E's talk about polymers, she is not about to take much real interest in her male fellow passengers, who remain just numbers, nor in the wine, whose name she can't spell, but keeps herself to her sober self and for her family. She is a good Chinese wife and mother at heart. (Does the contraption in the photograph suggest a traditional Chinese peasant hat, in shape if not in sheen, or an inverted wok?)

In Pragmatic terms the advert relies on a juxtaposition of two schemas: photography and air travel. These make possible a kind of punning in the underlined handwritten 'a few verbal snapshots from 34,000 ft'. The snapshot pun is obvious, but the 'from 34,000ft' demands a bit more processing. It's impossible to take a snapshot *from* 34,000ft, so, to dispel our bewilderment, we have to reprocess this to mean '*at* 34,000ft'. An alternative interpretation is to regard the fax as a kind of snapshot which is sent to her family *from* 34,000ft.

The photography schema also contributes to the visual informativeness of the advert. The black-and-white photograph of Mary Cheung – black hair and shoulders, white face – marked for cropping by the frame, is echoed in the text immediately below in its no-nonsense bold black-and-white font, something like Chicago. This rather impersonal font contrasts markedly with the handwriting which follows. Since handwritten letters are always sent to individuals it obviously symbolises a high level of informal Contact and synthetic personalisation.

The significance of fonts is very difficult to pin down and put into words. But a comparison between the *Emirates* under the picture and the *Emirates* below the logo alerts us to it. The second suggests style and sophistication, where the first connotes bare efficiency. The three graphic choices, at the centre of the advert's body, are in marked contrast with each other.

Let's return now to the interpersonal features of the text. In the handwritten section they include pronouns, markers of inclination/emotion, and punctuation. What is remarkable is the sudden intrusion of the first-person pronoun in the last sentence of the handwritten message. The impersonality of number '10B', suddenly gives way to the presence of the author 'I', 'my', 'I', '"you"', and the signature with first and second name. Markers of emotion/inclination are present throughout. At first they are applied to the other passengers: 'relishing', 'enjoyed', 'likes', 'is willing'. Note that they become less strong, though this contradicts the inference that 7E is probably quite absurdly keen to talk about industrial polymers. 'Unfortunately' probably expresses the disinclination of Mary Cheung, as does possibly the first ''ll'. In the last sentence the positive emotions of Cheung are forcefully expressed when they are paired with the first-person pronoun – 'miss', 'love'. The steady degree of informality and a crude marking of propositional attitude are also achieved by the punctuation, perhaps the dash, but certainly the exclamation marks.

Finally, in the signature line, there is an expression of emotion in the symmetry of sound and syntax. Taking the two phrases together there is both repetition of rhythm | / x x x | / x x x | / |, and overall symmetry / x x x / x x x /.

/ x x   x / x x   x /
Emirates the finest in the sky

If we take the second phrase as a unit, we have syntactic symmetry, emphasised by the repetition of [ai], which I have underlined:

Noun phrase	Prep	Noun phrase
the finest	in	the sky

Let us sum up the advertising strategy and linguistic features of the advert. The celebrity of the famous client rubs off on the product, and promises a similar distinction to customers buying the service. The features and awards of the offered service are downplayed and somehow become less important than the fact that a celebrity perceives and snaps them. Mary Cheung comes over very personally to the reader, through the handwritten note, the pronouns and expressions of feeling. She is portrayed ambiguously as part professional business woman, but more basically as a "family woman", slightly out of place in this wine-drinking, job-obsessed male company. The copy engages the reader through the schematically clashing puns, the three styles of print, one of which echoes the picture, and the use of parallel syntactic and rhythmical structures which convey both craft and an emotion of gentle admiration.

Case study 3: Unnecessary words and welcoming in style?

The paradox of the Luxury Collection advertisement (Plate 10) is that it keeps on reiterating that it is telling you nothing new: 'exactly what you'd expect'; 'there are no surprises; but then you knew that'; 'as you know you'll find just what you are looking for'. What is the point of this? It can be, as we noted earlier with phrases like *of course*, a ploy of modesty – the suggestion that the writer is communicating inefficiently by telling the reader things they know already. Alternatively, it may imply that these hotels need no special gimmicks to attract clients, simply the ordinary things a hotel offers but to a high degree of excellence. This second possibility is, however, undermined by the phrase 'special programs'. A third possible intention might be to suggest that most readers would be aware of the quality of ITT Sheraton hotels, and that, if the particular individual reader is not, then they are missing something which every other business traveller knows.

Evidence from the analysis of presuppositions supports the third of these interpretations. Perhaps in keeping with the pretence that the information in the copy is redundant, the existence of the properties making up the hotel group is also assumed rather than stated. The noun phrases which carry an existential presupposition are underlined.

> Allow us to welcome you at any of <u>the 48 properties in 20 countries that comprise The Luxury Collection</u>. Perhaps you'd like to sample <u>our hospitality</u> in Bangkok at <u>the Sheraton Grande Sukhumvit</u>, or Bali at <u>the Sheraton Laguna Nusa Dua</u> or even in Sydney at <u>the Sheraton On the Park</u>.

We don't dispute the existence of these hotels, or even their 'other special programs'. But more disputable and manipulative is the nominalisation of 'we are hospitable' to 'our hospitality'. This smuggles in an existential and possessive presupposition, assuming rather than stating the claim.

As far as the readers are concerned, there are several other presuppositions which position them. They are assumed to have travel professionals – 'your travel professional'. AT&T cardmembers are assumed to exist – 'For <u>AT&T cardmembers</u>' – and it is presupposed that they have calling cards – your AT&T Calling Card'. It is also assumed that they will use them to call home – 'when you call home using AT&T Direct Service'. (Clauses introduced by *when* carry the presupposition that the act has or will at sometime occur, in contrast with *if* which carries the presupposition that it may or may not occur.) These three presuppositions about AT&T cardmembers, their cards and their use of them, would have a different impact on different readers. Those who are not

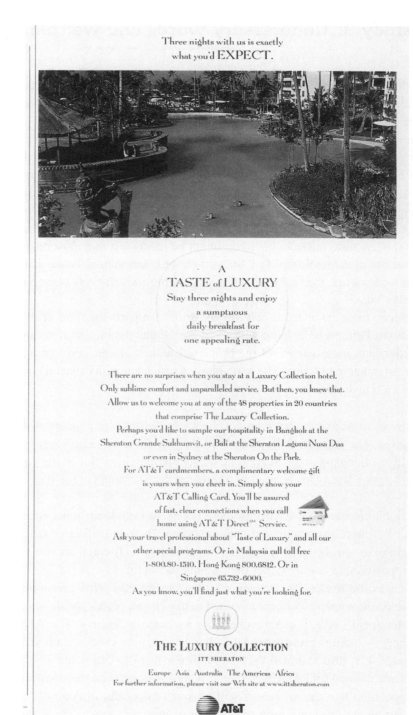

Plate 10 'A taste of luxury' (Advert for Sheraton hotels, *Asiaweek*, June 1997, p. 7)

cardmembers might feel they were losing out, without being explicitly told so, with the result that the advert seems to be indirectly advertising AT&T card-membership, as well as hotels. This interpretation fits nicely with our earlier suggestion – that the motive for insisting that the advert copy contains nothing new is to make readers for whom it is in fact new feel unusually ignorant and deficient. Notice that the *when* presupposition is also used about staying at one of the hotels, constructing it as something inevitable and normal:

There are no surprises when you stay at a Luxury Collection hotel

not

There are no surprises if you stay at a Luxury Collection hotel

The appeal of this advert is to a certain lifestyle, albeit one that can only be 'sampled' or 'tasted' for three days. And one strand of vocabulary underlines this selling point: 'luxury', 'sumptuous', 'sublime comfort', 'unparalleled ser-vice', 'welcome', 'hospitality'. Many of these adjectives, are, as is usual in adverts, quite empty affective ones – certainly 'sublime' and 'unparalleled' as well as 'appealing' and 'special', and possibly 'sumptuous' too.

Another aspect of the vocabulary is **upgrading** or euphemism. Instead of a *group* of hotels we have a 'collection of properties' – *collection* being associ-ated with fashion houses or high-class art, as though the hotels have been care-fully assembled over the years. Then we have the phrase 'travel professional' which sounds smarter than *travel agent* though the two phrases probably refer to the same people. And 'calling card' hints at the aristocratic milieu of previous centuries, Jane Austen's England, for example, when the idle rich spent their afternoons visiting fellow aristocrats and left behind a card if the people visited happened not to be 'at home'.

Some of this euphemistic upgrading suggests a degree of formality and deference, also detected in the relative tentativeness of the Directives at the beginning of the copy. 'Allow us to welcome you at any of the 48 properties in 20 countries that comprise The Luxury Collection', despite the imperative, counts as asking permission, a low degree of obligation, thereby recognising the authority of the client. The next request/offer is phrased 'perhaps you'd like to sample our hospitality in Bangkok at the Sheraton Grande Sukhumvit, or Bali at the Sheraton Laguna Nusa Dua or even in Sydney at the Sheraton On the Park'. Remember that to be tactful in Directives one should build optionality and in-directness. There is plenty of optionality in the 'perhaps' and the recurrent 'or'. Indirectness is achieved by guessing whether the reader wants the act to take place, this want being a condition for the speech-act offer. The indirectness is taken even further by having 'would like' rather than *want*, suggesting that the offer is hypothetical rather than actual (see Leech's hierarchy of tactful forms of request/offer, this volume, p. 152–3).

Synthetic personalisation surfaces in this advert from time to time. There are the explicit promises of hospitality and welcome, as though a friend is staying for the weekend, rather than a paying guest, though the extent of this hospitality is called into question when we learn that the welcome gifts are reserved for AT&T 'cardmembers'(used instead of *cardholders* to indicate a consumer club). More generally, there is the pervasive use of the pronoun *you*, often followed by the contracted *'ll,* and the less common *us* . In tandem with *you* is the imperative mood which recognises the existence of the reader, sometimes bordering on the Tactless, in the technical sense of that word:

Simply **show** your AT&T Calling Card (. . .)
Ask your travel professional about 'Taste of Luxury'
Or in Malaysia **call** toll free
For further information, please **visit** our Web site at www.ittsheraton.com

It's worth thinking a bit about the particular structure of the imperative clause + *and* + imperative clause, which is a stylistic peculiarity of advert copy. The example we have here is 'Stay three nights and enjoy a sumptuous breakfast at one appealing rate'. What exactly does it mean? Is it equivalent to 'if you stay three nights you enjoy a sumptuous breakfast' etc.? Almost, but on top of this promise is a stronger imperative invitation. The problem with this structure is that it is used by unscrupulous copywriters to promise things which will not be automatically delivered. 'Open an account with Standard Chartered Bank and win a Volvo', sounds like a promise, but in fact the Volvo is only a remote possibility.

To sum up our discussion. The existence and quality of the hotel chain, and of the services to AT&T cardmembers are taken for granted both through explicit claims that the reader knows this already, and through various kinds of presupposition. The apparent intention is to give the impression that these qualities are already well known to the vast majority of business travellers, so that if any readers haven't experienced them, they are somehow deficient. So, this is a covert appeal to join the consumer club of guests at these hotels. Especially at the beginning of the copy there is some deference, which meshes well with the personal pronouns, contractions, and the upgraded and euphemistic vocabulary to create a degree of interpersonal politeness, though without quite avoiding some empty fulsomely affective adjectives. Imperatives are also present, however, with the coordinated imperatives structure used to simultaneously persuade and promise.

(1) It was suggested that advertisements for some products, like whisky adverts, can use the appeal of tradition, rather than appeal to newness. By flicking through adverts, try to come up with two lists: one of those products where the appeal of tradition is prominent; and another where old means out of date or old fashioned. Does the same kind of product ever attract both techniques?

(2) Find an advertisement whose copy you think is interesting, and analyse it in the way that I analysed the four advertisements in this unit. To what aspects of human psychology does it appeal?

Project 3: Promotional or publicity material

This project gives you the opportunity to write some publicity (an advert or a brochure) for an organisation to which you belong, or with which you have contact. For example, a religious organisation, a student society, a club, your friend's business, your father's shop, or a school you have connections with, etc. This might be publicity advertising an upcoming event, a general recruitment advert for an organisation, or for goods and services.

(A) Decide what aspects of psychology you are going to appeal to in your advertisement:

- desire and greed;
- power to solve problems;
- acquiring personal qualities;
- choosing an identity;
- desire to be exclusive, distinguished;
- lifestyle change.

(B) Using the material in this chapter and from earlier parts of the coursebook, think carefully about:

- visual aspects of the text which might grab the reader's attention: fonts, colours, white space, and how you can use pictures to make implications (Chapter 1);

- whether you need to make the product or organisation seem powerful (Chapter 2);
- interpersonal aspects of the text, the desired degree of Contact and how you will achieve this (Chapter 3);
- how to get emotion into your text, through choice of adjectives, upgraded vocabulary, or rhythmic (syntactic) repetition (Chapter 3);
- the use of presupposition to avoid making claims that might not stand up, or to introduce knowledge everyone has (Chapter 4), or to position your reader (Chapter 5);
- whether to use metaphors and puns deriving from double schemas (Chapter 4);
- who the ideal reader is that you are targeting, and what speech acts you might use on them (Chapter 5).

(C) After a preliminary draft and discussion with other members of the client organisation, compose your first draft. This should include a commentary on the linguistic and visual features of the text and the psychological strategies you are employing.

Suggestions for further reading

- Judith Williamson's excellent book *Decoding Advertisements*, uses **semiotics**, the theory of signs and their meanings, to illustrate how advertisements are composed and understood both visually and verbally. It takes a Marxist perspective on advertising as a feature of capitalism.
- Guy Cook's *The Discourse of Advertising* is a more linguistic and less ideological exploration, which makes fruitful comparisons between the texture and discourse of adverts and of literary texts. Particularly interesting are the sections on how music and words combine with visuals in TV adverts, the intertextuality of one ad parodying another, the different voices of ads, and the structuring of vocabulary to reinforce stereotypes.
- Gillian Dyer's *Advertising as Communication* provides a fascinating historical perspective on advertising, discusses its current social importance and relates it to communication theory (rather than the narrower and more complex linguistic theory used here).
- Fairclough gives an interesting analysis of the relationship between adverts and lifestyle in *Language and Power*, pp. 191–211.

- The importance and the effects of consumer culture are both dealt with in Lester Faigley's *Fragments of Rationality*, where he discusses the post-modern subject and where he quotes from Baudrillard's *America*, another controversial text.
- No doubt my own ideological perspective on consumerism and advertising has been influenced early in my life by Vance Packard's *The Hidden Per-suaders* and Erich Fromm's *To Have or to Be* – this latter explores the warped psychology of consumerism and is a great antidote to the poisonous brainwashing undercurrents of advertising.

Chapter 8

Fiction and feminism

Aims of this chapter

To explore the origins of modern romantic love in medieval courtly love.

To investigate whether the text of a modern romance maintains aspects of courtly love by analysis of narrative structure, transitivity, politeness, vocabulary and inferencing.

To use the analysis as a feminist critique of the short story.

To give practice in creative writing of a story reflecting or rejecting in its language the ideology of romantic love.

- **8.0 Introduction: courtly and romantic love**
  Describes the features of medieval courtly love as the basis of romantic fiction.

- **8.1 Narrative Structure**
  Analyses the narrative structure of a romantic short story.

- **8.2 Transitivity and ideology**
  Shows the different degrees of power of the main characters and the importance of behavioural gestures and expressions to the "action".

- **8.3 Politeness and verbal processes**
  Demonstrates the change in the characters' relationships from the first to the second scene of the story.

- **8.4 Vocabulary and ideology**
  Shows how the ideology of the story can be detected in names, job titles, and the symbolic lexis for space and verticality.

- **8.5 Metaphor, irony and inferences**
  Exemplifies the importance of conceptual metaphor, irony and other inferential processes in making sense of the story.

- **8.6 Summary: courtly love, romantic fiction and feminist critique**
  Concludes on the sexism in the story and the token ideology of the "new" woman.

- **Project 4: A short love story**
  Writing a short love story for a student magazine, analysing how it adheres to or deviates from the norms of courtly love/romantic fiction.

8.0 Introduction: courtly and romantic love

Back in the twelfth century in the south of France there began an ideology of romantic love. It flourished in the Middle Ages under the name of *courtly love* and reached its climax in plays such as *Romeo and Juliet* or more precisely Wagner's *Tristan and Isolde*. And it still exists, curiously enough, in watered-down form in the romantic fiction much read by young and middle-aged women in the twentieth century.

What kind of ideology of love was this, and how did it position women and men? The important elements of the original courtly love can be gleaned from a typical scenario. A young man, often an adolescent page, would catch sight of a married lady. He would be physically and emotionally overcome by her appearance, and would worship her from a distance, perhaps not making much distinction between her and the Virgin Mary. He would be too timid or overwhelmed to show his love directly, but would go home and fantasise about her, suffering physically, from sleepless nights and loss of appetite, which over the weeks and months would come close to destroying his physical and mental health. When he could bear this no longer, he would finally pluck up the courage to send the lady a letter through an intermediary or confidante, asking for an audience. At the audience he would summon up the will to ask to become her knight, wearing her coat-of-arms or device on his shield. Before agreeing to this she would send him on some "errands" or tasks in order to prove his love and loyalty. This could be something as drastic as a pilgrimage to the Holy Land in a crusade. He would try to prove his chivalry by fighting in battle for her, perhaps acquiring a wound or bringing back to her a blood-stained handkerchief. After the successful completion of these tasks, which supposedly ennobled him, the lady might accede to his wishes; at least to the extent of allowing him to swear loyalty to her and fight for her in tournaments bearing her arms on his shield or wearing her device. After a long period of probation, the page, now ennobled into a knight, might finally be admitted to her sexual favours. End of story.

The main elements which we can extract from this scenario could be enumerated as follows:

- the love was passionate, physical and emotional;
- the love was adulterous;
- the man subjected himself to the will of the lady;
- the lady remained passive, apart from issuing him with orders and tasks;
- the carrying out of these tasks ennobled the man;
- the consummation of his passion was the end of the story and of his ennoblement.

Because this consummation was a hard act to follow, when courtly love developed later into Romantic love, a narrative solution was often the death of the lovers, as in *Romeo and Juliet* where Romeo poisons himself and Juliet kills herself with a dagger. Or, more romantic still, where Tristan tears off his bandages, and Isolde dies of love and grief. The main difference between courtly love and Romantic love is that in the latter the woman too has strong physical and emotional feelings.

One curious development is the domestication of this kind of passion, the attempt to incorporate it within and reconcile it to marriage. If we look back at the key features of courtly love we can see how much of this ideology of passion modern romance fiction has altered and how much it has preserved. The passion is no longer associated with adultery, and in many cases is assumed to be a good basis for marriage. Since marriage, or at least a steady relationship of cohabitation, is the sequel, the first consummation is not really the end of the story, and there is no need for death – the partners live together, if not happily ever after. What remains of courtly love in modern romance? Perhaps, the idea that men are ennobled or behave with more chivalry when in love, but certainly the emphasis on the physical and emotional nature of this passion, the lustful gaze, the throbbing of the heart, weakness at the knees, the obsessional thinking, if not fantasising about the loved one, the sleepless nights, the love-sickness.

Courtly romantic love is a passion beyond the control of the lovers, or at least of the young man. Like a sickness, it is something caught involuntarily, a force similar to gravity which we cannot resist. A "falling" in love. One question is 'how can such a love be compatible with a long-lasting steady relationship?' If we look at the Christian marriage service the couple are asked to promise to love one another. But in courtly love, the passion is not something we have control over; we can fall out of love as quickly as falling into it. Marriage or stable long-lasting relationships demand a different kind of love, where love is an act of the will. In other words, to equate a kind of short-term passionate love which in its origins is adulterous with married love is anomalous if not contradictory. 'The romantic moment, its [romance's] central tenet, cannot be reconciled with its promise of eternity' (MacRobbie 1991: 98). Some have seen the Arthurian figure of Guinevere as being destroyed by just such a contradiction (Pearce 1991: 114–15). And yet such is still the staple ideological position of much contemporary popular romantic fiction. And possibly one of the causes of the high divorce rates in modern society.

As we analyse our case study of romance fiction, let's bear in mind the origins of romantic love in courtly love and see how the story we dissect exemplifies or diverges from them.

Key
A = Action
ABS = Abstract
C = Coda
E = Evaluation
SA = Speech act
R = Resolution
O = Orientation

[Romance
in the air

Lizzie came to New York full of hopes and wishes for the future. Lieutenant Renard was a hard city cop who had settled for a life of routine ... until Lizzie appeared ABS]

[Lizzie [seemed out of place E] in the bustling Manhattan police station, her new winter jacket a spot of sunshiny orange in a field of dark blue uniforms O].

[[Even if her dress hadn't identified her as a tourist her face would have E]. A constant smile played around her mouth, and her translucent blue eyes met every stranger [as if they might become a good friend E] O]

[She shook her short fair hair and looked around for Officer Gregory A].

[He'd taken her statement and then gone away 10 minutes before O]. [She watched the hand of the wall clock ticking away the minutes of her first day in New York A].

['[Ms Engel? E]' Officer Gregory finally summoned her to an open door. ['Lieutenant Renard is ready to see you. E]' SA]

[He nudged her through the door and shut it A].

[Lizzie, more used to the wide prairies of the Midwest O], [thought the small dull office resembled a prison cell E]. [She stopped in front of an untidy desk A] [where the lieutenant was scowling down at a document O].

['[How are you? E]' she asked. SA]

['I'm Lizzie Engel from Iowa –' SA]

['I know.' SA] [He looked up A] [with a confused interest so sharp E] [it made her blush A].

['[You look like Iowa. E]' SA]

[Lizzie frowned. A]

['[I'm complimenting you, E]' he added and smiled. SA]

['Oh,' she smiled, [somehow pleased E]. SA]

[She noticed that his eyes were the colour of the grey tiles on her father's old farmhouse.

Somewhat reluctantly E] [he diverted his gaze from her and back to the document he was reading A].

['I'll just take two minutes to review this and then I'll be with you.' SA]

[She nodded then watched him read until he glanced up and noticed her looking. A]

['[Wouldn't you like to take a seat? E]' he asked. SA]

['No thanks.' SA]

[Her eyes searched the dingy office and found a grill-covered window framing the winter dusk as it descended on the city. She went over and peered between the skyscrapers and just caught sight of the Empire State Building. A] [Though far distant, the landmark tugged at her heart like a very old friend E].

[[For as long as she remembered E] [a model of that building had been on her Mom's dresser, a memory of her honeymoon.

'New York is magic,' she'd always told Lizzie. 'When you're older and get married, I'd like you and your husband to see the Empire State Building, just like your father and I did.'

'So then,' little Lizzie had always concluded the story, 'I'll live happily ever after, just like you, won't I?'

Her Mom had always nodded and chuckled, and Lizzie had been waiting for ages to visit New York City. O] [But just the previous week as she blew out the 28 candles [like a bush fire E] on her birthday cake, she suddenly became weary of waiting for the right man and made up her mind to go to New York without him. A]

[The drive was a long one alone in midwinter E], [but that city – that building – was pulling her on O].

['I can't understand why.' SA]

[Lizzie turned from the view and looked back at the lieutenant. A] [He was holding the stolen-car report Officer Gregory had attempted to make her sign O].

[Lizzie let out a sigh A].

[' [How can I sign a stolen car report, lieutenant, when my car wasn't stolen. E]' SA]

[He spoke [slowly and carefully as if to a child E] SA].

[' [In New York you can't let a stranger sit alone in a car with the engine running and expect to find it there when you get back. He stole it. E]' SA]

[Lizzie puckered her lips. A] [[' He was a kind E] [old man, waiting for his friends to pick him up. O]' SA]

['Yeah, really kind. E]' SA]

[Lizzie chose not to notice [the sarcasm E] A]. [['But his friends were late and he was freezing. O] [He said he'd look after my baggage SA] [as I ran into the cafe to get a coffee . A]' SA]

[He stared at her. A] ['[You left your baggage in a car with a complete stranger? E]' SA]

['[I'm perfectly aware there are people in this city that can't be trusted. But this wasn't one of them. E]' SA]

['[How do you know? E]' the lieutenant inquired. SA]

[Lizzie looked through the window. A] '[[I just know, that's all. E]' SA]

[The lieutanant sighed A] [with frustration E]. ['[If you won't sign this I won't be able to put out an APB E]' SA]

['[He didn't steal the car, E]' she insisted. '[It's missing E].' SA]

[He closed his lips together. A]

['[Pets go missing and persons go missing, Miss Engel, but there are no missing cars. They get stolen. E]' SA]

[Lizzie looked back at his serious face, [asking herself if it was the city or the job that had etched that line between his dark straight eyebrows, as if he had spent too long looking at things too close. E] A]

['[Don't you trust anybody, lieutenant? Surely there's someone. E]' SA]

['[My mother, E]' he grunted softly. '[Occasionally]' SA]

[Lizzie smiled a bit, and when he looked up and noticed, he smiled too, and the anxious line between his brows went away. A]

['Look, Ms. Engel, [I really want to assist you. But I can't do a thing if you don't sign this. E]' SA]

[Lizzie shrugged her shoulders then started to zip up her jacket. A] '[[I apologise for taking up so much of your time today, Lieutenant Renard. E]' SA]

[His eyes flickered. A] ['[That's it? Where are you off to? E]' SA]

[She smiled] ['The Empire State Building'. SA]

['[But how about your car, your baggage? How will you get home? E]' SA]

[She chuckled and stopped with her hand on the doorknob. A]

['I've got a whole week to worry about that. [I'm certain my car will turn up by then. E]' SA] [She looked back at him and smiled. A]

[Lieutenant Renard stared after her for a long moment, then grabbed the phone from its rest. A] ['Gregory, put an MCR on the Iowa plate in the computer ... [you don't know what an MCR is? E] A missing car report.' SA]

[It was chilly on the observation platform, but it was nine o'clock when Lizzie finally thought of looking at her watch O] [She had to drag her eyes away from the amazing view. It is the most magic place in the world, she felt, remembering her Mom's words. E]

[She pictured her mother and her father standing in the same place, sharing the amazement that would live with them in their future years. E] [She walked backwards towards the door to the lifts – right into the person coming out. A]

['Oh, sorry,' SA] [she tottered but felt strong hands steady her by the arms, then she turned her head and looked into Lieutenant Renard's eyes. A] [He seemed changed now E], [in a long overcoat and the wind tousling his hair O].

['Hi, Lieutenant.' SA]

['[We found your car. A]' SA]

['[Is that so? E]' SA]

[He scowled down at the concrete under his feet. A]

['It so happens it was in the car park at another district station most of the day.' SA]

['I see,' Lizzie nodded, her grin broadening. SA]

['[It appears you were parked on a double yellow line E], [and a officer going by asked your kind old man to drive off or be booked ... A]' SA]

[He lifted his eyes, A] [and Lizzie noticed [they weren't precisely the colour of those grey tiles on the farmhouse after all. They were a more intense blue. E] A] ['He went on driving round the block, hoping you would come out, and [I expect you just missed each other. E]' SA]

['[It was very nice of you to come up here to tell me. E]' SA]

['[It's nothing. E]' SA]

[He moved toward the door and then turned back. A] ['[I expect you've had dinner already? E]' SA]

[Lizzie grinned. A] ['[No, I'm famished. E]' SA]

[His whole countenance lightened. A]['There's [a good E] place just round the corner.' SA]

[He gazed at the panorama, his eyes mirroring the myriad lights below. A]

['[Hey, isn't that something?, E]' he whispered. SA]

[Lizzie gazed in the same direction. A] ['[It's wonderful isn't it? E]' SA]

[He nodded, then they both leaned on the rail. A]

['[I'm sorry to leave, E] she sighed. '[Is it this beautiful every time you see it? E]' SA]

[' [I wouldn't know, E]' he said. '[It's my first time. E]' SA]

['[First time? E]' she whispered. SA]

'[[Stupid, isn't it? E] [I've been in this city for years O], and it took a woman from Iowa to get me up here. CODA]' SA]

[Lizzie felt him turn to her, with eyes soft on her face, A] [and from deep inside she sensed a small fire kindling into life, something magic, something romantic R].

(A rewritten version of 'Magic in the air', by P. J. Platz, *Woman's World*, 14 January 1997 pp. 40–1 [Permission to use the original was refused.])

In describing the surface features of this short story we'll take a top-down approach, looking first at the overall narrative structure, considering the importance of Evaluation, the salient narrative clauses, and then quantitatively analysing the patterns of transitivity. We'll go on to a more interpersonal perspective and examine the patterns of mood/modality, speech acts (Verbal processes) and politeness which help us to discover in some technical detail how the main characters and their changing relationship is constructed. Finally, we analyse the oppositions established in the lexis of the story, which lead us into the Pragmatics of inference and symbolic interpretation.

8.1 Narrative structure

I have labelled the whole story using basically the categories provided by Labov. However, instead of simply using the rather general label 'Complicating Action' we can make a distinction between *actions* on the one hand, which, strictly speaking, are what constitute the narrative clauses, and *speech acts* on the other. This story in particular, and romance fiction in general, is heavily dependent on dialogue. And the "action" of the story is as much a matter of the dialogic tensions created by the cynicism of Renard and the innocent trust of Lizzie and how they are resolved, as it is about material doings.

The first problem we encounter in this analysis is that we may wish to identify two or even three narratives in this story. There is the narrative of how Lizzie used to talk to her mother when she was younger; the narrative concerning the old man and how Lizzie picked him up; and the main narrative that begins when Lizzie is summoned into Renard's office. The first of these "narrtives" can be discounted, on the grammatical evidence. The clauses of this passage, which begins 'For as long as she remembered' and ends 'to visit New York' are not in straightforward past or present tense, as are the typical narrative clauses, but are in **past perfect** (or past in past), using the **auxiliary verb** *had*. In addition, the adverb *always* recurs, so that these are habituative actions and speech acts rather than single ones forming a discrete sequence. For this reason I label this whole passage 'Orientation', as it provides background to the action of the main narrative.

The clauses involving the old man, do, however, constitute part of the main narrative, although they are narrated to us as part of the dialogue, disturbing the chronology of the story. The sentence which tells of Lizzie blowing out her candles and deciding to go to New York is also a flashback. On my reading, it constitutes the first sentence of the Complicating Action, and is significant in terms of romances since, in this genre, the city is where things really happen (MacRobbie 1991: 100).

Narrative theorists have made an important distinction between the narrative in its chronological sequence, which is called the *story*; and the actual way these chronological events are presented in the text, which is called the *plot*. If we reconstitute the story from the plot, we end up with the following narrative clauses in their chronological order.

(1) But just the previous week as she blew out the 28 candles on her birthday cake, she suddenly became weary of waiting for the right man

(2) and made up her mind to go to New York without him.

(3) {He [the old man] said he'd look after my baggage

(4) as I ran into the cafe to get a coffee.

(5) (You) she left (your) her baggage in a car with a complete stranger

(6) an officer going by told (your) her kind old man/complete stranger to drive off or be booked ...

(7) and ... (you) Lizzie and the old man just missed each other.

(8) (He) Officer Gregory (had taken) took her statement

(9) Officer Gregory (had) tried to make her sign the stolen-car report

(10) and then (had) gone away 10 minutes before}

(11) She shook her short fair hair

(12) and looked around for Officer Gregory

(13) She watched the hand of the wall clock ticking away the minutes of her first day in New York.

(14) He [Officer Gregory] nudged her through the door

(15) and shut it

(16) She stopped in front of an untidy desk where the lieutenant was scowling down at a document

(17) He looked up

(18) it [the confused interest] made her blush

(19) Lizzie frowned

(20) She nodded then watched him read

(21) until he glanced up

(22) and noticed her looking.

(23) Her eyes searched the dingy office

(24) and found a grill-covered window framing the winter dusk

(25) as it descended on the city.

(26) She went over and peered between the skyscrapers

(27) and just caught sight of the Empire State Building.

(28) Though far distant, the landmark tugged at her heart.

(29) Lizzie turned from the view

(30) and looked back at the lieutenant.

(31) Lizzie let out a sigh.

(32) Lizzie puckered her lips.

(33) Lizzie chose not to notice the sarcasm

(34) He stared at her.

(35) Lizzie looked through the window.

(36) The lieutenant sighed with frustration.

(37) He closed his lips together.

(38) Lizzie looked back at his serious face,

(39) Lizzie smiled a bit,

(40) and when he looked up

(41) and saw that,

(42) he smiled too,

(43) and the anxious line between his brows went away.

(44) Lizzie shrugged her shoulders

(45) then started to zip up her jacket.

(46) His eyes flickered.

(47) She smiled.

(48) She chuckled

(49) and stopped with her hand on the doorknob.

(50) She looked back at him

(51) and smiled.

(52) Lieutenant Renard stared after her for a long moment,

(53) then grabbed the phone from its rest.

(54) 'We found your car'.

(55) She walked backwards towards the door to the lifts – right into the person coming out.

(56) She tottered

(57) and felt strong hands steady her by the arms,

(58) then she turned her head

(59) and looked into Lieutenant Renard's eyes.

(60) He scowled down at the concrete under his feet.

(61) He lifted his eyes,

(62) He moved toward the door

(63) and then turned back.

(64) Lizzie grinned.

(65) His whole countenance lightened.

(66) He gazed at the panorama, his eyes mirroring the myriad lights below.

(67) Lizzie gazed in the same direction.

(68) He nodded,

(69) then they both leaned on the rail.

(70) Lizzie sense him turning toward her, with eyes soft on her face,

(71) and from deep inside she sensed a small fire kindling into life, something magic, something romantic

However, not all these narrative clauses have equal importance for the story and the plot. Probably the most crucial ones are (53), (57), (69) and (71). Clause (53) indicates Renard's sudden resolve to accede to Lizzie's unwavering insistence that the car be listed as missing rather than stolen, a kind of agreeing to undertake the courtly lover's task. Incidentally, we note the Upgrading of the verb here, 'grabbed' rather than *took*, a distinctive mark of romance and action fiction (Nash 1990: 48–51). Clause (57) represents the only physical contact between them. Symbolically, of course, he saves her from falling, physically, while she saves him emotionally from the pit of mistrust and cynicism into which he has already fallen. The gender roles are quite clear here, with the man showing physical strength and the woman emotional fortitude.

Another clause which is noticeable is (69), because, exceptionally, it has Lizzie and Renard as joint Subjects. The only other sentences in which there are joint subjects, significantly enough, feature her hypothetical husband, and Lizzie's mother and father:

> I'd like you and your husband to see the Empire State Building, just like <u>your father and I</u> did.

> She pictured <u>her mother and her father</u> standing in the same place, sharing the amazement that would live with them in their future years.

We infer, I suppose, that at the end of the story the same amazement, transcending time and generation, stays with Lizzie and Renard in their future. The last narrative clause has to be important as it constitutes the Resolution. Once she has this warm feeling of some kind, love or passion, we know the solution to being an unmarried 28-year-old woman is at hand.

I've isolated these few clauses, but for a more thorough-going quantitative analysis we ought to look at the patterns of transitivity in the story.

8.2 Transitivity and ideology

To analyse the transitivity we can perform a thorough analysis of the process types represented. There are 98 clauses, all in Active voice, with Lizzie as Subject (Actor, Experiencer, Token, Sayer) and there are 54 for Renard. This difference in numbers reflects the reader's focus of attention on Lizzie, rather than Renard. Given the readership of the magazine, female, American, conservative, aged 30 to 50, Lizzie must be the character the ideal reader is asked to identify with.

Close inspection reveals some more interesting patterns. Material processes, we remember, may either have an Affected as Object, traditionally called transitive clauses, or may have no Object, in which case they are intransitive. Of the clauses where Renard is Actor, 70 per cent are transitive, but when Lizzie is Actor only 40 per cent are transitive. The significance is obviously that Renard comes across as more powerful: his actions impinge on the environment and people more regularly than Lizzie's (see Wareing 1994: 122–6).

Let's look at Lizzie as Actor clauses first. If we discount the clauses in which she acts on herself and her clothing, we are left with only three clauses in which another Thing or Person (underlined) is actually Affected:

as she blew out the 28 candles like a bush fire on her birthday cake

as I ran into the cafe to get a coffee.

and it took a woman from Iowa to **get** me up here.

The most significant of these clauses is the last one. For it is a crucial point of the story that Lizzie exerts sufficient influence on a suspicious scowling Renard to take him out of his constricted and poky office, where he spends his days short-sightedly poring over documents, up the Empire State Building for the first time to develop a smiling and trusting appreciation of the extensive views. But this is not really a material act of Lizzie's so much as a spiritual influence. The *get* here is not as literal as in the previous case of getting coffee.

We can analyse the transitive Material process clauses with Renard as Actor in exactly the same way. We can ignore the clauses in which Renard acts on himself, and those clauses which describe him reading documents. But with these set aside, we still have a number of significant clauses which show effective actions which precipitate the narrative outcome. First, he has the knowledge of his power to do things for Lizzie, to help her, if only she will cooperate:

I really want to assist you. But I can't do a thing if you don't sign this ...

If you won't sign this I won't be able to put out an APB

Then there is the crucial decisive action which leads to the order to put out a missing car report (MCR):

then [Lieutenant Renard] **grabbed** the phone from its rest.

This leads to the police force in which he is an officer recovering her vehicle, perhaps a debased version of the knightly errand on which the courtly lady sends her admirer:

We **found** your car.

The need to tell her this news takes him up the Empire State Building, and here the most important symbolic Material process action takes place.

She tottered but felt strong hands **steady** her by the arms

In contrast with the woman from Iowa, 'getting him up here', this steadying is Material, but in so far as it indicates his power over Lizzie, the Affected, the two clauses resemble each other.

The inequality in material power is mirrored when we look at how frequently Lizzie is constructed as an Affected of Material processes and a Receiver of Verbal processes. The general pattern seems to be one in which Lizzie is controlled by how the Empire State Building influences her ('that building – was pulling her on', 'the landmark **tugged** at her heart'), by what her mother and men say to her ('"New York is magic," she'd always **told** Lizzie', 'Officer Gregory finally **summoned** her'), and what men do to her ('[Officer Gregory] **nudged** her through the door', 'I really want **to assist** you', 'she tottered but felt strong hands **steady** her by the arms'). Renard is physically controlled by other people to a lesser extent, though clearly what Lizzie says to him has a considerable effect on his attitude. It is quite an achievement to 'get [him] up here'.

Analysis shows just how few of the apparent Material process clauses actually convey actions in which an Actor brings about a physical change to an Affected. Rather, in this kind of story, the emphasis is on the inner life of thought and feeling and the body language which expresses it. Although nothing much happens materially, a sense of business is conveyed by the characters' frequent and intense reactions and responses to the other characters' utterances.

Indeed, what strikes one immediately about this story and others within this romantic sub-genre is the extent to which **behavioural processes**, that is facial expressions, looks and glances, constitute the action (see Nash 1990: 34–5, MacRobbie 1991: 127, 171). For example, look back at the narrative clauses (17)–(23), (38)–(43), and (50)–(52). Lizzie's smiles, laughs or grins are mentioned eight times in the course of the story, and she only frowns once. Renard smiles twice, and scowls twice. In part the story is about her smile infecting him,

Lizzie **smiled** a bit, and when he looked up and noticed he **smiled** too

In the scene on the ESB his dark scowls are lightened under the influence of her smiles and grins.

Of course, these facial expressions have to be perceived by the characters so there are many processes of looking. Lizzie has fifteen, and Renard has nine. What is interesting is the nature of the Experience they sense or towards which they direct their gaze. Occasionally, Lizzie looks out of the window or peers through the skyscrapers at the Empire State Building, but on the whole her gaze is directed towards the Lieutenant (20), (22), (30), (38), (50), (59), (67). As in courtly love, the visual sense, the lust of the eyes, is crucial to the onset of romantic feeling. However, having the man as the focus of the woman's attention is a reversal of the courtly love situation, where it is the young man's gaze which is directed towards the lady.

Renard, on the other hand, seldom intentionally looks at her specifically, and when he does it is with stares of amazement (34), (52). Only at the end is he shown 'with eyes soft on her face'. The transformation which takes place in his visual perception is obvious enough. A man in his cramped prison cell of an office, mean minded and short-sighted, ends up redeemed:

He **gazed** at the panorama, his eyes **mirroring** the myriad lights below.

8.3 Politeness and verbal processes

One way in which stories such as this strive for, and, perhaps, achieve effect is through Upgrading – the avoidance of the common core or ordinary vocabulary in favour of the more specific or glamorous word. This is nowhere more evident than in the choice of verbs for the reporting clauses that indicate the Sayer. We have only two occurrences of common verbs of saying: *told* and *said*. The author prefers something more specific: 'called', 'inquired', 'added', 'asked', 'insisted', 'grunted softly', 'whispered', 'sighed'. Along with these are the numerous facial expressions and gestures, the nods, the frowns, the shrugs. The Upgrading of Verbal process verbs and these almost obligatory responses to the other character's utterances achieve two effects. First, as we pointed out, in the absence of real material action they create a sense of busy activity. But, second, they label speech acts for us and convey the propositional attitude of the speaker.

They compensate for the inability of writing to represent directly intonation and voice quality, the normal ways of conveying propositional attitude in speech.

Propositional attitude is one aspect of the narrative element (known as) Evaluation. Look back at my labelling of elements of narrative structure, and note how loaded down this short story is with Evaluation, either in the strict Labov sense, anything which interrupts the narrative flow (the linguistic symptoms of which were listed in Chapter 1), or in the narrower sense of characters expressing their attitudes. Most of the dialogue is evaluation in one or both senses.

In fact, the real psychological plot of this piece hinges on the evaluation of the old man, and of whether he stole Lizzie's car. So although Lizzie is represented as physically weaker, less of an effective Actor than Renard, she wins psychologically. This emerges from the speech-act categories into which the characters' utterances fall.

Table 8.1 Speech-act types in 'Romance in the air' (adapted short story)

Speech act	Expression
(1) Summons	'Ms Engel?' Officer Gregory summoned her to an open door
(2) T Request (I)	'Lieutenant Renard is ready to see you.'
(3) P Greet	'How are you?' she asked.
(4) P Introduce	'I'm Lizzie Engel from Iowa –'
(5) IP Dismiss	'I know.'
(6) AP Compliment (I)	'You look like Iowa.'
(7) Performative	'I'm complimenting you,' he added and smiled.
(8) Accept	'Oh,' she smiled, somehow pleased.
(9) P Excuse	'I'll just take two minutes to review this and then I'll be with you'
(10) T Offer	'Wouldn't you like to take a seat? ' he asked.
(11) IP Decline	'No thanks.'
(12) Seek clarification	'I can't understand why.'
(13) DG Refuse/account	'I can't sign a stolen-car report, lieutenant because my car was not stolen'
(14) DP Advise/criticise	'In New York you don't let a stranger sit alone in a car with the engine running and expect to find it there when you get back'
(15) DP Assert/Accuse	'He stole it'
(16) DG Defend	'He was a kind old man, waiting for his friends to pick him up.'
(17) DG (Dis)Agree (I)	'Yeah, really kind.'
(18) Account/justify	'But his friends were late and he was freezing. He said he'd look after my baggage as I ran into the cafe to get a coffee.'
(19) Justify	
(20) DP/Criticise/wonder	'You left your baggage in a car with a complete stranger?'
(21) AG Admit	'I'm perfectly aware there are people in this city that can't be trusted.'
(22) DG Disagree	'But this wasn't one of them'
(23) DP Disparage	'How do you know?' the lieutenant inquired.
(24) DG Insist	'I just know, that's all.'
(25) P Explain	'If you won't sign this I won't be able to put out an APB'
(26) DG Disagree	'He didn't steal the car,' she insisted.
(27) State	'It's missing.'
(28) DG Disagree	'Pets go missing and persons go missing, Ms Engel, but there are no missing cars. They get stolen.'

(29)	DP Accuse (I)	'Don't you trust anybody, lieutenant? Surely there's someone.'
(30)	Answer	'My mother,' he grunted softly. 'Occasionally.'
(31)	S Sympathise	'Look, Ms. Engel, I really want to assist you.
(32)	P Account/request (I)	But I can't do a thing if you don't sign this.'
(33)	P Apologise	'I apologise for taking up so much of your time today, Lieutenant Renard.'
(34)	Question/Surprise	'That's it?
(35)	Question	Where are you off to?'
(36)	Answer	She smiled. 'The Empire State Building'.
(37)	S Advise/ remonstrate	'But how about your car, your baggage? How are you going to get home?'
(38)	IP Decline	'I've got a whole week to worry about that.
(39)	Predict	I'm certain my car will turn up by then.'
(40)	TL Command	'Gregory, put an MCR on the Iowa plate in the computer …
(41)	IP Reprimand	you don't know what an MCR is?
(42)	Inform	A missing car report.'
(43)	P Apologise	'Oh, sorry,'
(44)	P Greet	'Hi, Lieutenant.'
(45)	AG Inform/agree	'We found your car.'
(46)	IP Acknowledge	'Is that so?'
(47)	AG Inform	'It so happens it was in the car park at another district station most of the day.'
(48)	IP Gloat (I)	'I see,' Lizzie nodded, her grin broadening
(49)	Inform/concede (I)	'It appears you were parked on a double yellow line and a officer going by asked your kind old man to drive off or be booked …
(50)	Inform	he went on driving round the block, hoping you would come out, and I suppose you just missed each other'
(51)	P Appreciate	'It was very nice of you to come up here to tell me. '
(52)	T Minimise	'It's nothing.'
(53)	T Pre-offer	'I expect you've had dinner already?'
(54)	P Accept (1)	Katie grinned. 'No, I'm famished.'
(55)	P Offer	'There's a good place just around the corner.'
(56)	Appreciate	'Hey, isn't that something,' he wispered.
(57)	Affirm	'It's wonderful isn't it?'
(58)	AG Agree	He nodded.
(59)	Complain	'I'm sorry to leave,' she sighed.
(60)	Question/presuppose	'Is it this beautiful every time you see it?'
(61)	Concede ignorance	'I wouldn't know,' he said.
(62)	Disallow presupposition	'It's my first time.'
(63)	Question	'First time?' she whispered.
(64)	M Self-criticise	'Stupid isn't it?
(65)	Inform	I've lived in this city for years,
(66)	AP Appreciate	and it took a woman from Iowa to get me up here.'

Key:

P = politeness	DP = disapprobation	IP = impoliteness
AP = approbation	T = tact	M = modesty
TL = tactlessness	S = sympathy	DG= disagreement
(I) = indirect	AG = agreement	

The most interesting way in which to approach the psychological movement of this narrative and the changing relationship is in terms of politeness, which, of course, includes agreement and disagreement over the old man's honesty or whether the car was stolen. With this in mind, we can attempt to label the speech acts, and to allocate letter codes for those speech acts which appear to have some obvious consequences for politeness or lack of it. The letters *P* and *IP* are general labels, but all the other letters refer to the maxims of Leech's Politeness Principle: agreement, approbation, modesty, sympathy and tact, the latter achieved by building indirectness and optionality into the message (see p. 152–3).

General politeness (P) covers speech acts that are inherently polite: greetings, introductions, apologies, accounts/excuses for non-compliance. General impoliteness (IP) covers dispreferred seconds. For example, we would expect Lizzie's initial greeting and self-introduction (3), (4) to be reciprocated and acknowledged. Instead, Renard seems to interpret Lizzie's introduction as an attempt to inform him, but, rather than acknowledging this information, impolitely indicates he has it already (5). Lizzie seems to get her revenge a little later when his offer of a seat, showing Tact, is declined rather than accepted (11). And later still she declines his indirect advice to make plans for getting home.

The atmosphere when they first meet in Renard's office is ambiguous in terms of politeness. Added to the dispreferred seconds we have a number of disagreements over whether the car was stolen or not (22), (28); implied disagreements about whether she should make plans for getting home rather than go off to the Empire State Building (37); several speech acts which indirectly insinuate disapproval of Lizzie's behaviour in leaving her car unattended with the old man (14), (20), and her reciprocal criticism of Renard for having lost trust in humanity. But on the polite side we have an example of approbation, a compliment by Renard (6), albeit he has to label it for us before Lizzie or we recognise it; direct and indirect expressions of sympathy for Lizzie, with accounts/explanations of why he cannot help her (31), (32) and (25); and an apology by Lizzie for having wasted his time (though this may be ironic given her clock-watching and impatience to get to the Empire State Building).

Their second meeting is altogether different. Lizzie persists with her general politeness with an initial apology and greeting (43), (44), and thanks/compliment later on (51), which Renard acknowledges (52), though for a hint of impoliteness we might interpret Lizzie's 'Is that so?' and 'I see!' as indirect gloatings over proving him wrong. Renard still appears a little gauche and slightly ungracious in his conceding that Lizzie was right (49) (his scowl indicates this). But at the end he shows that he can swallow his pride and be modestly self-critical (64). He is very polite and shows Tact in offering to take her to eat at a restaurant – in technical terms he makes a pre-offer/request 'I expect you've had dinner already', followed by an indirect offer/request 'there's a good place just round the corner'. The tactfulness is partly conveyed by the indirectness, but especially by loading the pre-offer/request so that refusing is easy for her, by assuming she has had dinner already. Unlike the dispreferred second of declining the offer of a seat in their first meeting, Lizzie accepts the offer of food with alacrity and appetite (54). But perhaps most important, besides the implied agreement or concession that Lizzie had been right in her evaluation of the old man, is their symbolic agreement in appreciating the view (58); and his (indirect) approbation of her having got him up there so that he could enjoy it (66). The sense that she has made him a better man with a healthier, more trusting attitude comes over very strongly in this last speech act of his, and reminds us of the ennobling function in courtly love fictions.

We have seen how the patterns of polite and impolite behaviour change between the first and second meeting, and it is interesting to explore whether similar changes can be observed in the patterns of mood, questions and modals. Clauses in imperative mood show an obvious pattern. Three clear imperatives, perhaps four, come from the lips of Renard during the meeting in his office, underlining his authoritative work status ((9), (31), (40), (?14)). In this second meeting there are no imperatives from Renard.

As for interrogatives and questions, Renard has eight in the first meeting. The first four of these ((10), (23), (20), (41)) are hardly questions at all – and are labelled offer, disparagement, indirect criticism and reprimand. Genuine questions are concentrated towards the end of the first encounter. Though intrusive and persistent, they do show a genuine concern for Lizzie's welfare ((34), (35), (37)). By contrast, in the second encounter Renard only produces two questions, a tag-question (64), and a very indirect pre-offer/request (53). When we look at Lizzie's questions the pattern is reversed. She has more interrogatives and asks more questions in the second encounter ((46), (57), (60), (63)).

The significance of this pattern can be found partly in their roles and subject positions: a policeman is entitled, even expected, to ask questions of a member of the public who has come for help. From another point of view, the asking of questions intrudes on **negative face**, the right to remain undisturbed, and can be interpreted in terms of dominance as well as curiosity. Renard is less dominant in the second encounter, and Lizzie clearly more, with the confidence to ask questions, where before she had only managed to pick up clues from his facial expressions. Notice that her questions are largely centred on his experience of the Empire State Building and his reaction to the view. We could infer that she wants to know whether he has passed the test; does he share her excitement? It was this shared excitement that guaranteed lifelong happiness to her parents, and promises to do the same for her and Renard.

On the evidence of modals, and modal devices like verbs of knowing and perception, the rather dogmatic Renard of the first interview becomes the relatively diffident Renard of the second encounter. He is dogmatic in his generalisation 'pets go missing and persons go missing, Miss Engel, but there are no missing cars', as certain as he can be about his own future behaviour '"and then I'll be with you"'. But he is uncertain about who can be trusted, only 'occasionally' trusting his mother, and no one else (30).

But, by the time of the second encounter, having had his earlier cynical generalisation proved wrong, he is much more diffident, using modals of cognition, 'appears' and 'expect', partly because he does not wish to be forced to admit how right Lizzie had been (49), (50). Partly too, in this non-institutional setting, he may feel shy and vulnerable about inviting a woman out to dinner, though perhaps not as self-consciously vulnerable as a love-sick page trying to summon up the courage to meet his lady.

'I expect you've had dinner already?'

In the interview Lizzie can be just as certain as Renard. She is sure about the need for trust, 'Surely there's someone', her opinions of the old man, 'I'm perfectly aware ...', and the fate of her car, conveyed through the dogmatic 'I'm certain my car will turn up by then'. All these employ modal devices of high probability. The interesting contrast is the generality or universality of the claims made by Renard 'there are no missing cars', with the less than universal claims made by Lizzie 'there are people [i.e. some people] in this city that can't be trusted'. In this feminine focus on particular experience rather than a masculine striving after generalisations, she relies, stereotypically, on intuition rather than reason: 'I just know, that's all'.

In the Empire State Building (ESB) encounter, on the other hand, there is little to say about Lizzie's use of modality of possibility since the only statements she makes are about her perceptions, feelings and appetites ((51), (54), (57), (59)) about which she has no doubts. Perhaps this emphasis on inner feelings, longings and sense impressions, along with the not so enigmatic last sentence of the story, help to fit her neatly into the stereotype of the emotional female.

Let us sum up the changes in politeness and impoliteness, mood and modality between the first interview and the second encounter. In the first interview we have a rather dogmatic, authoritarian Lieutenant Renard, with his subject position institutionally assured, confident in his cynicism and disapproval, unwilling to accept Lizzie's opinions, and a little gauche in his compliments and social relations, though concerned enough about her welfare to exercise his right to ask questions. In the second encounter he is a more diffident human, grudgingly conceding his mistakes, and sharing her viewpoint, tactfully or hesitatingly offering to satisfy her appetite, as a way of reconstituting trust. Lizzie changes from a rather polite but assertive and critical young woman, insisting on her intuitive personal experience as the touchstone of judgement, and refusing offers, into the sensitive, gently inquisitive and acquiescent feminine lover.

3.4 Vocabulary and ideology

If we look at the vocabulary in this text we may notice or infer a number of ideologically marked terms, categorisations and oppositions:

> She suddenly became weary of waiting for <u>the right man</u> and made up her mind to go to New York without him.

The phrase 'the right man' betrays a certain view of relationships: everyone has a specific potential partner who is made for them and the only problem is finding this Mr Right or Ms Right. It follows from this that if a relationship hasn't worked, it is because the other member wasn't the ideal partner, who is waiting somewhere else, and we just have to shop around until we find them. The notion of the right person is incompatible with the idea that we should stick with less than ideal relationships and through mental discipline and emotional effort make that relationship work. We might think that by going to New York Lizzie actually distances herself from this ideology, but in fact by the end of the story we are reasonably sure that she has found her Mr Right – 'the small fire flickering to life, something magic, something romantic' is a good enough guarantee.

The way people are named in this story is also significant. The narrator consistently calls the female character 'Lizzie'. This is not only a first name, but also a diminutive form of the name, suggesting a young child. Women's youth is crucial to their childbearing function, and if they accept this as their main role in life then they can only be flattered to be addressed as girls. It is perhaps not so surprising that Lieutenant Renard 'spoke slowly and carefully as if to a child', since the narrator refers to her as if she were one. We might infer that her child-like representation integrates with the theme of innocence and trust versus mistrust and cynicism. In contrast with the narrator, Renard is quite formal and correct in the way he addresses her, either as Miss Engel or Ms Engel. Since the 'Miss Engel' is inserted into one of his most dogmatic statements 'pets go missing and persons go missing, Miss Engel, but there are no missing cars' it might indicate a particularly overbearing or patriarchal attitude at this point of the dialogue. Alternatively, the inconsistency might suggest the author wishes to hedge her bets: she cannot be sure whether her readers dismiss the use of *Ms* as an affectation of feminism or whether they are likely to welcome the abandoning of the practice of labelling women according to their marital status.

By contrast, the male character is called by the narrator 'Lieutenant Renard', and by Lizzie 'lieutenant'. Use of the surname gives him an air of maturity, and the rank or title 'lieutenant' identifies him by his job and status. We never hear if Lizzie has a job, and, even if she has, she is at present a (sex?)

tourist, but Renard's job seems to define him. He has a relatively high rank and all the business of interaction with his inferior Officer Gregory, and his rather petulant tone in explaining what an MCR is, construct this man with a 'serious face' as a person of power and authority. The critical discourse literature points out that while men are typically defined by job or profession, women are more often placed socially in terms of their family relationships as daughters, wives and mothers, and this story provides a clear example (Fowler 1991: 102).

The vocabulary describing Lizzie and Renard is significant. Lizzie with her fair hair and orange jacket is associated with lighter and brighter colours. By contrast, the police in their dingy office wear dark-blue uniforms. Much is made of the colour of their eyes. Hers are 'translucent blue'. To start with Lizzie perceives his as grey like the grey tiles on her father's farmhouse, but later, up the ESB, realises they are a deep blue. Renard's brows too are dark until she agrees to their dinner date when 'His whole countenance lightened'. I would imagine that the target readership of this magazine is largely white. Perhaps the bright/white v. dark/dingy vocabulary reinforces the racist overtones of white = good, black = evil.

If we look carefully at the patterns of vocabulary we notice that the story explicitly sets up oppositions between constricted and open spaces, and less explicitly between downwards and upwards orientation. The key section runs as follows:

> He nudged her through the door and shut it.
> Lizzie, more used to the **wide open spaces** of the mid-west, thought the **small dull office** resembled a prison **cell**. She stopped in front of an untidy desk where the lieutenant was scowling down at a document.

Lizzie manages to find a window which gives her a view out of this constriction and with difficulty, through the grill, catches a glimpse of the Empire State Building. Renard, however, as we first encounter him, is habituated to small distances, 'as if he had spent too long looking at things too close'.

Many of the Material processes associated with Lizzie are to do with movement through space, whether the 'long drive' from Iowa to 'go to' or 'visit' New York, or running into the cafe to get coffee, or simply walking across the room. She pointedly refuses to sit down. By contrast the Material process verbs associated with the more sedentary Renard are often to do with reading: 'I'll just take two minutes to **review** this', 'the document he was **reading**'.

Because he spends much of the early part of the story reading Renard's gaze is generally directed downwards, and it is Lizzie's presence and behaviour which forces him to redirect his gaze upwards.

He looked **up** with a confused interest

Lizzie smiled a bit, and when he looked **up** and noticed he smiled too

The visit up to the observation floor of the Empire State Building with its 'amazing view' is a vertical movement of larger physical and symbolic scope. However nice he was 'to come **up** here to tell me', when he first arrived, Renard was reluctant to admit his mistaken suspicions of the old man who Lizzie had helped, and 'scowled **down** at the concrete under his feet'. It was a little later before he '**lifted** his eyes'. Finally, of course, 'he gazed at the panorama, his eyes mirroring the myriad lights below'. He is redeemed from his suspicious short-sightedness by Lizzie – 'it took a woman from Iowa to get me **up** here'.

The Empire State Building represents both distance, in terms of the space opposition, and height, in terms of the up-down orientation. It is the influence which pulls Lizzie to New York, and the symbol of Renard's renewed faith in humanity, as well as being a subliminal phallic symbol. The theme of lost faith or lost trust is made explicit enough in the exchange:

'Don't you trust anybody, lieutenant? Surely there's someone.'

'My mother,' he grunted softly. 'Occasionally.'

And it is also evidenced in the use of the word 'stranger'. Lizzie treats all strangers as potential friends: 'her translucent blue eyes met every stranger as if they might be her next friend'. Renard expostulates with her about her trusting attitude to strangers:

'You left you baggage in a car with a complete stranger?'

The Empire State Building functions as a phallic symbol in the context of Lizzie's need to find a sexual partner. (Note that its model sat permanently on her parents' dressing table!) Her problem is to find him before she gets too old, presumably for childbearing. The received wisdom seems to be that once past thirty years old the process of childbirth becomes relatively less safe, so marriage at twenty-eight would still give her time to have the ideal two children before she is out of her twenties. But she will have to be quick about it, and cannot wait any longer for the right man, and so succumbs to the tugging of the building. She has no time to waste in New York, and impatiently 'watched the wall clock ticking away the minutes of this first day in the city'. The issue of her missing/stolen car still unresolved, she rushes off to the Empire State Building, the New York erection *par excellence*, not wishing to waste any more time. Once on the observation deck, however, she poses as a lingering image of isolation typical of romance fiction, 'a single figure against … a wonderful landscape' (MacRobbie 1991: 102), and the passing of time becomes relatively unimportant:

> It was nine o'clock before Lizzie finally thought of looking at her watch

Renard turns up, of course, and provides the real partner – and, we suppose, eventually the sex of which the building is a symbol. Neither of them has been up there before, and we might interpret this as an indication that they are both virgins.

8.5 Metaphor, irony and inferences

Although this carefully constructed story is not a particularly sophisticated piece of fiction, nevertheless it makes considerable inferential demands upon the reader. Of course, some of the inferential aspects of my explanation have been devoted to uncovering latent or subliminal symbolism. We have to know something about Freudian theory, at least in its popularised form, and perhaps some of the avowedly phallic symbolism of tall buildings, especially the lingams of Hindu and Buddhist culture, to make the inference about the ESB as a phallic symbol. The writer may not have intended us to do this.

However, there are points in the narrative where we are expected to make inferences about the symbolic opposition of vertical and horizontal space versus constriction. At one stage Lizzie has already looked out of the window once and caught a distant glimpse of the ESB, and this has set up the opposition between the tiny office and the elevated building. Some minutes later, the crucial point of disagreement between Renard and her surfaces in dialogue.

> 'I'm perfectly aware there are people in this city that can't be trusted. But this wasn't one of them'
> 'How do you know?' asked the lieutenant.
> Lizzie looked through the window. 'I just know, that's all'.

At this point we are invited to infer that she sees the building and this reinforces her trust in human nature and faithful relationships.

Part of the ESB symbolism depends upon, not Freud, knowledge of whose theories we may not be able to count on in a conservative middle-aged female American readership, but on the more universal conceptual metaphors or **root analogies** which are encoded in the English language (Goatly 1997: chapter 2).

For example, when we are told that, at the positive response to his dinner invitation, Renard's 'whole countenance lightened', we actually plug into two or three of these root analogies. EXCITEMENT = COLOUR, SERIOUS = HEAVY, HAPPY = UP. Lizzie brings colour, and presumably excitement into Renard's dingy life and office, lightening his face and using her smile to make the dark line on his brows disappear. But the ESB is one of the tallest buildings, and obviously by going up there they achieve happiness, and avoid the heavy responsibilities of Renard's working-day world. The open spaces are also a powerful metonymy or metaphor for freedom, FREEDOM = SPACE TO MOVE. Part of the problem of Renard's prison-cell attitude is his inability to see far, either into the future, or to grasp the whole picture, stuck as he is into the details – to understand this symbolism we tap into the analogy UNDERSTAND = SEE.

Not all the inferences are simply related to the understanding of metaphors and symbols. Inferencing is sometimes quite mundane, where we interpret in the light of information given before. An inferential process is needed, for example, to work out the consequences that the narrative has for the debate over trust versus cynicism. When Renard tells her that the police found her car and that it was sitting in the district and that he supposed that Lizzie and the old man just missed each other, this does not, on the face of it, count as conceding defeat for cynicism at the hands of trust. But if we supply information from earlier in the story, we recognise this as an indirect concession of defeat.

In some cases the genre will be crucial in giving guidance. What, are we supposed to infer, is Lizzie's motive, for example, in picking up the old man? Is her sexual frustration so strong that she wants to take the first man who presents himself, whatever his age? Or is this an indication of her helpful and generous nature, an attitude to life which she brings from her relatively rural background? The genre and the nature of the magazine in which we find the story makes the second inference much more plausible.

Finally, we might think of the choice of surnames in the story, since these tend to produce rather weak allusive implications. Both would appear to be the names of white people. Renard has something of a French, faded aristocratic ring. *Engel*, German for 'angel' suggests Christmas, given the mid-winter setting, the importance of lights, and Lizzie's fair hair.

8.6 Summary: courtly love, romantic fiction, and feminist critique

To begin our summary we can reconsider the main features of courtly love which we laid out in the introduction, and see how this story measures up:

(1)   the love was passionate, physical, emotional and uncontrollable;
(2)   the love was adulterous;
(3)   the man subjected himself to the will of the lady;
(4)   the lady remained passive, apart from issuing him with orders and tasks;
(5)   the carrying out of these tasks ennobled the man;
(6)   the consummation of his passion was the end of the story and of his ennoblement.

(1)   The love here certainly does seem to be physical. Lizzie's obsessive glances, finally reciprocated, are symptoms of the lust of the eyes. Renard does physically touch or steady her. She eagerly accepts his dinner invitation with 'I'm famished', which suggests displaced sexual appetite. A phallic interpretation of the Empire State Building is a possibility, and the euphemistic 'a small fire kindling into life' is certainly a flame of emotion if not visceral lust. This something warm is beyond her control, not an act of her will.

(2)   However, we have no doubt that this encounter is destined to end in life-long marriage. Their mutual appreciation of the Empire State Building which parallels that of her parents, suggests an equivalent relationship for Lizzie and Renard in the future. The grammatical use of joint subjects for father/mother and Lizzie/Renard underlines the equivalences.

(3)   After a struggle, Renard certainly submits himself to the will of the lady, by agreeing to list the car as missing rather than stolen, though this is hardly the heroic act of a would-be knight.

(4)   The transitive Material process clauses present Lizzie as rather passive, though she does go on a quest for love – the kind of journey which in the courtly love tradition would have been associated with a knight rather than the stay-at-home lady. Renard's issuing the report and bringing news about the finding of her car might be seen as performing the task she had set him, in courtly love style. His reporting back to her the successful completion of this errand is very similar to the typical medieval story sequence.

(5)   No doubt Renard is ennobled in the course of this story, by his relationship with Lizzie, which turns him from cynicism to trust. It may not be so much the task itself that ennobles him, as the attraction to Lizzie, and the influence of the building with a view, up which he chivalrously pursues her.

(6)   There is no consummation to their love, though the Empire State Building and the anticipated dinner provide symbolic substitutes for eroticism and satisfied appetite. Although the indications are that on the basis of this love they are going to attempt a lifetime's relationship, the story declines to give details.

The story illustrates that many of the courtly love themes and elements of plot and characterisation are still being recycled in romantic fiction, though with the stark difference that romantic love in the women's magazines is associated with marriage rather than adultery. However, there are a number of other ideological, stereotypical assumptions which have emerged in our analysis and which are worth underlining.

First, in this story woman is presented as incomplete without a man. This is something like a reversal of the courtly love situation, in which the lady has independent status (albeit as a married woman) before the page falls head-over-heels in love with her. Renard has his social roles and status as a police lieutenant, and is relatively independent of the influence of his mother. Lizzie's actions are defined by her mother's wishes for her, she has no job that we know of, and feels the need of a husband to be fulfilled, with twenty-eight a dangerously late age to linger beyond if she is to assume her motherly duties. Of course, Renard, in a sense, needs the influence of a generous and trusting Lizzie as well, but he is not conscious of this need, as Lizzie is.

Renard, too, is a strong authoritative man. There is something a little paradoxical in the fact that it is his institutional authority, conveyed by his imperative-mood clauses, his tough decisiveness with his opinions and generalisations, and his brusqueness with inferiors which attracts the female reader to him, at the same time that it makes it necessary for Lizzie to soften him. The way the transitive clauses represent him as impinging on people and the environment, but particularly the way 'his strong hands steady her by the arms' construct him as basically a macho male. The one concession to the new man is his ability, in the right circumstances, to appreciate beauty.

By contrast, Lizzie is intuitive, for example in her judgement of the old man, in which practical experience weighs more importantly than cynical generalisations. She is emotional, excited about New York and the Empire State Building. She is trusting in a sort of childlike way, spoken to by Renard and referred to by the narrator as if a child. Apparently, she submits to or courts institutional authority in the form of parents and the police. She is more socially adept than Renard, with her greetings, introductions, apologies and thanks, and a civilising influence on him. All these qualities fit the female stereotype. The two concessions to the new woman are her initiative in making the journey to New York in the first place, and her defiant insistence, modally reinforced, in the validity of her judgements about the old man and her missing car.

Lizzie, we suppose, is being proffered by the writer as the sort of woman with whom to identify, inviting the reader to construct herself as subject of/to her kind of femininity. And Renard is offered as the kind of man with which the ideal reader could imagine forging a permanent relationship. However, the magazine, *Woman's World*, as is clear from the problem-page extracts we analysed in Chapter 3, does not target an unmarried twenty-something readership, but rather middle-aged women/mothers. This suggests that the identification is to take place in the imagination rather than in real life. Lizzie could function as a fantasy figure, a symbol of escape from the boredom of Iowa, or other areas of the mid-west. Janice Radway (1987) found that, for housewives, reading romances was an act of independence, an escape from looking after husbands and children, but paradoxically a way of giving them the emotional strength to continue with the endless round of housework. Such a housewife readership might be comforted by some of the ideological slants of the story: the necessity for submission, that a woman is incomplete without a man; that though he is the intelligent breadwinner she uses her intuitive and interpersonal skills to build a family and social network .

It would be interesting to do a wider study to see how typical these ideologies are for stories within other issues of this magazine, or magazines targeted towards a similar readership, and to what extent the ideologies change in magazines for younger women (see MacRobbie 1991, chapter 6). And how tenacious, I wonder, in other stories, are the romantic themes that were first celebrated among the troubadours of twelfth-century southern France?

ACTIVITY 49*

You could find another romantic short story in a magazine and analyse it in the same way as 'Romance in the Air'. How do the two stories compare or differ in their depiction of male and female roles, and in the nature of the love they depict? Has this anything to do with the differing readership of the magazines from which they are taken?

Project 4: A short love story

For this project you could write a short love story, roughly of the length of 'Romance in the Air'. However, the ideal readership for your short story would be other students at your institution, not middle-aged white American women. Ideally you will be able to publish the best ones in an anthology or magazine.

The material in this unit is designed to help you think about your story, and also to revise the linguistic features and communicative strategies we mentioned in Parts one and two of this textbook. So when composing your story

(1) Consider how traditional you are going to be in terms of gender roles of your characters. Are they going to be very traditional, are they going to make a few concessions to the new man and the emancipated woman, or are they going to be radical departures from the norm? What elements of the courtly love passion, if any, are you going to adhere to in your story?

(2) When drafting and redrafting, think carefully about the following points:

- How are you going to organise the narrative structure? (Chapter 1.) Will there be a distinction between plot and story, or will the narrative be told chronologically without flashbacks? Will you have first-person narration, or will the narrator make evaluative comments? What will be the Complicating Action, and how will it be resolved? How much of the resolution will be left implicit, and how much actually stated?
- How do you conceive the relationships and personalities of your characters? What patterns of process type and participant roles will you establish as part of your characterisation? (Chapter 2.)
- How will the relationship between characters be reflected in the pattern of speech-act types which they use on each other? How polite will they be to each other? (Chapter 5.) Will this change in the course of the story, as it does in 'Romance in the Air'?
- How much will you, as a narrator, interfere with the speech of the characters when you represent it; will you use Free Direct, Direct, or Indirect Speech or Narrative Report, and in what proportions? (Chapter 6.)
- What names will you choose for your characters, and will they allude to other real-life or fictional characters? Will there be a symmetry in the way the characters in your story are named, for example in the use of title, surname, first name, diminutive?
- Will you use any ideologically loaded, contested or offensive terms to stimulate the reader or to tune them in to a particular ideology? (Chapter 3.)
- What use might you make of irony and metaphor? Will any of the objects or places or actions of your story acquire symbolic value, through the inferences you encourage the reader to make, for example the model of /climbing of the Empire State Building? (Chapter 4.)

This assignment will be more useful if you include notes where you justify the linguistic and discoursal choices you have made in your story.

Suggestions for further reading

- Two important books on this topic of courtly love and its development in Western literature are C. S. Lewis's *The Allegory of Love* and Denis de Rougemont's *Passion and Society*. C. S. Lewis examines the phenomenon of courtly love in medieval literature, and somewhat contentiously assumes that it was not simply a literary phenomenon but reflected societal practice. De Rougemont traces the development of courtly love into Romantic passion in European cultural history, and draws interesting contrasts with Chinese attitudes to gender, sex and marriage.

- Walter Nash's highly entertaining *Language in Popular Fiction* is recommended to anyone going on a long plane journey. He critically analyses in an accessible and lighthanded manner the linguistic and discourse style of romance fiction in magazines and action stories, concentrating on the structures of the narratives and the formulas to which they are written.

- Deirdre Burton's 'Through a glass darkly – through dark glasses' shows how the transitivity patterns in Sylvia Plath's *The Bell Jar* could be rewritten from a feminist perspective. This could be very useful supplementary reading before doing the 'love-story' project.

- Angela MacRobbie writes on teenage magazine fiction from a sociological perspective. Two chapters of her book *Feminism and Youth Culture* are the most relevant to Chapter 8 of this book. In '*Jackie* magazine: romantic individualism and the teenage girl' she describes the typical patterns of subject positioning of teenage girls in the magazine *Jackie* during the 1970s, concentrating on the fiction of their photostories. In '*Jackie* and *Just Seventeen*: girls' comics and magazines of the 1980s' she shows how fiction has been replaced with feature stories about 'pop boys' as the main field for the teenage imagination.

- Janice Radway's *Reading the Romance* is a study very relevant to Chapter 8, as it records research into the reports of middle-aged housewives on their motives for reading romances, and the effects that the reading has on them. 'Romance in the Air' obviously has such housewives as its intended readership since the short story on which it was based appeared in *Woman's World*.

Chapter 9

News and institutional power

Aims of this chapter

To argue that the idea of unbiased news is a myth, given the powerful economic and political interests behind the publishing and production of news.

To analyse the tendencies to sexism and racism/imperialism in the news, and ways of resisting the latter.

To give practice in the composition of a news report.

- **9.0 Introduction: freedom of the press?**
  Argues that the press is never entirely free but reflects the power structures of society.

- **9.1 Ownership of the press and other media**
  Demonstrates that ownership of the press will affect news coverage.

- **9.2 Newspapers' dependence on advertising**
  Explains how dependence on advertising revenue militates against serious working-class newspapers.

- **9.3 The selection of news**
  Explores in more depth the news values which lie behind news selection and how these tend to exclude the most ideologically and environmentally important issues.

- **9.4 The sources of news**
  Describes how news is predicted and gathered from the rich, famous and powerful and how this might influence its content and agenda.

- **9.5 Whose voices get into the news? A case study survey**
  Surveys whose voices are quoted in *Newsweek* and the Singapore *Straits Times*.

- **9.6 Participants in the news: a case study analysis**
  Analyses a newspaper report of an Australian One Nation party rally to reveal pro-Hanson bias.

- **9.7 Representation of nations and women: content analysis case studies**
  Surveys newspaper and magazine content to show more frequent and positive coverage of powerful nations and marginal/stereotypical coverage of women.

- **9.8 Fighting back against the US empire**
  Reports research on how Singapore *Straits Times'* representation of China and the US reacted against pro-Western news coverage.

- **Project 5: A news article**
  Writing a news article or feature for a student magazine, showing awareness of factors influencing your selection of news and of quotes, and sensitivity to linguistic strategies in the representation of characters.

9.0 Introduction: freedom of the press?

No one doubts the power of the media, and no one doubts the media is useful to those in power. Newspapers have vast circulations compared with any other published print, they are published frequently, and are accessible through wide distribution networks. For most people, they constitute the most substantial consumption of printed discourse. That the powerful in society should attempt to control and influence them is beyond question.

However there is also a conflicting myth of the freedom of the press, that journalists are free to give an objective account of anything they think newsworthy. And that, even if journalists on a particular newspaper may be constrained about what they can report, the reader has a choice because of the variety of newspapers on offer. Newspapers in this regard have been held up as the third estate, an essential ingredient of democracy; the information they give is supposed to be sufficiently important and trustworthy to allow voters to make judgements about the record of the political parties contesting elections, and to make informed decisions about which party to vote for.

In the first part of this Chapter I wish to challenge the view that the press is free, or that, for example, the citizens of the UK, or the US (or, especially, Singapore) have a diversity of points of view on offer in the news in their respective countries. I also want to challenge the view that it is even theoretically possible, let alone practically so, for the press to give an objective representation of the world.

Lord Northcliffe, the newspaper owner, once said that real news is something someone somewhere wants to hide, and that all the rest is advertising. He obviously saw the role of the press as a watchdog for any inefficiency, irrationality, injustice, corruption or scandalous behaviour for which those in power may have been responsible. However, the press as we know it has been hi-jacked by those with political and economic power. First, they have done this through ownership. Second, they have done so by the dependence of newspapers on advertising. Third, they have exploited the ambiguities in what is newsworthy to their own ends. And lastly they dominate the way the world is represented in the news since they are gatekeepers controlling the sources of the news and are being constantly quoted in it.

9.1 Ownership of the press and other media

Ownership of the press tends to be concentrated in the hands of a few companies. An extreme case of this is Singapore, where all the newspapers – *Berita Harian, Berita Minggu, Business Times, Lianhe Wanbao, Lianhe Zaobao*, the

New Paper, the *Straits Times*, the *Sunday Times* – are owned by Singapore Press Holdings. Additionally, a large proportion of the magazines are controlled by Times Periodicals. But in the UK, the situation is not much better. The best-selling tabloid newspaper is the *Sun* with a circulation of around 4 million. The most influential and the most widely read broadsheet newspaper is *The Times* (circulation around 800,000). Both the *Sun* and *The Times* are owned by News International Corporation. At the beginning of the 1990s News International, owner Rupert Murdoch, not only controlled newspapers with a weekly circulation of around 37 million but also published seven magazines, owned three satellite TV channels, as well as 50 per cent of the Eurosport satellite channel, and had a sizeable share in another publishing company, Pearson–Longman (publisher of the *Financial Times*). Another sizeable proportion of the readership of daily newspapers, about 2 million, has its news manufactured for it by United News and Media in the form of the papers the *Express* and the *Daily Star*.

In the US, control of media outlets is progressively in the hands of fewer and fewer corporations. In 1995, Walt Disney announced its intention of merging with Capital Cities/ABC, and Time–Warner was set to merge with (Ted) Turner Broadcasting System. Disney, already in 1994, had revenues from film entertainment of US$4.7 billion. It also produced prime-time television, home video and cable TV, with 14 million subscribers. Its theme parks and resorts produced revenues of US$3.5 billion. Another US$1.6 billion was made from retail, publishing and licensing. Capital Cities/ABC owned one major national TV network, TV stations in major cities, a radio network, cable interests including ESPN, the sports channel, multimedia (America Online) and publishing (books and newspapers). Time–Warner had the Warner Brothers film and TV studios, cable systems serving 11.5 million homes, Home Box Office, 50 record labels, the world's largest music publisher, and various publishing outlets (*Time*, *Life*, *Money*, *Fortune*, *People*, *Sports Illustrated*). Turner has two cable channels (CNN and TNT) and film production studios (Schiller 1996: 253).

This means to say that, particularly in Singapore, as well as in the UK, and even in the US, the owners of newspapers and other media have enormous scope, should they so wish, to exert pressure to suppress or highlight certain topics or events, or to mount campaigns, and to establish consensus, by denying alternative agendas, or silencing opposing views. The scope for influence is facilitated by the process of manufacture of news. The reporter's original text is filtered through a hierarchy including copy-editor, sub-editors, layout editor, and editor-in-chief, making it possible to reject, interfere with, cut and distort the original text in line with editorial policy.

Pressure to interfere with the news may come from government, but just as important are influential commercial interests. Newspaper publishing companies, especially in Australia, Europe and North America, are often subsidiaries of multinational corporations. At times there will arise a conflict of interest between investigative journalism and their other business interests. A good example is the case of Dioxin and its reporting in the *New York Times*. Dioxin is widely believed to be a highly toxic chemical, which as part of the defoliant Agent Orange, dropped on the jungles during the Vietnam War, was responsible for widespread birth deformities in the years following. However, in the 1990s the *New York Times* deliberately downplayed the dangers of this chemical. In one article with the headline 'US Officials Say Dangers of Dioxin Were Exaggerated' the newspaper stated 'Exposure to the chemical, once thought to be much more hazardous than chain-smoking, is now considered by some experts to be no more risky than spending a week sunbathing'. It is important to realise that the *New York Times* had financial interests in four paper mills. When the article was published these mills were facing a Canadian court claim of $900 million for polluting three rivers with Dioxin (Beder, 1999: 30)!

9.2 Newspapers' dependence on advertising

Newspapers are not simply a service to the public but must make a tangible profit for the corporations to which they belong or to their owners and shareholders. Where do newspapers get their revenue? The largest part is from advertising, not from the cover price charged to the readers. As Norman Fairclough puts it

> The press ... are eminently profit-making organisations, they make their profits by selling audiences to advertisers and they do this by achieving the highest possible readerships ... for the lowest possible financial outlay.
>
> (Fairclough 1995: 42)

There are two effects of this. For one, newspapers will not wish to run stories which might put off advertisers. This means that advertisers can threaten to withdraw their advertising if newspapers publish stories or implement policies which are critical of them or undermine their position. This may well restrict the range of political views, agendas or topics of investigative journalism to those which are acceptable to the particular companies advertising, or more generally to those which support the capitalist system of which advertising is a part.

But second, and more important, the dependence of newspapers on advertising makes it very difficult for newspapers representing the views of the poor and the working class to be viable. Papers with a less affluent readership get much less advertising revenue per copy than papers with richer readers. This is

Table 9.1 Circulation and cost of advertising in UK, Singapore and US newspapers

Newspapers	Circulation	Cost of full-page ad
Financial Times (B)	300,000	£35,272
Sun (T)	4,000,000	£34,700
Independent (B)	270,000	£14,000
Daily Star (T)	670,000	£9,432
Express (Median B)	1,200,000	£28,825
Mirror (T)	2,400,000	£27,500
Business Times (B)	34,000	S$4931
New Paper (T)	104,000	S$2797
Straits Times (B)	370,000	S$16,074
Christian Science Monitor (B)	78,200	US$4,000
Los Angeles Times (B)	1,000,000	US$7,800

Key
(B) = 'broadsheet'
(T) = 'tabloid'

because the advertisers can push more expensive products, not, for example, matches, soap powder or toothpaste, but televisions, mobile phones, computers, photocopiers and cars.

The 1997 figures for advertising cost compared with circulation given in Table 9.1 illustrates this. the *Financial Times* has less than 10 per cent of the circulation of the *Sun*, and yet is able to charge slightly more for a full-page advertisement. This is quite out of proportion, even allowing for the fact that the *FT* is a broadsheet, and the *Sun* a tabloid, with pages half the size. The explanation is that the readers of the *Financial Times* have much more buying power per head than readers of the *Sun*. The same goes if we compare the *Independent* and *Business Times* with the *Daily Star* and the *New Paper*, the latter pair having two-thirds of the revenue per page but two and a half times the circulation figures. The *Mirror* and the *Express* adverts cost roughly the same for a tabloid page, but the *Mirror*'s circulation is double that of the *Express*. The *Straits Times* has three and a half times the circulation of the *New Paper*, but charges six times as much for advertising. In the US, the highly prestigious *Christian Science Monitor* charges only half the rate of the less prestigious *Los Angeles Times* despite the fact that the latter has twelve times the circulation.

Since the financial viability of newspapers depends upon their advertising revenue, this makes it very difficult to run a national newspaper (in the UK) which represents the views of the poor, or takes their political agenda seriously. The history of radical working-class newspapers in the UK gives a clear picture of the problem. The *Daily Herald*, which was just such a paper, folded in 1964. At that time, it had 4.7 million readers, almost double the readership of *The Times*, the *Sunday Times* and the *Guardian* put together, that is 8.1 per cent of the newspaper circulation. However, it had only a 3.5 per cent slice of the available advertising revenue. This did not stop Sir Denis Hamilton, editor-in-chief of Times Newspapers, saying at the time 'The *Herald* was beset by the problem which has dogged nearly every newspaper vowed to a political idea; not enough people wanted to read it.'!

So, popular newspapers, in order to reach as wide a readership as possible, and to avoid tackling issues of inequality which may threaten the interests of advertisers and the capitalist system of which they are part, have to trivialise their news. In the UK there is at present no attempt to create a taste for anything much except sensationalism and prurient gossip about the private lives of celebrities. During the aftermath of Princess Diana's death, when the TV and radio were casting around for someone to blame for the accident, the first tendency was to blame the so-called *paparazzi*, the photographers who were pursuing her on motorcycles, and the newspaper editors who were in the habit of buying their photographs. The focus of blame then shifted to the readers and purchasers of these newspapers. The problem is that the majority of the UK population really have little choice if they wish to read a daily newspaper. What national newspaper is there in the UK which deals with serious issues and which a person of average education and intelligence can understand? The tabloid newspapers make no attempt to cultivate a taste for clear thought or discussion of serious political issues.

Indeed, because their main aim is entertainment and not education, the papers turn political issues into matters of personality, as though political matters can be reduced to a soap-opera drama. The 1997 economic and currency crisis in Malaysia was presented as a conflict between Malaysian Prime Minister Dr Mahatir Mohamed and the international financier George Soros – complex economic issues being presented as antagonism between characters in a play. Just as, before, the Gulf War was presented as a conflict between Bush and Saddam Hussein, or the conflict between Palestine and Israel was presented as a duel between Arafat and Netanyahu. Personalisation thus becomes one aspect in the selection and presentation of news, or news values, the topic of our next section.

9.3 The selection of news

What gets selected as news and why? We already looked at some of Galtung and Ruge's news values in Chapter 2, but here we have the space to consider all of them in more detail (Table 9.2). If we assume that newspapers have a role in informing and highlighting actions, events and processes which represent a threat to the general public, including political ineptitude or corruption, it will be obvious that most news will come over as bad news (1). No news is good news, as they say. The question is whether newspapers really do their job in this regard.

Table 9.2 News values

Number	Value	Explanation
(1)	negativity	generally bad
(2)	frequency	the span of the event/ action less than the length of time between publication
(3)	meaningfulness	familiar and comprehensible within the cultural mind-set of the reader
(4)	persons	interest in people acting/talking/suffering
(5)	consonance	the usual, predictable or expected
(6)	unexpectedness	the unusual or abnormal
(7)	continuity	the topic in the news continuing there
(8)	composition	variety in one particular edition of the newspaper
(9)	threshold	large-scale events, numbers of people involved
(10)	élite nations	reference to powerful nations – US, Japan, Europe
(11)	élite persons	reference to powerful people – politicians, monarchs, the rich and famous

One problem is the question of frequency (2). In order to get into the news, events, actions or processes should take place over a period of time which is shorter than the time between publications of the newspaper. This means to say that newspapers find it difficult to cope with major threats to the public, indeed to all of us, from processes like global warming and climate change which take place over years and decades. The only time these will be reported is when there is some discrete event, like a politician's speech, or the Rio Earth Summit, which has a shorter time-span. Our perceptual apparatus is not, of course, very good at taking in these more extended processes, so that we find short isolable Material or Verbal processes much more meaningful (3).

Another factor which makes global warming difficult to get into the news is that it is a rather new cultural phenomenon: it's difficult for us to believe that the solid land on which we stand may in fifty years or so be under water, or that the familiar weather patterns which we have experienced all our lives may be disrupted. Of course, scientific investigations of the mechanisms of global warming, of meteorology, and the chemical reactions of the ozone layer are very remote from most people, and perhaps difficult to understand. So they may not make it as news since they are distant from the human-life world as we understand it. Most newsworthy topics are those which involve human interest stories, are personal, and can be dramatised (4).

This brings us to the next pairs of values, which represent a tension between the expected and the unexpected. Generally, news might be thought of as the reporting of exceptional or abnormal events (6). If everything goes according to the schema it is hardly worth mentioning. The problem here is that certain normal and recurring events, and processes and states, which nevertheless represent a threat to many people, tend to be ignored in the news. Take for example the carnage on the roads caused by car transportation. The fact that 120 people are killed on the highways in the US every day and 30 people or so in the UK seem to be such accepted, frequent and predictable threats to the public that newspapers and media hardly think them worth mentioning, unless there is some spectacular accident, with a high death toll (9), or unless it involves an élite person such as Princess Diana (11). At present, road accidents are the world's ninth most common cause of death with half a million killed each year. Similarly, the background noise of human misery caused by poverty, malnutrition, disease, pollution and ignorance is effectively filtered out from the mainstream media. By contrast, what really makes the news is the much less frequent phenomenon of terrorism and violent crime. A programme on the Insight series of the BBC World Service (28 October 1998) about kidnapping suggested it was a very serious problem because there were 1,400 cases reported last year!

There are, of course, powerful ideological reasons why terrorism should make the news when car accidents, and infant mortality do not. Terrorism is often of a political nature, and depending on allegiances one person's terrorist is another's freedom fighter. As such, terrorism represents a challenge to the political or economic status quo, and threatens those who have an interest in maintaining it because they at present have authority, fame or wield political or economic power. By contrast, the World Bank's loan and repayment system, which means a poor country like Mozambique spends two and a half times as much on servicing debt as it does on health care (Hanlon 1999: 27), is very much part of the economic order. Consequently, to draw attention to the threat it poses to the well-being of poor nations is not a high priority among newspapers owned by transnational corporations. Highlighting the deaths of poor children in Mozambique might lead to political action to change the economic world order. But instead, deaths from "terrorism" are highlighted because it threatens existing political orders.

By ignoring the real and pervasive threats to the well-being of humankind, newspapers are accomplices in one aspect of the crisis of modernity: the fact that the system is so rotten and out of step with human well-being that cooperating with and abiding by social norms is non-sustainable or brings tragedy or suffering. It was the playwright Arthur Miller who pointed out the difference between the heroes of traditional tragedy and the heroes of his own modern tragedies, like Willy Loman in his play *Death of a Salesman*. The traditional tragic hero experiences suffering and death because he rebels against society's valid norms, for example by, like Œdipus, marrying his mother, or like Macbeth, killing King Duncan. But Willy Loman suffers because he wholeheartedly embraces the suspect values of the American Dream: the drive for status, money, possession of the latest consumer goods; the obsession with being liked, with indiscriminate sexual gratification, and with fame and success for one's children (Miller 1958: 22–36). The interesting, or vital, question is how long can the media go on ignoring the increasing background problems created by a flawed economic and political world order, simply because the human misery they cause is so widespread as to be no longer newsworthy?

On the other hand we have the expected nature of the news (5), and we can relate this to what we have said about stereotyping in Chapter 2. We expect certain nationalities to behave in predictable ways, and events or actions which conform to our stereotype are likely to be more newsworthy than those that do not. I shocked myself the other day, by realising the extent to which my stereotypes of Afghanistan had been shaped by years of media coverage of war in that country. I had bought a CD collection of love songs which began with a particularly tender poem

> Since you love me and I love you
> The rest matters not.
> I will cut grass in the fields
> And you will sell it for beasts.
>
> Since you love me and I love you
> The rest matters not.
> I will grow maize in the fields
> And you will sell it for people.

When I read the CD insert I had to do a double-take when the song was labelled as an Afghani love song. Somehow it didn't fit my schema at all. The stereotyping and demonising of Middle-Eastern Arab countries as belligerent and obsessed with jihad or holy war, had closed my mind. Indeed, this stereotype conflicts with the experience of many who have actually lived in the Middle East and have concluded that Arab cultures are among the most hospitable in the world.

Continuity (7), the bandwagon effect, is very noticeable in news, and obviously contributes to stereotyping. In 1995 there was a near hysteria generated by the newspapers about the dangers to the public of certain breeds of dog: Rottweilers, pitbull terriers, Dobermanns, and so on. Once one horrific case was reported in the British press with accompanying photograph of the remains of a man's mauled face, all other attacks, especially of dogs on children, were assiduously selected for the news, even from as far afield as South-East Asia. Some years later, as I write, this doesn't represent a particular agenda or item for a current press campaign, so, though there may be more such attacks at the moment than there were during that period, they do not receive newspaper coverage. Sometimes newspapers wage such campaigns, either of their own ideological making, or taking the cue from government.

News value (9) is threshold, the idea that the larger the event or action in terms of casualties, numbers killed, cost of damage and so on, the more likely it is to make the news. The fact seems to be that this value, an absolute one if we accept that each human life is as valuable as the next, is largely overridden by factors such as threat to the status quo (as already noted, deaths from terrorism have a lower threshold than deaths from car accidents or starvation), or by the notion of élite nations (10) and élite persons (11), the last two values. As we shall see, rich and powerful people, and rich and powerful nations are the ones who are more newsworthy.

9.4 The sources of news

The dominant members of society also exert considerable influence on the selection of news because they tend to be the gatekeepers and the sources of news. On a global scale, the international news which appears in national newspapers is usually provided by one or more of the Western-based news agencies: AFP, AP, UPI, Reuters, mostly, by the way, operating in English with all the cultural biases that that entails. At a more local level, news is routinely gathered by journalists from the established and powerful institutions of society. Reporters check with the police and the courts to find out if there are any interesting crimes or legal cases, and with hospitals to see if there are newsworthy accidents. Reporters attend the press conferences at which politicians, company chairpersons, and spokespersons for important organisations pronounce on political issues or company financial results, plans for expansion or streamlining, retrenchment and redundancy. Should a journalist's report be critical of the police, the courts and these other powerful figures, she might well find her sources of news drying up in the future. So this dependence is likely to dampen her campaigning zeal.

Every editor will keep a press diary so that the paper can routinely cover scheduled events featuring the rich, the famous, the very important people: international conferences, press conferences, sittings of parliament, political speeches, state visits by foreign politicians or monarchs, concerts and so on. While this kind of routine makes the news production manageable, and means that it can be planned for, it also reinforces the power structures of society. Only relatively rich organisations can afford to employ press officers and stage press conferences, for example. So it is these powerful institutions who become the originating Sayers. Their views and values, their versions of economic and political reality, are passed around and become common sense and natural, hiding their ideological nature, and exerting "untold" influence.

The news is not, therefore, objectively gathered, but is selected according to the values which suit and reflect the dominant élites of society, the predilections of the transnational corporations who own the newspapers, and through the powerful international agencies and local institutions who act as sources of news. But once a particular item has been selected as newsworthy it still has to be presented and shaped on the page of the newspaper and this provides further scope for "bias". We saw in discussing the article about Clinton and the IRA, that the selection of Lead and headline in a Deductive, point-first genre like news reports can distort the facts, and mislead the reader who only skims the paper.

Besides this, we explored in some detail in Chapter 2 how the language we use and the choices we make within it inevitably suppress some aspects of the world out there and highlight other features. For example, seniority was seen as being relatively important in the way Asian languages classify relatives. Language, then, is no transparent medium for representing reality, but inevitably highlights and hides, is essentially "biased". We can only conclude that the notion of objective unbiased news published by a free press is a myth and a mirage.

9.5 Whose voices get into the news? A case study survey

I wanted to test the claim that it is the dominant members of society and the most rich and powerful countries whose views get reported in the news. So I quickly analysed the news reports in the first nineteen pages of the Singapore *Straits Times* (*ST*) for Wednesday, 9 July 1997, and also all the quotations in direct speech which appeared in *Newsweek* (*NW*) 1 June 1998.

Table 9.3 Voices in the news

Voices in the news	*ST*	*NW*
Public in court	5	
Public: witnesses/victims of crimes; relatives/friends of criminals	5	4
Public opinion	3	4
Lawyers, courts, judges, etc.	27	1
Police and military	10	8
Political/military alliances: Nato, Asean	6	
Government: prime ministers/presidents	16	9
ministers	12	7
Politicians/leaders	19	9
Political activists		4
Officials and heads of organisations and spokespersons	27	18
Monarchs	2	
Commerce: business people, financiers, companies, economists	14	16
Professionals: doctors, scientists, academics, priests, etc.	8	17
Students		4
Entertainers: theatre, sport		4
Media: journalists, editors, writers, analysts	16	10

Since the news is supposed to serve the interests of the public one would expect the voices of the general public to be heard frequently. This is not the case. The public voice does get heard but only in a limited range of situations. First, there are cases where members of the public get into court or are charged with a crime, for example Kip Kinkel, alleged teenage murderer (*NW*), or an Israeli woman on a racism trial for putting up posters of Mohammed in the form of a pig (*ST*).

Next, there are the occasional voices of members of the public who witness, provide information on, or are victims of accidents and crimes, or their relatives. For instance, an anonymous telephone caller who warned of the planting of a bomb which killed twenty-five on a train in Punjab and one of the survivors of the same bomb blast.

Sometimes articles are more focused on public opinion. Four fans get their voices heard in *NW*, and in the *ST* two youngsters in Shanghai get to express their views on *tamagotchi* (lovable eggs, virtual pets).

The pattern seems to be that ordinary members of the public hardly have their own individual voices represented in news reports except on trivial entertainment topics, or when they find themselves caught up in a court case or victims/witnesses of an accident/terrorist act. (Letters to the editor are the only forum in newspapers for public opinion – which is partly why this genre was suggested as a project.)

By contrast, the voices of the courts and the law are very prominent as newspapers' Sayers. On the whole, it is the court establishment and the judges, magistrates and prosecutors whose voices outnumber the defence, though members of the public as defendants get their voices heard. Working in tandem with the courts (and generally the prosecution) are the police and the military, especially in the *NW* reports from Indonesia and on the IRA.

The largest power structures in our world are the governments in military or political alliances, such as NATO and ASEAN. Most political power is, however, concentrated at the level of national governments. Some of the most frequent Sayers are prime ministers and presidents. This particular day's newspaper was a field day for ex-prime ministers/presidents: Malcolm Fraser (Australia) – urging PM Howard to apologise for the aboriginal "assimilation policy" of taking children away from parents and fostering them out to white couples; and Canaan Banana (Zimbabwe) indicted for sodomy. We have the Italian, British, Cambodian, Israeli, Australian, South Korean, and Singaporean presidents/prime ministers all figuring as Sayers. Next in the government hierarchy are ministers and their ministries. In the *ST* we have ministers from Taiwan, Italy, UK, Portugal and India.

At a lower level still we have politicians of various kinds. Less clearly labelled, and to some extent overlapping with all these political categories of Sayers are leaders, though the latter may not be of a legitimated or elected kind.

With even less power are those labelled political *activists* and *organisers* who may not even have reached a position of leadership.

Other authority figures and government officials make their verbal remarks: diplomats, chairpersons of councils, committees and commissions, and heads of organisations like Alan Greenspan and Robert Rubin, or just plain *authorities* and *officials*. Alongside the leaders are the unelected monarchs – sometimes doubling as politicians like Prince Ranariddh of Cambodia.

A further major source of comment are Sayers representing capital, finance and business: bankers, business people, economists and companies. One might expect these Sayers to be concentrated in the financial pages of the newspaper, but they creep, in substantial numbers, into the main World and East-Asian news. This is not surprising as they are increasingly the real power behind the political puppets in our governments.

So far the Sayers have been powerful because they represent authority, and in some cases the authorities, like the military, police and courts, who actually have the power to use physical force on the citizens. But professionals whose power comes from expertise also get their say: the doctors, scientists, priests and pastors and, less prominently, sociologists, a psychologist and other intellectuals/scholars.

Four individual students are interviewed as part of an *NW* article on the thirtieth anniversary of the May 1968 student movement in France, and we have the collective voice of chanting students reported four times.

Entertainers and sportspeople figure as Sayers in *NW*: Stephen Sondheim, a Korean golfer, an actor, a film producer.

Finally, there are journalists, analysts, editors and writers and other newspapers and agencies, not including the news agency attributions at the end of many of the newspaper articles. This reminds us of the extent to which news comes to us through many hands and of the way the different aspects of the international news and publishing machine are parasitic on each other.

As far as the *NW* survey is concerned, one of the most remarkable facts is that out of the 180 or so direct-speech quotations only 11 of the Sayers are identifiably women! Two of these are labelled as 'wife' or 'ex-wife', getting in on the back of their husbands. If *NW* represents the country in which the modern feminist movement was born, then on the basis of this edition, the movement still has a long way to go.

To sum up we can consult Table 9.4. News is very much presented to us through the eyes of those in charge of law and order (15 per cent), governments and politicians (26 per cent), heads of organisations and other officials (15 per cent). All these represent the official institutional authorities, those who have the power to legislate, imprison or punish (see Sigal 1987). Then we take our information from the commerce and financial sectors (10 per cent), the businesses,

Table 9.4 Sayers in *Newsweek* and the *Straits Times*

Category of Sayers	Percentage of Sayers
Governments and politicians	26
Law and order	15
Officialdom	15
Commerce and finance	10
Media	9
Other professionals	8
Public	7

banks and companies, who control the global financial system and the working of capitalism, the power behind the political throne. Finally, there are the experts, the professionals who are supposed to know the way things work and to create new knowledge (8 per cent). Media professionals are an equally influential voice and have just as large a say as these (9 per cent). These powerful individuals, institutions, organisations and governments represent over 80 per cent of the Sayers in my survey. The public are only represented as 7 per cent of the Sayers, usually only reported as victims, or defendants and witnesses in the courts, or as eyewitnesses of accidents and unpredictable events, or because of relationships with the famous or infamous. To put it in a nutshell, public persons are called upon for their opinions while private persons are called upon only for their experiences (Fairclough 1995: 40, 164; Scannell 1992).

9.6 Participants in the news: a case study analysis

The importance of whose analysis of events and whose agenda gets reported in the news is very clear in one news report from 9 July which we will now look at in detail.

(1) Several hurt in protest against Hanson

[*Photograph of a man lying unconscious*]

[**(2) A supporter of race-row politician Pauline Hanson's One Nation party lying unconscious after being assaulted in a confrontation with protesters following a party meeting in Melbourne on Monday. (3) Ms Hanson was not present at the meeting – Reuter picture**]

MELBOURNE –   (4) Australian police said yesterday that they would tighten security at a country rally to be attended by race-row politician Pauline Hanson after several people were injured during anti-Hanson protests on Monday.

(5) Police said a small group of activists were responsible for the violence at the launch of Ms Hanson's One Nation party in the Victorian rural town of Dandenong, where protesters threw potatoes, eggs and urine-filled balloons.

(6) Those injured included a 60-year-old Hanson supporter attacked by protesters. (7) The man spent the night in hospital.

(8) Former Australian Deputy Prime Minister Jim Cairns, 82, joined the protests but was thrown out of the meeting after he started distributing anti-Hanson tracts.

(9) Queenslander Ms Hanson is due next week to attend a rally in the Victorian town of Geelong and another counter demonstration is being organised.

(10) 'We're taking certain precautions,' said acting Chief Superintendent Alan Maclean of the Geelong police.

(11) 'I will have sufficient police there on the evening to maintain the community peace,' he said.

(12) Up to 1,500 protesters disrupted the One Nation meeting in Dandenong on Monday night. (13) The party launch was attended by 150 Hanson supporters, but not by Ms Hanson herself. (14) Police Superintendent Jim Hart said he had no doubt that militant minorities, rather than genuine demonstrators, were responsible for the violence.

(15) 'A large number of those demonstrating are genuine people wishing to voice their concerns,' he said.

(16) Police said they were studying videos of the meeting to identify the protesters who attacked the 60-year-old man. (17) Seven arrests had been made and more could follow. (18) One Nation spokesman, David Ettridge, said the protest was the worst he had ever seen at a Hanson rally.

(19) But Mr Cairns, Deputy Prime Minister under Labor's Gough Whitlam government in the 1970s, said the protesters had not been violent.

(20) He said One Nation's private security 'muscle men' had bundled him out of the meeting.

(21) One Nation, which has an anti-immigrant platform and also campaigns against Aboriginal welfare, has attracted support away from Australia's main political parties to become the country's third political force.

(22) An opinion poll published yesterday showed a 6 per-cent support for the independent politician and her party, which was registered officially only last month. (23) She is the only elected member of her party, and it has yet to be tested in an election – Reuter.

(Straits Times, 9 July 1997, p. 5)

As police are the major Sayers in this report it is interesting, but not surprising, to see the way in which they represent themselves. In Material-cum-
Mental process clauses they come over as firmly in control of the situation, using
their intelligence and planning abilities:

> They were studying videos of the meeting to identify the protesters
> 'We're taking certain precautions,'
> ... they would tighten security at a country rally'
> ... to maintain the community peace'

When it comes to apportioning blame for the injury to the 60-year-old man
in the picture, and the other injuries, there seem to be three or four voices to take
into account. First, there are three versions by the police, which seem to concur,
though the last of these is ambiguous (all or some of the protesters?):

> Police said a small group of activists were responsible for the violence at
> the launch of Ms Hanson's One Nation party in the Victorian rural town of
> Dandenong.

> Police Superintendent Jim Hart said he had no doubt that militant minor-
> ities, rather than genuine demonstrators, were responsible for the violence.

> Police said they were studying videos of the meeting to identify the pro-
> testers who attacked the 60-year-old man.

Then there is the less discriminating version, which is the report by the
journalists/editors/agency and so claims more reliability. It seems to blame
the protesters in general:

> A supporter of race-row politician Pauline Hanson's One Nation
> party lying unconscious after being assaulted in a confrontation with
> protesters ...

> Those injured included a 60-year-old Hanson supporter attacked by
> protesters

Swinging far in the other direction is the alternative version by Jim Cairns:

> But Mr Cairns, Deputy Prime Minister under Labor's Gough Whitlam
> government in the 1970s, said the protesters had not been violent. He said
> One Nation's private security 'muscle men' had bundled him out of the
> meeting.

By the time we reach this last version of events, towards the end of the report, we have probably accepted the representation which is given prominently in the caption to the photograph and reinforced early in the body of the copy.

An analysis of the transitivity patterns reinforces the blaming of protesters/demonstrators as the trouble makers. Protesters figure as Actors but never as Affecteds, often with One Nation as the passive Affecteds.

> Up to 1,500 protesters disrupted the One Nation meeting in Dandenong on Monday night.
> ... where protesters threw potatoes, eggs and urine-filled balloons.
> ... protestors, who attacked the 60-year-old man.
> ... attacked by protesters.

By contrast the One Nation party are Actors only metaphorically or non-violently or as supine victims:

> ... and also campaigns against Aboriginal welfare,
> ... has attracted support away from Australia's main political parties
> A supporter of race-row politician Pauline Hanson's One Nation party lying unconscious

One Nation are also Actors paired with the less than forceful verb *attend*

> The party launch was attended by 150 Hanson supporters, but not by Ms Hanson herself.

The exception to this pattern of innocuous actions is the version by Jim Cairns who blames the One Nation "muscle men", but the use of scare quotes and the drift of the report suggest his version is unreliable:

> One Nation's private security 'muscle men' had bundled him out of the meeting.

There is a certain amount of background information given about One Nation in Relational process clauses:

> ... which was registered officially only last month.
> One Nation, which has an anti-immigrant platform ...
> Queenslander Ms Hanson is due next week ...
> She is the only elected member of her party ...
> ... to become the country's third political force.

However, no information is given about the protesting organisations.

There are various implications which we might detect in the last sentences of the report, sentences (21) to (23). The idea that One Nation has become 'the country's third main political force' makes it sound very significant; though we later learn that it only has 6 per cent support in an opinion poll. It is, however, implied that this low percentage is due to the fact that it was registered 'only last month', suggesting that the real level of support is higher. The last sentence is ambiguous: perhaps it implies that 'when it comes to the vote fewer people will vote for it in an election' or 'the opinion poll seriously underestimates the level of support which will become apparent in an election'. Either of these are fairly weak implicatures.

We can sum up by saying that this news report seems "biased" in favour of One Nation and against the protesters. The photo with its caption is worth a thousand words in this respect. The protesters take *carte blanche* blame in the words of the report, are only selectively blamed in the words of the police, and are exonerated by the words of Jim Cairns. The transitivity patterns paint the protesters as trouble makers, if not violent, and One Nation generally as passive Affecteds or Actors in innocent processes like attending and campaigning. And the background information on One Nation along with the implications that it is a considerable political force, help to give it some legitimacy.

9.7 Representation of nations and women–content analysis case studies

Nations in the news

A quick way to see the selectivity of news in operation is to make a count of head-lines to see which countries get into the news, and for what reasons. Let's look at the 1 June 1998 edition of *Newsweek,* which claims to be 'The International News magazine' which is 'written and edited for a world-wide audience'. The cover story of this edition is the fall of Indonesia's President Suharto. This, by objective standards, is of enormous significance, since he was ruler of the world's fourth most populous nation. However, despite its political importance and its cover-story status, when we look at the number of pages devoted to Indonesia (Table 9.5) we will see that stories about the US actually receive more space.

In some ways these figures actually underplay the coverage of the US. The story on Mexico, 'Busting the Bankers' is about Washington's attempt to catch money launderers. One of the Japanese articles is an interview with the actor Kenpachuro Satsuma, who starred as Godzilla in seven movies, to find out his reaction to the new Hollywood version of the story.

Table 9.5 Coverage of countries in *Newsweek*

Continent	Country	Number of pages
North America		
	United States	15
	Mexico	1
South America		
	Argentina	2.66
Asia		
	Indonesia	9
	Japan	2
	India	1.5
	S. Korea	1
	Cambodia	0.33
Middle East		
	Egypt	0.66
	Israel	0.33
Europe		
	Central Europe	2
	France	5.17
	UK	3.5
	Czech Republic	1
	Italy	0.2
	Russia	0.17

The figures show clear patterns. With the exception of Indonesia, rich nations predominate: US, Japan, France, UK, and one of the richer South American countries, Argentina. The poorest continent, Africa, does not figure at all, unless one counts Egypt.

Another pattern concerns the division into good news, bad news, and interesting news. When poorer nations are mentioned it is generally in relation to bad news: the financial crisis, the riots and the political upheavals of Indonesia (though the silver lining here is the resignation of President Suharto), and the negative repercussions for the world financial system. India figures because of the withdrawal of investment following its recent nuclear tests. These were clearly bad news for the US establishment, precisely because, like terrorism, they threaten a change to the existing world order, though for many Indians this seemed to be the best news they had had since the BJP government took office. However, the withdrawal of investments is, we are to suppose, not such good news for them. The article on Egypt is about mistakes in restoring the statue of the Sphinx. Cambodia is represented by three letters on a previous issue's cover story about Pol Pot. Mexico is associated with money laundering and Argentina with corruption ('Relentless pursuit: a tough judge follows a trail of corruption').

By contrast, for the US, there is only one article which really has to do with bad news: two pages on 'The Oregon teen charged with killing his parents and classmates'. The rest of the US news is either good or interesting.

For example, one six-page feature, 'Savior of the streets', is about Gene Rivers, a black ex-Harvard preacher, who is successfully fighting teenage crime in Dorchester, one of the poorest neighbourhoods of Boston. There is a full-page celebration of Stephen Sondheim, a piece on the removal of beggars from San Francisco's streets, and a report of success by UCLA scientists in isolating a gene connected with breast cancer. Much of the UK news is about the referendum in Ireland in which 70 per cent voted to accept the 'Good Friday agreement'.

Women in the news

Another question we might ask ourselves is which women get into the news and how they are represented. I analysed references to women in the first 12 pages of the *Straits Times* for 30 December 1996, and the only references to women are pasted in Plate 11. This suggest that they are grossly underrepresented. (Though by comparison with the Sayers from the *ST* 9 July 1997, see Section 9.5, on p. 256, none of which were identified as female, the reports from 26 December 1996 give women a much higher profile.)

When we analyse the references we notice that many of these women get in simply by "virtue" of their husbands, i.e. because they married (or are otherwise related to) a more famous man. This applies to 'the director and his wife', 'Hillary Clinton', 'Barbara Bush', 'Mrs Elizabeth Dole', 'Princess Diana', 'Nancy Reagan', 'Jacko's wife Ms Debbie Rowe', 'Fergie', 'Sinatra's mum', 'Remli's Irish wife'. Notice too the way the prosecuted couples' identity is represented in the last column: 'a 28-year-old man and his 24-year-old wife'; 'Mustakin Karim and his wife Rahimah Ismail'; why not 'Rahimah Ismail and her husband Mustakin Karim'?

Another set of females are represented largely as victims: the Chinese woman who dies in the riot; the two young girls whose hair was chewed by cabbage-patch dolls; the wives of the bigamist; the strangled daughter; the factory-working women who may be exploited.

A further group represents the stereotype of the caring woman: Mother Teresa; a legal-aid worker (making sure that her parents were all right); the Filipino lawyer who runs the free Fil-Am Vet legal clinic; Ms Sabariah Ahmad campaigning against child abuse.

The minority of women who make the news resist this male chauvinist representation or stereotyping. Madeleine Albright, Margaret Thatcher, Barbara Streisand and Queen Elizabeth are the legitimate and respectable ones. But it's quite interesting that one or two allegedly violent criminals or "guerrillas" are mentioned: a young woman who was in Mr Uday's vehicle at the time of the attack; and one of the youngsters in the Lima siege who told the Malaysian

Director's film awards stolen

ROME — Burglars have made off with the most prestigious awards which Italian director Michelangelo Antonioni had won in his career, police said on Saturday.

Items taken from his Rome flat included the Oscar he received last year for his lifetime's work, the Golden Lion from the Venice film festival awarded in 1983 for his career and the Golden Palm which he won at the Cannes film festival with his 1967 film, Blow Up.

Investigators said that the flat was burgled on Dec 25 or 26 while the director, 84, and his wife, Ms Enrica Fico, were spending Christmas in the Venice region. — AFP, Reuter.

Clinton tops most-admired list

WASHINGTON — US President Bill Clinton (above left), has topped a Gallup poll list of the most-admired people.

Among the top 10 men after him were Pope John Paul II, retired General Colin Powell, the Reverend Billy Graham, former Senator Bob Dole, former presidents Ronald Reagan and Jimmy Carter (tie), Mr Nelson Mandela, former President George Bush, basketball star Michael Jordan and retired General Norman Schwarzkopf.

Heading the list of most admired women for the third time was Mother Teresa (above right). The second most admired was Mrs Hillary Clinton, followed by Mrs Barbara Bush, talk show host Oprah Winfrey and Mrs Elizabeth Dole (tie), Lady Margaret Thatcher, Princess Diana, US Secretary of State designate Madeleine Albright, former First Lady Nancy Reagan, singer-actress Barbra Streisand and Queen Elizabeth. — AFP.

'DNA tests' for Jacko's wife

WASHINGTON — Singer Michael Jackson reportedly wants to be certain that his wife is carrying his baby.

A British newspaper said that he had ordered DNA tests before signing a contract with his spouse, Ms Debbie Rowe. The Daily Mirror said Ms Debbie Rowe would get US$1.25 million (S$1.75 million) when the baby is born, and US$280,000 a year as long as the marriage lasts. — AFP.

Meanwhile...

when stars Hollywood hear...

■ **MONUMENT FOR SINATRA'S MUM:** The city of Rossiglione in Italy announced on Saturday that it plans to erect a monument to commemorate the birth of Frank Sinatra's mother, Ms Natalina Garaventa, who was born on Dec 26, 1896, in the city.

■ **FERGIE TURNS TO WRITING:** Britain's cash-strapped Duchess of York has written two children's books to rescue her from threatened bankruptcy, according to a report in the Sunday Telegraph.

QUOTEWORTHY

Riots in W Java

District officials maintained that only two people died during the riot and that only one, a Chinese woman, pulled out of the charred remains of her shop in the town centre, was a direct victim of the violence.

But the actual process of recovery would take a much longer time, said legal aid worker Henasari who had driven the 116km from Bandung to Tasikmalaya on Thursday night to make sure her parents were all right. She returned to Bandung on Friday night.

30/12/96
REFERENCES TO WOMEN

■ **BIGAMIST JAILED:** A Canadian business executive was sentenced to two years' jail in Shanghai for having three wives in China, a report said yesterday.

the sou...

In 1993, he allegedly strangled his 22-day-old daughter because she slowed down the gang as it moved from hideout to hideout. — AFP.

...ate

The Sunday Times added that British police had also investigated Remli, who has lived in Britain since 1983 and has an Irish wife, but had not stopped his activities.

The conflict began in 1992

Iraqi opposition groups abroad have claimed they were behind the attack.

A diplomat in Jordan said that a young woman, who was in Mr Uday's vehicle during the attack, was suspected of being an accomplice and had also been arrested.

...Samorai told...

'They asked me a lot about Malaysia'

He said that when he was about to be released, the guerillas shook hands with him. "One of the youngsters told me to listen to some pop songs for her when I am out of there," he said, referring to a young woman rebel.

The workers are convinced that the closure programme is a Western plot.

"I think the G-7 countries want to protect their own nuclear industry. They are rich, they are obeyed," commented a middle-aged woman as she got into the bus to take her Chernobyl from the new town of Slavutich where the workers have lived since 1968.

p...

cheques...

The same federal equalisation legislation, introduced in Congress every year since 1993, will go back for consideration next year, said Ms Lourdes Santos Tancinco.

The Filipino lawyer who runs the free Fil-Am Vet Legal Clinic here says: "I'm not that hopeful, considering what's going on with the welfare cuts. Part of it is racism. Part of it is the budget."

She added that the veterans, in their 70s and 80s, are running out of time to enjoy their hard-won US benefits and their families in the same place if the government did not give them equal rights soon. — NYT.

Call to whip parents who abuse or abandon children

MUAR — Johor Wanita Umno has proposed that the Child Protection Act 1991 be amended to provide heavier penalties, such as mandatory whipping, for those who abuse or abandon their children.

Its chief, Ms Sabariah Ahmad, said it would set up a committee to study the Act and submit recommendations to the national Wanita Umno.

She said the Johor movement viewed seriously offences where children were found abandoned.

"Such cases create more social problems in the community," she said in Tangkak after meeting Muar Wanita Umno leaders.

She was commenting on two recent cases in Tangkak where siblings had been abandoned by their parents.

Meanwhile, in the cases referred to, Mustakim Karim and his wife Rahimah Ismail, both aged 33, have been charged under the Child Protection Act with abandoning their six children.

They are scheduled to be sentenced on Jan 20.

In the other case, a 28-year-old man and his 24-year-old wife have been detained on suspicion that they abandoned their three children at a Chinese temple in Tangkak on Dec 6.

Ms Sabariah, who is also the State Agriculture and Rural Development Committee chairman, added: "Parents can seek aid from the Welfare Department rather than take the easy way out and let their children suffer."

She said that Johor Wanita Umno had also set up a committee at all levels to help the government reduce social problems.

"We are taking a look at the worksites and factories to ensure the women are not exploited.

"We will continue to work to upgrade the status of women. We also want to create awareness among women on the importance of moral, spiritual and family values." — NST.

Then, the comely 29-year-old adds in Mandarin: "I was pretty helpless, and felt as if it was the end of the world

---

Hair-chewing dolls turn play sessions into nightmares

MIAMI — Voracious Cabbage Patch dolls turned play sessions into horror scenes for two young girls when the dolls chewed up their hair, giving their families a scare.

The dolls, designed to chew plastic food such as a toy licorice bar and french fries, got started on five-year-old Carla Fernandez's long hair — and would not stop munching.

"It chewed her hair up to her scalp," the girl's mother Carmen Fernandez said of the accident in Miami area on Thursday. "It kept going and going, and finally I had to cut off her hair."

The doll did not have an on-off switch.

On Friday, news media reported a similar incident in Indiana involving a seven-year-old girl. In that case, the doll's 20 screws had to be removed. But toy company Mattel's spokesman Glenn Bozarth has said the toy was safe. — AFP.

...ed a job as a car salesgirl. When she lan...

Plate 11 References to women in the press (Compiled from the *Straits Times*, 30 December 1996)

ambassador to listen to some pop songs for her. The suggestion might be that in the alternative societies represented by guerrillas and "terrorists" women are more likely to have power than within the existing validated social structures.

9.8 Fighting back against the US empire

Last in this Chapter, we look at the ways in which news can be consciously as well as latently manipulated to redress the balance against the domination of the West over the worldwide news machine. In 1994/5 Shieh Yee Bing made a study of the way in which China and the US were represented in the *Straits Times*. She analysed locally written editorials and features concerning China and the US for the month of May 1994, and also the whole of the *Straits Times* newspaper for 27 December 1994. The stance taken represented a conscious attempt to counter the values of American society. The pro-Western media and their news agencies often depict Europe and the US and its values as superior to those of the cultures and governments of the East, a position we observed in analysing the content of *Newsweek*. It was interesting to see that writers in a small nation-state like Singapore can use the linguistic tricks and subterfuges employed by the Western media to counter and overturn their cultural imperialism, and to construct a representation which gives credit to Confucian and Asian values.

Transitivity

Shieh's first finding was that Americans tended to be represented as Experiencers in Mental process clauses a whole lot more than the Chinese – 10.04 per cent versus 3.02 % in the December 27th paper (pp. 65–6). This can be interpreted in various ways. Probably most obviously that China's behaviour prompts the US to think and worry about it, to be emotionally or perceptually affected by the economic rise of China. China becomes something to be wondered at.

Reporting verbs

There is also widespread use of reporting clauses which make negative evaluative judgements about the US:

> While many Americans *claim* that China's treatment of 'dissidents' are crimes, it may come as a surprise to many Americans that 'dissidents' in the Chinese vocabulary is not a synonym for reformers.
>
> (p. 47)

The arguments about Americans *preaching* on 'universal individual freedom' is that human rights are also conditioned by local culture.

(p. 47)

Nominalisation

More subtle is the use of nominalisation to make existential presuppositions.
First, there are those which depict the US as weak, decadent or inconsistent:

It is difficult to see how capitalism can survive the decline of pax
Americana

(p. 52)

the inconsistencies evident in the US policy towards the Asia-pacific
region are partly a consequence of the end of the Gulf War.

(p. 52)

the afflictions of American society, from unwed motherhood to street
crime

(p. 58)

America's eroding economic power

(p. 57)

In contrast, Asians are successful and self-confident in the superiority of their
values:

their success is due to the superiority of Asian values over those of the
decadent West

(p. 52)

the new burgeoning self-confidence of Asian countries

(p. 53)

The economic growth of China is presupposed, as is its authoritarianism,
and the fact that it has opened, is opening or will be opening to outside influences:

the resounding expansion of Chinese economic growth has raised the possibility that such economic growth could undermine powerfully the authoritarian system

(p. 69)

China's economic boom

(p. 57)

robust economic development in China

(p. 69)

the opening of China

(p. 69)

Images of belligerence

The verbal and economic disagreements and unwelcome changes of trade policy are metaphorically represented as fighting, war, or, at the least, a confrontational staring match. Very often the US comes across as the initial aggressor, and China as the victorious party:

Bill Clinton could wield the MFN sledgehammer to advance US moral intervention in China

(p. 54)

the US brandishing trade threats to force China to respect human rights

(p. 54)

China and the other Asian nations are uneasy over US threats to unleash its prime trade weapon

(p. 54)

China is waging war against the invasion of fancy foreign liquor

China triumphs over the US in diplomatic victory

China hailed its success in facing down Washington

(p. 70)

Premodification

The pattern of conscious bias is probably most clear in the contrasting adjectives which are used to premodify China and the US, in the features and editorials, as in Table 9.6.

All these adjectives are intended as positive towards China and Asia, but negative towards the US and the West; though, personally, I contest the negative affect of 'static' – no-growth economies are certainly more sustainable and inflict less harm on the environment.

Table 9.6 Premodifying adjectives for China and the US (Shieh 1994/5: Figure 4.3, p. 63)

Attributive adjectives for China	Attributive adjectives for the US
booming China	weak dollar
rich East Asian countries	failed Western welfare states
prosperous East Asian societies	abysmal failure of US trade policies
spectacular economic growth in China	static economy
robust economic growth in China	feeble economic growth in America
collectivist Asia	individualistic Western societies
strong and different Asian cultures	hypocritical western liberals
China's 2,500 years of highly moralist teachings	decadent west
superior Asian values	violent America

One particularly interesting finding of Shieh's is the ambiguity of **pre-modification** and its relation to stereotyping. Adjectives before the noun can either be **restrictive** or **non restrictive**. In their more usual restrictive meaning, they define a subclass of the class picked out by the noun, e.g. in 'ginger cats are nervous', *ginger* defines one subclass of cats. In their non-restrictive meaning adjectives presume that all members of the class picked out by the noun share the quality referred to by the adjective. Take for example 'cacti are the only large plants to flourish in the barren desert'. 'The barren desert' refers to deserts in general, since they are all barren; it is not defining one particular kind of desert which is barren and distinguishing it from those deserts which are not. The interesting finding is that there is a potential ambiguity in many of the noun phrases which Shieh isolated. For example does 'fancy foreign liquor' mean 'the subclass of foreign liquor that is fancy' or 'foreign liquor, all of which is fancy'?

Table 9.7 Restricitive and non-restrictive interpretations of adjectives

Noun phrase	Meaning 1 Restrictive	Meaning 2 Nonrestrictive
the angry American middle class	'that part of the American middle class that is angry'	'the American middle class, all of which is angry'
failed Western welfare states	'the subclass of Western welfare states which have failed'	'Western welfare states, all of which have failed'
individualistic Western societies	'the subclass of Western societies that are individualistic'	'Western societies, all of which are individualistic'
the decadent West	'the decadent parts of the West'	'the West, all of which is decadent'
violent America	'the violent areas or parts of America'	'America, all of which is violent'
American individualism	'the special (prototypical) kind of individualism found in America'	'individualism, all of which is American in origin'

In summary, Shieh's analysis shows the *ST* as using:

- Mental process verbs to depict the US as wondering at the economic success and social and moral superiority of the Chinese;
- reporting verbs to represent US statements and criticisms of China as unreliable;
- presuppositions portraying the US's economic decline and social decadence;
- metaphors to paint a picture of a US aggressive towards but defeated by China;
- ambiguous modifiers to stereotype US and Western people as individualistic, violent and failed hypocrites.

The analysis suggests that the existing resources of grammar and vocabulary can be exploited for whatever ideological purposes – while much of the news is still post-imperialist there is the potential, given media access, to put forward an alternative ideology. However, our next chapter claims that there is something intrinsic to the grammar of English which makes certain

---

ACTIVITY 50

Take another newspaper and collect the headlines for the first fifteen or so pages. What countries get mentioned in these articles? Does the particular story reinforce the kind of stereotyping we hypothesised in our analysis of *Newsweek*?

It would be interesting to bring your collection of headlines to class for discussion purposes.

Project 5

Another possible project is to write a news article covering an event which you think may be of interest to your fellow students. The most interesting ones could be published in a magazine or student newspaper.

You should ask yourself the following questions about your report:

- How are you going to gather the news? Will this be the kind of scheduled event that an editor has in his press diary or are you going to aim

> for the rather trickier reporting of a surprising or unpredicted event?
>
> - What news values are you catering for in your selection of a news story – does your choice of news event conform to the stereotypes of what gets into the news, or are you going to attempt to cover usually neglected topics?
> - Whose voices are going to be represented in the news – the usual rich, powerful and important or those whose voices are hardly ever heard?
> - How do your transitivity choices in the clause represent power and responsibility, and do your reporting clauses interfere with the voices represented?
> - Does your text conform to the norms of representation of women (and other countries) that were found in the surveys in this chapter? Do you try to avoid stereotyping?
>
> In addition, you should revise the work we did on the generic structure of news reports in Chapter 1, where you rewrote the Red Ridinghood story. In the instructions for that rewriting activity note the hints on how to incorporate the more local features of newspaper language.
>
> This writing will be most useful if, besides the actual report, you produce notes explaining and justifying the linguistic choices which you have made.

ideology difficult to express, namely an ideology or world-view which matches that of modern ecological science.

9.9 Summary of Chapters 7 to 9

In Chapters 7, 8, and 9, we've looked at the discourse of advertisements, romance fiction, and newspapers. What overall pattern of cultural values and preoccupations does our analysis present? Not a very reassuring one. None of these discourses, if my samples are typical, deal both with serious political concerns and strive to encourage social engagement on the important issues facing the world in this coming century. Advertising unashamedly appeals to the individual consumer, and holds out the illusory promise of identity and social membership through the power of purchasing, or as personal dream fulfilment. Romance fiction must be partly escapist, at least the text we analysed about an unmarried 28-year-old, written largely for a married middle-aged readership.

Moreover, though serious newspapers deal with political issues, very few of them can be read by the powerless members of society, because of the economics of newspaper production. Also, issues persistently important to the powerless are not aired in the serious papers because of the values and controls which determine the content of the media. News for the working and middle classes has become a matter of entertainment and amusement rather than political debate and engagement.

As Frith (1981) puts it 'the problem [for capitalism] is to ensure that workers' leisure activities don't affect their discipline, skill or willingness to work'. Consumption advertising, reading romance, and being entertained by the news solve this problem quite neatly. The more important problems of survival of humans on earth and the degradation of the environment, vital to powerful and powerless alike, seldom stay in the centre of newspapers' agenda for long. So our next and last chapter is a case study in the representation of the nature–human relationship.

Suggestions for further reading

- Bell's *The Language of News Media* is a unique book since it is written by a linguist who is also a journalist, which gives him an insider's view of the context of news production. This is especially interesting for anyone considering a career in journalism as it shows the internal workings of news organisations as well as performing linguistic analyses.
- Fairclough's *Media Discourse* is centrally within the critical discourse field in a way in which Bell's book is not, and theorises, for example, on the nature of mass communication and the mixing of public and private genres. Despite the theoretical framework, the analysis of radio and TV shows is both riveting and revealing about discourse types and social relations.
- Roger Fowler's *Language in the News* has already been referred to several times. It is an accessible, clear and accurate work of linguistic analysis of media texts, and illustrates how ideological consensus is achieved in order to maintain the power structures of society. Another must for would-be journalists.

Chapter 10

Nature, vocabulary and grammar

Aims of the unit

To introduce the idea of an ecological critical discourse analysis.

To suggest how the existing grammar of English might be exploited or subverted to counter the technological ideology of the exploitation of nature.

To compare, in a case study, the grammatical representation of nature in *The Times* of London and Wordsworth's *The Prelude*.

- **10.0 Introduction: the need for an ecological critical discourse analysis**
  Points out that ecological critical discourse analysis should have priority over discourse analysis from other ideological perspectives.

- **10.1 Pro-ecologist metaphorical modification**
  Illustrates how metaphors can be chosen to reflect a more helpful representation of nature.

- **10.2 Grammatical modification**
  Argues that advances in scientific and ecological theory make changes in the use of English grammar imperative.

- **10.2.1 Challenges to Newtonian dynamics**
  Sketches major changes to scientific models this century, stressing the spontaneity and interdependence of natural systems.

- **10.2.2 Ordinary grammar and scientific theory**
  Argues that ordinary English grammar is out of step with the new scientific models of the natural world.

275

- **10.2.3 What can we do about grammar?**

  Suggests how we might exploit and modify grammar to better reflect science.

- **10.3 A case study in ecological CDA**

  Through computer analysis of transitivity in *The Times* and Wordsworth's *The Prelude* investigates the grammatical differences in the representation of nature – in Wordsworth more powerful, active in its existence and communicative than in *The Times*.

10.0 Introduction: the need for an ecological critical discourse analysis

So far in our case studies we have taken quite familiar ideology perspectives on discourse, explaining texts and their interpretations as sexist, capitalist and imperialist. Of course ideology is not monolithic (Williams 1977), and though these ideologies are dominant they coexist with a strong emergent ideology of feminism, and somewhat weakened oppositional ideologies of socialism and internationalism.

However, fashionable as feminist and socialist critiques are, they are a little beside the point. Our most urgent priority must be to address the ideology of the exploitation of nature which has developed over the last two hundred years since the Industrial Revolution in Europe at the end of the eighteenth century. The rather alarming result of our prevalent attitudes toward nature is that

> If today is a typical day on planet earth, humans will add fifteen million tons of carbon to the atmosphere, destroy 115 square miles of tropical rain forest, create 72 square miles of desert, eliminate between forty to one hundred species, erode seventy one million tons of topsoil, add twenty-seven hundred tons of CFCs to the atmosphere, and increase their population by 263,000.
>
> (David Orr, *Ecological Literacy,* p. 3)

In the context of the ecological crisis a single-minded preoccupation with sexist and capitalist-imperialist critical discourse analysis is rather like addressing the problem of who is going to fetch the deck-chairs on the Titanic, and who has the right to sit in them.

However, these ideological positions can reinforce the ecological one. A broader socialist view might be linked with a blueprint for a more sustainable way of living: a simple lifestyle in which consumer products are shared by neighbourhoods rather than owned by nuclear families, would reduce consumption and waste. High taxes with good publicly owned amenities make ecological sense. For, however hard we work, we are unlikely to be able to afford a garden with an Olympic-sized swimming pool, so we might just as well willingly pay taxes to fund civic swimming centres. Gross affluence and gross poverty undermine ecological sustainability. Equally, an anti-imperialist ideological perspective could feel free to celebrate the harmonious relationships with nature of many indigenous peoples; biological diversity and cultural–linguistic diversity must probably go hand in hand. Feminism too, may reinforce ecological positions. A feminist view which celebrates rather than regrets the gender construction of women as more caring, gentler people than the typical male, would fit well with campaigns to end the profligacy of arms spending and the threats of nuclear contamination.

10.1 Pro-ecologist metaphorical modification

An ecological discourse analysis has something, too, to learn from feminist critiques of language. In the popular consciousness the "politically correct" language of feminism is a result of a campaign to change vocabulary and pronouns (Fowler 1991: 96–7). Similar campaigns might be launched ecologically. For example, see what you make of the following text.

> Consumption tax may 'slow down' Japan's cancer
>
> The lesson for Singapore was never to take things for granted, he said, since it only had 25 years of cancer compared to 200 years for the Swiss, and half the Swiss population.

In cases of mature economies such as Japan, Switzerland or Singapore, the metaphor of 'cancer' can justifiably be substituted for 'growth'. It draws attention to the fact that growth in an already mature economy threatens the life-support systems of the planet, in much the same way as a cancerous growth eventually threatens the life-support systems of the human body. We might, while about it, point out the possible archaic metaphor of consumption (tuberculosis) in the headline.

Another candidate for lexical and metaphorical modification is the substitution of *ecology* or *nature* for the word *environment*. *Environment*, meaning "surroundings" tends to be interpreted according to the metaphor IMPORTANT = CENTRAL.

> **IMPORTANT/POWERFUL** = **CENTRAL**
> Central is important and powerful:
> *centre, hub, kernel, marrow, pith, inside (info), inner circle, pivotal, self-centred*
>
> non-central is less important/powerful:
> *satellite, spin-off, marginal/ized, side-effect/side issue/sidekick, side-lines/-ed*

If we use the word *environment*, presumably we suggest that humans are central and thus more important than nature. The candidates to replace the word *environment* are perhaps *ecology* and *nature*. *Ecology* which includes in its original semantics the Greek word for home, also suggests a rather anthropocentric attitude, but, as this metaphor is inaccessible to most of us perhaps that doesn't matter. Even so, *nature* seems a more "ecologically correct" word.

Besides these specific cases of using *cancer* and *nature* it might be possible to engineer vocabulary use on a wider scale. For example we could exploit the existing metaphorical equations HUMAN BODY = EARTH and LANDSCAPE = HUMAN BODY to blur the human/earth distinction.

HUMAN BODY = EARTH
Human bodies can be portrayed as earth/landscape

Part of body is part of the landscape:
alimentary canal, digestive tract, furrows on the brows, stubble (= unshaven beard), to crop hair (cf. grass)

Quality/state of a human is quality/state of the earth:
clod, craggy, devastated, grit/-ty, rugged

Action on/of a human is action on/of the earth:
bury your face in your hands, plant a kiss/blow/kick on someone, tremor, quake with terror

PLACE/LANDSCAPE = HUMAN/BODY
The state/characteristic of a place is the state/characteristic or behaviour of a human:
bald, bare, denuded, gaunt, sterile, virgin lands/forest, a sleepy place, a dead seaside resort, sprawling village/town/building, straggling village/town/suburbs, tame/untamed land/-scape, placid, treacherous ground/sea, hospitable /inhospitable soil, environment-friendly

Parts of the earth/landscape are parts of a human body:
arm/neck/tongue of land, backbone, bowels of the earth, brow/crest/crown of hill (cf. head), face of the earth, head of a valley, foot of a mountain, finger of land, mouth of a cave/hole/river, shoulder of a hill, heart of a city (= centre)

Action on the countryside/landscape is like action on a human body:
comb the countryside, dominate, lie, gash/scar on the landscape, the rape of the countryside

10.2 Grammatical modification

Besides tinkering with the vocabulary of the language, which is a fairly superficial kind of modification, we need a more fundamental approach where it is the grammar which is rejigged in directions favourable to ecology. My belief is that the English language in its most simple material process grammar represents the world in ways that are in tune with the view of the world which grew up out of Newtonian physics, but out of step with modern science and modern ecological theory. The next few paragraphs elaborate on this idea, and suggest how a few less obvious grammatical choices can be exploited for pro-ecological ends.

One of the main features of Newtonian theory is its emphasis on movement. Newtonian dynamics concerned itself solely with the laws of motion:

> There is only one type of change surviving in [Newtonian] dynamics, one process, and that is motion. The qualitative diversity of changes in nature is reduced to the study of the relative displacement of material bodies.
>
> (Prigogine and Stengers 1985: 62)

In concentrating on changes which involve movement (rather than chemical changes or evolutionary changes), Newton represented objects as basically inert until they were acted upon by some external force.

It was Newtonian physics, particularly dynamics, which made possible, two hundred years ago, the Industrial Revolution in whose aftermath we are struggling, ecologically, to survive. This paradigm of an external agent applying a force to an inert object to set it in motion has been transferred to our dealings with nature. We are the external actor, and we apply force to an apparently inert nature, which is seen as separate from us. The Newtonian world-view and the technological world-view is one which we should abandon if we are to stop desertification, species destruction, ozone depletion and those ills which Orr listed at the beginning of this chapter. As we shall see, and as modern scientific theory realises, we have for too long forgotten that nature is far from inert, that we are part of it, so that it may take revenge on us if we assume blindly that we can dominate it.

10.2.1 Challenges to Newtonian dynamics

There are at least two aspects of twentieth-century science which challenge the Newtonian view of matter – that nature is passive and controllable and that human observers and actors are separate from what they observe and act on.

The second law of thermodynamics and the theory of entropy challenged the idea that natural objects can be completely controlled. This law states that it is impossible to make an engine which will continuously take heat from a heat source and, by itself, turn it all into an equivalent amount of mechanical work. The law indicates that the energy in the universe is inescapably and spontaneously being lost, or dissipated.

> Thus the 'negative' property of dissipation shows that, unlike [Newtonian] dynamic objects, thermodynamic objects can only be partially controlled. Occasionally they 'break loose' into spontaneous change.
>
> (Prigogine and Stengers 1985: 120)

The study of the movement of fluids such as phenomena like convection and turbulence also suggests a spontaneity which Newtonian dynamic systems deny.

Viewed in terms of the second law, the universe is gradually winding down to a disordered state, a state of maximum entropy, a structureless, homogeneous, equilibrium. For example, if cold water and hot water are separated this is a relatively ordered state. But if they are put in the same container they will gradually become a homogenous mass of lukewarm water, relatively disordered and structureless.

However, spontaneity also operates in another direction to balance the tendency to increasing entropy. The biological sciences, and particularly the theory of evolution, show increasing order among living beings, more and more complex structures evolving, and more and more disequilibrium.

Second, quantum mechanics, as Heisenberg showed, implies that when scientific observations are taking place, the observed object and the observing instrument can no longer be regarded as separate (Bohm 1980: 134). It is as though they are inextricably interconnected, as if they are part of the same phenomenon. The scientific observer is not outside the system which she is observing and recording, for at least two reasons. Scientific observations are time-orientated, and time can only be measured through entropy: 'Entropy is time's arrow'. In addition, since scientists are living beings, they themselves are manifestations of the unbalanced system, a disequilibrium (Prigogine and Stengers 1985: 300).

A modern ecological theory, such as James Lovelock's *Gaia* hypothesis, reinforces these two challenges to the classical physics view of the natural universe. Lovelock believes the world, or the earth goddess *Gaia* – including the atmosphere, the oceans, living things, the rocks and minerals of the crust – functions as one large organism. It is rather like a giant redwood tree, of which more than nine-tenths is dead wood, with only the outer skin and leaves "alive". Such an organism is self-regulating. Active feedback processes, operated unconsciously and automatically by living things, keep the temperature, oxidation state, acidity, and aspects of the rocks and waters constant at any one time. For instance, one would expect that the oxygen and methane in the atmosphere would react in the sunlight to produce carbon dioxide and water vapour, and that the atmosphere would return to a state of stable equilibrium. In fact, the amount of oxygen and methane in the atmosphere remains more or less constant; we live in an environment of constant disequilibrium. It can only remain constant because the living sub-systems of the *Gaia* system actively and continuously work to keep the environment suitable for life. The interdependence of these various subsystems means that evolution and life concerns *Gaia*, not the organisms or the environment taken separately (Lovelock 1988: 19). One rather optimistic scenario along these lines suggests that the melting of the ice caps and rising sea levels will put more pressure on the earth's crust, leading to more frequent volcanic eruptions which will throw dust into the atmosphere and thereby reduce warming. An ingenious self-regulating device.

Gaia theory most obviously reinforces the first scientific challenge to Newton: the earth goddess *Gaia* is not inert, but is constantly organising and regulating herself. In addition, the theory underlines the second, emphasising the wholeness and interrelatedness of nature and of humans as (a small) part of nature. From a *Gaia* angle, exploiting nature as a resource becomes an obvious threat to the well-being of the ecosystem and the human race as part of it. Mining the earth for minerals is about as sensible as eating one's liver for nutrients.

10.2.2 Ordinary grammar and scientific theory

We have sketched briefly how modern physics and ecology undermined two assumptions in the world-view of classical science. But what has this to do with the grammar of English? I would suggest that English grammar typically structures reality according to a Newtonian view of the world. Let's take an example of a fairly ordinary sentence.

> Fishermen traditionally caught 100,000 tons of fish per year in the North Sea.

This grammatical construction of reality encourages us to think in ways which are Newtonian in essence, but wrong according to modern science. There are, at least, two things "wrong" with this kind of grammatical construction of the "world out there".

(1)   The division into the Actors who apply force or energy, the fishermen, and the inert or passive Affected, the fish. This makes us think of the fish as inac-

tive, not allowing for any feedback within the *Gaia* mechanism, as though cause and effect only operate in one direction. Take a clearer example: 'John drove the car'. In the longer term the Actor, John will be affected by the consequences of his actions: the car will produce sulphur dioxide and nitrogen dioxide which may contribute to John or his children suffering from asthma, and will definitely contribute to global warming which is already affecting him. He may appear to be doing things to the car, and the car to the atmosphere but the atmosphere will actually be doing things to him too.

(2) This sentence marginalises the 'environment' or location circumstance ('in the North Sea') suggesting that the North Sea is either powerless, or is not affected. In fact the catching of so many tons of fish obviously changes the North Sea's ecosystem.

10.2.3 What can we do about grammar?

We need a grammar which constructs a world-view more reflective of modern scientific/ecological theory. Here is a selection of structures and grammatical resources which could be used to reflect the views of the modern natural sciences more closely.

Location circumstance as actor

Instead of marginalising the environment by referring to it in a Location Circumstance, we have the option of turning it into a Subject, or Actor.

Ants are crawling all over the bed →
The bed is crawling with ants

The environment, the bed, and the participants, the ants, become, in the transformed version, mutual participants in the process.

Ergativity

There are a number of verbs which belong to what is called the **ergative** paradigm (Halliday 1994: 163–72), for example *sail, tear* and *cook (Table 10.1)*. The difference between ergative verbs and non-ergative verbs is that when two participants Actor and Affected are involved, in other words the transitive (or **effective**) version, the clause is extended in different directions (Table 10.2). With non-ergatives the clause is extended to the right, with ergatives to the left.

Table 10.1 Ergative clause patterns

| | Intransitive/middle | | | Transitive/effective | |
Medium	Process		Instigator	Process	Medium
The boat	sailed	v.	Mary	sailed	the boat
The cloth	tore	v.	The nail	tore	the cloth
The rice	cooked	v.	Pat	cooked	the rice

Table 10.2 Participants and ergativity

	Non-ergative	Ergative
intransitive	John swallowed	The cloth tore
transitive	John swallowed a grape	Paul tore the cloth
	---------->	<----------

Ergative verbs without an object, i.e. intransitive, represent changes to an entity as the result of some self-generating process. For example 'the door opened' suggests that the energy for this process originated in the door. When so-called inanimate things are Actors in such clauses they obviously represent nature as far from inert. Compare this, again, with Prigogine and Stengers's remarks:

> Unlike dynamic objects, thermodynamic objects can only be partially controlled. Occasionally they 'break loose' into spontaneous change.
>
> (p. 120)

Might the increases in the number of ergative verbs over the last 100 years, be some kind of adaptive response to the insights of modern scientific thinking?

Mühlhäusler, quoting Wilkins (1989: 71ff.), suggests that the use of intransitive ergative verbs is one of the features of Australian aboriginal languages which reinforce the identity between people and things (Mühlhäusler 1996: 123). The argument goes that the ergative verbs of these languages are usually used intransitively, making human agency a special case.

Animation or personification

We saw earlier that we can use metaphorical vocabulary already in the dictionary of English to blur the distinction between humans and the landscape. However, there are various ways in which, to represent nature as less than inert, as animate, we can systematically modify grammar.

First, metaphorically, we can reconstruct Experiences in mental process clauses as though they were Actors in material processes, e.g. *we noticed the river* → *the river arrested my gaze, we love the forest* → *the forest touches my heart.* Let's call this **activation of experiences**.

Second, metaphorically, we can reconstruct relational processes into material ones, so that instead of nature being static it is seen as active. For example *There are five trees in the valley/five trees are in the valley* → *Five trees stand in the valley, There is a boulder on top of the hill* → *a boulder tops the hill*. Let's call this **activation of tokens**.

Besides these more specific patterns of activation, there are general patterns in which verbs which normally take animals or humans as subject are used for natural, traditionally inanimate, objects. All verbal and mental processes, which are used in this way will count as **personification** and **animalisation** respectively.

We should sum up our discussion up to this point, so that we can bear it in mind as we proceed with our first case study. We discussed:

- the urgent need for an ecological critical discourse analysis as being more fundamental to our survival than feminist, anti-imperialist or socialist CDA;
- examples of how metaphorical vocabulary could be changed or exploited to influence our attitudes to and impact on nature;
- how modern science and ecological theory has challenged some of the assumptions of the Newtonian cosmology:

  – nature's passivity and controllability
  – the divisibility of nature from humans as observers and actors

- how basic grammar is essentially Newtonian, and has led us to think in terms of technological domination of nature;
- the possibility of grammatical modification using the following structures:

  – circumstances as Actors
  – ergativity
  – animation/personification
  – activating Experiences and Tokens

10.3 A case study in ecological CDA

One important question is how average modern urban educated humans think of nature or represent their relationships with nature. It would be a massive research project to investigate this, so I considered the easier question of how broadsheet newspapers represent nature and construct human relationships to it. The rationale claiming a link between these two questions lies in the importance of newspapers in our modern culture. For many people, newspapers are probably the only regular leisure reading, and are the most widely circulated print medium. So I chose to analyse the text of one copy of *The Times* of London, or, more precisely, those articles by *Times* journalists, ignoring press agency reports.

But, it is equally interesting to compare the treatment of nature in a modern broadsheet with her treatment in a text by a "nature poet". I chose Wordsworth, because his name is synonymous with nature poetry, and, incidentally, *The Prelude* provides a text of comparable length to one copy of *The Times*. In addition, Wordsworth was writing before the Industrial Revolution had taken hold, and one would therefore expect his attitudes to contrast with the technological attitudes of the last two hundred years.

Two specific questions were addressed in this case study.

(1)   What elements of nature figure most prominently in *The Times* compared with the *Prelude*?
(2)   What degree of power do *The Times* and *Prelude* confer on nature?

To answer the first question, the Concorder computer program was used to compile a frequency list of all the vocabulary in the two texts which referred to these classes of natural objects:

- animals;
- plants, flowers, fruit and vegetables;
- landscape;
- rivers, lakes, seas and other bodies of water;
- weather.

The second research question could then be addressed. For all the clauses in which this nature vocabulary occurred, either as Participant or Circumstance, a Hallidayan transitivity analysis was conducted.

What natural elements figure most prominently (Tables 10.3 and 10.4)?

The most obvious finding is that even if 25 per cent is added to these *Times* figures to compensate for the fact that *The Prelude* is 25 per cent longer (giving the figures in brackets in Table 10.4), nature is much more important in *The Prelude* than *The Times*.

It is startling, therefore, that animals are represented so strongly in *The Times*. This is largely due to the British preoccupation with horses, dogs and other pets and, during the period of publication, cattle suffering from BSE. Animals as

Table 10.3 Frequency of natural elements in *The Times* and *The Prelude*

	The Times			The Prelude	
	R	A	P		
Animals	117	156	122%	127	100%
Landscape	79	105	24%	436	100%
Weather	16	21	16%	133	100%
Lakes, seas, rivers	26	35	13.5%	259	100%
Plants	29	39	14%	277	100%

Key
R = Raw
A = Adjusted for differing length of texts
P = percentage frequency compared with *The Prelude*
Note
To make comparisons, the raw figures had to be adjusted because the rough word counts for the two texts are *Times* 43,500, and *Prelude* 58,000. This adjustment gives the A figure in Table 10.3 (and the figure in parenthesis in Table 10.4). The P figure was calculated by taking *The Prelude* as 100 per cent, and expressing *The Times* figures as a percentage of this.

Table 10.4 Rank order of natural elements in *The Prelude* and *The Times*

The Prelude		The Times		
Landscape	436	Animals	117	(156)
Plants	277	Landscape	79	(105)
Lakes, seas, rivers	259	Plants	29	(39)
Weather	133	Lakes/seas	26	(35)
Animals	127	Weather	16	(21)

pets (or horses on which to gamble), perhaps are a deliberate attempt to maintain some link with nature, even within an urban environment. For the British, dogs and horses also probably represent a displaced snobbery. You may not have much of a pedigree yourself, but by buying a pedigree dog you can vicariously experience a kind of canine aristocracy. (And the Royal Family is, of course, also famous for its love of dogs and horses, so you are expressing solidarity with them, as a member of the same consumer club.) Remember, the statistics come from the very establishment paper, *The Times*.

When the frequency list of lexical items had been produced by computer it had to be checked manually, otherwise the results would have been misleading, with inflated figures for animals and plants in *The Times*. Not surprisingly *plant* is often industrial plant. *Flora* was the name of the margarine company. The apparent prevalence of bats turned out to be references to BAT or British American Tobacco. Eagles mainly materialised as *Eagle Star Insurance*. Apparently, newspapers like *The Times* are content to refer to animals and plants simply as parts of company and brand names. It may well be, given the values of consumer capitalism, that the more we build industrial plant, eat margarine, insure ourselves against disasters, and smoke tobacco, the fewer and less diverse the plants, and the lower the population of eagles and bats. One tiger more in your tank might mean one tiger less in the jungle.

Before we compare the way these natural elements are treated in our two texts it is interesting to note what aspects of nature are present in the newspaper but absent in *The Prelude*. The main categories seem to be chemistry and disease. *The Times* refers to oxygen, steroids, ozone, CFCs, molecules, polymers, cellulose, acetic acid, and sulphuric acid. It also mentions flu, sickness, Creutzfeldt–Jakob disease, and BSE. Urban populations, though they may isolate themselves from nature to a large extent, still cannot cut themselves off from those small but dangerous natural organisms – bacteria and viruses. In fact, the more people are crowded into cities, the more virulent germs can afford to become – they can kill their victims and still be sure of finding another host.

Which of these texts represents nature as most powerful?

In order to answer this question I carried out a transitivity analysis of the clauses featuring natural elements. To draw conclusions about the representation of power, we have, of course, to make some assumptions about which kinds of participants tend to be more powerful, and which least powerful. For this purpose the following hierarchy might be used.

(1) Actor in Transitive Clauses: an active participant powerful enough to affect other entities.
(2) Actor (Medium) in Intransitive Clauses: an active participant though not affecting other entities.
(3) Sayer: powerful enough to send messages and therefore have an effect on the consciousness of other sentient participants.
(4) Experience: capable of impinging on the consciousness of others but non-volitionally.
(5) Experiencer: sentient and responsive to outside stimuli.
(6) Affected: powerless because acted upon, the victim of the power of Actors.

The details of this hierarchy may be rather debatable, but at least we probably accept that Actors and Sayers, (1) to (3) are rather more powerful than other participants.

Comparison of Actor and Sayer frequencies

One way, therefore, of introducing the general findings of my analysis is to total the numbers of Actors and Sayers and represent these as a percentage of

Table 10.5 Actor/Sayer participants as percentage of total for each natural category

Category	The Times	The Prelude
Weather	19	50
Animals	13	21
Lakes, seas, rivers	8	18
Plants	10	17
Landscape	0	9

all participants and circumstances, as in Table 10.5. Using these criteria we can say that when nature is mentioned, and of course it is mentioned much less in the newspaper, it is twice as active in *The Prelude* as it is in *The Times*. What is interesting, however, is that more or less the same rank ordering occurs in both texts, weather top, animals next, and landscape bottom, but with plants and bodies of water exchanging ranks.

We noted already that urban populations have successfully (or disastrously) isolated themselves from certain aspects of nature, with viruses and chemicals the major exceptions. A further exception, is, of course, weather. Although we do our best with our central heating and air-conditioning to escape it, it still impacts on our existence, even within an urban setting, where, on the other hand, plants, natural landscapes and bodies of water may be few and far between. This can be seen clearly in an article from the Singapore *Straits Times* newspaper, which illustrates the fact that Singapore has the highest number of deaths from lightning per head of population:

Lightning kills worker on board ship

A FOREIGN worker died after he was struck by **lightning** at Sembawang Shipyard on Monday afternoon, the second death due to lightning in eight days.

Mr Salauddin Hossain, 31, was a rigger on board the Rikhard Zorge, a tanker berthed at the yard for repairs. He was struck by **lightning** at around 1.45 pm, after tightening a mooring rope. There was only a slight drizzle and some thunder at the time.

A boy, seven, died last Monday after being struck by **lightning** while walking to a bus-stop in Jurong during a thunderstorm. His mother and sister were both seriously hurt.

[…]

Detailed results and discussion

Let's look, now, in more detail at the way nature is represented in our texts. The text-processing procedures and analysis gave the rough percentages for the different participant types and circumstantial elements with regard to each aspect of nature in Tables 10.6 to 10.10. References will be made to these tables in the course of our discussion. We'll start with more specific discussion on Sayers and Actors as these represent the most powerful participants.

Table 10.6 Participant status of animals and birds

Participant	The Times	The Prelude
Total nominal groups	117	127
Actor transitive	8.5%	0.7%
Actor intransitive	1.7%	9.2%
Sayer	2.6%	10.7%
Experiencer	2.3%	4.6%
Experience	7.7%	19.8%
Affected	41.9%	19.8%

Table 10.7 Participant status of bodies of water

Participant	The Times	The Prelude
Total nominal groups	26	259
Actor transitive	7.7%	5.8%
Actor intransitive		6.2%
Sayer		5.8%
Experiencer		1.2%
Experience	7.7%	4.6%
Affected	19%	9.3%

Table 10.8 Participant status of plants

Participant	The Times	The Prelude
Total nominal groups	29	277
Actor transitive	7.7%	5.8%
Actor intransitive	10.3%	9.7%
Sayer		1.8%
Experiencer		1.1%
Experience	6.9%	6.9%
Affected	48.2%	15.5%

Table 10.9 Participant status of landscape

Participant	The Times	The Prelude
Total nominal groups	79	436
Actor transitive	–	4.8%
Actor intransitive	–	3.2%
Sayer	–	1.1%
Experiencer	–	1.4%
Experience	–	4.4%
Affected	15.2%	16%

Table 10.10 Participant status of weather

Participant	The Times	The Prelude
Total nominal groups	16	133
Actor transitive	6.25%	22.6%
Actor intransitive	12.5%	24.8%
Sayer		3%
Experiencer		0.75%
Experience		3.8%
Affected	25%	16.6%

Nature as Sayer

The high incidence of Sayers and Experiences in *The Prelude* suggests Wordsworth's openness to messages from nature. Sayers in *The Prelude* tend to be associated with, on the one hand, animals and birds, and on the other hand with rivers and streams. Let's look first at some examples of animals and birds (Table 10.6).

> By the still borders of the misty lake,
> Repeating favourite verses with one voice,
> Or conning more, as happy as the birds
> That round us **chaunted**.

> The heifer **lows**, uneasy at the voice
> Of a new master; **bleat** the flocks aloud.

By contrast, the avian Sayers in *The Times* are comic:

Birdbrains fight ruff justice in court

A HEN and a duck will appear in court today as character witnesses for a dog branded a livestock worrier. Mark Hayes, 33, a smallholder from

Llangranog on the Dyfed coast, is relying on Gloria, a brown-feathered chicken, and Snowy, a white duck, to clear his pet dog Dino.

Mr Hayes insists it is a case of mistaken identity, but to be on the safe side the defence case will rely heavily on <u>the birds'</u> **testimony**. Gloria has shared the courtyard of Mr Hayes's farmhouse with Dino, a five-year-old Jack Russell–Cairn cross, for 18 months. Yesterday <u>the chicken</u> showed confidence in Dino, **clucking** quietly while it sniffed around.

<u>Snowy</u>, recently judged best of its breed at the Royal Welsh Agricultural Show, is owned by one of Mr Hayes's friends and **quacks** happily when Dino is around, seemingly unruffled by the dog's friendly attentions.

Mr Hayes hopes that by bringing Dino, Gloria and Snowy together at Cardigan Magistrates' Court he will prove that his dog is innocent. He was given permission at an earlier hearing to take them to court.

Mr Hayes says that he and Dino were away from the village at the time an informant claimed to have seen Dino worrying ducks belonging to Janet French, a neighbour. He said yesterday: 'Dino is a kind and affectionate dog without an ounce of malice in him'.

Mr Hayes faces a £200 fine if Dino is convicted.

Other animals to have had their day in court include <u>Barney the parrot</u>, which **'testified'** last year against a man accused of handling it as stolen goods. <u>The bird</u> **exposed** the guilty party by **whistling** and letting its chin be tickled when its real owner entered the witness box.

Let's now turn to bodies of water, and their representation as Sayers (Table 10.7). While oceans, in the newspaper, are used as labels for political entities ('The Pacific Forum', or 'on both sides of the Atlantic') in Wordsworth, water, personified, speaks for itself.

And when at evening on the public way
I sauntered, like <u>a river</u> **murmuring**
And **talking** to itself when all things else
Are still . . .

<u>The wild brooks</u> **prattling** from invisible haunts . . .

The sands of Westmoreland, <u>the creeks and bays</u>
<u>Of Cumbria's rocky limits, they</u> can **tell**
How, when the Sea threw off his evening shade . . .

. . . the roar of <u>waters, torrents, streams</u>
<u>Innumerable,</u> **roaring** with one voice!

Wordsworth is, by his own admission

... a spoiled child ... in daily **intercourse**
With those crystalline rivers, solemn heights,
And mountains, ranging like a fowl of the air

Indeed, in Wordsworth's ideal world, we should not interfere with rivers
and treat them as Affecteds since this will actually inhibit their powers of
communication:

The famous brook, who, soon as he **was boxed**
Within our garden, found himself at once,
As if by trick insidious and unkind,
Stripped of his voice and left to dimple down
(Without an effort and without a will)
A channel paved by man's officious care.

To sum up, water and to a lesser extent animals/birds are much more serious communicators than their counterparts in *The Times*. The idea that nature
can speak to us and that we should be receptive to its messages as Experiencers
can, of course, give us another trajectory for our scientific and technological
advances, perhaps a more positive one than when technology is used to
enhance our material power as Actors. Scientific measuring instruments convey
messages from nature which may lead to a more reciprocal relationship. Will
we respond to messages about the ozone layer and global warming which
nature is sending us?

Nature as Actor

Let's turn now, to see more details and examples of nature's active power in our
texts. In newspapers, when animals and bodies of water are Actors in material
process clauses, usually they are transitive (Tables 10.6 and 10.7):

LEMON'S MILL, the Martin Piper-trained mare, **took** over £18,000 in
recorded bets out of the ring

Supported down to 11–8 favourite, the mare **trounced** Maremma Gale by
24 lengths

Material, **washed** on to the minerals periodically by rain or tide.

The subtropical Jurassic seas that **covered** southern England.

To be newsworthy, animals, birds and water have to make an impact. We might contrast this with clauses typical of *The Prelude*, where their actions can be described, quite apart from any effect they may achieve beyond themselves.

> The eagle **soars** high in the element

> That lowly bed whence I had heard the wind
> **Roar** and the rain **beat** hard

Landscape also figures quite commonly as an intransitive Actor. The following passage describes the young Wordsworth ice-skating, and the highlighted clauses in the last ten lines illustrate a blurring of the nature–human distinction, as though the skater's movement makes him aware of an energy inherent in the banks and cliffs:

> So through the darkness and the cold we flew,
> And not a voice was idle; with the din
> Smitten, the precipices **rang** aloud;
> The leafless trees and every icy crag
> **Tinkled** like iron; while far distant hills
> Into the tumult sent an alien sound
> Of melancholy not unnoticed, while the stars
> Eastward were sparkling clear, and in the west
> The orange sky of evening died away.
> Not seldom from the uproar I retired
> Into a silent bay, or sportively
> Glanced sideway, leaving the tumultuous throng,
> To cut across the reflex of a star
> That fled, and flying still before me, gleamed
> Upon the glassy plain; and oftentimes,
> When we had given our bodies to the wind,
> And all the shadowy banks on either side
> **Came sweeping** through the darkness, **spinning** still
> The rapid line of motion, then at once
> Have I reclining back upon my heels,
> Stopped short; yet still the solitary cliffs
> **Wheeled** by me even as if the earth had rolled
> With visible motion her diurnal round!
> Behind me did they stretch in solemn train,
> Feebler and feebler, and I stood and watched
> Till all was tranquil as a dreamless sleep.

One of our grammatical modification devices seem quite prominent here: the use of ergative verbs: *sweep*, *spin*, *wheel*, *ring* and *tinkle*. (They are ergative, remember, because when transitive, the extra participant will be Subject rather than Object.)

Landscape Actors in intransitive clauses give us an example of a second kind of pro-ecological grammatical modification. The example below promotes what is literally a location Circumstance into an Actor

and all <u>the pastures</u> **dance** with lambs

Compare this with the more common sense 'Lambs dance in all the pastures'. And contrast it with the newspaper's

Residential areas already suffer enough from the noise and damage caused

Although superficially similar to 'the pastures dance with lambs' we interpret this rather differently: either it is the residents who suffer, or the pockets of the owners and developers.

We have been looking at the way landscape features as actor in intransitive clauses. However, Table 10.9 shows that more often landscape is an actor in transitive clauses, and it is this active nature of the landscape in Wordsworth which sets it apart from landscape as we commonsensically conceive it. Typically, mountains feature as these transitive actors:

I had seen ...
<u>The western mountain</u> **touch** his setting orb

<u>A huge peak, black and huge,</u>
As if with voluntary power instinct
Upreared its head.

And <u>mountains</u> over all, **embracing** all;

The last example suggests the unity, connectedness and indivisibility of nature as though Wordsworth were prefiguring Lovelock, or Lovelock echoing him.

Weather, too, is an important transitive actor, but whereas landscape seems to act on other natural objects, weather affects humans and the poet in particular. The very opening of *The Prelude* demonstrates:

Oh there is blessing in <u>this gentle breeze</u>,
A visitant that while <u>it</u> **fans** my cheek
Doth seem half-conscious of the joy <u>it</u> **brings**
From the green fields, and from yon azure sky.

In another famous passage, the boy Wordsworth feels the wind (and grass and rock) supporting him as he climbs steep crags:

> Oh! when I have hung
> Above the raven's nest, by knots of grass
> And half-inch fissures in the slippery rock
> But ill **sustained**, and almost (so it seemed)
> **Suspended** by the blast that blew amain,
> Shouldering the naked crag, oh, at that time
> While on the perilous ridge I hung alone,
> With what strange utterance did the loud dry wind
> Blow through my ear! The sky seemed not a sky
> Of earth – and with what motion moved the clouds!

The repeated representation of weather affecting humans in *The Prelude* is not very different from its representation in newspapers, for example the passage on lightning in Singapore quoted earlier. What distinguishes the Actors in *The Prelude* most from those in the typical newspaper is the energy and potential given to the landscape.

Personification/activation of experiences and tokens

We noted earlier, as two kinds of grammatical modification, the upgrading of Experiences and Tokens to Actors. This is a widespread and stylistically significant phenomenon in *The Prelude*. It applies most obviously to plants, landscape and weather. Many of these Actors are only metaphorically material. In a more common sense syntax they would be Experiences, though paraphrasing into such syntax (attempted in brackets) becomes increasingly problematical in the following examples:

> Till the whole cave, so late a senseless mass,
> **Busies** the eye with images and forms
> Boldly assembled

(cf. I saw the whole cave...)

> Oh there is blessing in this gentle breeze,
> A visitant that while it fans my cheek
> Doth seem half-conscious of the joy it **brings**
> From the green fields, and from yon azure sky.

(cf. I felt joyful (when the breeze fanned my cheek))

> ... my favourite grove,
> Tossing in sunshine its dark boughs aloft,
> As if to make the strong wind visible,
> **Wakes** in me agitations like its own

(cf. I am disturbed by my favourite grove)

> ... Lofty elms,
> Inviting shades of opportune recess,
> **Bestowed** composure on a neighbourhood
> Unpeaceful in itself.

(cf. I was calmed by the lofty elms)

> Yet, hail to you
> Moors, mountains, headlands, and ye hollow vales,
> Ye long deep channels for the Atlantic's voice,
> Powers of my native region! Ye that **seize**
> The heart with firmer grasp!

 (cf. I adore/love/worship/am obsessed with the moors, mountains, headlands, etc.)

> Oh! **wrap** him in your shades, ye giant woods
> And you, *ye groves*, whose ministry it is
> To **interpose** the covert of your shades

(cf. Ye giant woods and groves, prevent me seeing him)

The last two examples illustrate that the Actor potential of landscape and plants often coincides with the use of apostrophes or calls to nature, where the Actor nominal group is used as a vocative term of address: 'ye hollow vales', 'ye long deep channels', 'ye groves'.

A further very significant pattern in Wordsworth is the metaphorical transformation of a basically Relational Process into a Material one, which we refer to as activation of Tokens. Some quite common verbs like *surround*, *lie* are half Material half Relational, and these proportions may vary with the Subject of the verb (Martin and Matthiessen 1991). For example 'the moat surrounds the castle' pushes in the direction of a Relational process, whereas 'the soldiers surrounded the castle' pushes towards the Material. Exploiting such vocabulary is a widespread tendency in Wordsworth, so nature becomes more active than static:

> The visionary dreariness ...
> **Invested** moorland waste, and naked pool,
> The beacon **crowning** the lone eminence

> The garden **lay**
> Upon a slope **surmounted** by a plain
> Of a small bowling-green; beneath us **stood**
> A grove

> There **rose** a crag,
> That, from the meeting-point of two highways
> Ascending, **overlooked** them both

Instead of 'being at the top of' an eminence or slope or two highways, the plain or beacon or crag 'surmounts' or 'crowns' or 'overlooks' them. And in this environment of active existence even the quite normal *stood* seems to take on more energy than usual. The high percentage of landscape as Affected in *The Prelude* (Table 10.9) is partly due to those metaphorical Material processes, which represent the relative positions of one part of the landscape in relation to another.

Nature as Experience or Affected

Table 10.6 shows two significant patterns which we have not yet commented upon. There is a much higher number of animals as Experiences in *The Prelude* compared with *The Times*. This suggests that they are worth observing and noticing for their own sake, a corollary of their communicative potential:

> I **spied**
> A glow-worm underneath a dusky plume
> Or canopy of yet unwithered fern,

> At leisure, then, I **viewed**, from day to day,
> The spectacles within doors, birds and beasts
> Of every nature,

> ... **see** that pair, the lamb
> And the lamb's mother, and their tender ways

In *Tne Times*, on the other hand, there is a much higher frequency of animals as affected by humans but doing nothing (but suffer) in return. The following article is typical:

Tube drivers ran over injured dog to avoid delays

LONDON Underground ordered four trains to pass over a dog lying injured on the track to avoid causing rush-hour delays, it admitted yesterday. One driver who refused to carry out the instruction was replaced by another who was 'less squeamish', a spokesman said.

'Controllers were satisfied that the dog would not suffer further injury because it was lying between the rails. A lot of passengers had to get to work or important meetings.' He added: 'No disciplinary action was taken against the driver who refused to proceed.'

The National Canine Defence League called for the Underground to be prosecuted for causing unnecessary suffering to <u>the German shepherd-cross, which</u> strayed on to the line and **was hit** by two trains. <u>The dog</u> **was** eventually **taken** to a nearby station and **put down** by the RSPCA after suffering serious head and internal injuries and burns from the live rail. London Underground said it was lying on a sleeper between the tracks and would not have suffered further physical injury from trains passing over it.

The incident began at 7.07 am when the driver of a Northern Line train in the tunnel near Highgate station hit something on the track. He walked back and **found** <u>the dog</u> then radioed to control and was told to continue.

A second train at 7.10 am with two drivers was ordered to proceed over the dog. When the first driver refused he was replaced by the second. The next two trains were also forced to drive over the dog and at 7.28 am two managers who happened to be at Highgate went to the scene. One **muzzled** <u>the dog</u> by wrapping his coat around it and **lifted** <u>it</u> into the cab of another train, which **took** <u>it</u> to East Finchley. The RSPCA was contacted at 7.36 am, arrived at 8.47 am and the dog was destroyed at 8.51 am.

An RSPCA spokeswoman, who said the dog had a collar but no tag, added: 'We cannot understand why they did not give the original driver permission to **remove** <u>the dog</u>, which was in considerable pain. The decision is morally questionable to say the least. We believe the management seriously underestimated the feelings of their passengers who I am sure would not have minded waiting.'

Furthermore, the figures in Tables 10.7 and Table 10.8 show us that Affected bodies of water and plants are more frequent in the newspapers:

devoting formidable energies to **restoring** its mountains, <u>rivers and seas</u> to their primal beauty.

Britannia is liable to **rule** <u>the waves</u> in very sedate fashion for a season or two.

'**Investigate** <u>the plants and trees</u>.'

The children with her mother on Tuesday night **laying** <u>some flowers</u>

Teenage girls **laid** <u>floral tributes</u> in the road where Miss Allen was attacked

I **have** <u>tea</u> with the Conservative agent

We notice, too, that, even before they become Affecteds, the plants mentioned have undergone human processing to a lesser or greater extent; less with the floral tributes, much more with tea.

10.3.1 Summary and postscript

It is worth summing up the differences in grammatical practice in relation to nature:

- in *The Prelude*, nature is represented as twice as powerful as in *The Times*;
- in *The Prelude*, weather and animals are the most powerful natural elements, just as they are in *The Times*;
- in *The Prelude*, rivers are frequently represented as Sayers, in contrast with *The Times*;
- in *The Prelude*, mountains and landscape feature as transitive Actors, which never happens in *The Times*;
- in *The Prelude*, natural Actors figure intransitively without Affecteds, more so than in *The Times*.

Besides this we have seen that Wordsworth uses some grammatical modification techniques to mitigate the effects of a "Newtonian" grammar:

- ergative verbs are used to construct natural landscape as possessing its own energy;
- experiences are activated into Actors, especially in conjunction with vocatives of address: the experience of nature is very powerful;
- tokens and Values are activated into Actors: nature *does* rather than *is*;
- location circumstances are treated as Actors, so the environment is less marginalised.

In brief, nature is seen as a communicator and as active not inert.

I would like to suggest, as a parting polemical comment, that the view of the natural world represented by Wordsworth, along with aspects of his grammar, provides a much better model for our survival than that represented by *The Times*. The latter presents a domesticated, processed and relatively passive nature, mainly avoided apart from the impact of weather (and disease) and an interest in dogs and horses, and sometimes subordinated, as brand names or commodities, to economic interests.

In this new millennium, to survive we had better take note of Wordsworth, the physicists and the ecologists, rethink and respeak our participation in nature, before it rethinks or rejects our participation in it.

ACTIVITY 51

(1) Find a short lyric nature poem and analyse the patterns of transitivity which are found there. In what ways, if any, do these patterns resemble those I found in *The Prelude*?

(2) Working in groups, take one whole tabloid newspaper and note down all the references to nature (using the same categories of natural things which I used in this chapter). Which aspects of nature are represented in the newspaper? How do your findings compare or contrast with mine?

Texts analysed

The Times of London (excluding news agency reports), 2 May 1996;
William Wordsworth, *The Prelude*, 1850.

Suggestions for further reading

Ecological Linguistics is a relatively new area of research, and I hope this Chapter will awaken interest in it. But this means that publications on the topic are rather few and far between.

• Rob Pope has an interesting website at: <http://www.brookes.ac.uk /schools/humanities> with a section devoted to 'Ecological and Environmental Approaches'. It gives an overview and several further references to follow up. The site is associated with his *English Studies Book*, essential for students of English.

- Halliday's article 'Language and the order of nature' is seminal in bringing to light the problems of mismatch between grammar of scientific texts and the physical 'realities' discovered by twentieth-century science. These ideas are developed in conjunction with Jim Martin in *Writing Science: Literacy and Discursive Power*. However in 'Green grammar and grammatical metaphor' I take issue with Halliday and Martin's conclusions.

- These problems of mismatch have been eloquently expressed by David Bohm in *Wholeness and the Implicate Order* though his linguistic solutions to the problem are rather eccentric and impractical.

- A very exciting recent publication on Ecolinguistics is *Greenspeak: A Study of Environmental Discourse* (1999) by R. Harre, J. Brockmeier and P. Mühlhäusler, London: Sage.

- Kristin Davidse in 'Language and world view in the poetry of G. M. Hopkins' shows how this nineteenth-century English poet exploits the ergative vocabulary of English to depict the relationship between humanity, nature and God. The article would make an interesting complement to this chapter.

- From a more literary point of view, Jonathan Bate's *Romantic Ecology* devotes much attention to Wordsworth's relationship with nature, and its relevance to current ecological debates.

- Mary Schleppegrell, has written several articles on language in environmental education, especially 'Abstraction and agency in middle school environmental education', which concentrate on how textbooks often fail to identify the perpetrators of environmental degradation.

- On modern scientific theory and the move beyond Newton, Fritjof Capra's *The Tao of Physics* and *The Turning Point* are quite accessible. For a rather difficult and challenging book on one modern physical theory, chaos theory, you could try Prigogine and Stengers's influential *Order out of Chaos*. James Lovelock's popular *Gaia: a New Look at Life on Earth* and the more technical *The Ages of Gaia* are essential background to one modern ecological theory.

Comments on activities

Chapter 1

Comment 1

We can see that the most important new information in answering question (a) is that it was the eating that took place on Wednesday not the picking. So (5) is the best answer as 'eat' comes in the rheme. The information required by (b) is about the day on which they were eaten so (1) would be the most straightforward reply, with 'on Wednesday' ending the rheme. (c) demands to know who did the eating, so the Passive construction in (4) is the best answer with 'John' at the end of the rheme. (d), like (b), asks to know when the eating of tomatoes took place, so actually (1) could be an answer, but, since the question seems to be making a contrast between tomatoes and something else, then (2) would be the best option. (e) obviously demands a reply like (3) with 'tomatoes' at the end of the rheme.

Comment 2

I think (a) would be better rewritten as:

> It is generally recognised that persuasion depends on interrelationships between discourse and society.

This is because the main focus of emphasis is not on the

recognition of the fact, but on the fact itself, so putting 'recognised' at the end of the rheme seems awkward.

I think (b) would be better rewritten as:

> In this study I argue that ideological persuasion can be repeated so that later it becomes taken for granted.

Putting 'this study' (and arguing) near the end of the rheme is not a natural choice, since we all know that this dissertation is a study of some kind, so this knowledge is certainly Given information. And what is important is not the arguing itself but what is being argued.

I think (c) could be better rewritten:

> Essentially I will use the framework for studying discourse proposed by Fairclough (1992)

The writer may have taken to heart the maxim that academic writing should be impersonal, and this has driven her to use the Passive voice. However, the desire for impersonality is probably outweighed by the need for smooth distribution of Given and New information. If impersonality is insisted upon, then an alternative possibility would be:

> Essentially this study will use the framework for studying discourse proposed by Fairclough (1992)

Comment 3

Underlining indicates the Themes of the sentences in the two passages. In (1) there is no particular pattern for the choice of Theme, except that two out of the five Themes refer to trees and flowers. By contrast, (2) shows a very tight control in the choice of Themes, with all five referring to seasons.

Text 1

Spring and fall are the most beautiful time of the year here in the Blue Mountains. Millions of wild flowers and trees are in bud, and the many planned gardens in the region start to flourish in springtime. The North American species of trees introduced long ago into the region – oak, elm, chestnut, beech and birch – do the same in the Blue Mountains as they would in the Catskills: turn brilliant reds oranges and yellows in fall. Campers and hikers are found descending on the mountains in throngs in summer. <u>The mountains</u> are at their quietest and most peaceful in winter, offering perfect solitude for city escapees.

Text 2

<u>Spring and fall</u> are the most beautiful time of the year here in the Blue Mountains. <u>In springtime</u> millions of wild flowers and trees are in bud, and the many planned gardens in the region start to flourish. <u>In fall</u> the North American species of trees introduced long ago into the region – oak, elm, chestnut, beech and birch – do the same in the Blue Mountains as they would in the Catskills: turn brilliant reds oranges and yellows. <u>Summer</u> finds campers and hikers descending on the mountains in throngs. <u>Winter</u> is the time the mountains are at their quietest and most peaceful, offering perfect solitude for city escapees.

Comment 5

Murder mysteries, jokes, and sophisticated commercial adverts are invariably Inductive; classified adverts and news reports are Deductive; research articles are a mixture – insofar as their main point is made in the results or conclusion sections, which appear last, they are basically Inductive, but in so far as they announce their findings in the Abstract, which comes first, they are to some extent Deductive.

Comment 6

WB seems more visually informative. Under (2) NUSG only uses white space, centring of title, indentation of sender's address and paragraphing, but WB uses columns for the titles, white space to localise each true/false segment, vertical orientation for 'True', variable indentation for the main title, and some lettering on dark background, and various colours (though this is not apparent from the black-and-white reproduction). As for type (3) features, neither text is especially visual. In terms of (4) NUSG uses only one font type, Courier, and does not vary its size, and only highlights through underlining. Whereas WB uses at least two different fonts, in six or seven different sizes, and uses bold type.

Comment 7

Poems are generally not very informative, except for the spacing between stanzas, capitalisation of initial letter of the line, and line endings. Of course there are experiments with concrete poetry, e.g. a poem about a snake in the shape of a snake, but these are unconventional.

Textbooks no doubt vary but are probably the next least visual. They will probably have (numbered) headings which will be highlighted in some way, and use bullets and enumeration, especially in summary sections. Psychology textbooks seem to be more visual than others, often using columns and varying fonts.

Recipes often have two sections, one for ingredients, one for the cooking instructions, and these may be distinguished visually in blocks separated by white space. The separate ingredients are listed on separate lines, though this is not always the case with the steps in the cooking procedure, unfortunately – see the example of the Step (p. 19). Do you ever forget where you are up to?

Newspapers usually use columns, their headlines and sometimes the first paragraph (Lead) are in larger font, and they will often have sub-headings, use bold type and have boxed insets of extracts from the main article, etc.

Forms make liberal use of white space, boxes, different colours; bullets, enumerative devices, arrows; bold type, variation in font, font size, and so on.

Magazine advertisements will usually have coloured pictures, which occupy at least 60 per cent per cent of their area. They tend to employ many different fonts in different sizes, and may exploit the whole range of graphical resources mentioned above.

Comment 8

In some cases, assuredness does seem to be an explanatory factor. For example, poetry readers are generally pretty much assured, or the poet has a take-it-or-leave-it attitude. And this would explain why newspapers are more visually informative than textbooks; students are either motivated or forced to study their books, but newspaper readers are much more selective in the articles which they read. Cooks need recipes, and are not planning to give up half-way through cooking, so they can be relatively uninformative visually.

Forms seem to be the main exception here. Generally, one has no choice in filling out a form. But precisely because many are designed for all sections of the population, of varying degrees of literacy and education, bureaucrats have been forced to make them as filler-friendly as possible. Perhaps taking an assured readership for granted is no excuse for being visually mean; a richly visual textbook may well fulfil its purpose or convey its content more effectively, even if the readership is in any case motivated to keep reading.

Comment 9

Probably, the narrative can be divided into the following sections.

ABSTRACT *I think Peter's always been a bit foolhardy.* (the point of the story)

ORIENTATION *I remember once we were on holiday in Cornwall, and it was one of those lovely sunny breezy days which are just right for a picnic. So we'd decided to go down to Clodgy point, the rocky cliffs of the Atlantic coast.* (setting the scene; no simple past tenses except with stative/relational verbs)

COMPLICATING ACTION (the succession of narrative clauses in past tense describing a sequence of events) *After picnic lunch Peter and his brother asked if they could go for a walk while me and my husband had a nap. So off they went.* [EVALUATION *They hadn't come back in two hours* (negative)], *so we went to look for them. We walked quickly along the cliff for half an hour, and, as we came round a promontory, we caught sight of them at the foot of the cliff on the rocks at the opposite side of the cove.* [EVALUATION *I was terrified* (comment by narrator). *How had they got down there?* (question)] *We called frantically for them to come back. They climbed up the steep grassy slope,* [EVALUATION *which must have been about 60 degrees.* (modal clause) *I don't know how they did it* (negative, comment by narrator).] *When they met us at the top I said,*

[EVALUATION *'Why did you go down there? Don't you know it's dangerous?'* (questions, evaluative comment by character/narrator]

RESOLUTION *Peter held out a black and white striped snail shell, and all he said was* [EVALUATION *'If we hadn't gone down there I would never have seen this.'* (negative, modals)]

CODA *So nowadays I'm never surprised to hear he's involved in some dangerous adventure or other.* (brings us out of the narrative by the time reference *nowadays*, and the tense, present).

Comment 10

'Superman' may never walk again [HEADLINE]
SUPERMAN star Christopher Reeve is in hospital with
a suspected broken back (1) [LEAD/MAIN EVENT]
His family ordered hospital officials not to give out any
information — but sources say he is partially paralysed

307

(2) [VERBAL REACTION]
The actor's publicist, Lisa Kastelere, was plainly upset
[REACTION] as she revealed that horse-mad Reeve
was hurt show-jumping in Virginia (3) [VERBAL
REACTION [EVALUATION] [BACKGROUND]]
Witnesses saw him hit the ground hard as his horse
shied (4) [BACKGROUND].
As doctors evaluated his condition [REACTION] in the
acute care ward at the university of Virginia's Medical
Centre in Charlottesville [BACKGROUND], it was not
known whether he will walk again (5) [COMMENT]
Reeve, 43 and 6ft 4in, was flown to the hospital by air-
ambulance after doctors at the competition decided he
needed special care (6) [REACTION]
Reeve, who starred in 4 Superman movies, lived with
his British lover Gael Exton for 11 years. They had two
children (7).
Reeve then began a relationship with singer Dana Morosini (8).
[BACKGROUND]

Chapter 2

Comment 12

You probably found that there was no exact match for "brother" and "uncle" in your non-European language. For example, in East-Asian languages an important semantic feature in classifying siblings is seniority in relation to the speaker. This means that, for speakers of these languages, the "natural" way of thinking about siblings is in terms of seniority. However, in English, the primary means of classification is by sex. And yet this does not mean it is impossible for a monolingual speaker of English to understand the East-Asian concepts; she can simply paraphrase: 'younger brother' and 'older sister'; or 'elder brother of father' and 'elder brother of mother', etc. In French, there are two words *chaise* and *fauteuil*. The first has the English equivalent *chair* and the second is translated *armchair*. The difference is that whereas an armchair is a type of chair, a *fauteuil* is not a type of *chaise*. Perhaps more interesting is that the distinction between "brown" and "yellow" in English is not the same as the distinction between "brun" and "jaune" in French.

Comment 13

Obviously (b) is most hostile to the police and sympathetic to the victims, (c) makes it look as though the youths were responsible for the accident, while (a) is relatively neutral. The neutrality of (a) is due to the use of 'crash' suggesting an accident, and the turning of it from a verb into a noun (nominalisation) which makes it unclear who is responsible for the crash. In (c) the youths are made responsible as subjects of the reflexive verb 'killed themselves', and 'driving'. Whereas in (b) the police are the Subject of the verb 'murdered' and therefore responsible. The choices of 'murder' over 'kill' and of 'rammed' rather than 'driving'/'crash' suggest deliberate violence. And the phrase used to refer to the young people varies from 'men', which invites little sympathy, to 'youths' and '17 year-olds', which evoke progressively more.

Comment 14

I have noted the terms *cat-lovers* and *catarrh-sufferers* in adverts.

Comment 15

The most obvious categorisation is to put Jane Fondas (more than one?), and Ramsey Clarks into the class of 1960s hippies. The second emerging classification is to group Cambodia with South Korea as countries threatened by tyranny. The reason for doing this is presumably that North Korea still seems like an evil bully to a greater extent than the now "tyrannised" Cambodia.

Comment 16

We may have met some of these nationalities, but the ones we meet are not necessarily a representative sample. We will meet US tourists and expatriates in Europe and Asia but these will tend to be far richer than the average US citizen. Conversely, if we live in the US the Mexicans we meet may well be unrepresentatively poor, as they are often economic migrants. Many adjectives might come from the media or hearsay. If we confirm these media-based stereotypes on visiting their native country, this may simply be that the stereotypes have cued us to look for certain characteristics and to ignore others.

Comment 18

You probably felt that *tart*, *crumpet* and *honey* are used almost exclusively for women.

Comment 19

I would analyse the clauses as follows:

ACTOR	PROCESS	AFFECTED	
Rebel Myanmar group	sets up	radio station	= MATERIAL

TOKEN	PROCESS	VALUE	
Thatcher	to be	consultant with tobacco company	
			= RELATIONAL

EXPERIENCE	PROCESS	EXPERIENCER	
She	disgusts	me	= MENTAL
			(EMOTION)

SAYER	PROCESS		
Iraq	denounces	world population conference	
			= VERBAL

EXPERIENCER	PROCESS	EXPERIENCE	
Japanese parents	reconsider	cram school system	= MENTAL
			(THINKING)

AFFECTED (Beneficiary)	PROCESS	AFFECTED	ACTOR
I	was given	a present	by John
			= MATERIAL

EXPERIENCER	PROCESS	EXPERIENCE	
I	love	it	= MENTAL
			(EMOTION)

Comment 20

Material

ACTOR		AFFECTED
vitality	(1) **makes**	a difference

ACTOR		AFFECTED (Beneficiary) (AFFECTED)
It	(2) **gives**	your hair a superb feel and a new vitality.

ACTOR		AFFECTED
your L'Oréal hairdresser	(3) **perms in**	Dulcia Vitality

ACTORY		
Your hair . . .	(4) **shines**	(with a soft natural silkiness)

AFFECTED		AFFECTED
every single hair	(5) **receives**	a thorough beauty treatment

ACTOR		AFFECTED
only he	(6) can **add**	that finishing touch of brilliance (to . . . Dulcia Vitality)

The Material processes confer no power on the women, the potential consumers of the perm. Instead, power resides in the product and the hairdresser who uses it. Women are seen as relatively passive. Only part of the woman's body, the hair, has any agency attached to it.

Mental

EXPERIENCER	EXPERIENCE	
(you)	(1) **feel** the difference	= MENTAL (PERCEPTION)

EXPERIENCER	EXPERIENCE	
you	(2) **enjoy** a perm	= MENTAL (EMOTION)

EXPERIENCER	EXPERIENCE	
(you) [Just]	(3) **imagine** the difference	= MENTAL (COGNITION)

EXPERIENCE		
a soft natural silkiness that	(4) **feels** as good as it looks	= MENTAL (EMOTION/ PERCEPTION?)

EXPERIENCE		
a soft natural silkiness	(5) **looks** good	= MENTAL (PERCEPTION)

In contrast with Material processes, the women consumers are represented as indulging in Mental processes a whole lot more, either of emotion ('enjoy') or perception ('feels') or thinking ('imagine'). They are the explicit or implicit Experiencers in the first four of these clauses, this role being implied by the visuals. In the last clause the perceiver (Experiencer) is presumably whoever admires the hair of the woman consumer. Predictably enough, the Experiences throughout are either the perm or the qualities it produces in the hair.

Relational

Dulcia Vitality	**is**	a perm for you to enjoy
Your hair [not only]	**has**	vitality

These clauses concentrate on describing the product and the qualities it can transfer to the hair of the consumer.

Verbal

(SAYER)		
(you)	**ask** your hairdresser	for Dulcia Vitality

Again, women can't actually do much except verbalise what they want to their hairdresser, who, along with the product, is the only person with power.

Summary

Obviously, adverts are attempts to sell products, so it is not surprising that the focus is upon the product, what it can do, its qualities, and the way it can change the qualities or potential of the customer's hair. The depiction of the readers as indulging mostly in Mental processes centring on parts of their own bodies fits in with a stereotype of a woman worrying about whether she is an object beautiful enough to attract men. That the women themselves are not Actors in Material processes also reinforces this stereotype of the passive female, and in a sense thereby dehumanises her. The fact that the hairdresser, male, comes over as quite powerful, may be explained by the readership of *Good Housekeeping*: middle-aged women, who might appreciate the intimate touch of a 'male' hairdresser.

Comment 21

Her horse was given to me and she <u>was set</u> on it and so she <u>was brought</u> down the mountain. As I walked the sound of wailing <u>was heard</u>. Her face was observed, but she stared straight ahead. We rested at the hamlet till day-break. The men <u>were told</u> to take enough for their meal, no more. She <u>was sat</u> down in the headman's house, and the lamp <u>was lit</u>. Some supper <u>was brought</u>.

Comment 22

(a)

fail → failure
attract → attraction
deny → denial
inflate → inflation
silly → silliness
demand → demand
export → export
sensitive → sensitivity
complain → complaint (complaining)
end → end/ending
safe → safety

(b)

(i)   Applause followed the end of the play
(ii) (John's) eating the banana skin shows (his) stupidity
(iii) Our stay in Switzerland was wonderful
(iv) The jury agreed with the (judge's) suggestion that I was guilty
(v)   The coolness of the mountains causes the condensation of moist air that/when it goes over them

Comment 23

Three people were killed and fifteen injured in fighting on Friday with police during protests against prison sentences imposed on seven leaders of the Islamic Salvation Front (FIS).

This might become:

> The police killed three people and injured fifteen others when a large crowd of unarmed Algerian citizens protested against the prison sentences which the unelected military junta had imposed on the seven leaders of the Islamic Salvation Front.

313

Chapter 3

Comment 25

One possible rewrite is as follows.

Getting started
You <u>might</u> discuss the concept of the four dimensions with your pupils. This will prepare them for the reading as well. According to Collier's Encyclopaedia the four dimensions are length, width, height and time. The fourth dimension, which is time, also refers to any additional quality beyond what is ordinarily expected. You <u>must</u> ask pupils to think about the fourth dimension in this less specific sense, and <u>should</u> discuss the possibility of life on other planets. The poem is provided as a stimulus. You <u>ought to</u> check pupils' comprehension of it.

It <u>is suggested</u> you assign pupils to read on the topic ahead of the lesson, so that they can contribute to the discussion of aliens. You may choose to focus the topic as an oral book-review session.

Alternatively, you <u>could</u> use the kit to introduce pupils to science fiction, in particular the work of H. G. Wells.

Comment 26

One possibility is as follows:

As a matter of fact, till 1800 many English people were <u>mainly</u> a rural people – very rural. England <u>might</u> have had towns for centuries, but they have <u>seldom</u> been real towns, only clusters of village streets. The English character has <u>usually</u> failed to develop the real urban side of man, the civic side. Siena is a bit of a place, but it <u>could</u> be a real city, with citizens intimately concerned with the city. Nottingham is a vast place sprawling towards a million, and it <u>sometimes seems</u> to be <u>little</u> more than an amorphous agglomeration. There <u>may</u> be no Nottingham in the sense that there is a Siena.

Comment 27

The doctor in Doc's Corner is more measured in tone than the rather hectoring psychotherapist in Helping the Kids. Most obviously the contrast is apparent in the psychotherapist's many imperatives: 'get', 'let', 'encourage', 'stand back'. The doctor uses declarative mood, and his statements are almost constantly modalised whether with the high probability 'certainly' or the lower probability 'may', or the medium generality of 'some'.

It may be that because doctors have a higher, more scientific status than psychotherapists, they can afford to be less dogmatic and assertive.

The diarrhoea questioner suggests that she finds her obligations restricting by using the modal verb *have to*. The girlfriend questioner comes over as diffident, with her subjective verb 'I think' and as emotional with her strong expression of disinclination 'I'd hate '. On the other hand, her modals of frequency 'a lot', 'rarely', suggest a reasonable mother – she doesn't exaggerate with *all the time* or *never*. Both of them ask interrogative questions, of course, which reflect their position as seeking expert advice.

Comment 28

The first- and second-person pronouns are used in paragraphs one to five. But paragraphs six to ten use exclusively second-person pronouns.

In the first four paragraphs the 'you' is used to mean 'anyone', a general use, apart from the first sentence of four, which addresses the reader. But in paragraph five the 'you' seems to blur the distinction between Monica Lewinsky, 'bimbos', and people in general. In paragraphs six to eight the 'you' refers to and addresses adolescents in general. At some points, e.g. the end of eight, it's almost as if the writer is addressing her own teenage son or daughter. This use is a little odd – because one cannot assume that the only or even main readers of this column are teenagers. It's as though the middle-aged reader is invited to be an audience for a dramatic confrontation between mother and daughter or son.

In paragraph one the *we* shifts from referring to Linda Grant and whoever saw the show with her, to the Turkish cleaner's 'us', which refers to the middle-aged (women?) in general. It is, therefore, exclusive, or, after the shift, inclusive in a limited way. The 'us', 'we' of paragraphs four and five claim to be all inclusive – 'we all'. The strange thing is that Linda Grant is struggling not to belong to that group who are so fixated on Clinton's affairs that they ignore the real dangers in the geopolitical situation. She is therefore on the edge of this inclusive group. But think how she would sound if she used the pronoun *you* instead!

I is only used at one point, where Grant acknowledges her use of a sexist term *bimbo*. She is only alone in her role as writer. However, we might wonder whether the 'you' at the end of paragraph six actually refers to her – the sort of thing she worries about.

Comment 29

The only complete sentences are these:

That's the GOAL of every competitor
Altogether it's the heart and soul of a WINNER
The new TACOMA has arrived
And it's every inch a CHAMPION
Call 1800 GO-TOYOTA for a BROCHURE and the location of your
    NEAREST DEALER
I love what you do for me

Comment 31

I think that 'genocidal' has very strong negative emotions suggesting the delib-erate attempt to wipe out a certain racial group, rather than the unplanned killing that takes place in a civil war. It is not a subjective adjective, however, and whether Pol Pot's actions were genocidal or not could theoretically be verified or falsified. This is not true of 'monster' which is totally subjective in its nega-tive affect. 'Failed' is a word with negative spin, compared with the more neu-tral *omitted*. 'Holocaust' is generally applied to the Nazi killings in the deathcamps in the Second World War, and therefore is a little metaphorical here, and so fairly subjective. 'Displaced' sounds like a euphemism with positive spin which substitutes for *driven out*, or we could think of the phrase *displaced per-son* as a by now conventional euphemism for refugee. 'Terrorist' has plenty of negative spin, compared with the positive *freedom fighter* or the neutral *guer-rilla*. 'Invasion' could be negative in other contexts but seems more neutral or even positive here.

There are a group of words which would seem to have positive emotional spin elsewhere, but when connected to Pol Pot become tainted and negative: 'helped', 'support', 'reconstruct'. They exemplify the fluidity of emotional meanings according to context.

Comment 32

(1) The minor sentences are the replies to questions. 'Thanks, but no thanks.' (Section 3) 'False' (Section 4) 'True' (Section 5), 'Both' (Section 6) . There are also a number of sentences beginning with *but* (Sections 5 and 6), which might give the impression of incomplete sentences.

A sense of (mock) dialogue is created by:

- the (expository) questions and answers of the True or False segment (Sections 4–6)
- the title, which is a question
- the question (Section 3) which imagines an offer of 1,3,7-trimethylxanthine to the reader, with the reader's reply
- the follow up to this reply – 'Well, guess what' – in imperative mood.

The rhythm of Section 2 could be diagrammed thus, with each line constituting a repeated rhythm.

/   x   /   x /   x   / x   /   x
Whether you're a quivering caffeine junkie

or

/   x /   x /   x
just a casual sipper,

x   /   x   x   /   x x   /
there's more to that hair-raising jolt

x   /   x   /
than meets the eye.

(2) By deliberately substituting the technical scientific (chemical) term for coffee in the imagined dialogue, the whole passage seems to foreground/make fun of technicality. But it also seems to delight in mixing these technical scientific words with slang: 'fancy-schmancy' and 'go-go' come hard on the heels of 'trimethylxanthine'. 'Jump start' (colloquial) and 'metabolism' (medical) and 'revving up'(slang) and 'central nervous system' (medical) are similarly placed together in contrasting pairs. The level of formality also veers wildly from one sentence to the next: 'But, despite caffeine's *au naturel* origins, its chemical make-up belongs to the same family of potentially lethal compounds as emetine. But fear not the hot black brew.' The first of these sentences has six words of three or more syllables, and a very technical word 'emetine'. The next sentence is entirely composed of one-syllable words. It is interesting that this archaic expression *but fear not* ... has now become a quite fashionable colloquialism. Similarly 'maven' and 'chutzpah' are markedly slang, and 'full of beans' is (rather dated) slang, but brought in for the sake of the pun.

(3) Here are some examples I spotted of emotional vocabulary

Negative spin	Positive spin	Euphemism
junkie (cf. addict, user)	go-go (cf. active,	love handles (cf. belly fat)
fancy-schmancy	hyper-active)	
(cf. technical)	effortless (cf.	
overwhelming (cf.	indolent, lazy)	
impressive/		
prominent)		
myths brewing (cf.		
stories being		
created)		
fat (cf. large)		

'But fear not the hot black brew' looks to me racially insensitive. It suggests that coffee could be feared because it is black, thus preying on stereotypical metaphors of darkness as evil, which might be transferred to 'people of colour'. Table C.1 indicates the major markers of universality, subjectivity and probability.

Table C.1 Markers of universality, subjectivity and probability

Universality (frequency)	Subjectivity	Probability
In everything from soda to snickers (3) Caffeine can temporarily enhance athletic performance (6) Some cardiologists also warn that caffeine ... can raise blood pressure (6)	A recent study suggests that women who drink two or more cups of coffee a day are less likely to commit suicide (5)	What would you say (3) A cup of coffee will keep the love handles away (4) Sure (4) A moderate dose of caffeine might temporarily jump start your metabolism (4) In fact (4) It has no proven long term affect on weight (4) Potentially lethal compounds (5) Women who drink two or more cups of coffee a day are less likely to commit suicide (5) Caffeine can temporarily enhance athletic performance (6) The gym teacher might applaud you (6) The IOC could hand you your walking papers (6) Some cardiologists also warn that caffeine ... can raise blood pressure (6)

Chapter 4

Comment 34

- Existential presuppositions: >> there were bagloads of rubbish, there is a writer, etc.
- Comparison: >> there is some litter (if there is none, there is no possibility of more)
- Non-main clause: >> the writer saw the bagloads of rubbish
- Subordinate clause: >> more litter would be left behind if there had been no stiff $1,000 dollar fine
- *if* clause >> there is a stiff $1,000 fine
- main clause >> less litter is left behind [because of the fine]

The manipulative nature of some of these presuppositions is quite clear. Instead of giving any evidence that stiff fines reduce the amount of littering the writer simply assumes this to be the case.

Comment 35

The peculiar character of the metaphor depends on the clashing emotional associations of the metaphorical referent and the literal meaning: the negative feelings about venomous snakes, in contrast with the responses of attraction and protectiveness towards innocent babies feeding at the breast.

Comment 36

Irony

The stretch of text 'Hey, why not ask him ... European Union' seems ironic. These sound like genuine formulaic suggestions. However the writer does not really want the suggestions acted upon, so they are an ironic caricature of what Peter Mandelson did.

In paragraph two *Titanic* is called 'enjoyable tosh'. In paragraph three the experience of watching it is called 'bum-numbing' (i.e. uncomfortably boring). As both of these cannot be true it seems likely that one of these statements is tongue-in-cheek, ironic exaggeration, probably the second.

In paragraph eight parents are called 'cruel and oppressive' for insisting their children come home by midnight. The writer doesn't believe this – the adjectives echo the kinds of words teenagers might use, and so are an example of echoic irony.

Metaphor

The first text uses metaphor exclusively for explanatory purposes, with police force used as a metaphor for lymphocytes, police-training colleges for primary lymphatic organs, and police stations for secondary lymphatic organs. These explain how immunity is acquired, and infection resisted.

The second text uses the metaphor of a cucumber for a newspaper, probably as an attempt at humour, to cultivate intimacy. There is also a kind of (ideological) restructuring in suggesting Holland (which no doubt has its fair share of industry) is a kitchen garden.

Comment 37

The pupil thinks that 'what are you laughing at?' is a reprimand, part of the schema for keeping control or regulation in the classroom. In fact the question is part of another content-related schema for lessons: the teacher wishes to elicit an answer to a display question in order to get across to the rest of the class information about the social status of certain accents.

Chapter 5

Comment 39

Possible answers are as follows:

(1)   apology [and excuse]?
(2)   sympathising, or words to that effect
(3)   promise, or at least an undertaking
(4)   command or request
(5)   apology
(6), (7) promise or undertaking
(8)   advice (against)
(9)   promise or undertaking
(10)   condolence or commiseration
(11)   promise or undertaking
(12)   compliment
(13)   promise or undertaking

Keats seems to be constructing a subject position for his younger sister in which she is very dependent upon him. The high number of promises and undertakings suggest this, but so do the apologies – he assumes that his behaviour is a focus of her attention and any slight imperfection therefore demands apology. Fanny comes over as rather passive – one Directive simply demands verbal behaviour from her (and the actual action demanded will be by someone else); the other Directive is negative, advice against. In this he constructs himself as rather paternalistic. But he is also warm in the concern and sympathy and condolences which he expresses.

Comment 42

(1) Of course the subject positions are those of writer/composer and reader, but more particularly they are of advertiser/marketer and potential buyer/customer/client

(2) The ideal reader is someone interested in science and technology, with a computer and modem (of various specifications in the small print) and ideally a CD-ROM drive.

(3) The headline is a question. The main body of the ad is labelled as an invitation. The triangular bullets introduce what look like offers/commands, but they can also be taken as undertakings or promises. There is a promise to send the software and give ten hours free, and an undertaking that clients may cancel if not satisfied (in the form). Taken as a whole, the form is an acceptance of the invitation, but consists largely of indirect or elliptical questions equivalent to 'What is your name?', etc. The small print represents conditions for taking up the invitation – stipulations about the equipment necessary and the offer's limits.

(4) Because it is constructed as an invitation (of more benefit to the client than the company) we assume the imperative commands 'detach', 'mail', 'complete', 'select' and perhaps 'navigate', etc. are polite.

(5) We have 'must respond by' and 'you must have' 'requires'. These latter two are not Directives but still use modals of obligation.

(6) The form is largely indirect questions.

(7) 'America's # 1 online service', 'the nation's most exciting service', carry very immodest existential presuppositions. 'There is free software and trial membership' are further existential presuppositions. There are the possessive presuppositions 'we have science forums' and 'we have computing forums';

(8) Like most ads it is very visually informative, in ways I hardly need to spell out. What is interesting is that visual prominence is denied to the stipulations about the necessary equipment and the limits to the offer – the small print. It's the headline question and invitation itself, and the pictures of the Internet page which have most prominence, along with the arrow indicating where to write your acceptance.

(9)   They need to know if you have a Mac or Windows PC and if you have a CD ROM simply to send you the right software.

Chapter 6

Comment 44

(1)   Free direct speech: (6), (7), (8), (10), (12), (15), (16), (20), (23), (25), (33), (34), (35), (37)
(2)   'Cried', 'laughed', 'broke out', 'bridled', 'leaped lightly' seem to suggest manner of speaking.

'Went on', 'promised', 'asked', 'explained', 'stated', 'protested', 'carrying her point' are labels for speech acts.

'Gaily answered', 'returned in the same spirit' combine the labelling of speech act with adverbials of manner.

'Said' of course, is simply a neutral reporting verb.

Notice, incidentally, that *answered, returned* and *went on* define the speech acts in relation to other speech acts in the discourse; *answer* presupposes a question, *returned* presupposes a previous statement by another speaker, *went on* assumes a previous statement by the same speaker.

Comment 46

In the intertextual context of (1), the paragraph might count as a warning that the use of such sprays is dangerous to health because it undermines the body's use of pain as a defence mechanism.

As a reply to (2), the paragraph would be interpreted as a warning to politicians that unless they allow constituents or members of the public to give feedback or make comments, the political system, 'the body politic', is in danger of injuring itself, and may not survive. The organism would be society. The decision-making centre, the central nervous system, would be interpreted as the person in power (politicians or the government). The signals sent by the nerve cells to the spinal cord/brain would represent feedback from the less powerful members of society, and so on. The stifling of feedback messages would stand for the silencing of feedback or dissent.

References

No writing or research takes place in a vacuum. I have at some stage been in touch with the authors whose given or first names are spelled out in full.

A Course in Learning and Using English Book 2: Teachers' Guides (1994) Singapore: Federal Publications.

Althusser, L. (1984) *Essays in Ideology*, London: Verso.

Austin, J. L. (1962) *How to Do Things with Words*, Oxford: Oxford University Press.

Bate, J. (1991) *Romantic Ecology*, London: Routledge.

Baudrillard, J. (1989) *America*, trans. C. Turner, London: Verso.

Bazerman, C. (1992) *The Informed Writer: Using Sources in the Disciplines*, Boston, MA: Houghton Mifflin.

Beck, U. (1992) *Risk Society: Towards a New Modernity*, trans. Mark Ritter, London: Sage .

Beder S. (1999) 'Best coverage money can buy', *New Internationalist,* July 1999, 314: 30.

Bell, A. (1991) *The Language of News Media*, Oxford: Blackwell.

Bernhardt, S. (1985) 'Text structure and graphic design: the visible design', in Benson, D. and Greaves J. (eds) *Systemic Perspectives on Discourse*, vol. 2, Norwood NJ: Ablex.

Bex, T. (1996) *Variety in Written English*, London: Routledge.

Bohm, D. (1980) *Wholeness and the Implicate Order*, London: Routledge.

Booth, Wayne C. (1974) *A Rhetoric of Irony*, Chicago: University of Chicago Press.

Brown, P. and Levinson, S. (1987) *Politeness: Some Universals in Language Usage*, Cambridge: Cambridge University Press.

Burton, D. (1982) 'Through a glass darkly — through dark glasses', in Carter, R.A. (ed.) (1982) *Language and Literature: An Introductory Reader in Stylistics*, London: Allen & Unwin.

Butt, David, Fahey, R., Spinks, S. and Yallop, C. (1995) *Using Functional Grammar: An Explorer's Guide*, Macquarie University: National Centre for English Language Teaching and Research.

Capra, F. (1975) *The Tao of Physics*, London: Wildwood House.

Capra, F. (1982) *The Turning Point: Science, Society and the Rising Culture*, London: Flamingo.

Carter, Ronald and Nash, W. (1990) *Seeing through Language*, Oxford: Blackwell.

Christie, Frances and Martin, J. R. (1997) *Genre and Institutions: Social Processes in the Workplace and School,* London: Cassell. .

Cixous, H. (1981) 'Sorties', in Marks, E. and De Courtivron, I. (eds) *New French Feminisms*, Brighton: Harvester, pp. 90–9.

Colomb, G. G. and Williams, J. (1985) 'Perceiving structure in professional prose', in Odell, L. and Goswami, *Writing in Non-Academic Settings*, New York: Guilford, pp. 87–112.

Cook, G. (1992) *The Discourse of Advertising*, London: Routledge.

Davidse, Kristin (1994) 'Language and world view in the poetry of G. M. Hopkins', in de Graef, O. *et al.*, *Acknowledged Legislators: Essays on English Literature in Honour of Herman Seurotte*, Kapellen: Pelchmans.

Davis, H. and Walton, P. (1983) 'Death of a premier: consensus and closure in international news', in Davis, H. and Walton, *Language, Image, Media*, Oxford: Blackwell, pp. 8–49.

De Rougemont, D. (1956) *Passion and Society*, trans. Montgomery Belgion, London: Faber & Faber.

Downing, A. and Locke, P. (1992) *A University Course in English Grammar*, Hemel Hempstead: Prentice-Hall.

Dyer, G. (1982) *Advertising as Communication*, London: Methuen.

Eggins, S. (1994) *An Introduction to Systemic Functional Linguistics*, London: Pinter.

Faigley, L. (1992) *Fragments of Rationality*, Pittsburgh: University of Pittsburgh Press.

Fairclough, Norman (1989) *Language and Power*, London: Longman.

Fairclough, Norman (1995) *Media Discourse*, London: Arnold.

Fish, S. (1980) 'Is there a text in this class', in *Is There a Text in This Class?*, Cambridge, MA: Harvard University Press, pp. 303–21.

Fowler, R. (1991) *Language in the News*, London: Routledge.

Fraser, E. (1987) 'Teenage Girls Reading *Jackie*', *Media, Culture and Society* 19.

Freud, S. (1960) *Jokes and their Relation to the Unconscious*, Strachen, J. (trans), London: Routledge.

Friedan, B. (1964) *The Feminine Mystique*, New York: Dell.

Frith, S. (1981) *Sound Effects*, New York: Pantheon.

Fromm, E. (1978) *To Have or to Be?*, London: J. Cape.

Frye, N. (1957) *Anatomy of Criticism*, Princeton NJ: Princeton University Press.

Galtung, J. and Ruge, M. (1973) 'Structuring and Selecting news', in Cohen, S. and Young, J. (eds.) *The Manufacture of News: Social Problems, Deviance and the Mass Media*, London: Constable.

Geis, M. L. (1987) *The Language of Politics*, New York: Springer-Verlag.

Glasgow University Media Group (1980) *More Bad News*, London: Routledge.

Goatly, A. (1996) 'Green grammar and grammatical metaphor or language and the myth of power or metaphors we die by', *Journal of Pragmatics* 25: 537–60.

Goatly, A. (1997) *The Language of Metaphors*, London: Routledge.

Goatly, A. (1999) 'What does it feel like to be a single female 20-something Singapore graduate?', in Chew, Phyllis and Krämer-Dahl, Anneliese (eds) *Reading Culture: Textual Practices in Singapore*, Singapore: Times Academic Press, pp. 163–84.

Goodman, S. and Graddol, D. (eds) (1996) *Redesigning English: New Texts, New Identities*, London: Routledge.

Greene, J. (1986) *Language Understanding: A Cognitive Approach*, Milton Keynes: The Open University.

Grice, H. P. (1975) 'Logic and conversation', in Cole, Peter and Morgan, J. (eds), *Syntax and Semantics 3: Speech Acts*, New York: Academic Press, pp. 41–58.

Halliday, Michael (1987) 'Language and the order of nature', in Fabb, N., Attridge, D., Durant, A. and MacCabe, C. (eds) *The Linguistics of Writing*, Manchester: Manchester University Press, pp. 135–54.

Halliday, Michael (1994) *An Introduction to Functional Grammar*, 2nd edn, London: Arnold.

Halliday, Michael and Hasan, Ruqaiya (1976) *Cohesion in English*, Harlow: Longman.

Halliday, Michael and Hasan, Ruqaiya (1985) *Language, Context and Text*, Geelong: Deakin University Press.

Halliday, Michael and Martin, J. (1993) *Writing Science: Literacy and Discursive Power*, London: Falmer Press.

Hanlon, J. (1999) 'A pound of flesh', *New Internationalist* 310: 26–7.

Harre, R. Brockmeier, J. and Mühlhäusler, P. (1999) *Greenspeak: A Study of Environmental Discourse,* London: Sage.

Hasan, Ruqaiya (1989) *Linguistics, Language and Verbal Art*, Geelong, Victoria: Deakin University Press.

Hiraga, M. (1991) 'Metaphors Japanese women live by', *Working Papers on Language, Gender and Sexism*, vol.1 (1), AILA Commission on Language and Gender, pp. 38–57.

Hodge, G. and Kress, G. (1993) *Language and Ideology*, 2nd edn, London: Routledge.

Hoey, M. (1973) *On the Surface of Discourse*, London: Allen & Unwin.

Hutchinson, T. (1989) 'Speech presentations in fiction with reference to *The Tiger Moth* by H. E. Bates', in Short, M. (ed.) *Reading, Analysing and Teaching Literature*, Harlow: Longman, pp. 120–45.

Ivanic, R. and Simpson, J. (1992), 'Who's who in academic writing?', in Fairclough, N. (ed.) *Critical Language Awareness*, pp. 141–73.

James, H. ([1897] (1996)) *What Maisie Knew*, Harmondsworth: Penguin.

Jones, J. (1991) 'Grammatical metaphor and technicality in academic writing', in Christie, F., *Literacy in Social Processes*, Darwin, Northern Territories: Centre for Studies in Language and Education, pp. 178–98.

Juvenal (1979) *The Satires*, ed. John Ferguson, New York: St. Martin's Press..

Keats, J. (1965) *Letters of John Keats*, ed. Gardner, S., London: University of London Press.

Kress, G. (1985) *Linguistic Processes in Sociocultural Practice*, Oxford: Oxford University Press.

Krishnamurty, Ramesh (1996) 'Ethnic, racial and tribal: the language of racism?', in Caldas-Coulthard, C. R. and Coulthard, M. *Texts and Practices*, London: Routledge, pp. 129–49.

Kristeva, J. (1974) *La révolution de langage poétique*, Paris: Seuil.

Labov, W. (1972) *Language in the Inner City*, Philadelphia PA: University of Pennsylvania Press.

Larkin, P. (1955) 'Toads', in *The Less Deceived*, London: The Marvell Press, pp. 32–3.

Lawrence, D. H. (1950) 'Nottinghamshire and the Mining Country', *Selected Essays*, Harmondsworth: Penguin, pp. 114–22.

Lee, Penny (1996) *The Whorf Theory Complex*, Amsterdam: Benjamins.

Leech, Geoffrey (1974) *Semantics,* 2nd edn, Harmondsworth: Penguin.

Leech, Geoffrey (1983) *Principles of Pragmatics*, Harlow: Longman.

Leech, Geoffrey and Short, M. (1973) *Style in Fiction*, Harlow: Longman.

Levinson, S. (1983) *Pragmatics*, Cambridge: Cambridge University Press.

Lewis, C. S. (1936) *The Allegory of Love*, Oxford: Oxford University Press.

Lovelock, J. (1988) *The Ages of Gaia*, Oxford: Oxford University Press.

Lovelock, J. (1995) *Gaia: A New Look at Life on Earth*, new edn, Oxford: Oxford University Press .

Lucy, J. A. (1992) *Language Diversity and Thought: A Reformulation of the Linguistic Relativity Hypothesis*, Cambridge: Cambridge University Press.

MacRobbie, A. (1991) *Feminism and Youth Culture: From Jackie to Just Seventeen*, London: Macmillan .

Martin, J. R. (1985) *Factual Writing*, Geelong: Deakin University Press.

Martin, J. R. (1992) *English Text: System and Structure*, Amsterdam: Benjamins.

Martin, J. R. (1993) 'Life as a noun: arresting the universe in science and humanities', in Halliday, Michael and Martin, J. R. (1993).

Martin, J. R. and Matthiessen, Christian (1991) 'Systemic typology and topology', *in Literacy in Social Processes*, ed. Christie, F., Centre for Studies of Language in Education, Northern Territories University, Darwin.

Martin, J. R. and Rothery, Joan (1980) 'Writing report project no. 1', *Working Papers in Linguistics*, Department of Linguistics, University of Sydney.

Martin, J. R. and Rothery, Joan (1981) 'Writing report project no. 2', *Working Papers in Linguistics*, Department of Linguistics, University of Sydney.

Matthiessen, Christian (1992) 'Interpreting the textual metafunction', in Davies, M. and Ravelli, Louise (eds) *Advances in Systemic Linguistics*, London: Pinter, pp. 37–81.

Miller, A. (1958) *Collected Plays*, London: Cresset Press.

Mills, S. (1995) *Feminist Stylistics*, London: Routledge.

Montgomery, M. (1986) 'DJ talk', *Media, Culture and Society* 8 (4): 421–40.

Montgomery, M., Durant, A. Fabb, N. Furniss, T. Mills S. (1992) *Ways of Reading*, London: Routledge.

Mühlhäusler, P. (1996) 'Linguistic adaptation to changed environmental conditions', in Fill, A. (ed.) *Sprachokologie und Okolinguistik*, Tubingen: Stauffenburg Verlag..

Nash, W. (1980) *Designs in Prose*, Harlow: Longman.

Nash, W. (1990) *Language in Popular Fiction*, London: Routledge.

Nash, W. and Stacey, David (1997) *Creating Texts: An Introduction to the Study of Composition*, Harlow: Longman.

Nataf, Z. I. (1998) 'Whatever I feel…', *New Internationalist* 300, (4): 22–25.

Orr, D. W. (1992) *Ecological Literacy: Education and the Transition to a Postmodern World*, New York: State University of New York Press.

Packard, V. (1957) *The Hidden Persuaders*, New York: McKay.

Painter, C. and Martin, J. R. (eds) (1986) *Writing to Mean: Teaching Genres across the Curriculum*, Papers and Workshop Reports from the Writing to Mean Conference, University of Sydney, May 1985, Bundoora, Victoria Applied Linguistics Association of Australia.

Pearce, L. (1991) *Woman/Image/Text*, Toronto and Buffalo: University of Toronto Press.

Pinker, S. (1994) *The Language Instinct*, New York: Morrow.

Pope, Rob (1998) *English Studies Book*, London: Routledge.

Pope, Rob (1995) *Textual Intervention*, London: Routledge.

Postman, N. (1987) *Amusing Ourselves to Death,* London: Methuen.

Poynton, C. (1985) *Language and Gender: Making the Difference*, Geelong, Victoria: Deakin University Press.

Prigogine, Ilya and Stengers, I. (1985) *Order out of Chaos*, London: Flamingo.

Radway, J. (1987) *Reading the Romance: Women, Patriarchy and Popular Literature*, London: Verso 1987.

Saville-Troike, M. (1982) *The Ethnography of Communication*, Oxford: Blackwell.

Scannell, P. (1992) 'Public service broadcasting and modern public life', in Scannell, P. *et al.* (eds) *Culture and Power*, London: Sage.

Schark, R. and Abelson, R. (1979) *Scripts, Plans, Goals and Understanding*, Hillsdale NJ: Erlbaum.

Schleppegrell, Mary, J. (1996) 'Abstraction and agency in middle school environmental education', in Bang, J. C., Door, J., Alexander, Richard J., Fill, Alwin, and Verhagen, Frans (eds) *Language and Ecology: Proceedings of the Symposium on Ecolinguistics of AILA 1996, Jyvaskala*, Odense: Odense University Press, pp. 27–42.

Searle, J. R. (1969) *Speech Acts: An Essay in the Philosophy of Language*, Cambridge: Cambridge University Press.

Searle, J. R. (1979) *Expression and Meaning*, Cambridge: Cambridge University Press.

Schiller, H. (1996) *Media Ownership and Control: In the Age of Convergence*, London: International Institute of Communications.

Shieh, Yee Bing (1995) *Language in the Singapore News: Constructs of China and the United States,* unpublished academic exercise 1994/95, Singapore: National University of Singapore.

Short, M. (1988) 'Speech presentation, the novel and the press', in van Peer W. (ed.) *The Taming of the Text: Explorations in Language, Literature and Culture*, London: Routledge, pp. 61–81.

Sigal, L.V. (1987) 'Who? Sources make the news', in Manoff, R. K. and Schudson, M. (eds) *Reading the News*, New York: Pantheon, pp. 9–37.

Simpson, P. (1993) *Language, Ideology and Point of View*, London: Routledge.

Sperber, D. and Wilson, Deirdre (1995) *Relevance: Communication and Cognition,* Oxford: Blackwell.

Talbot, M. (1992) 'The construction of gender in a teenage magazine', in Fairclough, N. (ed.) *Critical Language Awareness*, Harlow: Longman, pp. 174–99.

Tan, Kim Luan (1993) 'Describing students' literature test essays using systemic linguistics', unpublished MA dissertation, Singapore: National University of Singapore.

Tanaka, K. (1994) *Advertising Language: A Pragmatic Approach to Advertisements in Britain and Japan*, London: Routledge.

Thomas, J. (1995) *Meaning in Interaction,* Harlow: Longman.

Thomson, J.B. (1984) *Studies in the Theory of Ideology*, London: Polity Press.

Toolan, Michael J. (1988) *Narrative: A Critical Linguistic Introduction*, London: Routledge.

Trew, T. (1979) '"What the papers say": linguistic variation and ideological difference', in Fowler *et al.* (eds) *Language and Control*, London: Routledge, pp. 117–56.

van Dijk, T. A. (1986) 'News schemata', in Cooper, C. R. and Greenbaum, S., *Studying Writing: Linguistic Approaches*, London: Sage, 151–85.

van Dijk, T. A (1988a) *News Analysis: Case Studies of International and National News in the Press*, Hillsdale NJ: Lawrence Erlbaum.

van Dijk, T. A. (1998b) *News as Discourse*, Hillsdale NJ: Lawrence Erlbaum.

van Leeuwen, T. (1987) 'Generic strategies in press journalism', *Australian Review of Applied Linguistics* 10(2): 199–220.

Wareing, S. (1992) 'And then he kissed her: the reclamation of female characters to submissive roles in contemporary fiction', in Wales, Katie (ed.) *Feminist Linguistics in Literary Criticism*, Cambridge: D. S. Brewer, pp. 117–36.

Whorf, B. L. (1956) *Language, Thought and Reality*, Carroll, J. B. (ed.) Cambridge MA: MIT Press.

Wilkins, D. P. (1989) 'Linguistic evidence in support of a holistic approach to traditional ecological knowledge', in Williams, N. M and Baines, G., *Traditional Ecological Knowledge*, Canberra: ANU Centre for Resource and Environmental Studies.

327

Williams, R (1977) *Marxism and Literature*, Oxford: Oxford University Press.

Williamson, J. (1978) *Decoding Advertisements: Ideology and Meaning in Advertising*, London: Marion Boyars.

Wilson, Deirdre and Sperber, D. (1986) 'An outline of relevance theory', in Alves, H. O. (ed.) *Encontro de Linguistas*: *Actas*, Minho, Portugal: University of Minho, pp. 19–42.

Wolfson, N. (1989): *Perspectives: Sociolinguistics and TESOL*, Rowley MA: Newbury House.

Index and glossary of linguistic terms

This is a form of combined glossary and index. Listed below are the main key terms used in this book, together with brief definitions. The bold page references will take you to the place in the book where the term is defined and most extensively discussed. On that page, the term will appear in bold. Some terms, however, will be best understood by exploring other parts of the book, in which case there will be more than one page reference provided.

This is not a full list of linguistic terms, and often the definitions are simplified. For students who are majoring in English language or linguistics, dictionaries or encyclopaedias such as David Crystal's comprehensive *A Dictionary of Linguistics and Phonetics* (3rd Edn, 1991, Oxford: Blackwell), Rob Pope's *English Studies Book* (1998, London: Routledge), or Ronald Carter's *Keywords in Language and Literacy* (1995, London: Routledge) would be indispensable.

abstract 31–34, 219ff., 307
A short summary of the story provided before a narrative begins, capturing the 'point' of the story. It signals that a narrative is about to commence, and is a bridge to make the narrative relevant to the preceding conversation.
activation of experiences 285, 296 (see **mental process**)
activation of tokens 285, 297 (see **relational process**)
active 95, 113, 227

One kind of grammatical voice. Clauses can differ according to whether they are in the active voice or the **passive** voice. In the active voice, the subject of the sentence is the participant who acts, speaks or experiences. In the equivalent passive sentence, this participant, if mentioned at all, will be in a *by* phrase, and the subject will be the participant affected or what is experienced. For example:

the dog bit the man	active
the man was bitten by the dog	passive
I noticed the bird first	active
the bird was noticed by me first	passive

actor (see **material process**) **60,** 67–70, 75–6, 277–80, 280–83, 293–97, 310–11

adjective 4, 54, 56, 76–7, 155, 270, 316

The part of speech which describes, modifies or gives extra meaning to a noun or noun phrase, for instance (1) 'the *green* bottles' (2) 'the bottles are *green*'. Most adjectives can have *very* in front of them. They can usually be used attributively, before the noun, as in (1), and, predicatively, following the noun, as in (2).

adverbial 15, 31

A word or phrase (or sometimes a clause) which gives information about the process described in the rest of the clause (or another clause). It gives information about the time, manner/attitude, position/direction, accompaniment, beneficiary or purpose of the process, e.g. '<u>Yesterday</u> (time) I <u>reluctantly</u> (manner/attitude) went <u>to a football match</u> (direction) <u>with my children</u> (accompaniment) <u>for my wife's sake</u> (beneficiary), <u>to give her a break from the kids</u> (purpose).' The first two of these adverbials are words, the next three are phrases, and the last one is a clause. They all give us extra information about 'I went'.

affected (see **material process**) **60,** 67–70, 73, 76, 277–8, 282–3, 298–9, 310–11

affective words 108–9, 209–10

I use this phrase to mean words which are empty or drained of conceptual meaning and simply convey emotion, e.g. swear words, which show negative emotion, and empty subjective words like *nice, fine, cool, good, great, wonderful, smashing, fabulous*, much used in advertising copy.

agreement maxim 153–4, 231–2

An aspect of the politeness principle which says it is more polite to agree than disagree (see also **preferred seconds**).

animalisation 284

Using a verb, adjective or noun normally associated with an animal for an insentient or non-living entity, e.g. the mountain *breathed* on my face, the *shivering* trees, the *blind* building.

approbation maxim 152–3, 231–2
An aspect of the politeness principle which says it is more polite to show approval or give praise, than to voice disapproval or criticise.
assured readers 28, **29**, 44, 306
Readers who are highly motivated to read or continue reading a text. **Non-assured readers** are reluctant or show little interest in the text. Texts for assured readers need to be less visually informative than those for non-assured readers.
auxiliary verb (see **verb**) **223**

background 35, 36–9, 138, 308
One of the elements in the generic structure of news reports. It includes references to previous events, even those stretching back into history, and details of the physical circumstances in which the event took place. It resembles Labov's **orientation**.
balance 22–3, 30, 153, 202
One basic design for paragraphs or texts, in which there is a weighing-up of descriptive facts, or arguments for and against a proposition, giving equal proportion to each side.
behavioural process 228
A process intermediate between a mental process and a material process, which describes the outward manifestation of an inner feeling or condition, or an intentional perception. Here we find verbs describing facial expressions, gestures, etc., and verbs like *watch* and *look at*, which contrast with the mental perception verbs like *see* and *notice*.
beneficiary (see **material process**) **60**

chain 21, 23, 30
A paragraph design where the sentences appearing in succession are linked most obviously only to the sentence before. Cohesive links are achieved by repeating vocabulary, or using pronouns to refer 'back' to something which has come in the previous sentence.
change-of-state presupposition 125ff.
When a text mentions a change of state and thereby assumes that the thing or person that changes is or was in a different or opposite state. For example, 'Your food will get cold' presupposes that the food is not cold, i.e. it is hot or warm.
coda 32–3, 37, 219, 223, 307
An element of generic structure by which a narrative is completed. It is a bridge out of the narrative and often uses changes of tenses and time adverbs to bring us back to the present.
cohesion 18–19, 22
The patterns of language in a text which help it to hang together across sentence boundaries to form larger units like paragraphs. Cohesion can be lexical or

grammatical. Lexically, chains of words related in meaning across sentences make a text cohere; grammatically, words like *this*, *the*, *it*, *the latter* can establish cohesion.

comments 36–9, 308

Part of the episode in the generic structure of news reports. It comprises evaluations of the other elements and speculations about what might happen next.

complicating action 32–4, 223–4, 307

The most essential generic element in a narrative. It contains clauses describing linked events or actions, in past or present tense, ordered chronologically. If the order of clauses is reversed we have a different narrative. For instance, 'He went to Harvard and got a bachelor's degree' is a different story from 'He got a bachelor's degree and went to Harvard.'

conjunction 22, 105, 127, 201

A word used to connect (or join) two or more phrases or clauses. Conjunctions are sometimes referred to as 'joining words'.

consequences 35–7

An element in the generic structure of news reports. The consequences are anything which was caused by the main event, namely another event, or a human physical reaction or verbal reaction.

contact 85–9, 94, 97, 99, 102–3, 106, 110, 115, 151, 154, 201–2, 205

The degree of intimacy or solidarity in social relationships. Frequency of meeting, variety of contexts in which we meet, and the time period over which our meetings last are all factors in determining contact.

contested terms 109–11, 132

Words which provoke an emotional or other reaction because of the ideology recognised in their use, and the fact that some people deliberately object to their use, e.g. *poetess*, *chairman*.

declarative 90, 150, 201, 315

The grammatical mood usually used to make statements (rather than issue commands or ask questions). The test for declarative mood is whether the Subject precedes the Finite verb, e.g.

Subject	*Finite*	
He	took	the chestnuts.
He	did	look a fool.

deductive structure 24, 34, 39–40, 177, 256, 305

The structure of a paragraph or text where the main point or idea comes first. In **inductive structures** the point comes last. Deductive structures allow skimming, or abandoning reading half-way through the text. Inductive structures emphasise the process of reading rather than simply the information as a product.

direct speech 166–7, 170

A form of reporting speech in which the words actually spoken are included within quotation marks, and in which there is a reporting clause preceding or following the quote. For instance, 'John said, "I will come tomorrow".' Or '"I did not have a sexual relationship with Monica Lewinsky," Clinton said.'

directive 148, 150, 152, 209, 321

A type of speech act in which the writer/speaker attempts to make the reader/hearer do something, e.g. 'Could you type out the agenda?'. Examples of directive verbs would be *ask, command, request, suggest, plead, beg*.

discourse 3–4, 6, 107, **118**, 122, 176

As I use the term, the interpersonal act of communication in which the writer intends to affect a reader, and the reader attempts to work out the writer's intentions. The writer may encode some of her meaning in Text as part of this act of communication. But beware, there are many conflicting definitions of this term in the literature.

discussion 30

A genre which presents information and opinions about more than one side of an issue: it may end with a recommendation based on the evidence presented. It is associated with the kind of text organisation known as a balance.

dispreferred second (see **preferred second**) **154**, 162, 231–2

effective 230, **283**

A term used to describe ergative material process clauses in which there are two participants. When there is only one participant the clause is called *middle*. The terms *effective* and *middle* are roughly equivalent to the more traditional *transitive* and *intransitive*.

emotion 85–6, 104–5, 108–10, 115 133–4, 202, 206, 310–11

An aspect of interpersonal relationships in which affect or feeling is expressed. It can be positive or negative, and fleeting or permanent.

emotive spin 108, 316, 318

Words may share the same conceptual meaning but differ in emotive meaning, and this difference could be called 'spin'. A famous trio are *slim, thin* and *skinny. Slim* spins positively, *skinny* negatively and *thin* doesn't spin at all.

episode 35–6

An element of the generic structure of news reports comprised of events and consequences.

ergative 283–4, 295, 302

A specific kind of verb (or language). The difference between ergative verbs and other verbs can be seen when we add a second participant to the clause. With non-ergatives, the clause is extended to the right, with ergatives to the left.

	non-ergative	*ergative*
1 participant	John ate	The boat sailed
2 participants	John ate a grape	Paul sailed the boat
	---------->	<----------

euphemism 108–10, 134, 209, 316, 318

A word used to avoid a direct reference to something considered impolite, for example, *comfort woman* for *sex slave*. Sex, urination and excretion, and death are the commonest topics for euphemism, though politically contested terms are also avoided by this technique.

evaluation 32–3, 219, 223, 230-2, 307

An element in the generic structure of narrative. Labov identified evaluation with those clauses which don't belong to the narrative action, but which delay its forward movement. These comprise comments by narrator or character, emotive devices, comparatives, *if* clauses, negatives, questions, exclamations and future tense clauses.

event 35–6, 39, 41, 252, 307

An element of the generic structure of news reports comprising the main event and the background.

existential presupposition 77, 122, 128, 207, 296, 298

The assumption that a (definite) noun phrase must refer to something that exists. If a new word or phrase is invented, such as *shopaholic*, then we assume that some people exist in the world who belong to this class.

experience (see **mental process**) **60**, 68, 71, 75, 267, 284–5, 288, 291, 296, 310–12

experiencer (see **mental process**) **60**, 66–8, 71, 75, 227

explanation 3–4, 71, 181, part three *passim*

The end point or aim of critical discourse analysis, showing what social and ideological forces underlie or determine text and discourse meanings.

exposition 20, **30**

A genre whose purpose is to advance or justify an argument, or put forward a particular point of view.

expository questions 89, 317

A question which the writer herself goes on to answer. It is a way of introducing or stimulating interest in an issue or discourse topic, or of providing a frame for the discourse which follows.

face 153, **233**

An aspect of interpersonal relationships. It has two aspects, **positive face** and **negative face**. Negative face is the basic claim to territories, personal preserves, rights to non-distraction – freedom of action and freedom from imposition. Positive face is the positive consistent self-image or 'personality', crucially including the desire that this self-image be appreciated and approved of.

free direct speech 160, 167, 322
A way of representing speech in which the words actually spoken are quoted, but without a reporting clause, e.g. "'I will resign on Monday.'"

free indirect speech 166
A way of representing speech in which there is no reporting clause, the lexical words actually spoken remain the same, but some of the grammatical words known as shifters change. For example, if the actual words spoken were "'I will visit you tomorrow'" in free indirect speech this would become 'He would visit him the next day'.

generic structure 29, 31–9, 44–5
The stereotypical structure of a particular genre, also known as a discourse schema. It provides a kind of template into which an author can fit her text. For example, the generic structure for each entry in a telephone directory is:

SURNAME followed by GIVEN (OR FIRST) NAME followed by ADDRESS followed by NUMBER

ideational meaning 5, chapter 2 *passim*
Conceptual meaning, which represents, sorts and classifies the outside world and the mental world.

ideology 3, 37, 39, 43, 52ff., 71, 132, 140, 167, part three *passim*, 277
As I use the term, it means the ways of thinking which (re)produce and reflect the power structures of society, or, more briefly, 'meaning in the service of power'. This term has many different definitions in different political philosophies.

imperative 19, 69, **87**–8, 150–1, 154, 210, 233, 315, 321
The grammatical mood most obviously associated with commands. Imperative mood uses the bare or base form of the verb without any Subject before or after it. For example: 'wash the dishes'; 'have a drink'; 'take a bath'; 'come on Tuesday morning'.

implying, **implication** 3–4, 57, 118, 122, 136–41, 238–9
The unstated message the writer wishes to convey beyond what is encoded in the text. The reader is expected to make **inferences** about the writer's implications. If someone says 'I can't open this briefcase' and you reply 'Here's a key' you are implying that the person should use the key to open the briefcase, and expecting the person to infer this. The process depends on familiarity with a schema in which keys are used for opening locks, and in which suitcases have locks.

indirect speech 166–7
A way of reporting speech where there is a reporting clause, no change to the lexical words, but changes to some words to bring them into line with the time, place and person of the reporting clause. E.g. 'John said "I will come here tomorrow"' becomes, in indirect speech 'John said that he would go there the following day.'

indirect speech act 89, **150**–2, 201, 209, 231–3
Using one kind of grammatical mood structure to perform indirectly a speech act associated with another mood. For instance, using the declarative mood, instead of interrogative, as a question, e.g. 'You went to Starbucks' last night?' Or the declarative mood, instead of imperative, as an indirect command, e.g. 'The dog needs to be fed' instead of the direct 'Feed the dog'. Indirect commands/requests are considered more polite than direct ones in imperative mood.

inductive structure (see **deductive structure**) **24**, 28, 34, 305
inference (see **implying**) 3–4, 57, 118, **122**, 136–41, 238–9
information report 30
A genre whose purpose is to represent factual information about a class of things, usually by first classifying them and then describing their characteristics.

interpersonal meaning 5, chapter 3 *passim*, 85–6, 131, 134, chapter 5 *passim*, 201, 205, 210, 231–34
The aspect of (textual) meaning which creates or reflects the roles and relationships between reader and writer (or speaker and hearer).

interrogative 89, 150, 210–12, 233, 315
The grammatical mood associated with questioning. The grammatical test for the interrogative is that the finite verb precedes the subject

	Finite	*Subject*	
	Did	you	eat the plums?
What	were	you	doing?

The only exception to this rule is with *wh-* interrogatives when the *wh-* word is the subject e.g.

Subject	*Finite*	
Who	ate	the plums?

intertextual chains 169–70
The process by which one text is passed on through a series of readers/writers and may be modified in the process. There are particularly long intertextual chains in the news-gathering process.

intertextuality chapter 6 *passim*, **165**, 171–2, 176, 178, 322
The way in which one text impinges on other later texts, or, to put it another way,

how texts feed off and relate to each other. Examples are quotation, paraphrase, reaction and parody.

irony 122, **129**–31, 134–6, 144, 238, 319

Saying or writing something very different or opposite from what one knows to be true, with the intention that the hearer/reader will realise that it is not true. (If you intend them not to realise this falsity it is lying rather than irony.) Irony often involves echoing or quoting what another speaker actually said or might have said and which turns out not to be true, as a way of showing dissatisfaction with or scorn for that person or their message.

latent ideology 50, 143, 147

The ideology which we accept in our everyday life and discourse without being aware of it. Ideology very often becomes hidden through a process of **naturalisation** in which we come to accept that the texts we encounter and their language are the only natural way of representing experience. It is only because ideology is so well hidden that people can believe in the ideal of 'objective' or 'unbiased' reporting. Learning an exotic language or doing critical discourse analysis are good ways of becoming aware of latent ideologies.

lead 35, 39–40, 107, 138, 306

The element of the generic structure of news which comprises the first paragraph of the news report. Along with the headline it gives a summary. It usually contains information about who did what, when, where and how.

linguistic relativity 49

The claim that the language we speak determines the way we think about the world and ourselves. The weak version claims that speaking one language makes it difficult to think as the speakers of another language do, the strong version that it makes it impossible.

localised texts 28, 44

Texts using graphic or visual devices to create easily perceptible sections which can be read selectively, and in any order. By contrast, texts that are not sectionalised by visual or graphic information tend to be **progressive**, and to be read in linear order from start to finish.

location circumstance 283, 295

An adverbial of place, telling where a process took place. It is possible to 'promote' a location circumstance into an Actor, a strategy which might give more syntactic prominence to the 'environment'. For example, 'snakes slithered over the rocks' could become 'the rocks slithered with snakes'.

material process 59–60, 68–72, 236–40, 280, 284–5, 293ff., 311–12

A process which is an action or event, and answers the question 'What happened?' The thing responsible for causing the action/event is called the **actor**.

The thing that the action or event affects is called the **affected**. An affected that benefits from the material process is called a **beneficiary**.

mental process 60, 66–7, 71–2, 75, 94, 261, 267, 284, 311–12
A process of perception, cognition or emotion. In grammatical analysis the 'person' who experiences these perceptions, thoughts or emotions we can call the **experiencer**, and these perceptions, thoughts or emotions are called the **experience**. Experiences in mental process can be coded in the grammar as though they were Actors in material processes. For example 'I noticed the river' -----> 'the river arrested my gaze', 'we love the forest' -----> 'the forest touches our hearts', and I refer to this as **activation of experiences**.

metaphor 57, 129–34, 136, 144, 199–200, 238–9, 269, 284–5, 296–7, 319–20
A figure of speech or tool of thought in which one thing is experienced in terms of another. Like irony, a metaphor often states something which the writer does not believe, but depends for its interpretation on similarities between what is stated and the actual state of affairs, not, as with irony, on dissimilarities.

minor sentences 99, 100–1, 201–2, 316
Stretches of text punctuated as sentences but which are incomplete either because the main finite verb or Subject has been missed out. In dialogue, such utterances or 'sentences' occur quite naturally, for example in response to questions.

modal constructions 33, **87**–92, 109, 115, 233–4, 307, 315
Verbs, adjectives or adverbs which express obligation/permission, probability, inclination or usuality. Modal verbs include the following: *may*, *might*, *can*, *could*, *will*, *would*, *shall*, *should*, *must*, *have to*, *ought to*, *need*. Examples of modal adjectives and adverbs are *permitted*, *allowed*, *expected*, *required*, *possible*, *possibly*, *inclined to*, *determined to*, *usually*, *sometimes*, *always*.

modesty maxim 152, 203, 207, 231
The aspect of the politeness principle which says that in order to be polite one should be modest – criticise oneself or underplay one's achievement rather than praise oneself or boast.

narrative, **narrative structure 19**, 30–5, 45, 223–6, 307
A genre in which one tells a story as a means of making sense of events and happenings in the world. It can both entertain and inform. The generic structure of narrative, according to Labov, is:

(Abstract) ^ (Orientation) ^ Complicating Action ^ Resolution ^ (Coda)
.... + (Evaluation)...............

narrative report of speech act 167, 174, 243
A means of reporting speech in which none of the original words need occur. '"I

will resign tomorrow"' might become in narrative report of speech act 'Jean Paul indicated his intention of relinquishing employment on 6 May'.

naturalisation (see **latent ideology**) **50**

negative face (see **face**) 233

news story **35**

The major element of the generic structure of news reports. The news story comprises the episode and comments.

nominalisation **76**–80, 82, 95, 128, 190, 207, 268, 309

A grammatical transformation which turns a verb or an adjective (or clause) into a noun (noun phrase). It is brought about most obviously by adding a suffix, (e.g. *rough* → *roughness*, *imply* → *implication*), but less obviously by using a noun which has the same form as a verb, e.g. *a catch*. Nominalisation allows the omission of both participants in a clause, e.g. actor and affected in material process clauses. Its other effects are to remove time or tense, and to introduce existential presuppositions.

non-assured readers (see **assured readers**) 28, 29, 44, 306

non-restrictive premodification (see **restrictive premodification**) 270

noun 54, 76, 82, 207

The part of speech typically used for referring to entities with dimensions in space – things, people, places etc. Structurally, nouns fit into frames like 'John noticed the …'. In terms of their form they regularly inflect or change form to mark the plural, e.g. *ship/ships*, *dog/dogs*, *mouse/mice*.

noun phrase 77, 95, 123, 201, 270

The phrase of which the noun is the head, the compulsory constituent. Noun phrases can vary in length from one word, e.g. 'dogs' to very complex structures with premodification and postmodification, e.g. 'my neighbour's scruffy black dog which you see every morning and which persists in burying bones in my garden …'.

object (see **subject**) 15, 60, 227, 295

Old English 105–6

The form of the English language up to around 1100AD, in contrast with Middle English, 1100–1500AD, and Modern English, 1500 to the present.

optionality **151**–2, 209, 231

The choice of saying 'yes' or 'no'. It is important in making polite requests to put them in question form, and even politer to put them in the form which makes it easy to say 'no', e.g. 'You couldn't drive me to the station could you?'

orientation **31**–2, 36, 219–20, 224, 307

An element of narrative structure which gives information about the time, place, persons and situation/activity type they are engaged in when the action takes place. Typically this section will include Adverbials of time and place, relational verbs like *to be* and progressive *-ing* forms of the verb.

overwording 64, 71

When a phenomenon, person or thing is referred to with unnecessary frequency and with a variety of different terms. This often betrays a preoccupation or obsession due to ideological struggle.

parody 172–3, 175–6

A kind of intertextuality used for humorous purposes, in which the content is presented in an inappropriate style. For example, 'I put it to you that when you should have been washing your hair in anti-dandruff shampoo last night, you were in fact watching TV all evening, is that not so? Do you plead guilty or not guilty to having dandruff?' This talks about hairwashing and dandruff in the style of legal cross-examination.

passive, passivisation (see **active**) 15, **75–6**, 78–9, 95, 303

past perfect (past in past) tense 223

A tense of the verb which takes the form of *had* + past participle. It refers to an event which occurred before the past events that you are already describing. For example, 'When he returned to his flat, Paul saw that the dog had chewed the carpet'. Paul's returning and seeing is already referred to in the past tense. The dog's chewing the carpet took place before he returned and saw it, so we use the past perfect *had chewed*. (Halliday calls this tense the *past in past*.)

past tense 32, 54, 167, 307

The tense typically used to refer to something which happens before it is reported. Many verbs mark the past tense with *-ed*, though some change their vowel sound *see/saw*, *come/came*, *take/took*.

personification 284–5, 296ff.

Using a verb, adjective or noun normally used to describe a human to describe an animal, plant or non-living entity, e.g. 'the hills danced for joy', 'the daffodil encouraged the tulip to bloom', 'the bald landscape'.

possessive presupposition 123–5, 207, 321

The kind of presupposition that is made when we use *'s* to indicate possession, or the pronominal 'adjectives' *hers/his*, *their*, *my*, *our*, *your*. For instance, 'I looked under Raymond's car for your rabbit' presupposes >> 'Raymond has a car' and 'you have a rabbit'.

power 85–8, 92, 110, 144, 151, 154

A major element in interpersonal relationships, indicating inequality between speakers . The power takes various forms: physical strength; the authority given to a person by an institution; status depending on wealth, education, place of residence; or expertise, the possession of knowledge or skill.

pragmatics 3, 141, 162, 205, part two *passim*

The branch of linguistics concerned with the production and interpretation of utterances in context. Whereas **semantics** answers the question 'how do we know what this sentence means?', pragmatics answers the question 'how do we know what X means by uttering/writing this sentence in this time and at this place?'. It studies topics like establishing the referent, the principles governing polite cooperative talk, speech acts, propositional attitude and inference.

preferred second 154, 162, 231–2

The preferred-second member of a pair of speech-acts. For example, in the speech act pair of invitation followed by acceptance or refusal, acceptance is preferred and refusal is **dispreferred**. The dispreferred is often accompanied by delays or voiced hesitation and an account or apology, e.g. 'Mmm, er, sorry I can't make it then because I've got to go to a meeting'.

present tense 54, 167, 223

The tense of the verb which refers to habitual actions or present feelings or states, e.g. 'I go to college by bus', 'I feel sick this morning', or 'The phone is dead'. With most verbs the present tense is the basic shortest form of the verb, that is the infinitive without *to*, e.g. (*to*) dive. But the third-person singular of the present tense adds an *s* to this base form, e.g. *he/she/it dives*.

presupposition 77, **122**–8, 130, 143–4, 158, 207–9, 268, 319, 321

An assumption made by a speaker or writer which is not explicitly stated. Strictly speaking, the presuppositions of a sentence remain unaffected when it is negated. This makes presuppositions less easy to argue against than their equivalent explicitly stated sentence. For example 'Clinton's dishonesty was frowned on by the majority of Americans' negated becomes 'Clinton's dishonesty was not frowned on by the majority of Americans'. But the negated sentence still presupposes, without stating it, that Clinton is dishonest.

procedure 19, 30, 306

A genre which shows how something can be accomplished through a series or steps of actions to be taken in a certain order. Examples are instructional texts like recipes.

progressive form of the verb 31, 32

The form of the verb which has -*ing* on the end. It indicates that the process referred to by the verb is still in progress, incomplete or unfinished e.g. 'I was driv*ing* to work when lightning struck my car'.

progressive texts (see **localised texts**) 28

pronoun 94–8, 103, 115–16, 201, 210, 315

A word which normally substitutes for a noun or noun phrase, e.g. *I, you, they, him, myself, some, these, any.*

propositional attitude 122, 128–30, 144

The attitude a writer or speaker has to the proposition which they have expressed, for example desirability in commands, uncertainty in questions and belief in statements. But note that in ironical or metaphorical statements the attitude is less than belief. Mood encodes some kinds of propositional attitude linguistically, but in graphic communication it is very difficult to encode.

reaction 36, 38
An element of the generic structure of news reports, namely, an action taking place in response to the main event.

reading position (see **subject position**) 118, **154**, 156–9

receiver (see **verbal process**) **60**, 228

recount 30, 33–4
A genre which constructs past experience by retelling events and incidents in the order in which they occurred.

relational process 59, 68, 70, 262, 285, 297
A process which describes states of affairs, static situations. It relates two things, or a thing and a property, the **token** and the **value**, e.g. 'John (token) is a teacher (value)', 'John (token) is poor (value)'. Common relational process verbs are *to be* and *to have*. Tokens in relational processes can be grammatically recoded as Actors in material processes. For example, 'There are five trees in the valley/five trees are in the valley' -----> 'Five trees stand in the valley', giving rise to what I call the **activation of tokens**.

resolution 32–4, 220, 226, 307
An element of the generic structure of narrative provided by the last of the narrative clauses. It brings the sequence of actions and events to a relatively neat end, by, for example, solving a problem.

restrictive premodification 270
When a premodifier, for example, an adjective before a noun, is used to define a subset of the things referred to by the noun, for instance *black* in 'black cars'. Adjectives can also be used with a **non-restrictive** meaning, indicating that all of the referents of the noun share the quality referred to by the adjective, e.g. 'The warm waters of the Gulf Stream'. This restrictive/non-restrictive ambiguity can be exploited for purposes of stereotyping.

rheme (see **theme**) **15**–16, 144, 303–4

rhetorical question 89, 97, 150, 201
A sentence in interrogative mood that looks like a question but is in fact an indirect way of making a statement, e.g. 'who left the window open?' could convey 'someone left the window open'.

root analogies 199, 238–9
The network of metaphors in the dictionary which conceptualise abstract concepts in more concrete terms, e.g. TIME = SPACE, SUCCESS = MOVEMENT FORWARD, EMOTION = HEAT.

sayer (see **verbal process**) **60**, 70, 75–7, 79, 167, 229, 255–65, 288, 290–2, 310, 312

schema 122, **136**–41, 144, 165, 171, 205, 252, 320
The mental organisation of stereotypical knowledge about objects, sequences of behaviour and discourse patterns. We generally rely heavily on schematic knowledge in making inferences when interpreting discourse.
semantics (see **pragmatics**) **3**, 5, 116, 118,
shifter 166
A word which changes its meaning according to who utters it, when and where. For example, *I*, *here*, and *now*. Also known as a *deictic* term.
stack 19–20, 23, 30, 202
A kind of paragraph structure common in argument or exposition which comprises lists of arguments or facts. These are often used to justify the thesis or argument stated in the topic sentence which precedes them.
step 19, 30, 306
A kind of paragraph/text structure associated with procedural genres. Each sentence or clause of the paragraph describes one step in a process and is presented in the order in which it occurs.
stereotyping 4, **55**–8, 136–41, 205, 234, 240–1, 254, 265, 270, 309, 312
Assuming, on the basis that some members of a class have a characteristic, that other members have that characteristic.
subject 15, 76, 99, 102, 226–7, 283, 285
Subjects and objects are major elements in a clause and are noun phrases. In the active voice in statements (declarative mood) subjects precede the verb and objects follow the verb. In 'John hit the ball', 'John' is the subject, and 'the ball', the other noun phrase, is the object. The Subject, not the Object determines whether the verb has the plural or singular form:

Ducks love the pond	Plural Subject + Plural Verb + Singular Object
The duck loves the ponds	Singular Subject + Singular Verb + Plural Object

Several pronouns in English have different forms according to whether they are subject or object. For example, *he* (subject), *him* (object), *she* (subject) *her* (object), *they* (subject) *them* (object), *I* (subject) *me* (object), *we* (subject) *us* (object).
subject positions 147–8, chapter 5 *passim*, 162, 165–6, 202, 233–4, 244, 320–1
The relative roles, positions and identities created for reader and writer through texts/discourse. These positions are culturally determined through subjection to societal institutions such as the educational system, religious organisations, the family and the media. The subject position of a reader is the **reading position**. This is more likely to be consciously learned/taught, for example we might learn to read literature or a religious text according to certain conventions of interpretation.

summary 35, 37, 39

The element of the generic structure of news reports consisting of the headline and the lead (first paragraph).

sympathy maxim 153–4, 231–2, 321

One of the maxims of the politeness principle. It states that one should at least take an interest in the readers' problems or successes, and ideally claim your feelings match theirs. Examples of sympathising would be condolences and congratulations.

synthetic personalisation 89, 98–9, 133, 165, 205, 210

Treating a mass audience as though they are individuals being directly addressed. It is very common in advertising and the media, and facilitated by the singular–plural ambiguity of *you*.

tact maxim 152, 210, 231–2, 234

One aspect of Leech's politeness principle which says that to be polite when making requests one should build in indirectness and optionality, for example, using statements or questions rather than commands.

text 3, 5–6, part one *passim*, 25

The physical form which the writing (speaking) takes on the page (in the air) and the meanings which this physical form encodes. I use it in contradistinction to the term 'discourse'. Decoding of text depends upon semantics and answers the question 'What does the text mean?'.

text population 64

The people and characters mentioned in a text.

textual meaning 5, chapter 1 *passim*, 25

The meanings involved in the organisation of a text, for example, the distribution of information within a clause and paragraph, or the overall generic structure.

thematic development 17–19

The pattern of themes over a whole paragraph or passage.

theme 15–18, 45, 80, 144, 174, 304

The informational starting point in the clause. In English it corresponds to the first of the basic elements of the clause – Subject, Object, Verb or Adverbial. The remainder of the clause constitutes the **rheme**. For example:

Theme	*Rheme*
The florist shop	stocks wonderful hollyhocks

It is normal to put old or given information in the theme and new information towards the end of the rheme.

token (see **relational process**) 59, 66, 227, 285, 296–7, 310

topic sentence 20, 23

The sentence in a paragraph which encapsulates the main idea. In 'stack' paragraphs it generally appears at the beginning (and/or end).

transitivity 59–75, 227ff., 262, 267, chapter 10 *passim*

The resources of the grammar devoted to ideational meaning, that is the representation of the physical and mental worlds and what goes on in them.

upgrading 209

The choice of a less common word when an ordinary one will do, in order to sensationalise or exaggerate the nature of the activity.

value (see **relational process**) 59, 66, 300

verb 15, 31, 54, 59–60, 67, 87–92, 127, 202, **223**, 226, 297, 309, 315, 322

A word class or part of speech which refers to a process – of doing, being, experiencing or saying (see **material**, **relational**, **mental** and **verbal processes**). Verbs can be inflected, that is change their form or ending to show tense. For example:

> she works hard (present tense)
> she worked hard (past tense)

Verbs can be either main verbs or **auxiliary** verbs. For example, in the sentences:

> I may decide to go to the match
> He did tell me to come at three

'decide' and 'tell' are the main verbs, and 'may' and 'did' are auxiliary verbs. Auxiliary verbs cannot usually stand on their own, for example, 'I open the fridge' and 'I can open the fridge' but not 'I can the fridge'. One type of auxiliary verb is a modal verb (see **modal constructions**).

verbal process **60**, 70–1, 75, 223, 228ff.

A process of saying or writing (or other symbolic expression). In verbal-process clauses, the participant doing the saying or writing is the **sayer**. The person addressed is the **receiver**. What is actually said is the **verbiage**.

verbal reaction **36**–8, 307–8

One element of the generic structure of news reports which refers to a spoken response to the main event.

verbiage (see **verbal process**) **60**, 70

visual informativeness **24**–5, 28–9, 45, 103, 128, 205, 305–6, 321

The extent to which a writer uses devices like graphics, pictures, colour, white space, different fonts, bullets, asterisks and highlighting to make a text more visually arresting than homogeneous print. Visually informative texts tend to be more localised and to cater to non-assured readers.

Index of names